In the warm, vibrant region of Southeast Asia, local scholars of mission, rooted in the land and the sea, the bamboo huts and the skyscrapers, have brought fresh questions and insights to bear on the classic cosmic truths of God in Christ-incarnate, crucified, resurrected, reigning, and sending us out as his witnesses throughout his world. Coming from diverse ethnic heritages but united in faith and place, these writers offer sharp, authentic interpretations and applications from this pivotal region.

Miriam Adeney, PhD
Associate Professor of World Christian Studies,
Seattle Pacific University, Washington, USA

Pulling threads from the diverse contexts and cultures of Southeast Asia, this book weaves a beautiful tapestry, exploring how the unchanging message of the Bible remains relevant in an endlessly evolving environment. The book challenges the reader to go beyond the reductionist, linear mindset that pervades Western thought. Instead, it calls us to embrace an interdisciplinary approach that welcomes diversity, complexity, fluidity, and fuzzy boundaries, which are essential to understanding the multicultural, multireligious, multi-economic, multi-political, multicolored, and multilingual mosaic realities of Southeast Asia. This book presents spirituality within the context and framework of traditional Southeast Asian worldviews and brings the Bible into conversation with each perspective.

Rev. Dr. Patrick Fung
General Director,
OMF International, Singapore

This is a book that I've wanted to see from the Asian church for a long time. All those involved in the tasks of missions today will benefit from the insights found here. While some big concepts, like Complex Adaptive Systems, are used, the editors carefully describe and illustrate what they mean from practical examples in the literature of other disciplines as well as in the missions context. They have brought together writers who incorporate the history of missions in different countries, mission thinking, planning and education, deployment, and use of resources. If you were a farmer, wouldn't you want to keep learning how best to prepare the soil, plant, and harvest? This book will help those planning, preparing, and planting spiritual seeds to improve their harvest yields for the Kingdom of God.

Anne C. Harper, DMiss
Editor, *Journal of Asian Mission*
Missionary, Action International Ministries, UK

This book is a needed resource for understanding Christian mission in Southeast Asia by thought leaders from the region. By tracing the history of mission in the region, against the background of colonisation, and the road towards nationalism and modernisation, the writers help to exegete the context and point to the presence of God in history. This can help to shape historical consciousness and identities of the people in the region. The discovery of how God has worked in the past can perhaps inspire new acts of faith and witness in the present. The book also offers a much needed holistic gospel and missional framework to address a web of complex issues in the local contexts, from social injustice to abject poverty. I commend this book to all believers seeking to engage the world as mature and effective witnesses of God's kingdom vision and values in this twenty-first-century world, especially in rapidly urbanising and globalising Southeast Asia. Congratulations on this precious resource in contextual missiology.

Lawrence Ko
National Director (2012–2022),
Singapore Centre for Global Missions

Congratulations to the editors and authors for compiling mission histories and contextual theologies in one book, giving voices to missiologists of Southeast Asia. This is highly recommended for students, scholars, and practitioners. Each chapter has contributed to the past, present, and even future challenges of missiology in this region. Southeast Asian scholars must continue writing and producing glocal theologies that will inform both the global and local churches.

Juliet Lee Uytanlet, PhD
Program Director of PhD Intercultural Studies,
Asia Graduate School of Theology, Philippines
Faculty, Biblical Seminary of the Philippines

This collection shows that any missiology in the 2020s must be contextually grounded, glocally adaptive, socially engaging, and eschatologically oriented toward God's redemptive purposes. More specifically, these essays indicate that missiological considerations have to be historically rooted, which is what we find in part I of this book. Our Southeast Asian colleagues show how Christian history and missiology have always been mutually informing, even more so now that we are observing how younger churches continue to mature and respond to the call of the *missio Dei*!

Amos Yong, PhD
Dean of the School Mission and Theology,
Fuller Theological Seminary, California, USA

Southeast Asia is one of the most complex regions in the world because of its variegated histories, convoluted politics, and multiplicity of cultures, languages and religions. Furthermore, Christianity in this region has been a largely neglected field of study until very recently. The significance of this exciting volume is that it opens up our understanding of the complex multifaceted nature of the encounter between the gospel and the peoples of the region. It will also help churches develop clearer indigenous Christian self-identities and more contextual approaches in mission. This book is a hugely welcome contribution to this field of study.

Bishop Emeritus Hwa Yung
Methodist Church in Malaysia

Missions in Southeast Asia

Missions in Southeast Asia

Diversity and Unity in God's Design

Kiem-Kiok Kwa and Samuel K. Law

© 2022 Kiem-Kiok Kwa and Samuel Ka-Chieng Law

Published 2022 by Langham Global Library
An imprint of Langham Publishing
www.langhampublishing.org

Langham Publishing and its imprints are a ministry of Langham Partnership

Langham Partnership
PO Box 296, Carlisle, Cumbria, CA3 9WZ, UK
www.langham.org

ISBNs:
978-1-83973-436-6 Print
978-1-83973-737-4 ePub
978-1-83973-738-1 Mobi
978-1-83973-739-8 PDF

Kiem-Kiok Kwa and Samuel Ka-Chieng Law hereby assert to the Publishers and the Publishers' assignees, licensees and successors in title their moral right to be identified as the Author of the General Editor's part in the Work in accordance with sections 77 and 78 of the Copyright, Designs and Patents Act 1988.

All rights reserved. No part of this publication may be reproduced, stored in a retrieval system or transmitted, in any form or by any means, electronic, mechanical, photocopying, recording or otherwise, without the prior written permission of the publisher or the Copyright Licensing Agency.

Requests to reuse content from Langham Publishing are processed through PLSclear. Please visit www.plsclear.com to complete your request.

All Scripture quotations, unless otherwise indicated, are taken from the Holy Bible, New International Version®, NIV®. Copyright ©1973, 1978, 1984, 2011 by Biblica, Inc.™ Used by permission of Zondervan.

Scripture quotations marked NRSV are from the New Revised Standard Version Bible, copyright © 1989 National Council of the Churches of Christ in the United States of America. Used by permission. All rights reserved.

British Library Cataloguing-in-Publication Data
A catalogue record for this book is available from the British Library

ISBN: 978-1-83973-436-6

Cover & Book Design: projectluz.com

Langham Partnership actively supports theological dialogue and an author's right to publish but does not necessarily endorse the views and opinions set forth here or in works referenced within this publication, nor can we guarantee technical and grammatical correctness. Langham Partnership does not accept any responsibility or liability to persons or property as a consequence of the reading, use or interpretation of its published content.

CONTENTS

Chapter 1: Introduction 1
    Kiem-Kiok Kwa and Samuel K. Law

Part I: A Diversity of Local Church Histories

Chapter 2: The Rebirth of the Church in Cambodia 13
    Samuel K. Law

Chapter 3: History of Christianity in Indonesia: The Witness of Protestant Mission through the *Pancasila*-Based State............27
    Benyamin F. Intan

Chapter 4: History of Christianity in Malaysia........................47
    Tan Sooi Ling

Chapter 5: History of the Church in Myanmar........................61
    Peter Thein Nyunt

Chapter 6: History of Philippine Christianity 77
    Narry F. Santos

Chapter 7: History of Christianity in Singapore 101
    Andrew Peh

Chapter 8: History of Christianity in Thailand......................119
    Karl Dahlfred

Chapter 9: History of Christianity in Vietnam: Evangelical Churches in Vietnam in the Early Twenty-Frst Century.......139
    KimSon Nguyen

Part II: A Unity of Interweaving Themes

Chapter 10: A Complex Systems Approach to Pedagogy and Research for Multicultural Contexts....................................151
    Samuel K. Law

Chapter 11: Glocal Complexities 177
    John Cheong

Chapter 12: The Churches in Southeast Asia 207
    Andrew Peh

Chapter 13: Southeast Asian Churches at the Global Church Roundtable 233
    Robert M. Solomon

Chapter 14: A Holistic Response to Social Justice..................................261
  Kiem-Kiok Kwa

Chapter 15: Case Study of Cultural Integration for
  Self-Theologizing in the Evangelical Church of Vietnam.....................287
  KimSon Nguyen

Chapter 16: Afterword: Beyond Southeast Asia – So the World
  May Know...309
  R. Daniel Shaw

CHAPTER 1

INTRODUCTION

Kiem-Kiok Kwa and Samuel K. Law

At the beginning of the twenty-first century, Southeast Asia is considered to be one of the most pivotal regions of the world. As American diplomat John Frankenstein captures well, the region is a strategic link between Middle East oil and the Pacific. While it may not be "at the cockpit of major power contention . . . this region is where the political and economic interests of India, China, the United States and Japan, rub up against each other."[1]

More than being merely a game board for world powers, the region's key political organization, the Association of Southeast Asian Nations (ASEAN), may also hold the key for global relations in an increasing conflictual world, beyond the clash of civilizations.[2] As Frankenstein notes, "The 'Asean way' has paid dividends in the relative peace, growing prosperity and political progress of the region."[3]

The region is also of importance in the kingdom of God. The area of 4.5 million square kilometers, less than half of Europe's 10.8 million square kilometers, with a population of about 650 million, almost 90 percent of Europe's 741 million, is a microcosm of the larger global community.[4] Here are followers of every major religion, along with their many local and primal folk religion variants. Here are vast rural lands and teeming urban centers where people of different religions, cultures, and socioeconomic classes live side by side. The traditions, interactions, and amalgamations of diverse cultures and religions provide a fertile test bed for theologizing, contextualizing, and ongoing Christian mission practice that can also guide the global church to

---

1. John Frankenstein, "A Strategic Link: The Complex Diversity of Southeast Asia," *America: The Jesuit Review* (31 March 2014): 19.
2. Scott Waalkes, "Beyond the Clash of Civilizations: Hermeneutical Hospitality as a Model for Civilizational Dialogue," *Christian Scholar's Review* 48, no. 3 (2019): 237–54.
3. Frankenstein, "Strategic Link," 19.
4. "What is ASEAN," ASEAN-US Business Council (24 October 2019).

resolve the emerging missional challenges of the twenty-first century.⁵ While Southeast Asia is the primary geographical region under discussion, it is part of wider Asia, and some writers wisely place the discussion in this milieu.⁶

Unfortunately, the region is often overlooked or misunderstood by the rest of the world. Concerning the continent of Asia, some people only consider the significances of large masses, such as China and India, and overlook the smaller nations that make up Southeast Asia. But this region is not merely a subset of Asia; it is a dynamic and lively area in itself. Herein ancient cultures like the Khmers expressed themselves in the context of being a young democracy. Here the world's most populous Muslim nation, Indonesia, is neighbor to communist Vietnam and the majority Christian Philippines. The city-state of Singapore is stable and economically prosperous while the Philippines is regularly beset by economic and political turbulence.

In all of these countries Christianity is present. The gospel, brought by missionaries over centuries, is bearing fruit. The church finds expression in all of these geographical, social, economic, and political contexts – growing in some instances and failing in others. While European colonization from the sixteenth century onwards was certainly a major factor in the church's development, what is often overlooked is that as early as 111 BC, China invaded Vietnam. Hence the Vietnamese have felt the effects of colonization for a long time, and not appreciating this results in a failure to properly contextualize the gospel in Vietnam. Indeed, understanding the Southeast Asian region in all its complexities and nuances is key to understanding the wider Asian context.

Thus this book arises initially out of two motivations. The first is to take stock of the fruit of the gospel that has been planted by Protestant missionaries from the early nineteenth century. For example ministry among university students, such as through Campus Crusade for Christ (now Cru) and the International Fellowship of Evangelical Students (IFES), is present in all of these Southeast Asian countries, and over the years, students and graduates from these ministries have made their quiet mark in their societies. Seeing this

---

5. John Roxborogh, "Contextualisation and re-contextualisation: Regional patterns in the history of Southeast Asian Christianity," *Asia Journal of Theology* 9, no. 1 (April 1995): 36–46.
6. See as an example H. S. Wilson, "Partnership in Preparing Leadership for Mission and Ministry: A Continued Story of the Foundation for Theological Education in South East Asia," in *Reflection on and Equipping for Christian Mission*, eds. Stephen Bevans, Theresa Chai, J. Nelson Jennings, Knud Jorgensen, and Dietrich Werner (Oxford: Regnum Books International, 2015), 362–73.

fruit also reveals where other branches are bare, and thus the spaces and places where the church needs to be.

The second motivation is the desire of those who live and work here to deeply understand the Southeast Asian context in order to see how God's hand has been present here even through all the political and social events and upheavals. As missions practitioners and educators, the writers and editors recognize the need for deeper contextualization so that the gospel can be more appropriately presented in Thai or Laotian cups.[7] Contextualization begins with exegeting the context.[8] This exegesis will be helpful and necessary for the global church not only to understand this multireligious context, but also to understand the people from this region who, riding on the waves of global migration patterns, are all over the world.

Southeast Asia, with all its layers of history and ancient cultures overlayed with world religions like Buddhism, Christianity, and Islam, is a complex system. Herein is the book's intention – to provide a way of being missional and doing missions by understanding complex systems. Since missions is the people of God responding to the world and needs of people with the truth of the gospel, Christians must be wise readers of the times. Current frameworks in mission studies, however, lack adequate approaches to analyze these events. For example while Samuel Huntington posits static cultures in his *Clash of Civilizations*, the twenty-first century has revealed its inadequacy in interpreting complex confluences.[9] David Brooks of the *New York Times* notes,

> I'd say Huntington misunderstood the nature of historical change. In his book, he describes transformations that move along linear, projectable trajectories. But that's not how things work in times of tumult. Instead, one person moves a step. Then the next person moves a step. Pretty soon, millions are caught up in a contagion, activating passions they had but dimly perceived just weeks before. They get swept up in momentums that have no central

---

7. E. Stanley Jones, *Christ of the Indian Road* (New York: Abingdon, 1925).
8. Paul Hiebert, "Critical Contextualization," *International Bulletin of Missionary Research* (July 1987): 104–12.
9. Samuel Huntington, *The Clash of Civilizations and the Remaking of World Order* (New York: Touchstone, 2011). See for example Amaryta Sen, "Democracy as a Universal Value," *Journal of Democracy* 10, no. 3 (1999): 3–17; and Edward Said, "The Clash of Ignorance: Labels like 'Islam' and 'the West' serve only to confuse us about a disorderly reality," *The Nation* (1 October 2001), https://www.thenation.com/article/archive/clash-ignorance/.

authority and that, nonetheless, exercise a sweeping influence on those caught up in their tides.[10]

A complex systems science (CSS) framework and complex adaptive systems (CAS) analyses are therefore necessary to understand the increasingly diverse, complex contexts of human interactions we face today. Economic crises like the Asian financial crisis of 1997, humanitarian catastrophes like the genocide in Cambodia (1975–1979), the Rohingya crisis of 2018, and the worldwide COVID-19 pandemic have torn all predictability and foreseeable patterns asunder. This volume is thus an attempt to integrate these approaches into missions research and practice in this diverse region. Thus this book will inform readers of the richness, diversity, and complexities of Southeast Asia and also equip readers and practitioners to develop appropriate frameworks by which to research and to minister in the diverse, complex contexts of the twenty-first century.

OVERVIEW OF THE BOOK

The book is in two parts. First is an historical survey of Christianity's journey in eight countries of Southeast Asia to provide a microlevel understanding of their churches and missions contexts. While not an exhaustive history that describes the state of Christianity in Southeast Asia,[11] these are accounts of Christian missions and the church in these countries written by national or international scholars who are familiar with the nuances of these countries. We note that where there are archives, especially in English, these histories are well documented, and the story of Christianity in that country can be readily told. However, civil war has torn apart Cambodia, so Samuel Law had to glean the story from available records in English, from his personal experiences, and from interactions with Cambodian Christians in Singapore. Knowing and understanding the history of each country is necessary to understand the regional churches today as well as the possibilities and obstacles for missions and ministry going forward.

The authors covering Malaysia, Myanmar, the Philippines, Singapore, and Thailand write about the common Western colonial experience and World War II and the Japanese Occupation. Because of each country's unique cultural

---

10. David Brooks, "Opinion Page: Huntington's Clash Revisited," *New York Times* (3 March 2011).
11. For a complete history, see Robbie G. H. Goh, *Christianity in Southeast Asia* (Singapore: ISEAS, 2005).

makeup however, the churches in these countries have emerged different. But like different parts of the body of Christ, all are important and necessary. What is common in these countries is the key role played by the early missionaries who appreciated and thus uplifted the local culture. In Malaysia and Myanmar, they learned the local languages and started printing presses; in Singapore they started schools for girls at a time when it was considered a waste of time to educate girls.

These nations also struggled with being occupied by the Japanese during the World War II (1942–1945) and with attaining independence from their respective colonial masters. This period is when Indonesian Benjamin Intan sets his account of the Indonesian church, and by doing so provides an example of how the church negotiated all of these aspects of nationhood.

Christianity came into a Southeast Asian context in which other religions already held sway. In Indonesia that religion was Islam, and in Cambodia, Thailand, and Vietnam it was Buddhism. With this background and history, the challenge for churches today is to be contextualized, expressing the gospel in languages, images, and rituals which are meaningful in each situation, as these histories show.

The second half of the book deals with broad issues which affect all the Southeast Asian countries, reinforcing the commonalities that arise from geographical proximity. Furthermore, since ASEAN is a regional grouping, it makes sense for the church to also view this region as a bloc with shared interests and concerns, though the uniqueness of each society still shines through.

This section uses complex systems approaches for research and analysis as explained in Samuel Law's chapter. The complex adaptive systems (CAS) framework raises awareness of the critical variables that are necessary to understand the trajectory of the *missio Dei*, thus enabling Christians, researchers, and practitioners to develop a more robust framework to navigate its metanarrative. The goal is to equip readers to understand the direction and shape of emerging trends and develop *prescriptive* long-term strategies. By understanding how CAS is applied to Christianity's trajectories in the Southeast Asian context, the lessons gained on the regional mesoscale hold the potential to shed insight on the macro-level scale of global Christianity.

While each chapter stands on its own merits, this book is more than a collection of articles; it is a complete whole in which each section and chapter are pieces of a larger puzzle (see Figure 1).

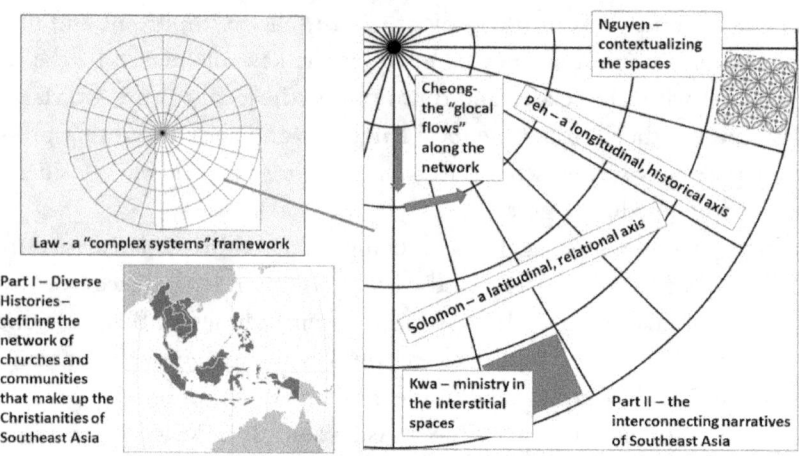

Figure 1: *Missiology for Southeast Asia* **Structure**

John Cheong explains globalization in broad strokes, such as its scapes and flows. As the twenty-first century is a study of processes rather than nation states, it is meaningful to understand the world in terms of flows and trajectories. Charting the forward direction, especially for Christian missions, requires an informed understanding of the past and present trajectories. People, including Christians, move with these flows and reflect some of these global values, such as the preference for worship songs from the West. Herein is the local expression of globalizing forces, which is called "glocalization."

The next two chapters by Andrew Peh and Robert Solomon are complementary as they describe the complex personal and organizational relationships which characterize Christian mission. Peh introduces the common longitudinal thread of the colonial legacy in the patchwork context that is Southeast Asia. He shows how colonialism has shaped Southeast Asian contexts, its cultures, its societies, and its churches. His insights reveal that the thread is not monolithic but multicolored and that the dyes in these threads, when mixed with different local contexts, create a mosaic of ever changing patterns. Informed Christians, researchers, and practitioners would do well to heed Peh's insights to ensure that proper forms of ministry and missions will be developed to navigate the changing trajectories of local contexts in the ocean of globalization.

Solomon introduces us to the latitudinal network relationships that define the push-pull factors of the diverse contexts of Southeast Asia. Unlike

Introduction

twentieth-century research methods that focus on describing states of being, twenty-first century complex systems methods and models focus on relationships and the dynamic interactions between entities. Like the multidirectional thrusters on a rocket ship, these connections define the forward trajectories in a given context. But more than this, Solomon also reminds us that these connections are multidirectional. Any change in one node of the web inevitably alters the course of its neighbors. Hence for any context, we need to be aware not only of the internal factors, but more importantly the external drivers and how the trajectory of one piece impacts all the other surrounding pieces.

The next two chapters deal with specific issues which when addressed will bring the church in Southeast Asia into a new level of maturity. A look at the meso- and microlevel of global flows reveals eddies, peaks, and valleys. These interstitial spaces are filled with abject poverty, rampant injustice, and the search for self-identity (as opposed to identities provided by colonial powers or globalization) that impact hearts, minds, and souls.

Kiem-Kiok Kwa's chapter sheds light on the role of churches in addressing social justice issues that arise from, among others, the deleterious effects of globalization and crowd the interstitial spaces of society. While Christian communities have been balms to smooth the symptoms of those who dwell in the interstitial spaces, Kwa reminds us that the church needs to respond holistically to social ills. Only in the coordinated efforts of networks and nodes can we create a safety net of social justice, and more importantly mitigate the forceful damage of global flows and transform them into channels of grace to a hurting world.

KimSon Nguyen offers an insightful case study of contextualization of ancestor veneration, an ongoing issue for Christians in this region. He integrates longitudinal and latitudinal variables to identify a fruitful trajectory that can help churches and mission agencies translate Christianity into the local context through the example of a self-theologizing exercise for evangelical Vietnamese churches. In his proposal for these evangelical Vietnamese churches, Nguyen provides a template for how gathering the individual pieces of the context can form a map by which to navigate into the future. The chapter contrasts the traditional, linear approach used in the past that resulted in a "foreign religion" which was ill-fitted to the local context and shows how a complex, systemic analysis can help produce a fertile faith that is rooted in Southeast Asian soil.

Since this work is intended to be used as a textbook, the chapters in the second half include case studies and exercises as heuristic tools for both understanding the content of the chapter and applying a complex analysis to real situations. These tools will help Christians, researchers, and practitioners develop richer frameworks and lenses to understand not only the twenty-first century complexities of Southeast Asia, but also the wider world.

Finally, Daniel Shaw's afterword reflects on the connections between the book's reflections on Southeast Asia and the broader missiological discussions in the world. This broadened horizon highlights the uniqueness of the region and allows both practitioners and researchers to better appreciate the insights of the book as well as see key paths for further study.

ACKNOWLEDGMENTS AND THANKS

We are grateful for the opportunity to work together with the contributors of this book. We have learned much through the lenses of their lives and experiences as we try to understand what God is doing in Southeast Asia. We thank them for responding positively to our invitation, even when we didn't know each other, and then waiting patiently through the various delays towards its completion.

We wish to especially thank the series editors, Drs. Steve Pardue and Andrew Spurgeon for their support and encouragement. They met with us regularly, giving helpful guidance, and keeping us on track in the midst of the COVID-19 pandemic and the lockdowns that we all experienced. Using the Zoom online platform for all our meetings, we spanned the globe, working from home, praying together, and encouraging each other through the surges and sadness of the pandemic's toll.

We thank ATA for entrusting us with the project and as well for our respective institutions Biblical Graduate School of Theology and Singapore Bible College for giving us the time to work on it.

Finally, we thank God for His daily grace through the entire process. As the pandemic raged around the world, God preserved all the authors and editors, and enabled us to see the larger narrative of God's work unfolding throughout Southeast Asia. It is our hope that you the readers will share the same hope and optimism of His faithfulness as you see His work in the pages to follow.

REFERENCES

Brooks, David. "Opinion Page: Huntington's Clash Revisited." *New York Times* (3 March 2011). http://www.nytimes.com/2011/03/04/opinion/04brooks.html.

Chong, Terence, and Evelyn Tan. "Why Christian expansionism is a quiet storm in Southeast Asia." *South China Morning Post* (21 November 2019). https://www.

Introduction

scmp.com/week-asia/politics/article/3038665/why-christian-expansionism-quiet-storm-southeast-asia.

Evers, Georg. "'On the Trail of Spices:' Christianity in South Asia: Common Traits of the Encounter of Christianity with Societies, Cultures, and Religions in Southeast Asia." In *The Oxford Handbook of Christianity in Asia*, edited by Felix Wilfred, 66–79. Oxford: Oxford University Press, 2014.

Frankenstein, John. "A Strategic Link: The Complex Diversity of Southeast Asia." *America: The Jesuit Review* (31 March 2014): 15–19.

Goh, Robbie G. H. *Christianity in Southeast Asia*. Singapore: ISEAS, 2005.

Hiebert, Paul. "Critical Contextualization." *International Bulletin of Missionary Research* (July 1987): 104–12.

Huntington, Samuel. *The Clash of Civilizations and the Remaking of World Order*. New York: Touchstone, 2011.

Jones, E. Stanley. *Christ of the Indian Road*. New York: Abingdon, 1925.

Roxborogh, John. "Contextualisation and re-contextualisation: Regional patterns in the history of Southeast Asian Christianity." *Asia Journal of Theology* 9, no. 1 (April 1995): 36–46.

Tan, Eugene K. B. "Faith, Freedom, and US Foreign Policy: Avoiding the Proverbial Clash of Civilizations in East and Southeast Asia." *The Review of Faith & International Affairs* 11, no. 1 (Spring 2013): 76–78.

Waalkes, Scott. "Beyond the Clash of Civilizations: Hermeneutical Hospitality as a Model for Civilizational Dialogue." *Christian Scholar's Review* 48, no. 3 (2019): 237–54.

"What is ASEAN." ASEAN-US Business Council (24 October 2019). https://www.usasean.org/why-asean/what-is-asean.

Wilson, H. S. "Partnership in Preparing Leadership for Mission and Ministry: A Continued Story of the Foundation for Theological Education in South East Asia." In *Reflection on and Equipping for Christian Mission*, edited by Stephen Bevans, Theresa Chai, J. Nelson Jennings, Knud Jorgensen, and Dietrich Werner, 362–73. Oxford: Regnum Books International, 2015.

PART I

A DIVERSITY OF LOCAL CHURCH HISTORIES

CHAPTER 2

THE REBIRTH OF THE CHURCH IN CAMBODIA

Samuel K. Law

Although the history of Christianity in Cambodia spans centuries, possibly to the Nestorians, the modern church in the twenty-first century in Cambodia is at the dawning of rebirth. As a consequence of the Pol Pot regime of the Khmer Rouge from 1975 to 1979, which resulted in a genocide of about two million people, sadly including the exodus or extermination of the vast majority of Christians, Christianity effectively ceased to exist in Cambodia. Today, however, the church in Cambodia is a testament to God's faithfulness as it emerges from one of the darkest moments of human history. Not only do the numbers of Christians and churches exceed pre-1975 numbers, the Christian witness of redemption has been woven into the rebuilding of the nation through the transformative testimonies of thousands of former Khmer Rouge members who have converted to Christianity.

From a missiological perspective, the story of the twenty-first century Cambodian church is also a reflection of "glocalization," in which the forces of globalization are contextualized through the lens of the local narrative, in particular the recent events of the nation's history. Tobias Brandner concludes, "Christianity in Cambodia today is a church in its infancy. It illustrates vividly how a church develops in a context of global religious exchange and how global mission activism and local context interact."[1]

This chapter explores these global and local forces. The chapter first provides a brief history of Christianity prior to 1975, continues by providing vignettes of the reemergent Cambodian church in the early twenty-first century, and concludes with exploring the challenges the church faces in the future.

---

1. Tobias Brandner, "Emerging Christianity in Cambodia: People Movement to Christ or Playground for Global Christianity?" *International Bulletin of Mission Research* 44, no. 3 (2020): 280.

Note that there is a paucity of comprehensive and definitive histories of the church post 1979, and what exists is mainly field-researched interviews and surveys.[2]

THE HISTORY OF CHRISTIANITY THROUGH 1979

It is highly likely that Christianity has been in Cambodia for over a thousand years. The first three waves, Nestorian, Roman Catholic, and Protestant missions, are similar to the rest of the Christian narrative in Southeast Asia. It is the fourth wave after the turbulent Khmer Rouge period of 1975–1979 that sets Cambodia apart from its Southeast Asian counterparts.

Although there are no historical records mentioning Christianity in Cambodia in the first millennium AD, there are credible accounts that Nestorian Christians were in Thailand, Burma (modern-day Myanmar), and Cambodia. The earliest report from eyewitness accounts of this first wave comes from Cosmos Indicopleustes. John C. England writes, "His report of those he discovered in the years AD 520–525 includes not only Socotra, along with southwest and central India, but also Taprobane (Sri Lanka), Pegu (southern Burma), Cochin China (southern Vietnam), Siam, and Tonquin (northern Vietnam)."[3] England concludes that, while a fuller picture remains to be completed, continuing discoveries of manuscripts, building ruins, and physical artefacts such as crosses increasingly support an early Christian presence in Indochina, including Cambodia.

The second wave came in the 1500s when the Roman Catholic Church sent missionaries to Cambodia. The beginnings were turbulent as several early missionaries were martyred. The Portuguese and the Spanish arrived first in the sixteenth century followed by the French in the eighteenth century. Portuguese Gaspar de Cruz was the first missionary, visiting Lovek in 1555, then meeting with King Chan the following year. Cruz was followed by Dominican Sylvestro de Azevedo in 1574 who established a church with a number of Cambodians. However, he was killed in 1576. Another Dominican missionary came in 1588, but he too was also martyred. In the early seventeenth century, about seventy Japanese Christians with a few Portuguese missionaries arrived in Cambodia as a consequence of the repression and persecution of Christianity in Japan

---

2. Brandner provides a list of resources in Brandner, "Emerging," 287–88.
3. John C. England, "The Earliest Christian Communities in Southeast and Northeast Asia: An Outline of the Evidence Available in Seven Countries Before A.D. 1500," *Missiology* 19, no. 2 (April 1991): 205–6.

under the Tokugawa shogunate. The Jesuits arrived in Cambodia shortly after, but they came to serve the Japanese Christians there.[4]

It was not until 1768 that the Catholic Church sent missionaries to work primarily for the Cambodians. This time the missionaries were French, the first being Nicholas Lefaser from Paris. In his love for Cambodia, Lefaser translated the catechism into the Khmer language. There were 222 Cambodian Christians in 1842, and by 1850, the number had grown to six hundred.[5] However, the spread of Christianity was limited as services were held in Latin; it was not until after the Second Vatican Council that worship services were held in Piesa Khmer. By 1970, there were an estimated sixty-six thousand Roman Catholics in Cambodia – though about fifty thousand were ethnic Vietnamese.[6]

The third wave of Christianity in Cambodia, Protestant missions, began in 1897 when the British Bible Society sent a Bible translator and distributor to Phnom Penh. But it was not until the arrival of two Christian and Missionary Alliance (CMA) missionaries and their wives in 1923 that missionary work began to take root. Other Protestant denominations were present in Cambodia, but due to the Comity agreements by the Protestant mission agencies to divide the work in Southeast Asia, the C&MA was the primary Protestant missions force in Cambodia until the 1980s. Protestant Vietnamese also made efforts to share their faith with Cambodians about this time.[7]

Protestant Christianity never fully developed in Cambodia because it was limited by anti-proselytization laws enacted by the Catholic-biased French colonial government, and because of a variety of social and historical factors. King Monivong banned all evangelistic activities in 1932. In 1941 the Japanese Occupation saw all missionaries interned. And in 1965, all Western missionaries were banned.[8]

Despite these barriers, the C&MA nevertheless made several notable contributions. They were the first to open a seminary in 1925. Second, they established a principle of self-support that called pastors to be bi-vocational. Third, their efforts led to the translation of the Bible into Khmer, the New

---

4. Joseph Keo Thyu, Hanns Hoeschelmann, and Anne Juergensen, "Cambodia," *The Ecumenical Review* 64, no. 2 (July 2012): 104. Note that there is a paucity of histories of the Cambodian church. This article is perhaps one of the best. See also the article of Tobias Brandner, a Catholic priest, who provides several additional sources, though mostly covering Catholic missions. Brandner, "Emerging."
5. Thyu, Hoeschelmann, and Juergensen, "Cambodia," 104.
6. Thyu, Hoeschelmann, and Juergensen, "Cambodia," 105.
7. Thyu, Hoeschelmann, and Juergensen, 105.
8. Brandner, "Emerging," 281.

Testament in 1934 and the Old Testament in 1940, with the first fully printed edition in 1953.[9] By 1975, there were roughly ten thousand Protestant Christians in Cambodia.[10]

But outside of the Khmer catechisms and Bible translations, the progress of Christianity up to 1975 was effectively obliterated by the Khmer Rouge and Pol Pot regime that devastated Cambodia until the Vietnamese army overthrew them in 1979. In the five year period known as the "Killing Fields," an estimated 1.5 to 2.5 million people, about 20 to 25 percent of the population, were killed.[11]

The Khmer Rouge brutally tortured and killed the people, targeting the intelligentsia, even those who merely wore eyeglasses, and those who appeared to be aligned with Western interests, while Christians were earmarked for their adherence to a foreign religion.[12] Many Christians fled the country, including fifty thousand Catholics, mostly Vietnamese, leaving some ten thousand Christians, both Catholic and Protestant, in 1975.[13] All records indicate that only two hundred Christians remained by 1979.[14] Kate Shellnutt writes, "One church in Phnom Penh was said to have gathered 600 Christians for a prayer service just weeks before the revolution. The members promised to return to the church and write their names on the wall to let each other know they survived. Years later, there were only three names listed."[15] Christianity in Cambodia effectively ceased to exist.

In 1979 the Vietnamese army invaded Cambodia, resulting in more than a decade of civil war. Finally, with the Paris Peace Agreement of 1991, Vietnam withdrew its forces. Freedom of religion was restored under the United Nations Transitional Authority (UNTAC).[16]

THE CHURCH IN CAMBODIA TODAY

With the return of peace in the early 1990s, Cambodia is experiencing a fourth wave of Christianity, and what may be deemed a "glocal" church is

---

9. Thyu, Hoeschelmann, and Juergensen, "Cambodia," 105.
10. Thyu, Hoeschelmann, and Juergensen, 106.
11. Brandner, "Emerging," 281.
12. "Cambodia," Center for Holocaust and Genocide Studies, College of Liberal Arts, University of Minnesota (n.d.).
13. Thyu, Hoeschelmann, and Juergensen, "Cambodia," 106.
14. Thyu, Hoeschelmann, and Juergensen, "Cambodia," 106; Brandner, "Emerging," 281; Kate Shellnutt, "Unlocking Cambodian Christianity," *Christianity Today* (June 2017): 36.
15. Shellnutt, "Unlocking," 36.
16. Thyu, Hoeschelmann, and Juergensen, "Cambodia," 112.

The Rebirth of the Church in Cambodia

emerging out of the country's ashes. It is a church that is young, vibrant, and new. According to Kate Shellnutt,

> Like everything in Cambodia, Christianity skews young. In the aftermath of the civil war and resulting genocide, epitomized in the notorious and haunting Killing Fields, 60 percent of the country's population is under 30. Few Christians can say their faith dates back to before Pol Pot and the Khmer Rouge took power in 1975.[17]

In other words, many Christians are first-generation believers.[18] Ninety-nine percent of today's churches were founded after 1993.[19]

Perhaps the most detailed statistics of the Christian population in Cambodia come from Mission Kampuchea 2021 (MK2021) which estimates that in 2017, there were 171,000 Protestant Christians, or 1.29 percent of the population. Including Catholics, about twenty-five thousand believers (though many are of Vietnamese origin), Christianity accounts for 1.5 to 2.0 percent of the population.[20]

MK2021 counts 3,205 churches in Cambodia.[21] The C&MA churches, now known as the Khmer Evangelical Church (KEC), remains the largest denomination. However since 1993, all major denominations are now present and growing in numbers. In terms of networks, the Evangelical Fellowship of Cambodia (EFC), founded in 1996, includes 75–80 percent of all Cambodian Christians, while another is the Kampuchea Christian Council (KCC), founded in 1998 and affiliated with the World Council of Churches.[22]

Missionaries are no longer just from the West. Many are Cambodians who emigrated as refugees and returned to bring the gospel to their homeland. Seven hundred missionaries, or one for every three hundred believers, come from South Korea. Two other significant groups come from affluent churches in Singapore and Hong Kong.[23]

Churches in Cambodia have broad, hope-filled visions to evangelize their country. They recognize that they have a window of opportunity, for "while persecution still percolates in other Southeast Asian countries, Cambodian

---

17. Shellnutt, "Unlocking," 36.
18. Thyu, Hoeschelmann, and Juergensen, "Cambodia," 115.
19. Brandner, "Emerging," 282.
20. Brandner, 282.
21. Brandner, 283.
22. Brandner, 283.
23. Brandner, 283.

Christians enjoy a promising sense of openness from leaders and neighbors. . . . They want to see Cambodia's Christian population reach 10 percent, surging 'the same way God changed South Korea.'"[24] MK2021 sets out a vision to plant a church in every village. New Life Church, a megachurch in Phnom Penh, on its own wants to plant five hundred churches throughout Cambodia's twenty-four provinces.[25]

THE CHURCH AS A CATALYST FOR NATIONAL HEALING

I can attest to this youthful enthusiasm among Cambodian Christians. Our family had the chance to observe the reemergence of Christianity over several short-term mission trips to Cambodia between 2005 and 2019, and we heard the testimonies of God's work there from missionaries from Singapore as well as Cambodian students studying at Singapore Bible College. My first visit to Cambodia was to a Christian Nationals Evangelism Commission (CNEC) student hostel in Phnom Penh where I taught preaching for ten days to group of twenty young men and women in their early twenties. These young Christians had come to Christ through a Cambodian contextualized form of evangelism in which churches and mission agencies offer free or subsidized dormitory accommodation for poor students.[26] Through building relationships, many became Jesus followers. This practice draws from the local custom of young people when they reach puberty spending a year in a local Buddhist temple or living in a temple during their university studies. During the trip, I followed a team of young Christians who went back to their village to share the gospel, another common pathway of evangelism.[27] We also went to Batambang, the third largest city, where we visited a CNEC hostel and vocational center for young women who were exploited as sex workers in human trafficking, many sold by their parents. I was told that in the Buddhist worldview, fealty and honor to parents takes such a high precedence that prostitution is not necessarily seen as pejorative. One young woman was in her second time at the center, for after CNEC returned her to the village after the first time, her parents immediately resold her into prostitution.

My family's later visits from 2018 to 2019 focused on building projects for orphanages. Though most of the work was manual labor, nevertheless such

---

24. Shellnutt, "Unlocking," 35–36.
25. Shellnutt, 35.
26. Brandner, "Emerging," 284.
27. Brandner, 284.

trips provided opportunities to build relationships with the orphans and with the surrounding community.

The above snapshots of ministry in Cambodia reflect the gospel characteristics of loving relationships, sacrifice, and human dignity, values which are in stark contrast to the brutality, violence, and senseless slaughter of human beings by the Pol Pot regime. These attributes are why Christianity faces less resistance in Cambodia compared with other Southeast Asian countries and is welcomed by Cambodians. "Christianity attracts through being a good community, a helping community, a sharing community. This is the most important factor that makes Christianity grow."[28]

During my visit in 2005, the local CNEC (Christian Nationals' Evangelism Commission, known as Partners' International in North America) missionary shared that during the Pol Pot regime, people were forced to inform on their neighbors and students on their teachers; even children were made to inform on their parents and other relatives. Many of the accusations were false fabrications given to preserve the teller's own life. Such tactics by the Pol Pot regime essentially tore and ripped asunder the social fabric of Cambodia.

The consequence of the Pol Pot regime was that people focused on self-preservation. Every student in the Christian hostel I visited had experienced being forced to bring accusations against someone else and had lost members of their family. A missionary shared that as a consequence, very few Cambodians after 1979 had relationships with more than five people and generally kept to themselves; trust became a very scarce commodity after the Killing Fields.

Also the stain of guilt, particularly in the Buddhist karmic worldview, is a burden that everyone bears, both perpetrators and victims. There is "an element of disillusionment with Buddhist belief, particularly the belief in karma. Considering the atrocities of the Khmer Rouge and the extent of suffering, the framework of karma offers little comfort or meaningful interpretive help."[29]

But this national trauma is exactly why Christianity is now intertwined with rebuilding the Cambodian nation, particularly through the witness of thousands of Khmer Rouge soldiers who converted to Christianity. "For example, in one Khmer Rouge district, among converts to Christianity, some seventy percent were estimated to be former Khmer Rouge. Recent commentary and analysis further indicate the significance of conversion among former Khmer

---

28. Brandner, 285.
29. Brandner, 286.

Rouge as a social and political phenomenon."[30] The redemptive aspect of the gospel plays a unique and contextualized role in the Christian witness in Cambodia. "Conversion to the Christian faith signifies a clear and liberating break with the past, not only for victims but also for perpetrators."[31] Much like South Africa's Truth and Reconciliation Commission brought healing to that nation torn apart by apartheid, the conversion of former Khmer Rouge to Christianity has created a platform for peacebuilding and transitional justice in Cambodia. Conversion "acts as a lens for understanding one's own past, through which all experience is reconsidered, while furnishing a new way of organizing recollections of past experiences, imposing its own sequences and temporalities, and staking out its own narrative points of renewal."[32] One convert writes,

> We know that the Khmer Rouge regime killed a lot of people. So, we tell young people not to follow that path again. So, if many people believe in Christianity, the killing would be reduced. Those who believe in Christianity do not kill each other. We love each other as we are all the children of God. But those who do not believe they said that they are not children of God. If we believe in God, there is no killing, only loving each other.[33]

Conversion to Christianity "has emerged as a conviction of ex-members of the Khmer Rouge in ways that make their experiences of a chaotic, changing post-conflict landscape meaningful, independent of a formal peace or reconciliation process." "Khmer Rouge conversions to Christianity have implications for peace building and transitional justice trajectories in Cambodia, in so far as they furnish different lenses for thinking about experiences of suffering, violence and atrocity."[34]

Of course, there may be doubts as to whether these conversions are genuine, and conversion may serve as an addiction in the catharsis of the nation. One phenomenon is that of multiple baptisms. One church leader wryly notes, "People receive baptism until the fishes recognize their faces."[35] Coupled with

---

30. Peter Manning, Keo Duong, and Daniel Kilburn, "Faith in forgiveness? Exploring conversions to Christianity within a former Khmer Rouge community," *Critical Asian Studies* 51, no. 1 (2019): 52.
31. Brandner, "Emerging," 286.
32. Manning, Duong, and Kilburn, "Forgiveness," 62.
33. Quoted in Manning, Duong, and Kilburn, 66.
34. Manning, Duong, and Kilburn, 66, 69.
35. Brandner, "Emerging," 286.

the Buddhist karmic worldview, some believe repeated baptisms can tip the scales toward good as "bad sin" is removed.[36] Yet despite these concerns, few can dispute how the Christian worldview and conversion to Christianity has played a role in the healing process of the nation.

One pastor summarizes the current openness and opportunities Christianity has in Cambodia: "When the church can do this kind of work in society, it creates a positive view and [neighbors] aren't scared of Christians anymore. They'll say 'I came here to learn English only, no Jesus.' But then they'll come to Sunday school and fall in love with Jesus."[37]

CHALLENGES FACING THE FUTURE OF CHRISTIANITY

But as much as the presence of Christianity has spread since the 1990s, the rapid growth and a fragile and broken society coupled with an onslaught of international and global influences have resulted in major challenges for the future of the Cambodian church. Four challenges are highlighted in this section: (1) the need to develop a local Christian identity; (2) self-sufficiency; (3) the critical need for contextual theology and the lack of theological education for both clergy and laity; and (4) an appropriate missional model for the future Cambodia.

The first challenge is the confusing and often competitive nature of foreign agencies and organizations that have imprinted a foreign form of Christianity without any regard for the Cambodian context. Brandner writes, "mission agencies have made Cambodia a battleground."[38] Thyu, Hoeschelmann, and Juergensen note, "Many missionaries also teach Cambodians to evangelize in a very offensive and aggressive way: If you don't convert to Christianity, you will go to hell."[39]

On the flip side, because of the onslaught of global players, Cambodian Christianity lacks an indigenous identity. Subsequently, non-Christians in Cambodia see Christians as following a foreign religion.[40] For example a typical worship service in Cambodia bears no resemblance to local culture and traditions. In his travels, Brandner observed the following of church services:

---

36. Manning, Duong, and Kilburn, "Forgiveness," 62.
37. Shellnutt, "Unlocking," 37.
38. Brandner, "Emerging," 285.
39. Thyu, Hoeschelmann, and Juergensen, "Cambodia," 122.
40. Thyu, Hoeschelmann, and Juergensen, 113.

> The worship [in Phnom Penh] could be from any international church in the Global South: modern praise songs from Hillsong, testimonies, a charismatic sermon offered by a young American pastor with simultaneous on-stage translation into Khmer – simple, effective, and reflecting a global worship culture. A week later, at a rural church in a village twenty kilometers outside the capital, the Christian community is small. Foreigners are largely absent: the band on stage is even younger than the one in Phnom Penh, and the preacher is a local woman. Looking below the surface, however, the similarities are evident: the atmosphere and worship style of both congregations are reminiscent of a generic church culture that is nowhere and everywhere at home, connecting with every context without belonging to anyone.[41]

Hence churches in Cambodia are being shaped and defined by external, global agencies.

The second challenge is a heavy reliance on foreign support. Cambodia is one of the poorest countries in the region and has the highest incidence of HIV.[42] Subsistence farming employs 70 percent of the workforce.[43] Churches in Cambodia are highly dependent on foreign aid to survive. A Cambodian Bible costs US $7.00, but the average monthly offering of a typical Cambodian church is US $8.06.[44] Thyu, Hoeschelmann, and Juergensen note that many church leaders and churches disappear after support is removed. "Serious dependency issues [exist] with foreign money, foreign control, or self-promotion with foreign backing. They may not have even realized it, but everything they did was further creating dependence. Once the source was gone, the church and leaders rapidly declined."[45]

In an interview a missions pastor from a large Singapore church shared a similar story with me. Their goal was to plant twenty churches by giving a local Cambodian church planter SG $200 (US $150) a month for two years and SG $100 (US $75) a month in the third year, hoping that by the fourth year, each church planted would be financially independent. Unfortunately, the pastor lamented that after three years, all of the local pastors told the Singapore

---

41. Brandner, "Emerging," 280
42. Ladislav Bucko, Elena Rauschova, and Jana Tretiakova-Adamcova, "The Search for a Current Mission Model in Cambodia," *International Review of Mission* 109, no. 1 (May 2020): 29.
43. Thyu, Hoeschelmann, and Juergensen, "Cambodia," 107.
44. Thyu, Hoeschelmann, and Juergensen, 110.
45. Thyu, Hoeschelmann, and Juergensen, 111.

church that they could not survive without additional support. Though congregations ranged from twenty to fifty people, mostly in rural villages, the monthly offerings were insufficient to sustain the pastor or the church. Many Cambodian churches are totally reliant on foreign support to survive.

These two global challenges conflate each other. An interviewee said,

> There is a lot of division in the church because of payments from mission societies. Many missions do not focus on gospel ministry. They try to influence church members by using their resources. They come with money and try to win over the people. I want foreign missions to make the local church, not themselves, visible.[46]

These first two challenges lead to the third challenge, the need for theological education to develop sound, contextual theology for the Cambodian church. With the rapid growth of the Christian population, clergy and laity alike are in great want of theological education. The majority of pastors have only received theological education through short-term programs or seminars.[47] Without reflective, contextual theology, callously imprinting a global Christianity that ignores the local context results in unintended consequences. While evangelism has been contextualized somewhat as earlier mentioned in the adoption of youth hostels and bringing the gospel to rural villages through urban migrants, the failure to understand the local religious and historical context has led to unsound practices, such as the phenomenon of multiple baptisms to balance bad karma, "bad sins." Baptism should be the means of identification with Christ, not an absolution ritual. Thyu, Hoeschelmann, and Juergensen conclude that

> although there is a big need for theological education in Cambodia today, it is not just any education or teaching. There is a huge need for theological education that is qualified and reflective, and teaches students to think for themselves so as to be able to apply and contextualize in a constructive way.[48]

Finally because of the lack of both local contextual theology and theological education, the fourth challenge is the need for a contextualized mission model for a maturing, self-sustaining, and "glocal" Cambodian church.

---

46. Brandner, "Emerging," 285.
47. Thyu, Hoeschelmann, and Juergensen, "Cambodia," 113.
48. Thyu, Hoeschelmann, and Juergensen, 122. However, see Solomon in chapter 13 of this volume for an account of setting up theological education by the Methodist church.

Current mission models must take into account the local context, especially its history. Otherwise they are damaging the Christian witness in Cambodia and creating unsound dependency on foreign agencies.

In summary, the challenges are conflated and interdependent. Only a holistic model can address all four challenges simultaneously and constructively. Thyu, Hoeschelmann, and Juergensen write that they, "see a need to develop a Cambodian Christian culture: how to live with Buddhists in families and in communities; how to contribute as Christians to the reconstruction of the society, culturally, ethically, socially and financially."[49]

Some mission agencies have begun to realize that the early C&MA model of self-sufficiency is the more appropriate approach considering Cambodia's context. Pastors should be trained to be bi-vocational to support themselves and their ministry. According to Brandner, "Such bi-vocational leadership, independent of mission agencies, is a contextually appropriate form of ministry."[50]

One Singapore-based mission agency has met with some success in developing such bi-vocational pastors. A village is selected, and the local pastor gives a pair of piglets to some villagers. They are required to rear them and then to return to the pastor a pair of piglets from the first litter. This missional scheme is both self-propagating and multiplicative.

The pastor assigned to the village is trained in veterinary skills to care for the pigs, and this approach offers several benefits. First, the pastor has an opportunity not only to care for the pigs, but also to open a natural door to homes and build relationships with the villagers. Second, payment of the pastor's living expenses is not dependent on the meager church offerings, but is derived from the income or bartered goods of monthly veterinary visits. When the pair of piglets are returned to the pastor at the end of the year, the pastor keeps some for his own drove of pigs which he can breed or sell. Unlike the Cambodian pastors who received the monthly allowance from the Singapore church for three years, these bi-vocational pastors became self-sufficient by the second year, only receiving theological and veterinary training thereafter. Moreover, natural relationships were enabled between the pastor and the villagers, and the village community as a whole benefited materially and spiritually.

For the long term, one approach that provides a forward trajectory is a hypothetical model being developed for the Catholic mission in Cambodia. The nation's religious, historical, and socioeconomic contexts are all taken

---

49. Thyu, Hoeschelmann, and Juergensen, 124.
50. Brandner, "Emerging," 285.

into account. For example to address the issue of multiple baptisms, they recommend that new converts undergo discipleship for at least three years, possibly four.[51] This discipleship follows the practice of the early church and was proposed for Taiwanese converts.[52] To differentiate between community development and faith, they argue that

> Conversion to Christianity is not a goal of the mission. Here we see Christianity as one of the world religions with its ideology, history, and tradition, which is somehow in competition with other world religions. In this context, we must distinguish between Christianity and the church. We see the church as the way, means, and sign of mission. . . . the aim of mission in Cambodia is rather to bring the witness of God's love, to help people to gain a fuller and dignified life, and to help them to understand and to live the gospel values. The main goal of the mission is to help people establish personal contact with Jesus.[53]

Hence missionaries focus on "value orientation, such as the concern for the good of others, living in truth, the protection of life, and no corruption, rather than the specific elements of a material culture. They mediate values of the gospel to the Cambodians, but the way they understand it as a new way, their own way."[54] A reflective theology, sensitive to the local context, provides a missional way forward that helps Cambodian Christians and churches form a "glocal" identity that not only strengthens the church, but also communities and the nation as a whole.

It remains to be seen how long the window of opportunity will remain open and whether or not the church in Cambodia can fulfill its vision. Brandner prophetically concludes,

> Christianity plays an important role in supporting Cambodians as they cope with globalization and modernization. Yet divisions imported from global Christianity and inequalities spread by the global economy have deeply shaped Cambodian Christianity. It remains to be seen whether, out of this Christian body strongly

---

51. Bucko, Rauschova, and Tretiakova-Adamcova, "Mission Model," 30.
52. Jim Courson, "Deepening the Bonds of Christian Community: Applying Rite of Passage Structure to the Discipling Process in Taiwan," *Missiology* 25, no. 3 (July 1998): 301–13.
53. Bucko, Rauschova, and Tretiakova-Adamcova, "Mission Model," 30.
54. Bucko, Rauschova, and Tretiakova-Adamcova, 33.

dominated by global players, a contextual form of Cambodian Christianity will grow and flourish.[55]

REFERENCES

Brandner, Tobias. "Emerging Christianity in Cambodia: People Movement to Christ or Playground for Global Christianity?" *International Bulletin of Mission Research* 44, no. 3 (2020): 279–89.

Bucko, Ladislav, Elena Rauschova, and Jana Tretiakova-Adamcova. "The Search for a Current Mission Model in Cambodia." *International Review of Mission* 109, no. 1 (May 2020): 27–39.

"Cambodia." Center for Holocaust and Genocide Studies, College of Liberal Arts, University of Minnesota (n.d.). https://cla.umn.edu/chgs/holocaust-genocide-education/resource-guides/cambodia.

Courson, Jim. "Deepening the Bonds of Christian Community: Applying Rite of Passage Structure to the Discipling Process in Taiwan." *Missiology* 25, no. 3 (July 1998): 301–13.

England, John C. "The Earliest Christian Communities in Southeast and Northeast Asia: An Outline of the Evidence Available in Seven Countries Before A.D. 1500." *Missiology* 19, no. 2 (April 1991): 203–15.

Manning, Peter, Keo Duong, and Daniel Kilburn. "Faith in forgiveness? Exploring conversions to Christianity within a former Khmer Rouge community." *Critical Asian Studies* 51, no. 1 (2019): 51–74.

Shellnutt, Kate. "Unlocking Cambodian Christianity." *Christianity Today* (June 2017): 34–38.

Thyu, Joseph Keo, Hanns Hoeschelmann, and Anne Juergensen. "Cambodia." *The Ecumenical Review* 64, no. 2 (July 2012): 104–25.

---

55. Brandner, "Emerging," 287.

CHAPTER 3

HISTORY OF CHRISTIANITY IN INDONESIA

THE WITNESS OF PROTESTANT MISSION THROUGH THE *PANCASILA*-BASED STATE

Benyamin F. Intan

INTRODUCTION

Indonesia is the largest archipelago in the world and has a population of 265 million, making it the world's fourth most populous country.[1] With almost twenty thousand islands covering an area of more than 9.8 million square kilometers, Indonesia is arguably one of the most ethnically and culturally heterogeneous nations. The population includes over three hundred different ethnic groups who speak more than 250 distinct languages.[2] With regard to religious life, all the major world religions are represented in Indonesia, along with a wide range of folk religions and animistic beliefs. Among these faiths, Islam is held by approximately 87 percent of the population, making Muslims the largest religious group in Indonesia. The 2010 Indonesian census recorded the population as 87.18 percent Muslims, 6.96 percent Protestants, 2.91 percent Catholics, 1.69 percent Hindus, 0.72 percent Buddhists, 0.05 Confucians, and 0.13 percent who are designated as "Others."[3]

The history of Christianity in Indonesia follows a similar pattern with the other Southeast Asian countries. Christianity was introduced in a first wave by the Eastern Orthodox Church in the twelfth century with some settlements; however, the rise of Islam from the thirteenth century soon eclipsed

---
1. See Bappenas, "Proyeksi Penduduk Indonesia 2010–2035," Subdirektorat Statistik Demografi (2013).
2. Hildred Geertz, "Indonesian Cultures and Communities," in *Indonesia*, ed. Ruth T. McVey (New Haven: HRAF Press, 1963), 24.
3. "Sensus Indonesia 2010," Badan Pusat Statistik (n.d.).

them. A second wave of Christianity was driven by the Roman Catholic Church through Portuguese missionaries from Malacca in the sixteen century. However, the history of Christianity in Indonesia has been heavily dominated by the third wave driven by the Dutch Reformed Church whose missionaries arrived with the Dutch East India company in the seventeenth century.[4] The other denominations that came to Indonesia after World War II – Methodists, Baptists, Assemblies of God, Seventh-Day Adventists, and others – comprise only seven percent of the Protestant churches.[5]

Today while Christians enjoy freedom of religion as defined and protected by Indonesia's Constitution, nevertheless the future of churches and missions in Indonesia is increasingly shaped by how *Pancasila,* Indonesia's founding five-fold state ideology,[6] is being interpreted or reinterpreted. Robbie Goh writes,

> while in theory this leaves room for considerable freedom of religion, in practice the overwhelming socio-political dominance of Islam clearly makes it the privileged religion. Islamic societies and parties hold considerable socio-political influence, especially on the central island of Java and in the capital of Jakarta; with their vast numbers of members who are prepared to vote and even demonstrate on behalf of their party, they confer upon their religious leaders the weight to influence top political decisions.[7]

This chapter explores the history, current factors, and future trajectory of *Pancasila* as it relates to religion and state relationships. Within the context of the entire book, this chapter reminds us that every context is unique, and the shape and trajectory of Christianity must be analyzed through the local lens. For Indonesia, this lens is not cultural or social, but political.

CONSTITUTIONAL DEFINITIONS OF RELIGION AND STATE RELATIONSHIPS

As Indonesia is religiously pluralistic, early on the founding fathers fully realized the potential danger of the majority religion rising to tyranny and had accordingly paid careful attention to the problem of relations between

---

4. Robbie B. H. Goh, *History of Christianity in Southeast Asia* (Singapore: ISEAS, 2005): 57–58.
5. Goh, *History of Christianity*, 60.
6. Pancasila which derives from the words "Panca" (five) and "Sila" (guideline) meaning "five guidelines" consists of five principles – Lordship, human rights, nationalism, democracy, and social justice. J. Verkuyl, *Contemporary Missiology: An Introduction* (Grand Rapids: Eerdmans, 1978), 383.
7. Goh, *History of Christianity*, 60.

religion and the state. Their concern is expressed in chapter 29 of the 1945 Constitution, or *Undang-Undang Dasar* (UUD), which states that "[t]he State shall be based on [the principle of One Lordship]" and that "[t]he State guarantees the freedom of every inhabitant to embrace his/her respective religion and to worship according to his/her religion and faith as such."[8] These statements contain three basic thoughts. First, Indonesia is not a theocratic state since no religion is explicitly mentioned in the Constitution. This means that the State should be fair to all religions and not take sides with any one religion. Second, being founded on the principle of "One Lordship," the State appreciates and encourages the contributions of diverse religions in the life of the nation.[9] Third, the Constitution guarantees the freedom of each individual to change his or her beliefs or religion.

However, while the Constitution guarantees freedom of religion to Indonesian citizens, it does not specify, for example, how religion and state should properly relate to one another to avoid both the politicization of religion and the religionization of politics. Two other important matters left unaddressed are how religion should fulfill its responsibility toward the state and the state toward religion in encouraging the role of religion in the public sphere.

In spite of the Constitution's protections, violations of religious freedom and tolerance still occur among the religious minorities. The Setara Institute for Democracy and Peace notes that in 2012 there were 264 cases of violation against the freedom of religion or belief that involved 371 types of violent acts. The highest numbers of violations of religious freedom were those committed against Christian congregations (50 cases), apostates of minority religious beliefs (42 cases), and the Shiah and Ahmadiyah congregations (34 and 31 cases respectively).[10] Violence against people of particular religions and violations

---

8. The Constitutional Court of the Republic of Indonesia, *The 1945 Constitution of the Republic of Indonesia* (Jakarta: The Office of the Registrar and the Secretariat General of the Constitutional Court of the Republic of Indonesia, 2015), 30. See https://www.mkri.id/public/content/infoumum/regulation/pdf/uud45%20eng.pdf (accessed on 22 June, 2022).
9. See Benyamin F. Intan, *"Public Religion" and the Pancasila-based State of Indonesia: An Ethical and Sociological Analysis* (New York: Peter Lang, 2006).
10. Out of these 371 acts of violence, 226 were perpetrated by Indonesian citizens and 145 by the state, involving state officials as its initiators. The most conspicuous of the 226 violations committed by Indonesian citizens comprised 169 cases of criminal offense, 42 cases of religious intolerance, and 15 cases in which violence was condoned. Out of the 145 violations committed by the state, 117 were actually perpetrated by the state and 28 were not prevented by the state. The state institutions involved in the highest number of violations of religious freedom included the police (40 cases), the District Administrator (28 cases), the City Administrator (10 cases), the Ministry of Religion (8 cases), the Subdistrict Administrator (8 cases), and the

against religious minorities resulting in many human rights issues in Indonesia were highlighted in the Universal Periodic Review (UPR) of the Human Rights Council of the United Nations on 23 May 2012.

The Christian witness in Indonesia is complex due to the interplays between religion and politics. For example, Indonesian Christians are among the staunchest defenders of human rights and freedoms in the country. Yet because the Dutch most recently brought Christianity to Indonesia, Indonesian Christians are often associated with Western values and colonialism. Unfortunately, this minority sociopolitical position has resulted in the loss of social standing, and for some even the loss of life. This chapter explores four aspects of the Christian witness in Indonesia. First, the role of Indonesian Christians in fighting for freedom and defending human rights will be explored. Second, the various discriminative regulations used to restrict the freedom and rights of non-Muslims, especially Christians, will be examined. Third, the government's discriminative attempts from the perspective of Christian witness in Indonesia will be critically and reflectively evaluated. And fourth, a number of practical strategies that not only protect the freedom and rights of minorities in Indonesia but more importantly preserve the founding fathers' spirit of *Pancasila* will be recommended. The chapter will seek to demonstrate how the principles that founded the Christian witness provide a critical voice in Indonesian politics (descriptive) that preserves the aspirations of the founding fathers (prescriptive) as expressed in the Constitution.

THE WITNESS OF PROTESTANT MISSION

It has not been easy for Protestant Christians to exist and bear witness in Indonesia due to Dutch colonialism. While the Dutch did introduce Protestantism to Indonesia, their initial concern was only for their own people who were residing in the country. Colonialism did create an infrastructure for the coming of Western missionaries to propagate the Protestant faith. Protestant missions eventually freed themselves from colonial rule when the Dutch powers were forced out by the Japanese who occupied Indonesia in 1942. These three and a half years of the Japanese Occupation became a blessing in disguise for the development of the Indonesian churches. In order to

---

Office of the Attorney General (6 cases). Bonar Tigor Naipospos, ed., *Presiden tanpa Prakarsa: Kondisi Kebebasan/Beragama Berkeyakinan di Indonesia 2012* (Jakarta: Pustaka Masyarakat Setara, 2012), 31–49.

pursue their agenda of establishing "the Greater Asia Co-prosperity Sphere,"[11] the Japanese administration expelled the Dutch and replaced the European leadership of the churches with local Christians.[12] The transfer of church leadership into the hands of local Christians made the local Christians realize their responsibility to the faith they embraced.[13] This experience, in spite of the difficulties which ensued, actually worked to prepare the churches to become self-reliant. The realization of these self-reliant churches, freed from colonial rule, reached its peak when Indonesian independence was declared in 1945.

Historians note that from the very beginning, Protestant Christians played a pivotal role in the nationalist movement. During the pre-independence period, they participated in promoting national unity in several ways, one of which was to involve themselves in regional fights against the Dutch colonists. Thomas Matulessy, also known as Pattimura (1783–1817), led an insurrection against the Dutch in his hometown of Saparua in the Moluccan islands. The eminent Protestant T. B. Simatupang considers Pattimura, later honored as a national hero, as one of the "early Christian nationalists."[14]

Another significant way of promoting national unity was pioneered by the younger generation of Christian Protestants. While each of the Protestant churches at the time maintained their ethnic identity, the younger generation named themselves ethnically as for example Young Batak, Young Minahasa, Young Ambon, and Young Timor and participated in a national Youth Congress held on 28 October 1928.[15] In this meeting, representatives of the Indonesian youth unanimously pledged allegiance to Indonesia, endorsing the *Sumpah Pemuda* (Youth Pledge) in which they acknowledged that they belonged to One Nation, Indonesia; to One Motherland, Indonesia; and to One Language, Indonesian.[16]

---

11. Th. van den End and Jan S. Aritonang, "1800–2005: A National Overview," in *A History of Christianity in Indonesia*, eds. Jan Sihar Aritonang and Karel Steenbrink (Leiden, Boston: Brill, 2008), 179.
12. van den End and Aritonang, "1800–2005," 182.
13. John Titaley, "From abandonment to blessing: the theological presence of Christianity in Indonesia," in *Christian Theology in Asia*, ed. Sebastian C. H. Kim (Cambridge: Cambridge University Press, 2008), 76.
14. R. A. F. Webb, *Indonesian Christians and Their Political Parties 1923–1966: The Role of Partai Kristen Indonesia and Partai Katolik* (North Queensland: James Cook University, 1978), 24.
15. The twenty-eighth of October has been nationally commemorated as *Hari Sumpah Pemuda* (Youth Pledge Day).
16. T. B. Simatupang, "Dynamics for Creative Maturity," in *Asian Voices in Christian Theology*, ed. Gerald H. Anderson (Maryknoll: Orbis, 1976), 93–94.

These young Christians choosing the national identity "Indonesian" over tribal identities led to the establishment of *Christen Studenten Vereniging* (CSV, Student Christian Movement) in 1932. It was CSV that made it possible for students to be both nationalist and Christian at the same time. CSV was the pioneer of *Dewan Gereja-gereja di Indonesia* (DGI, Council of Churches in Indonesia), which appeared in late May 1950 with the intention of founding the *Gereja Kristen yang Esa di Indonesia* (the Single Christian Church in Indonesia). Simatupang states that one of the reasons for founding DGI was the growth of "a national consciousness, in the sense that the ethnic churches were seen as being called to grow into one church in order to express together the Christian presence in the nation."[17] In short, the Christian church played a critical role in the formation of a national Indonesian consciousness.

Protestant Christians also founded *Partai Kristen Nasional* (PKN, the National Christian Party), later renamed *Partai Kristen Indonesia* (Parkindo, the Indonesian Christian Party), on 10–11 November 1945. According to Martinus Abednego, one of its founders, Parkindo was "an organization of the Protestant Christians from various Protestant churches" functioning as "a working communion to struggle on the calling and responsibility of the Protestant Christians to the nation and the country."[18] Thus the presence of Parkindo disclosed the commitment of Protestant Christians to contribute to the nation and the state.

Furthermore, Protestant Christians had participated in the reconciliation process between Indonesia and the Netherlands to end the war. Johannes Leimena and T. B. Simatupang were among the Indonesian delegates who met with the Dutch at the Dutch-Indonesian Round Table Conference in The Hague in late 1949 to finalize the settlement of the war and to achieve constitutional acknowledgement of Indonesia's independence.[19]

The pinnacle of the Protestant Christians' contribution to national unity was seen in the strategic role they played in the formulation of *Pancasila*, Indonesia's national ideology, whereby a united Indonesia could be secured. From 29 May to 1 June 1945, *Badan Penyelidik Usaha Persiapan Kemerdekaan Indonesia* (BPUPKI, the Investigating Committee for Preparatory Work for Indonesian Independence) met to discuss the formulation of Indonesia's

---

17. T. B. Simatupang, "Doing Theology in Indonesia Today," *CTC Bulletin* 3, no. 2 (August 1982): 25.
18. Martinus Abednego, *Suatu Partisipasi* (Jakarta: BPK Gunung Mulia, 1976), 39. Quoted in van den End and Aritonang, "1800–2005," 190–91.
19. Simatupang, "Dynamics," 100–101.

ideological basis of the state (*Weltanschauung*). The discussion reached a deadlock due to the ideological confrontation between *golongan Islam*, a Muslim nationalist group who wanted Islam to be the ideological basis of the state, and *golongan kebangsaan*, a secular nationalist group who wanted Indonesia to be a secular state in which religion is separate from the state. Soekarno's address to the meeting about *Pancasila* on 1 June 1945 was well received by both parties, and he succeeded in breaking the deadlock.

On 22 June 1945, *Pancasila* was reformulated in a document known as the *Piagam Jakarta* (Jakarta Charter). In this document the first principle of *Pancasila*, namely the principle of Lordship, was reformulated by adding the clause "*dengan kewajiban menjalankan syariat Islam bagi pemeluk-pemeluknya*" (with the obligation to carry out the Islamic law by its adherents)[20] after the word "Lordship." Although it had been repeatedly asserted that the clause known as "the seven words" would apply to Indonesian Muslims only and not to other religious groups, the clause soon attracted rigorous objections, especially from the Christians. Latuharhary, a strong Protestant figure and member of BPUPKI, expressed his objection by stating that the seven words "could have considerable consequences regarding other religions, and moreover could lead to difficulties in connection with the *adat-istiadat* (customary law)."[21]

On 18 August 1945, one day after the Proclamation of Independence, in the first meeting of *Panitia Persiapan Kemerdekaan Indonesia* (PPKI, the Preparatory Committee for Indonesian Independence),[22] the Jakarta Charter was abrogated. Shortly before the opening of PPKI's formal meeting, Muhammad Hatta, who later became the first vice president of Indonesia, proposed changes to the draft of the Preamble of the Constitution. Hatta had been informed by a Japanese naval officer that in the eyes of Christians, the seven words were "discriminatory against all minority groups," since the clause served only part of the Indonesian people.[23] That is if these words remained, Christians living predominantly in the eastern part of Indonesia would not join the republic. This objection resulted in the removal of the seven words from the Preamble and the body of the Constitution. In short through the

---

20. B. J. Boland, *The Struggle of Islam in Modern Indonesia* (The Hague: Martinus Nijhoff, 1971), 25.
21. Boland, *The Struggle of Islam*, 28.
22. PPKI was founded on 7 August 1945 to replace BPUPKI and was led by Sukarno and Muhammad Hatta as its chairman and vice chairman respectively.
23. Deliar Noer, *Partai Islam di Pentas Nasional, 1945–1965* (Jakarta: Pustaka Utama Grafiti, 1987), 40.

Christians' contribution, *Pancasila* gives Indonesian citizens equal rights without prejudice of religion, race, and ethnic background.

The Protestant Christians' persistence in bringing about the independence of Indonesia was attributed to their conviction that independence is a gift of God,[24] and as such Indonesia should treat all of its citizens equally without differentiating between people according to their religious background. For this reason, the Protestant Christians insisted on the removal of the seven words from the *Pancasila*. They held that Indonesia should not allow any discrimination against certain citizens and should guarantee the freedom and rights of minorities. They therefore preferred the leadership of a Muslim president who upheld freedom and human rights to a Dutch governor-general who was a Christian but who did not resist violence and violations against freedom and human rights.

Nevertheless the struggle of Christians for Indonesia to extend equal treatment of its citizens still had a long way to go. The state's policy of giving Islam a privileged status had in fact disregarded the freedom and rights of non-Muslim minorities, especially Christians.

THE PROBLEM OF RELIGIOUS FREEDOM IN INDONESIA

At the beginning of the twenty-first century, the Indonesian government faces tremendous challenge in preserving the *Pancasila* as certain religious groups, primarily Muslim, attempt to politicize religion and assert a religious hegemony, threatening the religious freedom and equality for all citizens guaranteed by the Constitution. Specifically, the Ministry of Religion and the Indonesian Constitution of Criminal Law (KUHP) have been religiously politicized.

The Ministry of Religion and the Rights of Minorities

In this section we will see how far the Ministry of Religion has been influenced by religious groups and used as a means to politicize religion and religionize politics in such a way that religious violence would inevitably ensue.[25]

---

24. T. B. Simatupang, "Christian Presence in War, Revolution and Development: The Indonesian Case," *The Ecumenical Review* 37, no. 1 (January 1985): 81.

25. The Ministry of Religion was initially intended to administer the affairs of Islam only. Although it was later expanded by providing sections for non-Muslim religions – Protestant, Catholic, and Hindu-Buddhist – the ministry's existence, as Clifford Geertz has put it, "is for all intents and purposes a *santri* [devout Islam] affair from top to bottom." Clifford Geertz, *The Religion of Java* (Chicago: University of Chicago Press, 1976), 200. The *santri* are Muslims who follow the Islamic orthodox teaching and practices strictly and carefully. Intan, *'Public Religion,'*

The state's concession to Islam as a majority religion whose adherents demand privileges has naturally caused discrimination against non-Muslim minorities, especially Christians. On 13 September 1969 the Minister of Religion, together with the Minister of Internal Affairs, issued the *Surat Keputusan Bersama* (SKB, or Joint-Decision Letter) regarding the construction of worship places. This law required that permission from the head of the local government be gained for the construction of every worship place, and it allowed officials to request the opinions of representatives of local religious organizations and spiritual leaders.[26] The decree was issued in response to the large number of conversions from Islam to Christianity in certain areas of the country.[27] Although it was supposed to apply to all religious groups, the decree was in reality enforced to regulate only the construction of worship places for non-Muslims, especially Christians.[28] This decree made it difficult, if not impossible, for non-Muslims and Christians to build their worship places in a community where Muslims were a majority.

The decree was also used as an excuse for closing churches or even destroying and burning them. From 1969 to 2001 the number of churches closed, burned, or demolished increased yearly, from only two during Sukarno's presidency (1945–1967) to 456 during Suharto's dictatorship (1967–1998), and subsequently from 156 during the Habibie administration (1998–1999) to 232 during Abdurrahman Wahid's presidency (1999–2001). From 1945 to 2001, the average incidence increased from 0.008 per month to eleven per month.[29] The largest number of churches were demolished during Wahid's presidential term because of the efforts of certain groups to discredit his vision of a tolerant Islam.

---

36. Thus by giving Muslims special privileges, the presence of the Ministry of Religion had in the first instance discriminated against non-Muslim minorities and Christianity, in particular, by disregarding their freedom and rights.
26. Weinata Sairin, ed., *Himpunan Peraturan di Bidang Keagamaan* (Jakarta: BPK Gunung Mulia, 1996), 3–6.
27. In the early 1969, the World Council of Churches (WCC) reported that from 1965 to 1968, 2.5 million *abangan* (nominal Muslims) had converted to Christianity. Allan Arnold Samson, "Islam and Politics in Indonesia" (PhD diss, University of California at Berkeley, 1972), 237, quoting *Angkatan Baru*, 23 January 1969. See also M. C. Ricklefs, "Six Centuries of Islamization in Java," in *Conversion to Islam*, ed. Nehemia Levtzion (New York, London: Holmes & Meier, 1979), 124; Avery T. Willis, *Indonesian Revival: Why Two Million Came to Christ* (Pasadena: William Carey Library, 1977).
28. T. B. Simatupang, *The Fallacy of a Myth* (Jakarta: Pustaka Sinar Harapan, 1995), 198.
29. Paul Tahalele and Thomas Santoso, *The Church and Human Rights in Indonesia: Supplement* (Surabaya: Surabaya-Indonesian Christian Communication Forum, SCCF-ICCF, 2002), 1.

The Situbondo incident on 10 October 1996 is known as "Black Thursday." Twenty-four churches were demolished and burned. Among the victims was a pastor of the Gereja Pentakosta Pusat Surabaya (Pentecostal Church of Surabaya) who together with his wife, child, nephew, and an evangelist of the church died when their church in Situbondo was burned down.

During the Reformation Era after Suharto, the SKB was revised in 2006 and renamed the *Peraturan Bersama* (PERBER, Joint-Regulation) of Two Ministers. However, there is basically no difference in the content of the PERBER from that of the SKB. The new regulation imposes restrictions on religious freedom, particularly in the building of worship places. It requires at least sixty signatures of adults living in the proximity of the location where the new place of worship is to be built indicating their approval of the building project. Another ninety signatures of adult members of the congregation are required indicating that they live in close proximity to the location of the new church.

Following the implementation of the PERBER, the closing and destruction of worship places that belong to minority religious groups continues. A couple of days after the PERBER was promulgated, an angry mob expelled Christians from a Pentecostal church in Bogor and then closed it.[30] The Jakarta Christian Communication Forum observed that sixty-seven churches had become victims from 21 March 2006 to 17 August 2007.[31] According to Franz Magnis Suseno, Indonesia has become "a world champion in damaging and burning churches."[32] As of 2015, more than fifteen hundred church buildings have been either burned or demolished, mostly due to the religious intolerance expressed by the major religion of Indonesia.[33] Although the Ministerial Joint-

---

30. N. Hosen, "Substantive Equality and Legal Pluralism in Indonesia: A Case Study of Joint Ministerial Decrees on the Construction of Worship Places," paper presented to the Commission on Folk Law and Legal Pluralism International Conference, Depok, 29 June–2 July 2006, unpublished, 6, quoted in Arskal Salim, "Muslim Politics in Indonesia's Democratisation: The Religious Majority and the Rights of Minorities in the Post-New Order Era," in *Indonesia: Democracy and the Promise of Good Governance* (Singapore: Institute of Southeast Asian Studies, 2007), 121.
31. For a detailed discussion of PERBER, see Benyamin F. Intan, "Peraturan Bersama Kontraproduktif," *Seputar Indonesia* (21 September 2010): 4.
32. Franz Magnis Suseno, "Dialog Antar-Agama di Jalan Buntu?" in *Agama dalam Dialog: Pencerahan, Perdamaian dan Masa Depan, Punjung Tulis 60 tahun Prof. Dr. Olaf Herbert Schumann*, eds. Soegeng Hardiyanto, et. al. (Jakarta: BPK Gunung Mulia, 2003), 19.
33. Aulis Bintang Pratama, "Pembakaran Gereja Capai 1.000 Kasus Pasca Reformasi," CNN Indonesia (14 October 2015).

Regulation proves to be counterproductive and has even instigated religious violence, it is still retained.

It is certainly regrettable that the presence of the SKB and PERBER have created such a negative impact on certain groups of society. These two laws have made building a place of worship in the religious country of Indonesia far more difficult than building a massage parlor. Even more ironic is the fact that while churches can be built only with so much difficulty, they can be closed, demolished, and burned with so much ease.

The Constitution of Criminal Law and the Rights of Minorities

A deviation from the constitutional requirement for the government to be neutral toward all religions happened in 1965 when President Soekarno issued Presidential Decree No. 1/1965 concerning the Prevention of Abuse and/or Disrespect of Religion. Article 1 of this decree reads as follows:

> Every individual is prohibited in public from intentionally conveying, endorsing or attempting to gain public support in the interpretation of a certain religion embraced by the people of Indonesia or undertaking religious based activities that resemble the religious activities of the religion in question, where such interpretation and activities are in deviation of the basic teachings of the religion.[34]

This decree listed the six religions to which most Indonesian people adhere – Islam, Protestantism, Catholicism, Hinduism, Buddhism, and Confucianism – but it does not imply that these were the only official religions acknowledged. However in 1974 and onwards, when religion became a decisive factor in validating a marriage, these six religions became official, thus creating discrimination of citizens who subscribe to *aliran kepercayaan* (mysticism).[35]

Following this decree, a new article – Article 156a – was added to the Constitution of Criminal Law (KUHP) with imprisonment as penalty. It states the following:

---

34. Amnesty International, *Prosecuting Beliefs: Indonesia's Blasphemy Laws* (London: Amnesty International Ltd, 2014), 11. Available online: https://www.amnestyusa.org/files/_index-_asa_210182014.pdf (accessed on 22 June, 2022).
35. *Suara Pembaruan*, 28 November 2006, 2.

By a maximum imprisonment of five years shall be punished for whosoever in public deliberately express their feelings or engages in actions that: a. in principle is hostile and considered as abuse or defamation of a religion embraced in Indonesia; b. has the intention that a person should not practice any religion at all that is based on belief in [one Lordship].[36]

One implication of this rule is followers of an official religion no longer have the freedom to give an interpretation of their religion, as in doing so they could be convicted of desecrating their religion and thus committing a criminal act.

It is also important to note that Article 156a of KUHP has often been "expanded" indefinitely to entrap anybody regarded as desecrating religion, and the victims are usually minority groups. One example involves the recent prosecution of Basuki Tjahaja Purnama, also known as Ahok, the Chinese-Christian governor of Jakarta who was falsely accused of insulting the Qur'an based on a particularly controversial, edited video of a speech he delivered in September 2016. He was eventually convicted on blasphemy charges, had to resign from his office, and was sentenced to two years in prison. A curious matter to be noted in this case is the judges' final decision on his conviction, which they based on Article 156a of KUHP, even though the prosecutors had previously dropped those charges. Many viewed the former governor's trial and conviction as a case of injustice and protested it publicly.

THE RELATIONSHIP BETWEEN STATE AND RELIGION

From the previous analyses we can deduce that the main issue behind religious violence in Indonesia is the politicization of religion and the religionization of politics. The state dominates the religious sphere by subordinating religious groups to political power. Religious groups also position themselves as the only solution for the state's concerns, demanding subordination of the state on their own terms. For minority religious groups, including Christians, this set of circumstances is clearly far from ideal.

The religionization of politics is an effort by religion to bring the state under its power in order to protect and maintain its existence. Under the pattern of the religionization of politics, the state allows itself to become merely a tool for the pursuit of certain religious interests. When this happens, the state is not able to perform its primary task of promoting public justice and

---

36. Amnesty International, *Prosecuting Beliefs*, 12.

public morality in society. Instead, the state immediately loses its most noble function as a non-discriminating guardian dedicated to the good of its citizens. It segregates its citizens on the basis of their religion. The initial nature of the state has changed from inclusive and nonsectarian to discriminative and authoritarian.

Official religions that make use of the state's power are often unaware that this power could have counterproductive effects on their religious legitimacy conferred by the state. For example, Confucianism was acknowledged as an official religion during Sukarno's government through the Presidential Decree No.1/1965, together with Islam, Protestantism, Catholicism, Hinduism, and Buddhism. However, a Ministerial Decision issued by the Ministry of Home Affairs on 18 November 1978 announced that Confucianism was no longer acknowledged as an official religion and was therefore banned in Indonesia.[37] Not until the administration of Abdurrahman Wahid in 2000 was it once again declared an official religion.

With regard to our present discussion, the use of Article 156a of KUHP in the blasphemy case of Basuki Tjahaja Purnama, the governor of Jakarta, could be seen as reflecting a subordination of the state to religion in the pattern of the religionization of politics which could in the end produce a "theocratic state." Religious believers who do not exercise their faith according to the official religious interpretation can be punished through this KUHP. Religious believers who welcome the state's intervention in their religious life may initially have a good and noble intention to encourage believers to be more honorable and faithful to their religion. But in reality, the state's intervention fosters hypocrisy and taints the image of those religions. When the state regulation compels believers to exercise their faith according to the state's official interpretation, believers settle on a superficial religiosity that can only be judged from outside. Consequently, hypocrisy enters in and destroys the true and honorable values of the religion.

It is true that in the interventions of the Ministry of Religion and KUHP into the internal affairs of religion, one may find the manipulation of the state by religion for its own interests. But on the other hand, what happened in these cases was not merely the religionization of politics. It was also the politicization

---

37. Chandra Setiawan, "Khonghucu dalam Kemajemukan Agama-agama di Indonesia," in *Bergumul dalam Pengharapan: Buku Penghargaan untuk Pdt. Dr. Eka Darmaputera*, eds. Ferdinand Suleeman, Adji Ageng Sutama, and A. Rajendra (Jakarta: BPK Gunung Mulia, 2001), 463–64.

of religion in which religion was dragged into the public sphere and made into a symbol of contention and a tool for the state's political interest. The subordination of religion to the state in the form of the politicization of religion will produce a "state religion" in the end. When this happens, such a religion will lose its transcendental character since its infinite self will be matched with the temporal and mortal power of the state. Without a transcendent identity, religion will be crippled. It can no longer function critically and prophetically. As a result, it ceases to carry out its mission as the guardian of the state's morality.

The politicization of religion employed by the Indonesian state essentially receives consent from religion; in fact, religion even becomes the main architect. Religion acts in this way to sustain and prolong its existence. The politicization of religion thus is not only a deviation from state authority but also an investment of religions in politics.

It is true that in Basuki Tjahaja Purnama's case one may find the manipulation of the state by religion for its own interests. However seen from another perspective, what happened in that case was not merely the religionization of politics, in which a certain religion demanded a greater role as a decision-maker on matters of the state. It was also the politicization of religion. Many observers saw the prosecution of Basuki Tjahaja Purnama as politically motivated and a case in which religion was dragged into the public sphere and made into a symbol of contention and a tool for winning votes.

In sum, Christians in Indonesia should seek to ensure that religion and the state must never be totally fused. Both the *politicization of religion* and the *religionization of politics* are counterproductive and could even become a suicidal measure for all the parties concerned. Abraham Kuyper uses the term "sphere sovereignty" to designate the theological impossibility of unifying religion and the state since each has its own autonomy, identity, and responsibility.[38] But as each sphere receives its authority from God, Kuyper concludes that there must be "a free [religion] in a free state."[39] Without this freedom, the *politicization of religion* and the *religionization of politics* is inevitable. Because unifying religion and the state is problematic, it is not surprising that in the meeting of BPUPKI, Indonesia's founding fathers rejected the idea of an Islamic state that would unify religion and the state as proposed by Muslim nationalists.

---

38. Abraham Kuyper, "The Antirevolutionary Program," in *Political Order and the Plural Structure of Society*, eds. James W. Skillen and Rockne M. McCarthy (Atlanta: Scholars, 1991), 242.
39. Abraham Kuyper, *Lectures on Calvinism* (Grand Rapids, MI: Eerdmans, 1931, reprint 1987), 99.

It does not follow as a matter of course that a secular state promoting absolute separation between religion and state will automatically solve the problem of violence against people based on religion. State and religion are two separate and distinct entities. However absolute separation between them as proposed by the secular state is not feasible for several reasons. First, state and religion are in fact united or integrated in the very self of each individual who is at the same time a citizen of the state and a member of a religious institution. As prominent Protestant Eka Darmaputera has put it, "Every person is simultaneously a religious and political creature at the same time."[40] Second the secular state with its absolute separation of religion from state, signifying a Western way of thinking, is not the best alternative with respect to *Bhinneka Tunggal Ika*, the "unity in diversity" principle characteristic of Indonesia. Darmaputera explains that the secular state concept does not fit Indonesians, who are strongly religious.

> The very strong religious orientation of the Indonesian people in general makes a secular alternative very unlikely. Of course this is not a general truth. Turkey, for example, is a secular state and yet the majority of its population [is] Moslem. But Turkey and Indonesia are different in one important respect: Western influence is not as deep in Indonesia as in Turkey. India is also a secular state where the majority of its people are strongly religious. But we must not forget that it had to pay the price of the separation of Pakistan.[41]

In short, if Indonesia becomes a secular state, then the diversity of Indonesia will be preserved "but without a sufficient unifying factor to make Indonesia united as a nation."[42]

RELIGIOUS FREEDOM IN THE *PANCASILA*-BASED STATE OF INDONESIA

The above discussion has shown that both the theocratic state and the secular state are incompatible to the Indonesian context. The solution for Indonesia is

---

40. Eka Darmaputera, "The Search for a New Place and a New Role of Religion within the Democratic Order of Post-Soeharto Indonesia: Hopes and Dangers" (paper presented at the Third Annual Abraham Kuyper Award, Princeton Theological Seminary, Princeton, NJ, 1 December 1999, unpublished), 6.
41. Eka Darmaputera, *Pancasila and the Search for Identity and Modernity in Indonesian Society: A Cultural and Ethical Analysis* (Leiden: Brill, 1988), 179.
42. Darmaputera, *Pancasila*, 150.

that it should be neither a secular state nor a theocratic state, but a *Pancasila*-based state. Being a non-secular state means that Indonesians acknowledge the role of religion in the life of the nation. Confining religion to the narrow space of the private sphere is therefore not legitimized by the law. On the other hand since Indonesia is a non-theocratic state, by implication religion does not have the right to control the state. Nevertheless, the state acknowledges the social role of religion, since the various religions in Indonesia made significant contributions to the nation's fight for independence. The declaration that Indonesia is a non-theocratic state in no way trivializes religion. On the contrary, it is the prerequisite for religion to have an honorable position. The state not only preserves religious life but also encourages its growth, thereby confirming that no religious hegemony exists in Indonesia.

As noted above, *Pancasila* bridges the differences between Muslim and secular nationalists. Its formulation made a compromise between the ideas of an Islamic state and a secular state. While the first principle – that of One Lordship – delineates a "religious" element, the other four principles of humanitarianism, of nationalism, of democracy, and of social justice relate to "secular" matters. According to Darmaputera, the principle of One Lordship has become not only "the first in terms of order," but primarily "the guiding principle" to which the other four principles, to some extent, are "subordinated."[43] Thus within the framework of *Pancasila*, where the first principle functions as the regulating principle, Indonesian religions have to provide religious ethical guidance for the other four principles.

In other words, the state not only ensures within the framework of *Pancasila* freedom of expression for religion, but also stimulates the political and social role of religion in the public sphere. As mentioned above, the first principle of *Pancasila*, the principle of One Lordship, and its implementation in chapter 29 of the 1945 Constitution guarantee the religious freedom and rights of every citizen of Indonesia. Insofar as the first principle of *Pancasila*, "the principle of One Lordship," is concerned, it is certainly true that this principle must come to terms with the problem of religious pluralism, and thus promote the idea of religious freedom in Indonesian society. This is, however, a narrow interpretation of the principle. If it is only the idea of religious freedom that needs to be secured, then the second, third, or fourth principles in the *Pancasila* should be enough of a guarantee. The first principle of *Pancasila* recognizes unequivocally that the state will be based on religious beliefs, and

---

43. Darmaputera, 152.

that Indonesian society believes in "God." This "religious state," according to Sukarno, should promote what he calls "the interests of religion."[44] In the words of Simatupang, the *Pancasila*-based state is responsible "not only for ensuring religious freedom, but also for promoting the role of religions in society."[45] In this religiously accommodating state, religious communities not only maintain their autonomy but are also encouraged to make indispensable contributions to the nation's public life in accordance with their particular beliefs.

CONCLUDING REMARKS

If the Christian witness in the life of the nation and the state is to persist in the future, there must no longer be a gap between the aspirations of Indonesia's founding fathers as expressed in the Constitution and the reality of Indonesian politics. Christians and Christian churches must navigate the political realm in Indonesia. As they fought for freedom and defended human rights for the nation in the past, they must continue to do so in the present and the future. Through a proper relationship among religions, each citizen can enjoy his or her freedom and fundamental human rights. Without this proper relationship, Indonesian democracy will also be threatened. The reputation of being the third largest democratic country in the world would become only in memory.

REFERENCES

Bappenas. "Proyeksi Penduduk Indonesia 2010–2035." Subdirektorat Statistik Demografi (2013). https://old.bappenas.go.id/files/5413/9148/4109/Proyeksi_Penduduk_Indonesia_2010-2035.pdf, accessed on 23 June 2022.

Boland, B. J. *The Struggle of Islam in Modern Indonesia*. The Hague: Martinus Nijhoff, 1971.

Darmaputera, Eka. *Pancasila and the Search for Identity and Modernity in Indonesian Society: A Cultural and Ethical Analysis*. Leiden: Brill, 1988.

———. "The Search for a New Place and a New Role of Religion within the Democratic Order of Post-Soeharto Indonesia: Hopes and Dangers." Paper

---

44. Sukarno, "Lahirnya Pantja Sila," in Pantja Sila: *The Basis of the State of the Republic of Indonesia* (Jakarta: National Committee for the Commemoration of the Birth of Panca Sila, 1964), 29, cited in George McTurnan Kahin, *Nationalism and Revolution in Indonesia* (Ithaca: Cornell University Southeast Asia Program Publications, 2003), 124.

45. T. B. Simatupang quoted in Robert Lumban Tobing, "Christian Social Ethics in the Thought of T. B. Simatupang: The Role of Indonesian Christians in Social Change" (PhD diss., The Iliff School of Theology and the University of Denver, 1996), 166.

presented at the Third Annual Abraham Kuyper Award, Princeton Theological Seminary, Princeton, NJ, 1 December 1999, unpublished.

Geertz, Clifford. *The Religion of Java*. Chicago: University of Chicago Press, 1976.

Geertz, Hildred. "Indonesian Cultures and Communities." In *Indonesia*, edited by Ruth T. McVey, 24–96. New Haven: HRAF Press, 1963.

Goh, Robbie B. H. *History of Christianity in Southeast Asia*. Singapore: ISEAS, 2005.

Intan, Benyamin F. "Peraturan Bersama Kontraproduktif." *Seputar Indonesia* (21 September 2010), 4.

———. *"Public Religion" and the Pancasila-based State of Indonesia: An Ethical and Sociological Analysis*. New York: Peter Lang, 2006.

Kahin, George McTurnan. *Nationalism and Revolution in Indonesia*. Ithaca, NY: Cornell University Press, 1952.

Kuyper, Abraham, "The Antirevolutionary Program." In *Political Order and the Plural Structure of Society*, edited by James W. Skillen and Rockne M. McCarthy, 235–64. Atlanta: Scholars, 1991.

———. *Lectures on Calvinism*. Grand Rapids, MI: Eerdmans, 1931, reprint 1987.

Naipospos, Bonar Tigor, ed. *Presiden tanpa Prakarsa: Kondisi Kebebasan/Beragama Berkeyakinan di Indonesia 2012*. Jakarta: Pustaka Masyarakat Setara, 2012.

Noer, Deliar. *Partai Islam di Pentas Nasional, 1945–1965*. Jakarta: Pustaka Utama Grafiti, 1987.

Pratama, Aulis Bintang. "Pembakaran Gereja Capai 1.000 Kasus Pasca Reformasi." CNN Indonesia (14 October 2015). https://www.cnnIndonesia.com/nasional/20151014065145-20-84852/pembakaran-gereja-capai-1000-kasus-pasca-reformasi.

Ricklefs, M. C. "Six Centuries of Islamization in Java." In *Conversion to Islam*, edited by Nehemia Levtzion, 100–128. New York, London: Holmes & Meier, 1979.

Sairin, Weinata, ed. *Himpunan Peraturan di Bidang Keagamaan*. Jakarta: BPK Gunung Mulia, 1996.

Salim, Arskal, "Muslim Politics in Indonesia's Democratisation: The Religious Majority and the Rights of Minorities in the Post-New Order Era," in *Indonesia: Democracy and the Promise of Good Governance* (Singapore: Institute of Southeast Asian Studies, 2007), 115–137.

Samson, Allan Arnold. "Islam and Politics in Indonesia." PhD diss., University of California at Berkeley, 1972.

"Sensus Indonesia 2010." Badan Pusat Statistik (n.d.). https://sp2010.bps.go.id/.

Setiawan, Chandra. "Khonghucu dalam Kemajemukan Agama-agama di Indonesia." In *Bergumul dalam Pengharapan: Buku Penghargaan untuk Pdt. Dr.*

Eka Darmaputera, edited by Ferdinand Suleeman, Adji Ageng Sutama, and A. Rajendra, 462–80. Jakarta: BPK Gunung Mulia, 2001.

Simatupang, T. B. "Christian Presence in War, Revolution and Development: The Indonesian Case." *The Ecumenical Review* 37, no. 1 (January 1985): 75–85.

———. "Doing Theology in Indonesia Today." *CTC Bulletin* 3, no. 2 (August 1982): 20–29.

———. "Dynamics for Creative Maturity." In *Asian Voices in Christian Theology*, edited by Gerald H. Anderson, 87–116. Maryknoll: Orbis, 1976.

———. *The Fallacy of a Myth*. Jakarta: Pustaka Sinar Harapan, 1995.

Suara Pembaruan. 28 November 2006: 2.

Suseno, Franz Magnis. "Dialog Antar-Agama di Jalan Buntu?" In *Agama dalam Dialog: Pencerahan, Perdamaian dan Masa Depan, Punjung Tulis 60 tahun Prof. Dr. Olaf Herbert Schumann*, edited by Soegeng Hardiyanto, et. al., 19–31. Jakarta: BPK Gunung Mulia, 2003.

Tahalele, Paul, and Thomas Santoso. *The Church and Human Rights in Indonesia*: Supplement. Surabaya: Surabaya-Indonesian Christian Communication Forum, SCCF-ICCF, 2002.

Titaley, John. "From abandonment to blessing: the theological presence of Christianity in Indonesia." In *Christian Theology in Asia*, edited by Sebastian C. H. Kim, 71–88. Cambridge: Cambridge University Press, 2008.

Tobing, Robert Lumban. "Christian Social Ethics in the Thought of T. B. Simatupang: The Role of Indonesian Christians in Social Change." PhD diss., The Iliff School of Theology and the University of Denver, 1996.

van den End, Th., and Jan S. Aritonang. "1800–2005: A National Overview." In *A History of Christianity in Indonesia*, edited by Jan Sihar Aritonang and Karel Steenbrink, 137–228. Leiden, Boston: Brill, 2008.

Verkuyl, J., *Contemporary Missiology: An Introduction*. Grand Rapids: William B. Eerdmans, 1978.

Webb, R. A. F. *Indonesian Christians and Their Political Parties 1923–1966: The Role of Partai Kristen Indonesia and Partai Katolik*. North Queensland: James Cook University, 1978.

Willis, Avery T. *Indonesian Revival: Why Two Million Came to Christ*. Pasadena, CA: William Carey Library, 19.

CHAPTER 4

HISTORY OF CHRISTIANITY IN MALAYSIA

Tan Sooi Ling

Christianity in Malaysia has grown since its inception in the sixteenth century to register 2.39 million adherents (9.2 percent of the population) in 2010.[1] Since Malaysia is a Malay-Muslim majority country of 61.3 percent Muslims, this number of Christians is commendable. Not only has there been numerical growth but also progress in the areas of local leadership development, establishing vernacular language congregations, missional involvement, and ecumenism. The goal of this chapter is to understand and evaluate the historical developments that have led Christianity in Malaysia to this point so as to be in a better position to move forward.

The history of Christianity in Malaysia can be divided into four distinct periods:

1. Seeds (before 1874);
2. Footholds (1874–1941);
3. Redefining in Adversity (1942–1963);
4. Maturing (1963–present).

Three milestone years mark the transitions: 1874, when the British gained broad control in West and East Malaysia; 1942, when the Japanese occupied the country; and 1963, when the new nation of Malaysia was formed. Each period contributes material to the rich and complex tapestry of Malaysian Christianity today. Malaysian Christianity has thrived in times of adversity; it is the fruit of the faithful work of both foreign and local missionaries; and it is adaptable to change. Migrants and the church's social engagement with society have played a prominent role in this growth.

---

1. *Population and Housing Census of Malaysia: Population Distribution and Basic Demographic Characteristics* (Kuala Lumpur: Department of Statistics Malaysia, 2010), 82.

SEEDS: EARLY CHRISTIAN ACTIVITY (BEFORE 1874)

Malaysia was first populated by the *Orang Asli* (Original Peoples)[2] and later by the *Melayu* (Malays) who emigrated from south of Sumatra in the fifteenth century. In the ensuing centuries, West Malaysia experienced an influx of various influences, a phenomenon most aptly phrased as "Indianization, Islamization and Westernization" by Abdul Rahman.[3] Since Malaysia lies strategically at the crossroads between India and China, traders plying that route would stop at ports such as Melaka, Singapore (formerly part of Malaysia), and Penang. They not only brought their trade but also their cultural and religious influences. In particular, Muslim traders from Indonesia paved the way for Islam to be adopted by the Malays as their religion. Following this time, three waves of Western Europeans invaded West Malaysia. In 1511, the Portuguese conquered the port of Melaka and set up residence and rule there. The Dutch upstaged the Portuguese in 1641 and were in turn ousted by the British in 1786. After Melaka lost importance as a trading port, the British expanded their presence to Penang in 1786 and to Singapore in 1819.

Early Christian Presence

The Portuguese fleet that conquered Melaka in 1511 had Franciscan and Dominican monks on board.[4] Soon a small Catholic community of Chinese and Indians developed in Melaka, and a church on St Paul's Hill was built. When the Dutch took over Malacca in 1641, Catholicism was prohibited and replaced by the Dutch Reformed Church.[5] The Reformed Church had one hundred and fifty members and was led by two ministers, several elders, and a church council.[6] Despite the ban, the Catholic Church continued to grow to two thousand adherents as local leaders led and Catholic priests conducted

---

2. Colin Nicholas, "The Orang Asli: First on the Land, Last in the Plan," *Kajian Malaysia* 21, nos. 1 & 2 (2003): 315–29.
3. Abdul Rahman Haji Ismail, "Bumiputera, Malays and Islam: A Historical Overview," *Journal of Malaysian Studies* 20–21 (2003): 108; also in *The Bumiputera Policy: Dynamics and Dilemmasi*, eds. R. Mason and S. M. O. Arrifin (Pulau Pinang, Malaysia: Penerbit Universiti Sains Malaysia, 2003), 105–121.
4. John Roxborough, "A Short Introduction to Malaysian Church History: A Guide to the Story of Christianity in Malaysia and How to Go About Discovering the History of Your Church," 2nd rev. ed. *Malaysian Church History Series*, No. 1 (Kuala Lumpur: Seminari Theoloji Malaysia: Catholic Research Centre, 1989), 1.
5. However after the British took over, Christ Church Melaka was re-consecrated in 1838 from Reformed to Anglican use.
6. John Roxborough, *A History of Christianity in Malaysia* (Kuala Lumpur: Genesis Books and Seminari Theoloji Malaysia, 2014), 9.

mass in secret. The French Catholics arrived in 1781, first in Kuala Kedah and then in Penang where they built the Assumption Church in 1786, and thereafter College General in 1810 for the training of regional and local Catholic priests.[7]

Meanwhile, the London Missionary Society sent William Milne to Melaka to explore the possibility of setting up a base beyond India. Milne was known to be someone who appreciated Malay sensitivities, cultural appropriation, and language learning, as he had already founded the Anglo-Chinese College in Malacca in 1818. The Anglican mission followed the British move to Penang and Singapore, and they established St George's Church in Penang in 1818, the first Anglican Church constructed in Southeast Asia.

In summary, Christians made few inroads during these early years, but they did lay the foundation for the Malaysian church today. The seeds of growing faith were planted, local leadership was trained, and a sensitivity for cross-cultural mission was nurtured.

FOOTHOLDS: MISSIONS, MIGRANTS AND SERVICE (1874–1942)

Significant social, religious, political, and ethnic changes dominated the landscape of Malaysia during the period of 1874 to 1942. Greater British political control created stability that allowed Christianity to expand more extensively.

British Political Expansion

From 1842 onwards, the British extended their political influence over Malaysia. In Borneo, the Sultan of Brunei granted James Brooke the governorship of the First Division of Sarawak state in exchange for help against the Iban Dayaks, an indigenous people group. In Sabah, the British North Borneo Company established control in 1881. In West Malaysia, the British signed the Treaty of Pangkor in 1874 with the Malay rulers of the states of Perak, Selangor, Negri Sembilan, and Johor, promising protection in exchange for political control. This watershed treaty would have long-lasting impact in two ways: first, the Malay rulers retained control over matters of religion and culture, thus defining the boundaries of proselytizing, and second, the potential economic opportunities brought a large influx of Chinese and Indian migrants to West Malaysia who were to reshape the ethnic and religious composition of the land.

---

7. John Roxborough, "The Catholic Church," in *Christianity in Malaysia: A Denominational History*, eds. Robert Hunt et. al. (Selangor, Malaysia: Pelanduk, 1992), 10–11.

The British adopted a "divide and rule" policy by implementing an ethnic division and separation of labor and a four-language school system (Malay, Chinese, Tamil, and English) that eventually sowed the seeds of separatism.[8]

Churches and Social Engagement

Fresh missionary overtures occurred during this period. Migrant Indians brought to their estates Christians who were Lutheran, Methodist, Anglican, and Mar Thoma. The Chinese, such as the Basel Hakka, came to Sabah and the Methodist Foochow to Sibu and Sitiawan. The Anglicans extended their reach to towns in Perak and Kuala Lumpur, with Chinese and Tamil worship services beginning in 1929 and 1930 respectively.[9] New denominations also made their entry. Under John Chapman's leadership, a Brethren congregation was formed in Penang in 1860 and in Kuala Lumpur in the 1880s, and a Chinese Assembly was formed in 1893. The Methodists under William Oldham started their first missions in Singapore and West Malaysia in 1885. Worship services for their expatriates in Penang and Perak were initiated by the Presbyterians. Importantly, not all mission efforts were from the West. Renowned Chinese evangelist John Sung's revival meetings in Sibu and Sitiawan among the Methodists and Presbyterians enabled Chinese churches to flourish, and as Roxborough asserts, "helped lay the foundation of a local Christianity which would follow its own path."[10]

The Mill Hill Fathers brought the Catholic mission to Sabah and Sarawak in 1881, and by 1885 they had set up seven stations.[11] In Sabah, they worked among the Kadazan of Papar and the Kadazan Dusun of Penampang and Tambunan before the end of the nineteenth century.[12] In 1928, three young Australians arrived to evangelize in the Limbang river area, and their efforts resulted in significant conversions among the Lun Bawang and Kelabit peoples in Sarawak.

Evangelism also went hand in hand with social engagement. The demand and need for education in the English language was met by Methodist schools

---

8. Peter Rowan, *Proclaiming the Peacemaker: The Malaysian Church as an Agent of Reconciliation in a Multicultural Society* (Oxford: Regnum Books International, 2012), 77.
9. Roxborough, "Catholic Church," 40–43.
10. Roxborough, *History of Christianity*, 56.
11. Maureen Chew, *The Journey of the Catholic Church in Malaysia: 1511–1996* (Kuala Lumpur, Malaysia: Catholic Research Center, 2000), 122.
12. Jacqueline Pugh-Kitingan, "Cultural and Religious Diversity in Sabah and Relationships with Surrounding Areas," in *Islam and Cultural Diversity in Southeast Asia*, ed. Ikuya Tokoro (Tokyo: University of Tokyo, 2015), 284.

built in Penang, Taiping, Ipoh, Teluk Anson, and Kuala Lumpur by 1900. Catholics schools began in Penang, Malacca, Kuala Lumpur, Seremban, and Ipoh through the dedication of the La Salle Brothers and the Infant Jesus nuns. The Anglicans founded St Mary's high school for girls in 1912, a Tamil school in 1916, and the Yun San Chinese Mission School in 1921. Medical service for the outlying areas of Malacca was also initiated in 1911.

In retrospect, opportunities and constraints were present during this period. Christians extended their influence through the work of foreign (including Asian) missionaries and migrants and through the provision of educational, medical, and welfare services. Chinese and Tamil language congregations were also initiated. At the same time constraints such as the prohibition against proselytizing Malay-Muslims as well as the seeds of separatism set the trajectory for the current racial-religious divide.

REDEFINING IN ADVERSITY (1942–1963)

The Japanese Occupation ushered in a period of unrest and instability that would eventually lead to the formation of an independent Malaysia in 1963. Despite these upheavals, the church courageously defied the odds as Christians consolidated their faith, redefined their roles, and stepped up in leadership.

Shifting Winds

The British surrender to the Japanese in 1942 shattered the myth of Britain's invincibility and severed their domination in the region. When the British returned to Malaysia in 1945, their grip was considerably weaker. Nationalistic fervor swept through the Southeast Asian region as countries fought to achieve independence from their colonial masters. Indonesia attained independence from the Dutch in 1948, and the Federation of Malaya, including Singapore (which became independent of Malaysia in 1965), from the British in 1957. In Malaysia the precarious political situation was exacerbated by a communist insurgency that forced Britain to declare a state of emergency from 1948 to 1960.

Christian Growth Through Adversity

During the difficult years of the Japanese Occupation, the Christian community experienced loss, hardship, and persecution. Practicing their faith was not easy as Christians experienced harassment, persecution, and even loss of life. Christian activities were restricted, and churches, schools, and mission buildings were bombed, looted (such as St Georges, Penang), or taken over by the Japanese for governmental use. However, the church emerged much stronger. The loss of expatriate leaders who were either evacuated or incarcerated in Changi Prison in Singapore paved the way for local leaders to take responsibility for the churches. These leaders were aptly described by Hwa Yung and Robert Hunt as "heroic and competent," and they note that "under the most difficult circumstances, they kept the church alive, protected members and laid foundations for the future growth."[13] Undeterred, Christians continued to meet regularly, and in particular Tamil and Chinese Christians came to the forefront during this time. The experience of mutual suffering among Christians also brought about a greater spirit of unity as well as closer cooperation across denominations. As a result, the Council of Churches of Malaysia and Singapore was formed in 1948.

New Impetus for Mission Work

After the Japanese defeat in 1945, a fresh impetus of mission work ensued, brought about partly by the influx of missionaries who were expelled from China in 1948 and reassigned to Southeast Asia. These included Southern Baptist missionaries like Jessie Green who organized the Baptist Malaya Mission in 1952 with Lora Clement. Baptist churches were established in Alor Setar (1952), Penang (1953), and Ipoh (1954). In 1955, there were eighteen missionaries, eight churches and 750 members.[14] From these small beginnings, the Baptists grew to 188 churches and 30,301 members in 2018.[15]

New mission opportunities also emerged. The work in the New Villages is a case in point. In an effort to curb the communist (mainly ethnic Chinese) insurgency, during the emergency of 1948–1960, the British government forcibly moved many Chinese living at the edge of the Malaysian jungles into tightly controlled settlements known as New Villages. Over six hundred of these villages were created. To address the abysmal social and living conditions there, the British government encouraged missionaries and welfare workers to provide medical, social, and educational services. In response, the Lutheran Church ministered in the New Villages in Perak and Selangor, with

---

13. Hwa Yung and Robert Hunt, "The Methodist Church," in *Christianity in Malaysia: A Denominational History*, eds. Robert Hunt, et. al. (Selangor, Malaysia: Pelanduk, 1992), 175.
14. Hwang Wei-Tjang, "The Baptist Church," in *Christianity in Malaysia: A Denominational History*, eds. Robert Hunt, et. al. (Selangor, Malaysia: Pelanduk, 1992), 245.
15. Email correspondence with the Malaysia Baptist Convention, 30 January 2020.

Petaling Jaya as their base.[16] China Inland Mission (now known as the Overseas Missionary Fellowship) worked with the Anglicans to establish medical clinics and followed up with home visitations. Chinese converts established churches in New Villages in Teluk Anson, Bidor, and Slim River.[17]

Despite adversities, Christianity continued to grow as churches consolidated, Christians practiced and declared their faith, local Christians took leadership responsibility, and non-English language congregations came to the forefront. At the same time several challenges emerged including the widening divide of churches along linguistic lines and hence a greater need for "local" and stronger ecumenical cooperation. As the nation gained independence and developed its own identity, the church too had to find ways to recalibrate a path for this new phase in the nation's history.

MATURING: TOWARD A MALAYSIAN CHURCH (1963 TO PRESENT)

Malaysia became an independent nation on 16 September 1963. With nationhood, fresh and exciting opportunities to govern and to determine the nation's future opened. At the same time, nation building also brought a new set of challenges.

Nation Building

The nation of Malaysia is comprised of a diversity of cultures, ethnicities, and religions. While this diversity is often lauded as an asset, it has also spawned problems for national harmony and integration. Beneath the surface, inter-ethnic tensions simmered and at times erupted, as in the 13 May 1969 racial riots. Then the bone of contention was the privileged position and rights held by *Bumiputeras* (original peoples) over the *non-Bumiputeras* (migrants). These ethnic tensions were further complicated by religious competition. Although the state professes to be secular and religious freedom is guaranteed for all citizens, Islam is the official religion. The ambiguous interpretation of these state professions and actual legal practice resulted in contentions over issues such as the implementation of Islamic law and the erosion of religious liberties for minority religions. Other challenges to nation building included federal-state

---

16. Gideon Chang, "The Lutheran Church of Malaysia," in *Christianity in Malaysia: A Denominational History*, eds. Robert Hunt, et. al. (Selangor, Malaysia: Pelanduk, 1992), 253.
17. Michael S. Northcott, "Two Hundred Years of Anglican Mission," in *Christianity in Malaysia: A Denominational History*, eds. Robert Hunt, et. al. (Selangor, Malaysia: Pelanduk, 1992), 60.

tensions, national identity formation, and economic instability due to financial mismanagement and corruption.

The Church: Maturing

It is against this social, religious, and political backdrop that the Malaysian church began journeying toward becoming a true Malaysian church. Five key developments during this period shaped the mosaic of Christianity.

Indigenous Movements, Broadening Diversity

It is fitting to begin in the states of Sarawak and Sabah where 70 percent of Malaysian Christians are located and where waves of conversions and spiritual revitalization have been experienced among the indigenous peoples. The most significant events took place among the Lun Bawang and Kelabit tribes in northern Sarawak. The first revival broke out in 1971 at Lawas Bible School which had been founded in 1968.[18] Four waves of renewal which were characterized by experiences of repentance, reconciliation, revitalization of worship, prayer, and mission zeal followed in 1973, 1975, 1979, and 1984 in northern Sarawak, which later rippled to other parts of Sarawak.[19] A significant outcome was the emergence of Sidang Injil Borneo (Borneo Evangelical Church), an independent church which was instrumental in planting indigenous churches and training local Christian workers in Malaysia.[20] The work of the Methodist Iban Annual Conference grew among the Ibans in central Sarawak, while the Baptists expanded in the Sri Aman area. The global charismatic renewal also brought about the "mushrooming" of independent churches in Sabah and Sarawak.[21] All of these factors made Sarawak in 2010 become the only state in Malaysia with Christians as the largest religious population at 44 percent.[22] These indigenous movements provided a broader ethnic texture to Malaysian Christianity and consequently strengthened the Christian voice in the nation.

---

18. Tan Jin Huat, *Planting an Indigenous Church* (Oxford: Regnum Books International, 2011), 230.
19. Solomon Bulan and Dorai Lillian Bulan, *The Bario Revival* (Kuala Lumpur, Malaysia: Home Matters, 2004), 130.
20. Brian Newton, "A New Dawn over Sarawak: The Church and Its Mission in Sarawak, East Malaysia" (MA thesis, Fuller Theological Seminary, 1988), 60.
21. These churches include Churches of the Little Flock, Miri Gospel Chapel, the Baptist Churches, Full Gospel Church, Good News Fellowship, New Life Fellowship, Abundant Life Fellowship, Calvary Charismatic Center and Covenant Fellowship Centre. Newton, *New Dawn*, 71.
22. Department of Statistics Malaysia, *Population and Housing Census*, 92–93.

History of Christianity in Malaysia

Malaysian Christian Leadership

Over time as denominations and churches became fully autonomous, Malaysians took over higher leadership positions. In 1968, Yap Kim Hao was elected the first Asian Bishop of the Methodist Church of Malaysia, and in 1970, the Right Reverend Roland Koh was appointed the first bishop of the Anglican Church of West Malaysia.[23] Local pastors and lay leaders also led the growing Pentecostal/Charismatic churches. In Sabah, the closing of doors to non-Sabahan missionaries led to the expulsion of forty-one missionaries in 1970 which proved to be a blessing as local leaders then capably stepped in.

Growing Leaders, Theologians, and Resources

The need to train local Christian leaders naturally led to the growth of theological education offered at all levels and taught in different languages, and not just in English. Existing seminaries like Sibu Methodist Theological Seminary strengthened their Iban and Chinese departments. The Bible College of Malaysia inaugurated their Chinese and Bahasa Malaysia departments in 1980 and 2003 respectively, and Malaysia Evangelical College in Miri, Sarawak also spearheaded programs in Bahasa Malaysia. Malaysia Baptist seminary worked steadily to include more local Malaysian faculty. There were also interdenominational collaborations such as Seminary Theology Malaysia, a venture between the Methodists, Anglicans, Lutherans, and Presbyterians. Sabah Theological Seminary, which began as a ministry of Basel Christian church in the 1980s, now includes partners from other denominations.[24] Malaysia Bible Seminary, an interdenominational seminary started in 1978, and AGST Alliance (1984), a consortium of nine seminaries in Southeast Asia, began to offer post-graduate courses. Schools like Alpha Omega International College (1998) and St Paul's Theological College (2016) offer innovative programs for the urban workforce.

The Pentecostal/Charismatic Renewal

The Pentecostal movement contributed significantly to conversions and church planting in both urban and rural Malaysia. In the 1960s, English-speaking Assembly of God (AG) churches under the leadership of David Baker and

---

23. Robert Hunt, Lee Kam Hing, John Roxborough, eds., *Christianity in Malaysia: A Denominational History* (Selangor, Malaysia: Pelanduk, 1992), xi.
24. Partners include the Anglican Diocese of Sabah, the Protestant Church in Sabah, Sabah Evangelical Mission, Sidang Injil Sabah, the Anglican Diocese of Sarawak, the Grace Chapel of Sabah, the Lutheran Church of Malaysia and Singapore, the Evangelical Lutheran Church of Malaysia and Sabah, and the Methodist Church.

Lula Ashmoe Baird were established in the major towns of Penang, Ipoh, Taiping, and Kuala Lumpur. By 1970, nearly every town in West Malaysia had an AG church. In 1982, a church growth seminar conducted by South Korean pastor Dr. Paul Yonggi Cho stirred pastors to make an impact in the city by establishing large urban churches, which resulted in the birth of many member churches such as Calvary, Glad Tidings, and Grace Assembly in the Klang Valley. By 2000, there were 291 English-language AG churches throughout Malaysia.[25]

Simultaneously, the charismatic renewal that burst into prominence in the late 1970s and 1980s resulted in conversions as well as in the revitalization of Christians in the mainline denominations. University students were converted, spiritually revitalized, and imbued with missionary zeal. The Full Gospel Businessmen encouraged professionals and businesspeople into the charismatic experience. This effort led to the birth and proliferation of independent charismatic churches, notable ones being Full Gospel Assembly (1979), Full Gospel Tabernacle (1981), and New Life Restoration Center (1981). By 2018 there were over one hundred independent charismatic churches registered as members of the Evangelical Charismatic Churches of Malaysia.[26] Most of the leaders of these churches are Malaysians.

Cooperation and Collaboration

In the climate of religious repression, the battle to ensure religious liberties called for greater ecumenical cooperation. When religious tensions heightened in the 1980s because of the partial ban of the *Alkitab*, the prohibition of the use of certain Bahasa Malaysia words including the word "Allah," and the limits on the number of worship sites, evangelical Protestant denominations and churches gathered to form the National Evangelical Christian Fellowship (NECF) in 1983.[27] About 60 percent of all churches in the country are now NECF members. Two years later, the Roman Catholic Church, the Council of Churches Malaysia, and NECF Malaysia combined to form the Christian Federation of Malaysia (CFM). Two of their objectives were to represent the Christian

---

25. Timothy T. N. Lim, "Pentecostalism in Singapore and Malaysia: Past, Present and Future," in *Global Renewal Christianity: Spirit-Empowered Movements Past, Present, and Future, Volume I: Asia and Oceania*, ed. Amos Yong (Florida: Charisma Media/Charisma House Book Group, 2015), 126–135.
26. Interview with Ron Hee, Overseer, Evangelical Charismatic Church Malaysia, 1 November 2021.
27. See the NECF website: http://www.necf.org.my/.

community on issues and matters affecting the church and society and to address the shrinking public space for religious expression. CFM has since issued important statements regarding concerns over controversies such as the translation of the Bible in Bahasa Malaysia and Rooney Rebit's case of reverting from Islam to Christianity.[28] On the national platform, Christians joined with other non-Muslim religions to establish the Malaysian Consultative Council of Buddhism, Christianity, Hinduism, Sikhism, and Taoism (MCCBCHST) in 2000 with the goal of promoting goodwill and unity among all Malaysians.[29]

From being a client of mission, the church is steadily moving toward being missional. Proclamation is done with greater sensitivity by demonstrating the gospel through broader engagement with society. Excellent examples include the Salvation Army's residential homes for children, the elderly, and those with special needs; care of The Little Sisters of the Poor for the poor and elderly; Catholic work with the homeless, those with special needs, migrants, and refugees; and the Evangelical Lutherans' home for those with special needs. Non-church organizations also played a prominent role in non-sectarian advocacy. One notable example is Malaysian CARE, established in 1979 to provide services in three core areas: rural and urban community development, the prison drugs problem, and aid to people with special needs regardless of ethnicity or religion.[30] Another notable example is Dignity, a ministry offering holistic care and education for urban poor children in Kuala Lumpur since 1998.[31]

These developments shaped the present character of Malaysian Christianity. In summary, the Malaysian Christian community today is multilingual, multicultural, and multiethnic. The church is led by Malaysians, is spiritually vital, practices holistic mission, increasingly collaborates rather than competes, and values training local leaders. Though far from ideal, the church continues to take steps in a healthy, holistic, and missional direction.

PATHWAYS TOWARD A TRUE MALAYSIAN CHURCH

As the Malaysian church looks to the future, cues can be taken from historical precedents in several ways. The fact that historically adversity was not a deterrent but a catalyst for growth is an encouragement for Malaysian churches today as they continue to battle against growing religious restrictions. Also

---

28. "A United Malaysia, Vigilant and Resilient." CFM Statements, Christian Federation of Malaysia (30 August 2021).
29. See the Harmony Malaysia website: https://harmonymalaysia.wordpress.com/.
30. See the Malaysian CARE website: https://www.malaysiancare.org/.
31. See the Dignity for Children Foundation website: https://dignityforchildren.org/.

history confirms that migrants play a vital role in the Malaysian Church's growth. Non-citizen migrant workers from Nepal, Vietnam, Bangladesh, and Indonesia make up nearly 20 percent of Malaysia's population and should be recognized not as a social threat but as a growing mission field. Historically, the Malaysian Church's strong educational and social engagement with the community remains a vibrant example of how the church today can be an authentic and innovative witness in every sphere of society. Additionally, the Malaysian Church's ability to adapt and change as evidenced in the steady transitions from foreign to local leadership and from sectarianism to collaboration have contributed to its maturity.

However, challenges loom on the horizon as the Malaysian Church continues to engage with issues such as ethnic tensions, constructing and owning a Malaysian Christian identity, and being authentic witnesses in word and deed to all their neighbors. The steady process of Islamization resulting in restricted religious liberties and a growing fear among Christians are also causes for concern. Looking ahead, the Malaysian Church may need to become an agent of reconciliation in a multicultural but divided society.

The Malaysian Church is contextualized in that Christian leadership is Malaysian, local languages particularly Bahasa Malaysia are used, churches are self-supporting and self-governing, and indigenous/tribal groups are well represented in the Christian demographics. However, there are still areas for growth, particularly the need to express Christianity in contextually appropriate ways and to develop local theologies and theologians.

What is hopeful, however, is that embedded in the Malaysian Church's history are the wonderful stories of men and women of faith who braved all odds to bring the gospel to Malaysia, who stood against persecution, who served the poor and needy unconditionally, and who were humble enough to change and to effect change in innovative ways. They leave a strong legacy for the next generation of Malaysian Christians as they lead the church forward.

REFERENCES

Abdul Rahman Haji Ismail. "Bumiputera, Malays and Islam: A Historical Overview." In *The Bumiputera Policy: Dynamics and Dilemmas. Journal of Malaysian Studies*, edited by R. Mason and S. M. O. Arrifin, 315–29. Pulau Pinang, Malaysia: Penerbit Universiti Sains Malaysia, 2003.

Bulan, Solomon, and Dorai Lillian Bulan. *The Bario Revival*. Kuala Lumpur, Malaysia: Home Matters, 2004.

Chang, Gideon. "The Lutheran Church of Malaysia." In *Christianity in Malaysia: A Denominational History,* edited by Robert Hunt et. al., 251–258. Selangor, Malaysia: Pelanduk, 1992.

Chew, Maureen. *The Journey of the Catholic Church in Malaysia: 1511–1996.* Kuala Lumpur, Malaysia: Catholic Research Center, 2000, Denominational History. Selangor, Malaysia: Pelanduk,1992.

Hunt, Robert, Lee Kam Hing, and John Roxborough, eds. *Christianity in Malaysia: A Denominational History.* Selangor, Malaysia: Pelanduk, 1992.

Hwa Yung, and Robert Hunt. "The Methodist Church." In *Christianity in Malaysia: A Denominational History,* edited by Robert Hunt et. al., 142–198. Selangor, Malaysia: Pelanduk, 1992.

Hwang, Wei-Tjang. "The Baptist Church." In *Christianity in Malaysia: A Denominational History,* edited by Robert Hunt et. al., 243–250. Selangor, Malaysia: Pelanduk, 1992.

Lim, Timothy T. N. "Pentecostalism in Singapore and Malaysia: Past, Present and Future." In *Global Renewal Christianity: Spirit-Empowered Movements Past, Present, and Future, Volume I: Asia and Oceania,* edited by Amos Yong, 126–135. Florida: Charisma Media/Charisma House Book Group, 2015.

Newton, Brian. "A New Dawn over Sarawak: The Church and Its Mission in Sarawak, East Malaysia." MA thesis, Fuller Theological Seminary, 1988.

Nicholas, Colin. "The Orang Asli: First on the Land, Last in the Plan." Kajian Malaysia 21, nos. 1 & 2 (2003): 315–29. http://web.usm.my/km/KM%20 21,2003/21-13.pdf.

Northcott, Michael S. "Two Hundred Years of Anglican Mission." In *Christianity in Malaysia: A Denominational History,* edited by Robert Hunt et. al., 34–74. Selangor, Malaysia: Pelanduk, 1992.

Population and Housing Census of Malaysia: Population Distribution and Basic Demographic Characteristics. Kuala Lumpur: Department of Statistics Malaysia, 2010. https://www.dosm.gov.my/v1/index.php?r=column/cthemeByCat&cat=117&bul_id=MDMxdHZjWTk1SjFzTzNkRXYzcVZjdz09&menu_id=L0pheU43NWJwRWVSZklWdzQ4TlhUUT09#.

Pugh-Kitingan, Jacqueline. "Cultural and Religious Diversity in Sabah and Relationships with Surrounding Areas." In *Islam and Cultural Diversity in Southeast Asia,* 269–94. Tokyo: University of Tokyo, 2015.

Rowan, Peter. *Proclaiming the Peacemaker: The Malaysian Church as an Agent of Reconciliation in a Multicultural Society.* Oxford: Regnum Books International, 2012.

Roxborough, John. "The Catholic Church." In *Christianity in Malaysia: A Denominational History,* edited by Robert Hunt, et. al. Selangor, Malaysia: Pelanduk, 1992.

———. *A History of Christianity in Malaysia.* Kuala Lumpur: Genesis Books and Seminari Theoloji Malaysia, 2014.

———. "A Short Introduction to Malaysian Church History: A Guide to the Story of Christianity in Malaysia and How to Go About Discovering the History of Your Church." 2nd rev. ed. Malaysian Church History Series, No. 1. Kuala Lumpur: Seminari Theoloji Malaysia: Catholic Research Centre, 1989. http://roxborogh.com/sea/country/shmalaysia.htm.

Tan, Jin Huat. *Planting an Indigenous Church.* Oxford: Regnum Books International, 2011.

"A United Malaysia, Vigilant and Resilient." CFM Statements, Christian Federation of Malaysia (30 August 2021). https://cfmsia.org/2021/08/30/a-united-malaysia-vigilant-resilient/.

CHAPTER 5

HISTORY OF THE CHURCH IN MYANMAR

Peter Thein Nyunt

One of the largest Southeast Asian nations in terms of land mass, Myanmar, formerly Burma, is an area of more than 250,000 square miles. It is comprised of 135 ethnic groups, including eight who make up the majority: Burmese (Bamar), Shan, Kayin, Rakhine, Kachin, Mon, Kayah, and Chin. Their diverse cultures make up the Union of Myanmar. The official language is Burmese, and Buddhism is promoted as the state religion. While there is freedom of religion in the country, Buddhists are the vast majority at 88 percent followed by Christians (6 percent), Muslims (4 percent), and others (1 percent).[1] The nation has seen political structures including monarchy (1044–1885), colonialism (1824–1947), parliamentary democracy (1948–1962), socialist regime (1962–1998), military junta (1998–2010), and democracy (2010 to the present).[2]

Christianity is not a young religion in Myanmar, as a Christian presence has been in the land for more than five centuries. Like other religions in the country, Christianity was imported and introduced by traders, colonial armies, and missionaries. The contributions of the pioneer missionaries and their methods are very impressive. The faith was presented and adapted to meet the needs of the people and to address the nation's different cultures. Today the church that was built upon their hard labor is steadily growing in three dimensions: spiritual, numerical, and geographical. Currently Christians in Myanmar make up about 6 percent of the population, with a large percentage found among the tribal peoples. This chapter will highlight the prominent factors that have contributed to this growth.

---

1. Thein Swe, "Census Report Volume 2-C: The Union Report: Religion," in *The 2014 Myanmar Population and Housing Census* (Nay Pyi Taw, Myanmar: Ministry of Labour, Immigration and Population, 2016), 14.
2. Myo Thant, et. al., *Myanmar: Facts and Figures 2002* (Yangon: Printing and Publishing Enterprise, 2002), 8–12. In February 2021, the military junta again seized power.

THE MISSIONARY PERIOD (1511–1966)
Roman Catholic Missions

The first Christians in Myanmar were Portuguese soldiers, a few traders, and some adventurers who came in the sixteenth century. In 1511, an agent sent by Albuquerque, the Portuguese leader in Melaka, Malaysia, came to Moktama and Bago to investigate the people and the land. In 1519, Antonio Correa signed a trade agreement with the chief of Martaban. By 1540, about seven hundred Portuguese mercenaries and soldiers had arrived in Myanmar, many of whom were Catholic Christians.

Cing Khua Khai says, "From that time onward Portuguese armies and traders came and served the land. In 1554, the first Catholic priest and two Dominicans friars arrived to serve the Portuguese mercenaries. However, they left after three years as they were not well accepted by the Portuguese."[3]

Eventually two Italian Catholic priests were appointed in 1720. As a result of their work and that of their successors, it is estimated that there were approximately two thousand Christians scattered all over the country by the last quarter of the eighteenth century. Thirty-seven missionaries were sent to Myanmar between 1800 and 1856. By 1862, there was one college, one bishop, one native priest, and approximately six thousand members attached to the mission.[4]

The efforts of the early Catholic mission prospered among the Europeans and the Anglo-Burmese but not among the native people. As the mission expanded, a slow growth developed among the tribal groups, especially among the Kayin, Kachin, and Chin, although there is limited information available regarding their work in the nineteenth and early twentieth centuries. By 1990, the Roman Catholic church had a total membership of over three hundred thousand with nine bishops and 212 priests serving in nine dioceses.[5]

Baptist Missions

The foundation of Protestant missions in Myanmar is attributed to the American Baptist missionary Adoniram Judson who began work in 1813. However six years prior to Judson's arrival, Richard Mardon and James Chater from the English Baptist Missionary Society had travelled from Bengal to

---

3. Chin Khua Khai, *Cross amidst Pagodas: A History of the Assemblies of God in Myanmar* (Baguio, Philippines: APTS Press, 1995), 37.
4. Khai, *Cross amidst Pagodas*, 37–39.
5. Khai, 39.

investigate the possibility of establishing a Protestant mission in Myanmar. They were joined later by Felix Carey, son of William Carey, and they worked together for some years. But the English Baptist mission work was not very successful. It was when Judson arrived in Yangon under the American Baptist Mission that the Protestant mission movement ultimately took root.[6] Today the Myanmar Baptist Convention is the largest Protestant Christian organization in the country.

The Baptist mission efforts initially focused solely on the Burmese Buddhists. Shortly after his arrival, Judson began to communicate the gospel to them using Christian literature as a starting point.[7] After six years of labor in Yangon, Judson saw the first convert – Maung Naw, a Burmese Buddhist – baptized in 1819.[8] Judson hoped that the baptism of Maung Naw would lead to the conversion of more Burmese Buddhists to the Christian faith, and that these Buddhist converts would become a strong church which God would use to convert many Buddhists to the Christian faith. Judson's primary strategy was to make Burmese converts and incorporate them into a church. Accordingly, the first Burmese church was established in 1822 with a membership of eighteen converts from Buddhism. They were both poor and rich, ordinary and educated.[9] However, the mission to the Burmese people led to severe persecution, and Judson's hopes of planting a powerful church soon faded.[10]

In 1825, Judson moved to Kyaikkhami, southern Myanmar to establish a new station for missions and evangelism. Judson's biographers note that he went there because he knew that it was virtually impossible to see mass conversion in the Burmese Buddhist society in Yangon. In hindsight, he saw Yangon "only as a stepping stone."[11] As he reflected on his evangelistic tours and movements in Amherst and Moulmein, that stepping stone was used to reach Kayin and Mon tribes in southern Myanmar. Judson spent the rest of his life in Myanmar, from 1831 to 1835, visiting and preaching in the Kayin and Mon jungle villages north and east of Moulmein.

The response to the Baptist outreach to the Kayin people who were animistic was great. The first Kayin convert, Ko Tha Byu, was baptized in 1829.

---

6. Maung Shwe Wa, *Burma Baptist Chronicles* (Rangoon: Burma Baptist Convention, 1963), 6.
7. Wa, *Burma Baptist Chronicles*, 6.
8. Wa, 16–18.
9. Committee of History, *A Brief History of the First Baptist Church in Myanmar 1816–1991* (Yangon: U Naw Memorial Baptist Church, 2006), 7.
10. K. T. Vuta, "A Brief History of the Planting and the Growth of the Church in Burma: Dr. Price, the First Medical Missionary" (PhD diss., Fuller Theological Seminary, 1983), 51–53.
11. Faith C. Bailey, ed., *Adoniram Judson: Missionary to Burma* (Chicago: Moody, 1955), 33.

Judson realized that missions among the Kayin might be more successful than the mission to the Burmese Buddhists. Hence the mission was extended to the SaGaw-Kayin in 1828, the Pwo-Kayin in 1836, and the Kayin hill tribe in 1853. Today the Kayin (SaGaw and Pwo) represent a large portion of the Christian population in the Baptist mission in Myanmar. Compared with the Kayin, the number of Burmese Buddhist converts was extremely low, and even today, the growth of Burmese Buddhist converts remains small and stagnant. Baptist missions also extended to the Pa-o in 1838, the Asho Chin in 1856, the Shan in 1860, the Kachin and the Lisu in 1877, the Chin in 1899, and the Naga in 1953.[12] Judson and the American Baptist missionaries generally employed four types of outreach: literature, "zayat ministry,"[13] education, and medical ministry. To better illuminate the contribution of these approaches to the growth of Christianity in the nation, we will examine each in more detail.

Literature Ministry

Within a few days of his arrival, Judson began to study the Burmese language. Soon Judson and his wife, Ann, were engaged in translating and distributing Scripture portions and tracts while preaching the gospel in many areas. In October 1816, George H. Hough, a new missionary from America, arrived in Yangon with a printing press and a typewriter.[14] Then it seemed that Judson's dream could become a reality. After a discussion, Judson and Hough made an agreement to employ literature ministry as the first means and method to communicate the gospel to the people in Myanmar. Their commitment is described as follows:

> We agree on the position that our sole object on earth is to introduce the religion of Jesus into the Empire of Burma. The means by which we hope to affect this are: translating, printing, and

---

12. Theodore Lim and Dengthuama, "An Overview of Christian Missions in Myanmar," Tahan Theological College and Seminary, April 2016.
13. Zayats are small buildings by roadsides customarily constructed of bamboo and thatch which serve as reception shelters and resting places for travelers. Sometimes Buddhist monks delivered messages at zayats. Judson built his own zayat and used it as a point of contact. He also dialogued with the Burmese and held worship services at the zayat. This zayat ministry illustrates two reasons for the success of his mission work with the Burmese people: adaptation of the gospel to the Burmese Buddhist worldview and utilization of Burmese local cultural forms for communicating the gospel. As a result, hundreds of Burmese were won to Christ during Judson's lifetime.
14. Vuta, "Brief History," 45.

distributing the Holy Scriptures, preaching the Gospel, circulating religious tracts, and promoting the instruction of native children.[15]

Based on this agreement, this method of communication was enhanced. They started printing Christian literature and propagating the gospel extensively. Pa Yaw explains, "Judson could produce more pamphlets, religious tracts, and booklets for his mission work. He completed his translation work of the entire New Testament into Burmese on July 12, 1823. The translation of the whole Bible was completed on January 31, 1834."[16]

Judson continued to revise his translation. He completed a revision of the Old Testament on 26 September 1835, a revision of the New Testament on 22 March 1837, and a revision of the entire Bible, published in quarto format, on 24 October 1840.[17] Besides the Bible, another of Judson's prominent contributions to Myanmar society was an English-Burmese Dictionary completed in 1843.[18] Judson saw Christian literature as a significant means to communicate the gospel to the Buddhist indigenous people in Myanmar, and he saw the printing press as the "grand engine" to turn the local people to Christ.[19]

Zayat Ministry

Judson decided early in his ministry that he would preach the gospel rather than promote negative ideas about Buddhism. He observed that the Burmese people often gathered together in rest houses along the road which they called zayat. These were places for public discussion and sharing their thoughts and beliefs. After work in literature ministry, Judson diligently spent time at the zayat he had built, distributing Christian literature to inquirers and visitors.[20] Consequently, many people read the pamphlets and booklets when they visited this zayat.[21] After reading, many were stirred in their interest toward this

---

15. Wa, *Burma Baptist Chronicles*, 12.
16. Pa Yaw, "Christian Conversion: An Evaluation on Judson's Mission Approach," in *Our Theological Journey: Writings in Honor of Dr. Anna May Say Pa* (Insein, Yangon: MIT Festschrift Committee, 2006), 116.
17. Francis Wayland, *A Memoir of the Life and Labors of the Rev. Adoniram Judson*, vol. 2 (Cambridge, MA: Harvard University, 1853), 163.
18. Yaw, "Christian Conversion," 116.
19. Wa, *Burma Baptist Chronicles*, 85.
20. Wa, 84–98.
21. Wa, 15–16.

new religious teacher, and they brought many others to the zayat to hear. Wa emphasized this approach as follows:

> Mr. Judson preached for the first time in the new zayat . . . it must be regarded as an event of no ordinary importance. Here was the first altar erected in Burma for the worship of the Eternal and Everlasting God. Plain and simple as were its walls compared with the magnificent pagodas that surrounded it, [it] was perhaps the fitter emblem of that spiritual religion which delights not in temples made with hands, but in the service of the heart.[22]

Judson used a conversational style when he communicated with the people in the zayat. Lazarus Fish states that "Judson did not preach a sermon; instead, he listened to the people and engaged in one-on-one discussion with individuals, first about the weather, crop conditions, and other matters of mutual interest, and then about religion in general, and then about Christianity."[23] In his dialogues, Judson built up the common ground before he communicated the gospel. This method of communication is still relevant in Burmese society today. To emphasize this new approach, Francis Wayland states,

> The essence of Judson's *communication* was a combination of conviction of the truth and rationality of the Christian faith, a firm belief in the authority of the Bible, and a determination to make Christianity relevant to the Burmese mind without violating the integrity of the Christian truth, or as he put it, to *communicate* the gospel, not anti-Buddhism.[24]

It was as a result of this contextual method of communication, Maung Naw became the Baptist Mission's first convert to confess Christ in Yangon. His conversion had a great impact on fellow Burmese Buddhists.[25] It took Judson twelve years to make eighteen converts. By the end of August 1822, the young Burmese church grew to eighteen members.[26]

Judson's efforts through this zayat approach can be seen as "a web movement," "the process of people becoming Christians along the line of families

---

22. Wa, 15–16.
23. Lazarus Fish, "Reclaiming the Zayat Ministry: Witness to the Gospel Among Burmese Buddhists in Myanmar" (PhD diss, Asbury Theological Seminary, Lexington, KY, 2002), 8.
24. Wayland, *Memoir of the Life*, 126, emphasis added.
25. Vuta, *Brief History*, 46–47.
26. Wa, *Burma Baptist Chronicles*, 17–25.

and relatives."[27] U Shwe Ngong, a highly intelligent Burmese master teacher of learning and influence who argued with Judson many times, finally became a Christian, one of the eighteen converts. Unfortunately at his time, Christianity was questioned before the viceroy Mya-day-min who did not tolerate any Burman subject embracing a religion different from Buddhism. Consequently, visitors stopped coming to Judson's zayat.[28] So the infant church became stagnant, and even this web movement which had seemed so promising proved otherwise because of the hostility and resistance of the Buddhist society.

Educational Work

Judson and the Baptist missionaries also promoted the instruction of native children. Ann Judson, with the help of Ma Min Lay, the first Burmese woman convert of the Baptist mission, opened a school where village boys and girls could be taught to read and write instead of attending Buddhist monastic schools. Many of these students were converted through the school. Moreover, the school became the first of a long line of schools that helped to train young people over the following 143 years.[29]

Medical Ministry

The Baptist missions suffered from both persecution and natural disasters during this first period. Plagues such as cholera, dysentery, malaria, smallpox, and tuberculosis were prevalent. Life expectancy was short for both the Burmese and the missionaries.[30] Due to lack of medical knowledge, indigenous people could not control these diseases, and in addition, most medical services were inaccessible for the masses. Because of this public health situation, the missionaries felt they needed to provide medical services to the people and used this opportunity to communicate the gospel to the patients.

On 13 December 1821, Dr. and Mrs. Jonathan Price arrived and were warmly welcomed as the first medical appointees. Price's medical knowledge and skill were to prove most valuable in the treatment of diseases, and his fame spread all over the country, including the capital, Ava.[31] Even the Burmese King Bagyidaw was interested in the missionaries' medical science, and he

---

27. Donald A. McGavan, *Understanding Church Growth* (Grand Rapids, MI: Eerdmans, 1990), 243.
28. Wa, *Burma Baptist Chronicles*, 12–23.
29. Khai, *Cross amidst Pagodas*, 45–46.
30. Wa, *Burma Baptist Chronicles*, 110–11.
31. Yaw, "Christian Conversion," 118.

was always on the lookout for the medical scientific advances of Dr. Price. In fact, medical science remains one of the great contributions of the Baptist missions to Myanmar.

The first mission dispensary in Myanmar was established in 1866 in Taungoo by the American Baptist Mission, and in the first year over four thousand patients were treated. The American Baptist Mission established many hospitals and dispensaries around the country until the late nineteenth century.[32] Encouraged by the results, in 1887 the missionaries opened a women's hospital and nurses' training school on Mission Road, now known as Duffering Hospital in Yangon. Even today it is considered to be the best women's hospital in the country.[33] Despite the fact that not many people in Myanmar know of this hospital's Christian beginnings, many patients have experienced the compassion of its nurses and doctors and have had opportunities to hear about the love of God while they were admitted in the hospital.

These medical ministries offered key opportunities for Christian missionaries to communicate the gospel widely and to build the credibility of the Christian witness. Such ministries were well appreciated because they met a long-standing need. In spite of many hardships, the missionaries involved in these ministries not only saved souls but healed those who were physically sick.[34]

Assemblies of God Mission

Leonard and Olive Bolton were the first missionaries from the Assemblies of God to set foot in Myanmar in 1924. In reality, however, the Assemblies of God Missions in Myanmar started in the northern part of the country among the Lisu in the 1930s.[35] According to Stafford, the first Assembly of God church was established in Putao, Kachin state, probably in 1933.[36] Mission outreach in Yangon commenced only in 1957 through the work of Glenn and Kathleen Stafford. Until the 1970s there was not much growth in the Assemblies of God missions, especially in Yangon. According to Khai, at the time of the departure of foreign missionaries under Ne Win's government (1962–1988), there was only one Assembly of God church in Yangon, the

---

32. Vuta, *Brief History*, 107–8.
33. Wa, *Burma Baptist Chronicles*, 244–55.
34. Peter Thein Nyunt, *Missions amidst Pagodas: Contextual Communication of the Gospel in the Burmese Buddhist Context* (Carlisle, UK: Langham Monographs, 2014), 68.
35. Herbert Kane, *Understanding Christian Mission* (Grand Rapids: Baker Book House, 1975), 150.
36. Glen D. Stafford, *A Brief History of the Assemblies of Burma* (Springfield: Central Bible College, 1977), 2–3.

Evangel Church which was established in 1956 during the first phase of its mission in Yangon. When foreign missionaries left the country, the Evangel Church in Yangon had only a few members including Burmese Buddhist converts.[37] However after 1975, church membership grew tremendously in Yangon and all over the country.[38] Today the Assemblies of God is the second largest denomination in the Myanmar Protestant Church with a total of around three hundred thousand members.

Anglican Missions

The Anglican Christian community is represented in Myanmar by the Church of the Province of Myanmar. Anglican missionary work originated in the chaplaincy of the British soldiers in Myanmar soon after the first Anglo-Burmese War (1824–1826) and later included the efforts of the Society for the Propagation of the Gospel (SPG) and the Bible Churchmen's Missionary Society in 1850s. Their communicational approach was primarily carried out through educational work.[39] By 1857, after the Second Anglo-Burmese War (1852), an Anglican church was established for military personnel in Yangon, and the Yangon Diocese was inaugurated in 1877.[40] Following the footsteps of the American Baptist missionaries, Anglicans established educational ministries to communicate the gospel. They worked in Yangon, Moulmein, Henthada, Myan-aung, Thayet, Mandalay, and Taungoo. By the end of the nineteenth century, the Anglican Church had 105 schools with thirty-seven foreign workers and 329 native workers. St. John's College and St. Michael's Mission to the Blind, both in Yangon, became well-known centers of learning and ministry.[41]

Two decades ago, the Anglican Church had twenty-five thousand members throughout the country; today there are about sixty thousand members affiliated with the Anglican Christian community.[42] In spite of this considerable growth, Anglicans remain a relatively small percentage of the total Christian population.

---

37. Khai, *Cross amidst Pagodas*, 70–73.
38. Aye Min, "A Brief History of Myanmar Evangelical Fellowship. A Term Paper," (PhD diss, Asia Graduate School of Theology, Yangon, Myanmar, 2004), 22.
39. William C. R. Purser, *Christian Mission in Burma* (Westminster, UK: Society for Propagation of the Gospel in Foreign Parts, 1913), 118.
40. Purser, *Christian Mission*, 132–33.
41. Alexander McLeish, *Christian Progress in Burma* (London: World Dominion Press, 1929), 24–27.
42. Kane, *Understanding Christian Mission*, 150.

Methodist Missions

Methodist missionaries entered the country with the British after Myanmar became a British colony in the late 1880s. The American Methodist Episcopal Mission was started in 1879 in Lower Myanmar by James Mills Thoburn, and the English Methodist mission was started in Upper Myanmar in 1886 by G. H. Bateson, an army chaplain.[43] Before Thoburn arrived in Myanmar, Robert E. Carter, an American, was sent to Yangon to start a work there.

In its first phase, the Methodist missionaries focused on Indians, Chinese, and Bamar people in Yangon. The work was not as easy as in other parts of Myanmar, as Rev. H. J. Hawood stated, "Burma has been one of the most difficult and unresponsive fields for Christian evangelism, and the walls of spiritual lethargy will not collapse through human agency."[44] Out of these three people groups, the Bamar people may have been the most difficult with whom to communicate the gospel. This difficulty is evident in the first church established in 1880: the worship services were only in the Tamil and Telegu languages and not in Burmese. Methodist membership, including both English Methodist and American Methodist, in 1970 was approximately fifteen thousand, but today there are about one hundred thousand members.[45]

The Seventh-Day Adventist Mission

The Seventh-Day Adventists work started in 1919 with pioneer missionaries such as R. A. Beckner, G. A. Hamilton, D. C. Ludington, Eric B. Hare, Mr. and Mrs. H. A. Skinner, Mr. and Mrs. Denoyer, and Mr. and Mrs. Shannor. These early efforts were organized under the Southern Asia Division Headquarters in Poona, India.[46] The first mission headquarters in Myanmar was organized in Yangon in 1919 and reorganized in 1938. Within twelve years, by 1931, there were 277 members in eight churches and a church school in Yangon.[47] In 30 June 2019, the Church of Seventh Day had 239 churches and a membership of 33,692.[48] This growth was enhanced by communicating the gospel through educational ministry in Yangon, which makes it similar to the trajectories of the Baptist and Anglican missions.

---

43. Khai, *Cross amidst Pagodas*, 50.
44. Rev. H. J. Hawood quoted in Harmine G. Tegenfeidt, *A Century of Growth: The Kachin Baptist Church of Burma* (Pasadena, CA: William Carey Library, 1974), 28.
45. Kane, *Understanding Christian Mission*, 150.
46. Khai, *Cross amidst Pagodas*, 53.
47. Vuta, *Brief History*, 90–92.
48. Khai, *Cross amidst Pagodas*, 70–75.

The Church of Christ Mission

The origin and growth of the Church of Christ was centered around the Kachins and through the efforts of the J. Russell Moerse family. In the 1920s, they started a mission service on the border of Tibet, among the Lisu beyond the Mekong and Salween rivers of Yunnan, China. A second center for mission work was established near Putao in 1950 by the Moerse family and another missionary woman.[49]

The Salvation Army Mission

The work of the Salvation Army Mission commenced in Burma in 1915 under the administration of India. Thirteen years later, the mission became a separate entity. Despite restrictions on the entry of officers and lay workers from overseas, Myanmar Salvationists continued to develop their services in the nation, particularly in Upper Myanmar. Throughout the years, they have established a network of social services to meet a range of needs in the community. Their program reaches out to children who require care, communities living in the rural villages, and other needy segments in our society.[50]

Presbyterian Mission

British soldiers and traders first introduced the Presbyterian Mission to Myanmar after the third Anglo-Burmese War (1885–1886). But no chaplain or missionary ever came. The Presbyterian church today, established among the Mizo-Chins, is the result of a revival among the Mizos in India, which was passed down to the Mizo ethnic group in Myanmar. In 1981 the membership numbered 21,280, and the growth took place mainly among the Mizos and Dai people in southern Chin State. By 1983, the Presbyterian Church had grown to twenty-two thousand.[51] The church extended their activities to the southern Chin Hills, Rakhine State, Upper Sagaing Division. Today the total membership is around thirty thousand.

Evangelical Free Church of Myanmar Mission

The Evangelical Free Church Mission began with an indigenous church leader, Reverend Lalthanliana, in the 1955. The church adopted fundamental

---

49. Chin Khua Khai, "The Growth of Churches in Myanmar with a Special Reference to the Assemblies of God" (MTh thesis, International Theological Seminary, West Covina, CA, 1991), 2.
50. McLeish, *Christian Progress*, 51.
51. Khai, *Cross amidst Pagodas*, 72–73.

evangelicalism and is opposed to the ecumenism of the Myanmar Council of Churches. Their mission had a great impact among the Mizo, the Tedim, and the Matu people among the Chin. In 1980, the community had seventeen thousand members.[52]

THE NATIONAL CHRISTIAN CHURCH (1966 TO THE PRESENT)

Due to the declaration of Buddhism as the state religion by Prime Minister U Nu in 1962, the revival of Buddhism became an important aspect of state activity. Thus during this era of democratic government in Myanmar (1948–1962), it became more difficult for Christians to propagate the gospel in the country.[53]

In 1962 under the leadership of General Ne Win, the Myanmar Armed Forces seized power and set up the Revolutionary Council, and the rule of U Nu's parliamentary democracy came to an end. Then the Council established a military dictatorship and began to develop socialist rule over the country, publishing the statement of their ideology, "The Burmese Way to Socialism," in April 1962. In 1974, the Revolutionary Council transferred their power to the socialist government.[54] One of the main characteristics of the socialist government was Buddhism, including promotion of "the middle way" based on Buddhist philosophy. The government's motto was "man matters most," a conglomeration of Buddhism and Marxism.

The Revolutionary Council's act of implementing the socialist program had a great impact on Christianity. From 1962 to 1964, the government expelled all missionaries. They also demonetized the currency and nationalized all Christian mission schools and mission hospitals and dispensaries, along with other non-religious institutions such as farms and orphanages. These government actions brought an end to foreign Christian missions in Myanmar, and a new page opened for the national Christian leaders to carry the mission of the church in Myanmar. To highlight the situation of churches after the missionary era, Zau Lat states the following:

> In the post-missionary period, under the former Socialist Military Government, beginning with the 1960s, the Churches became limited both in resources and trained personnel to engage in active mission work among non-Christians. The Churches at

---
52. Vuta, *Brief History*, 251.
53. Nyunt, *Missions amidst Pagodas*, 76.
54. Nyunt, 76.

that time were busy fighting for their own "survival," for they had suddenly become independent autonomous Churches from being "mission fields of the American Churches. . . ." There were very few missions works the churches could do outside of the Church compounds. Christians were free to worship inside the church building at all times, but it was hard to get permission to hold big gatherings like Annual Conventions. The churches had no access to their once most effective arms of evangelization – mission schools, hospitals, and mission farms. Once again, all Church activities were confined to the Church compounds and thus, Christians in Myanmar began to develop a form of *"Mission Compound Mentality,"* establishing *"self-contained kinds of Churches,"* very rapidly, thereby sharing the good news of the Lord only in the churches, among its members, and thus limiting their mission work, *in the world.*[55]

In this statement, Zau Lat does not mean that the church in Myanmar after the missionaries left was stagnant, but his emphasis is on how the churches faced hardships that led the flocks into "the valley of the shadow of death" under the Marxist-oriented military government of the Myanmar Socialist Program Party.

Despite the end of foreign missions in Myanmar after 153 years, the church in Myanmar continues to grow in the midst of challenges. In the 1970s, a great revival came to many parts of Myanmar which caused rapid growth. Almost all of these new Christians were in the evangelical and Pentecostal churches. This shift reflects the lasting effects of renewal movements, evangelism, and church planting in urban and rural areas. Some of the products of these movements are the United Pentecostal Church, Believers' Church of Christ, Evangelical Church of Christ, The Gospel Baptist Church, the Christian and Missionary Alliance, the Four-Square Church, the Fundamental Baptist Church, the Nazarene Church, the Full Gospel Assembly Church, the Revival Baptist Church, and many parachurch organizations. All have their own programs and projects in Christian education, evangelism and mission, and church planting.[56]

---

55. Zau Lat, "Rereading the Great Commission Matt. 28:18–20," in *An Evaluation on Judson's Mission Approach: In Our Theological Journey: Writings in Honor of Dr. Anna May Say Pa* (Insein, Yangon: MIT Festschrift Committee, 2006), 86–87. Emphasis in the original.
56. Khai, *Cross amidst Pagodas*, 74.

CONCLUSION, AND ONGOING QUESTIONS

Churches in Myanmar, though founded by foreign missions, are largely indigenous today and are enjoying steady growth. Christianity is the second largest religious group in the country. The majority of Christians come from major ethnic groups such as the Kayin, the Chin, and the Kachin who are from tribal animistic backgrounds, with only a small fraction from the Burmese Buddhist background. The church has suffered political, social, and economic turmoil throughout its history, but it stands firm because of its solid foundation.

However, there are areas which still need deep theological reflection and development.

Theravada Buddhists and Christianity

According to the report of the 2014 census, the population of the country of Myanmar is over fifty million. Over 86 percent are Theravada Buddhists, and their culture has been deeply embedded as a powerful resurgent socio-politico-cultural religion. Many suggest that all Burmese owe loyalty to Theravada Buddhism because it is the only unifying foundation of the creativity, philosophical thinking, and way of life of the Burmese. The Theravada Buddhists' philosophy of *Abhidharma* expresses their worldview, their conception of the meaning of human existence and destiny, and the idea of the Ultimate or God. Religion and culture are, for them, just two sides of a coin.

Given that Christianity has been in Myanmar for more than five centuries, it is no longer a young religious practice. Hundreds of missionaries, thousands of dollars, and countless pages of translation have been utilized to propagate the faith. Today Christians in Myanmar are 6.2 percent of the entire population. Even though they are the second largest religious group in the country, the vast majority of Christians are from minority groups such as the Kayin, the Kachin and the Chin tribes. The Bamar, who are predominantly Buddhist and comprise the majority of the population, are only about 0.1 percent of the Christian community. In other words, Christianity among the Bamar people is still regarded as a "potted plant" as it has not been successfully transplanted onto the Burmese Buddhist soil. Christians are looked upon as unpatriotic, embracing a Western religion rather than being rooted in the soil of their "mother land."

Reflection Question: If the gospel is relevant for all, why is it still alien and unfruitful especially among the Burmese Buddhists in Myanmar?

Mission Communication

There are apparent missiological weaknesses in the mission strategy of the church in Myanmar, including ineffective communication and in particular a lack of indigeneity. In regard to mission strategy, the churches in Myanmar still venerate the imported mission outreach strategies inherited from the past centuries without critical appraisal of their relevance and empowering vitality. In the past, especially during the colonial period, the "mission station approach" was common. At that time, this approach may have been the only viable way to help Christians survive and to get the church started. But the "gathered conglomerate" often separates converts from their people and society and has seldom had a major impact on the Buddhist people groups. In addition, due to the tactless approaches used by some Christian fanatics to convert people in Christianity, Christian communication has largely failed in most of the fertile grounds of Buddhists soil.

Reflection Questions:

1. What kind of communication methods and strategies should the church employ in order to effectively reach the Buddhists?
2. What are some challenges for the churches in Myanmar as they try to accomplish God's kingdom ventures?

REFERENCES

Bailey, Faith C., ed. *Adoniram Judson: Missionary to Burma*. Chicago: Moody, 1955.

Committee of History. *A Brief History of the First Baptist Church in Myanmar 1816–1991*. Yangon: U Naw Memorial Baptist Church, 2006.

Fish, Lazarus. "Reclaiming the Zayat Ministry: Witness to the Gospel among Burmese Buddhists in Myanmar." PhD diss., Asbury Theological Seminary, Lexington, 2002.

Kane, Herbert. *Understanding Christian Mission*. Grand Rapids: Baker Book House, 1975.

Khai, Chin Khua. *Cross amidst Pagodas: A History of the Assemblies of God in Myanmar*. Baguio, Philippines: APTS Press, 1995.

———. "The Growth of Churches in Myanmar with a Special Reference to the Assemblies of God." MTh Thesis. USA: International Theological Seminary, West Covina, 1991.

Lat, Zau. "Rereading the Great Commission Matt. 28:18–20." In *An Evaluation on Judson's Mission Approach: In Our Theological Journey: Writings in Honor of Dr. Anna May Say Pa*. Insein, Yangon: MIT Festschrift Committee, 2006.

Lim, Theodore, and Dengthuama. "An Overview of Christian Missions in Myanmar." Tahan Theological College and Seminary, April, 2016. http://ojs.globalmissiology.org/index.php/english/article/view/1884/4197.

McGavan, Donald A. *Understanding Church Growth*. Grand Rapids: Eerdmans, 1990.

McLeish, Alexander. *Christian Progress in Burma*. London: World Dominion Press, 1929.

Min, Aye. "A Brief History of Myanmar Evangelical Fellowship. A Term Paper." D Min. diss, Asia Graduate School of Theology, Yangon, Myanmar, 2004.

Nyunt, Peter Thein. *Missions amidst Pagodas: Contextual Communication of the Gospel in the Burmese Buddhist Context*. Carlisle, UK: Langham Monographs, 2014.

Purser, William C. R. *Christian Mission in Burma*. Westminster, UK: Society for Propagation of the Gospel in Foreign Parts, 1913.

Stafford, Glen D. *A Brief History of the Assemblies of Burma*. Springfield, MO: Central Bible College, 1977.

Swe, Thein. "Census Report Volume 2-C: The Union Report: Religion." In *The 2014 Myanmar Population and Housing Census*. Nay Pyi Taw, Myanmar: Ministry of Labour, Immigration and Population, 2016.

Tegenfeidt, Harmine G. *A Century of Growth: The Kachin Baptist Church of Burma*. Pasadena, CA: William Carey Library, 1974.

Thant, Myo, et. al. *Myanmar: Facts and Figures 2002*. Yangon: Printing and Publishing Enterprise, 2002.

Vuta, K. T. "A Brief History of the Planting and the Growth of the Church in Burma: Dr. Price, the First Medical Missionary." PhD diss, Fuller Theological Seminary, 1983.

Wa, Maung Shwe. *Burma Baptist Chronicles*. Rangoon: Burma Baptist Convention, 1963.

Wayland, Francis. *A Memoir of the Life and Labors of the Rev. Adoniram Judson*, vol. 2. Cambridge: Harvard University, 1853.

Yaw, Pa. "Christian Conversion: An Evaluation on Judson's Mission Approach." In *Our Theological Journey: Writings in Honor of Dr. Anna May Say Pa*. Insein, Yangon: MIT Festschrift Committee, 2006.

CHAPTER 6
HISTORY OF PHILIPPINE CHRISTIANITY

Narry F. Santos

The history of Christianity in the Philippines began in the sixteenth century and developed through interactions between European colonial forces beginning with Spain, missionaries, and the Filipino people.[1] The Philippines – an archipelago with 7,100 islands and a nation belonging to the Malay race – has the longest history of Christianity and the second largest Christian majority in Southeast Asia.[2] Before the arrival of the Spanish, the Filipinos practiced an indigenous religion, engaged in trade and cultural relations with China and India, and experienced Islamic inroads via Indonesia. Roman Catholicism came into the country as a product of more than three centuries of Spanish dominance, while Protestantism entered the religious space as a result of almost five decades of American colonial rule after the Spanish-American War that concluded in 1898.

This chapter will present a summary of the history of Philippine Christianity over five hundred years, from the early sixteenth to early twenty-first centuries. It will begin with the context of the indigenous religion of the early Filipinos. Then it will discuss the arrival and influence of Roman Catholicism through Spain (1521–1898), the coming and impact of Protestantism through the United States (1898–1946), and the development of Philippine Christianity after World War II (1946 onwards). This chapter will conclude with an exploration of three major issues related to Philippine Christianity and Christian mission.

---

1. Christl Kessler and Jurgen Ruland, *Give Jesus a Hand! Charismatic Christians: Populist Religion and Politics in the Philippines* (Quezon City, Metro Manila: Ateneo de Manila University Press, 2008), 30.
2. The Southeast Asian country with the largest Christian majority as a percentage of population is East Timor. The 2005 World Bank report showed that the population of East Timor (about 1 million people) was 98 percent Catholic, 1 percent Protestant, and less than 1 percent Muslim, for a total of 99 percent Christian. The Philippine Statistics Authority reported in 2015 that 80.58 percent of the total Filipino population (about 102 million people) were Roman Catholic, 10.8 percent were Protestant, and 5.57 percent were Muslim, for a total of almost 92 percent Christian.

INDIGENOUS RELIGION

The early Filipinos had their own traditional religion before the Christian missionaries came to the Philippines in the sixteenth century.[3] The indigenous Filipinos of Luzon (Tagalogs) believed in a Supreme Being called *Bathala*, "who stands at the apex of a scale of powerful spirits."[4] However, *Bathala* was remote and inaccessible, so the Tagalogs appealed to the *anitos*, lesser divinities who served as ministers of *Bathala*, to intercede for them.

The indigenous Filipinos were closely connected with nature[5] and believed that there were *anitos* for the rice fields, for the sea, for battles, and for curing diseases, and that these *anitos* presided over the whole gamut of life including birth, sickness, courtship, marriage, planting, harvesting, and death.[6] Thus it was the *anitos* that the sixteenth century Filipinos called upon and offered sacrifices when they desired anything, believing that these beings sufficiently guided their temporal and spiritual needs.[7] Indigenous religious specialists – *catalonan* for the Tagalogs and *babaylan* for the Bisayans – performed ceremonies for the sacrifices and food offerings to the *anitos*. These specialists were responsible for solving the religious and medical problems of the people before the Catholic missionaries came.[8]

SPANISH ROMAN CATHOLIC MISSION (1521–1898)

With the arrival of the Spanish in the middle of the sixteenth century came the introduction of Catholic Christianity. Ferdinand Magellan arrived in 1521, representing both the Catholic Church and the Spanish crown. Thus Christianity came to the archipelago as a supplement and through the aid of the sword. In fact, "The process of Christianization was intimately related to

---

3. Fides del Castillo, "Gospel-Culture Relationship of Traditional Filipino Religion and Catholicism," *The International Journal of Religion and Spirituality in Society* 6, no. 2 (2015): 41–46. See also Pablo Fernandez, *History of the Church of the Philippines* (Metro Manila: Navotas, 1979).
4. Valentino Sitoy, *A History of Christianity in the Philippines* (Quezon City: New Day, 1985), 12.
5. Leonardo Mercado, *Spirituality on Creation* (Manila: Logos, 1998), 7–10.
6. Eduardo Domingo, "Re-reading the Contexts of Historical Records," *Philippiniana Sacra* (2007): 417–32.
7. Jose Francisco, "Tagalogs at the Spanish Contact," in *The Beginnings of Christianity in the Philippines*, ed. Christian Quirino (Quezon City: Vertex, 1965), 176–200; Lewis Hofpe, *Religions of the World* (New York: Macmillan, 1983), 8–9.
8. For more details on the autochthonous religion of early Filipinos, see F. Landa Jocano, *Filipino Prehistory: Rediscovering Precolonial Heritage* (Quezon City, Metro Manila: Punlad Research House, 1998).

the entire process of establishing Spanish civil rule in the colony. . . . [The] missionaries . . . were agents of the State as well as servants of the Church."⁹

Five Augustinian friars arrived with Legaspi in the central Philippines in 1565, and other missionaries followed soon afterwards. The Franciscans came in 1577, the Dominicans in 1578, the Jesuits in 1581, and the Augustine Recollects in 1606. By the end of the century, more than 450 regulars had embarked for the islands, though not all arrived.¹⁰ The period of 1578 to 1609 can be called the "golden age" of Christian evangelization in the Philippines through this first wave of Spanish missionaries, who were described as "fired with apostolic zeal . . . inspired by a seemingly boundless enthusiasm."¹¹ These early friars showed missionary zeal, learned the language of the people, emphasized instruction, and encouraged indigenous religious forms. They also introduced new methods of farming and increased the variety of produce by importing seeds. Most importantly, these missionary friars taught the basics of the Roman Catholic faith.¹² By the early 1600s, less than fifty years of sustained presence, approximately 250 missionaries saw the conversion of most of the people to Christianity.¹³

Aside from the zeal and commitment of the friars, three other factors propelled these early Catholic missionaries toward tangible success. First, Islam had not yet taken firm root in the archipelago except in the southern islands such as Sulu and Mindanao, though conflict between Catholics and Muslims continued throughout the Spanish rule.¹⁴ In fact, the Spanish arrival in the context of Islam's advance in Manila and the Southern Philippines can been

---

9. Arthur Tuggy, *The Philippine Church: Growth in a Changing Society* (Grand Rapids, MI: Eerdmans, 1971), 47–48.
10. Kenneth Latourette, *A History of the Expansion of Christianity*, vol. 3 (Milton Keynes, UK: Paternoster, 1971), 309–11.
11. John L. Phelan, *The Hispanization of the Philippines: Spanish Aims and Filipino Responses, 1565–1700* (Madison: University of Wisconsin Press, 1959), 70. Only a few baptisms occurred in the first few years, but twenty-five years after their arrival it was claimed that four hundred thousand had been baptized. Bishop Salasar in 1588 reported a more realistic 146,700 pacified Christian Filipinos. By 1622 this number had risen to half a million. Latourette, *History of Expansion*, 313.
12. Lorenzo Bautista, "The Church in the Philippines," in *Church in Asia Today: Challenges and Opportunities*, ed. Saphir Athyal (Singapore: Asia Lausanne Committee for World Evangelization, 1996), 178.
13. John L. Phelan, "Prebaptismal Instruction and the Administration of Baptism in the Philippines during the Sixteenth Century," in *Studies in Philippine Church History*, ed. Gerald H. Anderson (Ithaca, NY: Cornell University Press, 1969), 43.
14. For more information on the presence of Islam in the Philippines when the Spanish colonizers arrived, see Cesar A. Majul, "Succession in the Old Sulo Sultanate," in *The Muslim*

seen in this way: "If the islands had gone to Islam, the whole history of missions in this area would have been different, and evangelization immensely more difficult."[15] Second, the colonization of the Philippines was far less bloody than the Spanish conquest of Mexico and Peru. In fact, the first generation of friars vigorously defended the rights of the Filipinos. Third, the indigenous religious system was conveniently compatible with Spain's version of Catholicism.[16] *Bathala* corresponded with Catholic monotheism, and the *anitos* coincided with the role of saints and angels.[17]

Thus even when the early friars directly identified *anitos* with demons and destroyed all old images and religious paraphernalia, burning whatever indigenous materials they came across and destroying the vestiges of the early Filipinos' indigenous religion, the people did not violently rebel.[18] To replace the local religion, the missionaries adopted some of the native religious forms and provided Christian substitutes for previous rituals.[19] On the other hand, the early Filipinos enlarged and syncretized their indigenous religion with Catholic practices,[20] which led to the development of folk Catholicism, or the "Filipinizing" of Catholicism.[21]

Filipinos, eds. Peter G. Gowing and Robert D. McAmis (Manila: Solidaridad, 1974), 61–73. The Spanish and Muslim conflict led to the Moro Wars (1565–1898), with very lasting fruit in evangelism. Cesar A. Majul, *Muslims in the Philippines* (Manila: St. Mary's, 1973), 102.
15. Tuggy, *Philippine Church*, 67.
16. Patricio N. Abinales and Donna J. Amoroso, *State and Society in the Philippines* (Lanham, MD: Rowman and Littlefield, 2005), 51.
17. Ramon C. Reyes, "Religious Experience in the Philippines: From Mythos through Logos to Kairos," *Philippine Studies* 33 (1985): 203–12.
18. Teodoro A. Agoncillo, *A Short History of the Philippines* (New York: New American Library, 1969), 53. Vicente Rafael cites the insistence of Augustinian Thomas Ortiz that his fellow missionaries understand their duty to "examine their doctrines, customs, abuses, and superstitions, and, having examined them, impugn them and disabuse the said Gentiles of them because unless their roots are cut, the bad weeds will sprout again, no matter how many times you cut them." Vicente L. Rafael, *Contracting Colonialism: Translation and Christian Conversion in Tagalog Society Under Early Spanish Rule* (Durham, NC: Duke University Press, 1993), 107. Moreover, Gowing comments, "[T]he missionaries sought to destroy paganism, root and branch. With the help of the military, and assisted by many of their Filipino converts, they destroyed pagan holy places, burned idols, and obliterated the native literature [because of its religious character]." Peter Gowing, *Islands Under the* Cross (Manila: National Council of Churches, 1967), 16.
19. Phelan, "Prebaptismal Instruction," 38.
20. F. Lando Jocano, "Conversion and the Patterning of Christian Experience," in *Acculturation in the Philippines*, eds. Peter G. Gowing and William Henry Scott (Quezon City, Metro Manila: New Day, 1971), 55.
21. With regard to folk Catholicism, de Mesa wonders if Christianity had simply been Filipinized. José M. de Mesa, "Primal Religion and Popular Religiosity," *East Asian Pastoral*

However unlike the first waves of friars who skillfully appropriated Christianity for the indigenous people, the latter waves of friars from different orders were opposite in character. Friar cruelty and corruption, and political abuse and oppression,[22] especially the murder of three Filipino reformist priests, played major roles in the Philippine Propaganda Movement (1872–1892) that called for reforms.[23] The ensuing Revolutionary Movement (1892–1896), which was catalyzed by the public execution of Dr. Jose Rizal who had written two novels criticizing the abuse of the friars, called for revolt after more than three centuries of Spanish domination.[24] On 12 June 1898, the Philippine forces under the leadership of General Emilio Aguinaldo declared independence from Spain.

Moreover, the marginalization of the indigenous Filipino priests led to the formation in 1902 of the indigenous *Iglesia Filipina Independiente* (Philippine Independent Church) or Aglipayans.[25] This church organization called for a Philippine national church, a Filipinized Roman Catholic Church that maintained allegiance to Rome but rejected the authority of the Spanish bishops.[26]

AMERICAN PROTESTANT MISSION (1898–1946)

The "mock battle of Manila" between the United States and Spain in 1898 triggered the American occupation of the Philippines. The Treaty of Paris put

---

Review 37, no. 1 (2000): 73–82. In addition Phelan observes that in this process of what he calls "Philippinizing" Catholicism, the early Filipinos showed a remarkable selective process of stressing and de-emphasizing certain features of Spanish Catholicism. Phelan, *Hispanization*, 72.
22. Tuggy describes this later friar abuse: "As time went on, the Orders obtained more and more property and power. By not encouraging the development of a native clergy they extended the period of 'mission' too long and eventually set the stage for the great revolt against the friars at the end of the nineteenth century." Tuggy, *Philippine Church*, 66.
23. The murder of Fathers Jose Burgos, Mariano Gomez, and Jacinto Zamora by the Spanish authorities inspired the Philippine Propaganda Movement in the 1880s. The movement for political and civil liberties denounced Spanish discrimination but did not call for independence from Spain. See John N. Schumacher, *The Propaganda Movement 1880–1895: The Creation of Filipino Consciousness; The Making of the Revolution* (Quezon City, Metro Manila: Ateneo de Manila University Press, 1997).
24. Reynaldo C. Ileto, *Pasyon and Revolution: Popular Movements in the Philippines (1840–1910)* (Quezon City, Philippines: Ateneo University Press, 1979); and Renato Constantino and Leticia R. Constantino, *A History of the Philippines: From the Spanish Colonization to the Second World War* (New York: Monthly Review, 2008).
25. Although Catholic missionaries began work in 1565 and the numbers of converts grew fast, no Filipino was made a priest before 1702, and during Spanish rule not a single Filipino was made a bishop. Richard L. Deats, *Nationalism and Christianity in the Philippines* (Dallas, TX: Southern Methodist University Press, 1967), 28.
26. Teodoro A. Agoncillo, *Introduction to Filipino History* (Quezon City, Metro Manila: Garotech, 1974), 172.

an end to the Spanish-American War, and Spain ceded the Philippines to the United States for twenty million dollars.[27] American Protestants viewed the unexpected possession of the Philippines as a providential opening for missions. "Even President McKinley, speaking as a Methodist, spoke of the duty to 'Christianize' the Filipinos who at the time he believed to be 'unfit for self- government.'"[28]

Thus the "White Man's Burden formed part of the missionary urge of the nineteenth century,"[29] especially in light of the beginnings of American Protestant mission in the Philippines (1899–1901). Despite sometimes questionable motivations, American missionaries contributed constructively to the spread of Protestantism: "they sincerely labored as missionaries and addressed both spiritual and material needs of the people. They started churches and then also educational and medical institutions. They were also a pioneer test case in the new reality called freedom of religion."[30]

In the short period between 1893 and 1905, various missionaries arrived. First were the Episcopalian missionaries followed by Methodists and Baptists, then the United Brethren, Disciples of Christ, the Christian and Missionary Alliance, the Congregationalists, and the Seventh Day Adventists.[31] The Protestant missionaries met in 1901 to form the Evangelical Union in order to prevent duplication, undue competition, and divisive conflicts among them. These missionaries also approved a Comity Agreement, which assigned them each to the evangelization of certain well-defined areas in the country.[32]

The beginning of Protestant mission in the Philippines was marked by missionary enthusiasm and the people's responsiveness, especially the educated and upper middle classes. In fact, from forty-five mainline Protestant churches and four thousand members in 1903, the churches grew to 594 with 125,000

---

27. Horacio de la Costa, *Readings in Philippine History* (Makati, Metro Manila: Bookmark, 1992), 211.
28. De la Costa, *Readings*, 180; see Mariano C. Apilado, *Revolutionary Spirituality: A Study of the Protestant Role in the American Colonial Rule of the Philippines, 1989–1928* (Quezon City, Metro Manila: New Day, 1999), 57; and Gerald H. Anderson, "Providence and Politics behind Protestant Missionary Beginnings in the Philippines," in *Studies in Philippine Church History*, ed. Gerald H. Anderson (Ithaca, NY: Cornell University Press, 1969), 279–300.
29. Anne C. Kwantes, *Presbyterian Missionaries in the Philippines* (Quezon City, Metro Manila: New Day, 1989), 14. The white man's burden is the belief that colonizers had to impose Western civilization onto the indigenous inhabitants of the colonies.
30. Bautista, "Church in the Philippines," 180.
31. Kessler and Ruland, *Give Jesus a Hand*, 45.
32. Mariano C. Apilado, "The United Church of Christ in the Philippines," in *Chapters in Philippine Church History*, ed. Anne C. Kwantes (Metro Manila: OMF Literature, 2001), 340.

members in 1918. This growth continued, and in 1940 there were two thousand churches and 250,000 members.[33]

Three factors help explain the immediate success of Protestant expansion efforts. First was the open support of the United States colonial administration and the people's widespread aversion to the Catholic Church due to the corruption of the Catholic friars. The American colonizers immediately established public schools, mainly to promote the pacification of the islands.[34] The second factor was the democratization of religiosity by emphasizing the value of Scripture. From 1899 to 1910, the American Protestants initiated the translation of the entire Bible, or at least portions, into the vernacular regional languages. The Spanish Bibles were popular especially among the elite, but translation into the local languages was deemed necessary to make the Bible accessible to the common people.[35] Third, Protestant missions were quick to ordain Filipinos. The Methodists ordained their first pastor in 1900 and the Presbyterians in 1904. They gave also Filipino pastors a part in church leadership. In 1914, a Filipino was elected as Presbyterian moderator of the Evangelical Church of the Philippines. In 1923, a Filipino was elected president of the Evangelical Union, and in another two years, Filipinos outnumbered missionaries by ten to one in voting power at the Methodist Annual Council.[36]

Though Filipino leadership in Protestant churches was encouraged, indigenizing the churches was not pursued. The Protestant churches were mostly Americanized, influenced by the degree of Americanization of the culture.[37] Protestantism in the Philippines was also closely identified with Western foreign expression to the point that nationalistic sentiments and reactions against Western power negatively affected Protestant churches during the American control of the Philippines.[38] As a result, numerous indigenous churches were formed, like the *Iglesia Evangelica Metodista en las Islas Filipinas* (IEMELIF) in 1909 – an indigenous branch of the Methodist denomination.[39] Another was

---

33. Gowing, *Islands Under the Cross*, 154.
34. José de Mesa, "Tuloy Po Kayo sa Loob: Some Guidelines in Understanding Filipino Culture," *East Asian Pastoral Review* 27 (1991): 141.
35. Kwantes, *Presbyterian Missionaries*, 38.
36. Deats, *Nationalism and Christianity*, 96, 99.
37. Tuggy, *Philippine Church*, 159.
38. Dionesio Miranda, *Buting Pinoy: Probe Essays on Value as Filipino* (Manila: Divine Word, 1992), 6.
39. Nicolas Zamora, the first ordained Filipino Methodist pastor in 1900, founded this indigenous Methodist religious group. See José M. de Mesa, "Nicolas Zamora: Religious Nationalist," in *Studies in Philippine Church History*, ed. Gerald H. Anderson (Ithaca, NY: Cornell University Press, 1969), 325–36.

the *Iglesia ni Cristo* which, objecting to the Western Catholic and Protestant churches, was developed in 1914 with their own brand of indigenous faith.[40] In addition, the American efforts to integrate the Muslim people into the Protestant culture by encouraging them to immigrate to Mindanao did not reach the equality hoped for. Muslim resistance continued because they found themselves disadvantaged and powerless.[41]

The next decade of Protestantism saw a series of mergers, schisms, and leadership transitions in Protestant churches. Independent congregations and denominations like the Union Church of Manila (1914), United Church of Manila (1924), United Evangelical Church in the Philippine Islands (UECPI) (1929), and *La Iglesia Evangelica Unida de Filipinas* (1932) worked toward mergers and unions. The American-controlled Evangelical Union transitioned to the National Christian Council (1929), which shared leadership between American and Filipino Protestants, while Filipino Protestants took full leadership of the Philippine Federation of Evangelical Churches (PFEC) in 1938.[42]

The Pacific portion of World War II ended American rule in the Philippines. Japan invaded the Philippines in December 1941 and occupied the country until July 1945, causing 1.2 million deaths and massive physical destruction in the land. During this period, 257 priests and Catholic leaders were killed,[43] while 250 Protestant missionaries were imprisoned. Protestants who did not cooperate with the Japanese were harassed and prosecuted by the Japanese imperial army.[44]

CHRISTIANITY AFTER INDEPENDENCE (1946 ONWARD)

World War II ended with the surrender of Japan on 2 September 1945. Then on 4 July 1946, the Philippines was granted independence by the United States. Despite the devastation of war, the Philippines displayed hopeful political recovery and remarkable religious revitalization.[45] In February 1946, the

---

40. Felix Manalo founded the indigenous *Iglesia ni Cristo*; see Albert Sanders, "An Appraisal of the *Iglesia ni Cristo*," in *Studies in Philippine Church History*, ed. Gerald H. Anderson (Ithaca, NY: Cornell University Press, 1969), 350–65.
41. W. K. Che Man, *Muslim Separatism: The Moros of Southern Philippines and the Malays of South Thailand* (Manila: Ateneo de Manila University Press, 1990), 25.
42. Raymundo Go, *The Philippine Council of Evangelical Churches* (Carlisle, UK: Langham Monographs, 2019), 69–82.
43. James H. Kroeger, "The Catholic Church in the Philippines: A Brief Historical and Contemporary Overview," *Philippinia Sacra* 37, no. 109 (2002): 87.
44. David E. Gardiner, "Ecumenism among Philippine Protestants, 1945–1963," *Philippine Studies* 50, no. 1 (2002): 118–28.
45. Gowing, *Islands Under the Cross*, 171.

Catholic Church founded the Catholic Welfare, a relief organization which in 1967 became known as the Catholic Bishop's Conference of the Philippines (CBCP) – becoming the authoritative and official decision-making body of the Roman Catholic Church in the Philippines.[46] In addition, the 1950s saw the rise of a new lay movement through the formation of Catholic organizations for the laity.[47] From the second half of the 1960s, the *Cursillos de Cristianidad* (Little Courses in Christianity) or the *cursillo* renewal movement drew hundreds of thousands of followers.[48]

Consolidation of Philippine Catholicism in the postwar period was evident in the building of new churches, creation of new parishes, and opening of new schools. Between 1960 and 1967 alone, the number of Catholic schools rose from 916 to 1,637, while the number of students increased from 368,987 to nearly one million. With this growth came the challenge of a lack of priests, as seen in the ratio of one priest for every 5,600 Catholics in the middle of the 1960s.[49] The related challenge of nominalism or large segments of Filipino Catholics remaining unchurched is reflected in that "67 percent of all Filipinos live in Catholic families in which nobody goes to Mass on Sundays . . . (and) at most 3 percent of all Filipino families are regularly practicing Catholic families."[50]

The mainline Protestant churches also experienced significant mergers after the Japanese Occupation. In 1948, the United Church of Christ of the Philippines (UCCP) became the largest and most influential Protestant denomination in the country.[51] UCCP was a merger of the UECPI, the Philippine Methodist Church (1933), and the remnants of the wartime Evangelical

---

46. Kroeger, "Catholic Church," 87–88.
47. A prominent example of these lay organizations is the *Barangay* of the Blessed Virgin Mary which organized processions and promoted catechetical instruction. This group reportedly had more than five million Filipinos register for it in 1956. Other groups are the Legion of Mary, Knights of Columbus, and Catholic Women's League. Gerald H. Anderson and Peter G. Gowing, "The Philippines: Bulwark of the Church in Asia," in *Church and Christ in Southeast Asia*, ed. Gerald H. Anderson (New York: Friendship Press, 1968), 141–42.
48. For details on the *cursillo* movement, see Marcene Marcouxm, *Cursillo: Anatomy of a Movement; The Experience of Spiritual Renewal* (New York: Lambeth, 1982).
49. Jaime C. Bulatao, "A Socio-Psychological View of the Philippine Church," in *Phenomena and Their Interpretation: Landmark Essays 1957–1989* (Quezon City, Metro Manila: Ateneo de Manila University Press, 1992), 12.
50. Anderson and Gowing, "Philippines," 140.
51. Oscar S. Suarez, *Protestantism and Authoritarian Politics: The Politics of Repression and the Future of Ecumenical Witness in the Philippines* (Quezon City, Metro Manila: New Day, 1998), 151.

Church of the Philippines that was configured in 1943.⁵² In 1963, another decisive merger for mainline Protestant denominations was the formation of the National Council of Churches of the Philippines (NCCP) which replaced the prewar group of the PFEC that was formed in 1938. The churches that coalesced with NCCP were the Apostolic Catholic Church, the Baptists, the Episcopalians, the IEMELIF, the Aglipayans, the Lutherans, the Salvation Army, the Methodists, and the UCCP, plus nine Christian organizations as associate members. Under the UCCP, the Protestant Christians became ecumenical and more involved in developing activities that were designed to address the growing social injustices in society.⁵³

New conservative groups were also formed in the postwar period. In 1947, the Christian and Missionary Alliance Churches of the Philippines was established under Filipino leadership. In that same year, the Far East Gospel Crusade – a new missionary agency born out of the ministry of American military personnel in the Philippines – was started. In 1948, missionaries of the Association of Baptists for World Evangelism and Filipino pastors put together the Association of Fundamental Baptist Churches of the Philippines.⁵⁴

In 1964, the new "wave" of conservative missionaries who came to the Philippines after World War II chose to become part of the Philippine Council of Fundamental Churches (PCFC). These new missionaries including the Conservative Baptist Foreign Mission Society, the Overseas Missionary Fellowship, and the Southern Baptist Convention did not align with the theology of the NCCP.⁵⁵ In 1969, PCFC was renamed the Philippine Council of Evangelical Churches (PCEC) as a result of a doctrinal schism between the fundamentalist and evangelical churches. The PCEC sought to engage in both proclamation and social ministry, though with greater emphasis on evangelism and church planting.

In other words, the Protestant churches in this period progressed through a series of mergers, conciliar unions, schisms, and controversies that reflected the doctrinal and denominational issues that had been rigorously debated earlier in the United States.⁵⁶ However, despite the postwar gains of Protestants and

---

52. Raymundo Go, *The Philippine Council of Evangelical Churches* (Carlisle, UK: Langham Monographs, 2019), 101.
53. Kessler and Ruland, *Give Jesus a Hand*, 66.
54. Go, *Philippine Council*, 103–4, 109.
55. Averell U. Aragon, "The Philippine Council of Evangelical Churches," in *Chapters in Philippine Church History*, ed. Anne C. Kwantes (Metro Manila: OMF Literature, 2001), 372–73.
56. Aragon, "Philippine Council," 375. The doctrinal debates related to fundamentalist and evangelical issues, along with modernist-liberal/fundamentalist-evangelical issues of theology and

cooperation for more than two decades, the numerical growth of the early Protestant denominations was modest – as seen in the following government census statistics regarding the percentage of Protestants relative to the total population: 2.3 percent in 1948; 2.9 percent in 1960; and 3.2 percent in 1970. The percentage of Catholics in the same years were 83 percent, 83.8 percent, and 85 percent respectively.[57]

After two and a half decades of recovering from the ruins of war, the Philippines entered into a nation-altering experience. In September 1972, President Ferdinand Marcos declared martial law, using student activism, the communist insurgency, and Muslim secessionism in Mindanao as reasons to extend his rule beyond his allowable two terms in office. Marcos dissolved Congress, suspended the writ of *habeas corpus*, prohibited political parties, and arrested tens of thousands.[58] This reign of repression and authoritarianism extended for eleven years, culminating in the assassination of opposition leader Benigno Aquino in August 1983. This murder eventually led to the ouster of Marcos in February 1986 through the EDSA Revolution or bloodless "people power" revolt and to the installation of Corazon Aquino, Benigno Aquino's wife, as the president of the Philippines.[59]

President Aquino restored democratic processes in the land, though she had to go through six aborted military coups. The next president, Fidel Ramos, pushed for deregulation and privatization which lead to considerable economic growth, though the Asian crisis of 1997 to 1998 abruptly disrupted this gain.[60] The next two presidents, Joseph Estrada and Gloria Macapagal-Arroyo, were not able to sustain the economic growth of the previous administration. Rodrigo Duterte, elected in 2016, was a strong advocate on the war on drugs, though questions have been raised on extrajudicial killings.[61] The social and economic issues that were exacerbated during martial law – poverty, corruption,

---

practice, like evangelism and social concern. See Al Tizon, *Transformation after Lausanne: Radical Evangelical Mission in Global-Local Perspective* (Eugene, OR: Wipf and Stock, 2008), 24–28.
57. Bautista, "Church in the Philippines," 180.
58. Kessler and Ruland, *Give Jesus a Hand*, 67.
59. Bautista, "Church in the Philippines," 184.
60. Kessler and Ruland, *Give Jesus a Hand*, 80.
61. Jayeel Cornelio and Ia Maranon, "A 'Righteous Intervention': Megachurch Christianity and Duterte's War on Drugs in the Philippines," *International Journal of Asian Christianity* 2 (2019): 211–12.

exploitation, social injustice, and the growing gap between the rich and the poor – continue to persist.[62]

In this context of upheaval and turmoil, the churches responded actively. Though their perspectives were different and their contributions diverse, the Roman Catholics and mainline and evangelical Protestants took steps to speak against the abuses of martial law and to address the social and economic ills of the land. The Catholic approach to social action in the Philippines has been heavily influenced by Vatican II (1962–1965), which strongly urged Catholic churches to play an active role in the struggle against social injustice and poverty. Because of this impact, Catholics continue their commitment to education and health. In 2001, the Catholic Church ran 965 high schools and 275 colleges, along with operating 147 hospitals and clinics, 236 orphanages, and sixty-nine homes for the elderly.

The mainline Protestants through the NCCP "became more involved in development activities which were designed to target the growing social injustices in the country. It was nevertheless a sign of progress that the Protestant Churches became a more vocal voice in their call for greater social justice."[63] The evangelical Protestants of the PCEC created the Philippine Relief and Development Services as a systematic way to help those in crisis and to care for the needy.[64] Mission as transformation was also initiated, examples of which are the Centre for Community Transformation (1992) and the Studies in Asian Church and Culture.[65]

CONTEMPORARY CHRISTIANITY AND MISSION

Having discussed the indigenous religion, Roman Catholicism during the Spanish colonial period (1521–1898), Protestantism during the American rule (1898–1946), and the development of Philippine Christianity after the Japanese Occupation (1946 onwards), we will now explore three major issues in early twenty-first century Christianity and mission. First is the rise of charismatic and evangelical Christianity; second is the need for more contextualized

---

62. José de Mesa and Lode Wostyn, *Doing Theology: Basic Realities and Processes* (Quezon City: Claretian, 1990), 37–38. Enriquez called the separation between the educated (Anglicized) Filipinos and the masses the "Great Cultural Divide." Virgilio Enriquez, *From Colonial to Liberation Psychology* (Manila: De La Salle University Press, 1992), 2. See Melba P. Maggay, "Crossing the Cultural Divide: Reflections from Down Under," *PATMOS* 11 (1995): 15.
63. Kessler and Ruland, *Give Jesus a Hand*, 66.
64. Go, *Philippine Council*, 149.
65. Tizon, *Transformation after Lausanne*, 155–57.

and indigenized Christianity; and third is the phenomenon of the Filipino diaspora mission.

The Rise of Charismatic and Evangelical Christianity

Since the 1970s, and especially in the 1980s and 1990s, charismatic Christianity, composed of Catholic charismatic groups and evangelical and Pentecostal churches, have experienced tremendous growth in the country.[66] Christian religious groups also have mushroomed in this period, and some have become veritable mass movements.[67] El Shaddai, a Catholic group which began as a radio program in 1981, claims two million registered members and an estimated seven million unregistered followers. Couples for Christ, another Catholic charismatic mass organization founded in 1981, claims 1.4 million followers.[68] Jesus Is Lord, the largest Protestant charismatic organization started in 1978, claims a membership of one million.[69]

In addition, evangelical Christianity in the Philippines grew from five thousand congregations in 1975 to fifty-one thousand in 2000. This growth was mainly due to the collaborative efforts of eighty-one evangelical denominations in the campaign Discipling a Whole Nation (DAWN 2000) which had the goal of planting one evangelical church in each of the 41,500 *barangays* (communities) in the country by the year 2000.[70] In 2001 DAWN, which was adopted by the PCEC as their main strategy of evangelism and church planting, was reported to have exceeded that goal by planting 51,500 churches nationwide, though it reached less than half of the total *barangays*.[71]

---

66. In light of many similarities between the charismatic evangelicals, charismatic Catholics and Pentecostals in the Philippines, it is a helpful categorization to subsume Pentecostalism, Roman Catholic Charismatics, mainstream Charismatics and Evangelical Charismatics under Charismatic Christianity, with Catholic Charismatics outnumbering Protestant Charismatics in the Philippines. Kessler and Ruland, *Give Jesus a Hand*, 8–9.
67. Kessler and Ruland, *Give Jesus a Hand*, 2–3.
68. Estimates of El Shaddai adherents vary. Gorospe-Jamon places the number at eight to ten million. Grace Gorospe-Jamon, "The El Shaddai Prayer Movement: Political Socialization in a Religious Context," *Philippine Political Science Journal* 20 (1999): 88. Mercado puts the number at six to seven million. Leonardo N. Mercado, *El Shaddai: A Study* (Manila: Logos, 2001), 1.
69. Kessler and Ruland, *Give Jesus a Hand*, 3.
70. For more details on DAWN 2000, see Jun Balayo, "Historical Sketch of the DAWN 2000 Movement in the Philippines," in *Making Missions Practical: A Compendium of the Regional Consultation on Missions*, ed. Averell U. Aragon (Davao, Mindanao: Mindanao Challenge, 1990); and Jim Montgomery, *DAWN 2000: 7 Million Churches to Go* (Pasadena, CA: William Carey Library, 1989).
71. Go, *Philippine Council*, 148.

Evangelical megachurches have also been observed as "among the fastest-growing religious groups in the Philippines today."[72] Located in urban centers, they attract young, educated members, though not necessarily affluent, and imbibe the middle-class disposition.[73] Many of these megachurches were started at a time of deteriorating economic and political conditions. One reason for their attractiveness is the fact that political and social movements have not been successful in recent Philippine history.[74] Mirroring the work of other influential religious groups in the history of the country, these megachurches have the social capital that can influence politics,[75] though a number of them are apolitical in the pulpit and are not as vocal about social justice issues compared to earlier mainline and evangelical churches.[76]

A common thread that connects the rise of charismatic Christianity, evangelical Christianity, and megachurches is the indigenous nature of their development; that is they were developed in the Philippines, not imported from the West. Jesus Is Lord was founded by a Filipino pastor.[77] DAWN was hatched as a national mission strategy in the Philippines and has spread to other countries.[78] Many evangelical megachurches were started by Filipino

---

72. Cornelio and Maranon, "Righteous Intervention," 225.
73. Jayeel Cornelio, "Religious Worlding: Christianity and the New Production of Space in the Philippines," in *New Religiosities, Modern Capitalism and Moral Complexities in Southeast Asia*, eds. J. Koning and G. Njoto-Feillard (New York: Palgrave Macmillan, 2017), 169–97; see also Omni Elisha, "Moral Ambitions of Grace: The Paradox of Compassion and Accountability in Evangelical Faith-Based Activism," *Cultural Anthropology* 13, no. 1 (2008): 154–89.
74. Kessler and Ruland, *Give Jesus a Hand*, 79.
75. Jayeel Cornelio, "Jesus Is Lord: The Indigenization of Megachurch Christianity in the Philippines," in *Pentecostal Megachurches in Asia: Negotiating Class, Consumption and the Nation* (Singapore: ISEAS, 2019), 137.
76. David S. Lim, "Consolidating Democracy: Filipino Evangelicals between People Power Events, 1986–2001," in *Evangelical Christianity and Democracy in Asia*, ed. D. Lumsdaine (Oxford, England: Oxford University Press, 2009), 235.
77. Jesus Is Lord was started by Eduardo "Brother Eddie" Villanueva in 1978. For more details on this non-denominational evangelical charismatic group and Brother Eddie, see Cornelio, "Jesus Is Lord."
78. DAWN 2000 began in 1966 when Filipino leaders from five mission groups attended a church growth workshop in Winona Lake, Indiana. Go, *Philippine Council*, 146–47.

preachers.[79] This development has been called the third wave of missions in the Philippines, while the first two waves came from foreign mission agencies.[80]

Need for More Contextualized and Indigenous Christianity

The significant influences of more than three hundred years of Roman Catholicism under Spain and of almost fifty years of Protestantism under the United States are evident in the current Philippine religious demographics. The 2010 census reports 74,211,896 followers of the Roman Catholic Church, or 80.6 percent of the Philippine population. In 2015 the Philippine Statistics Authority reported that 80.58 percent of the total Filipino population were Roman Catholic, 10.8 percent were Protestant, and 5.57 percent were Muslim. In 2013, the Center for the Study of Global Christianity projected that the Philippine population in 2020 would be 109,742,000 and the Christian population of Catholics and Protestants together would be 99,614,000, or 90.8 percent of the entire population, an annual growth rate of 2.22 percent. Thus the Philippine religious space is still predominantly Catholic with a minority of Protestants.

Despite all the growth in Philippine Christianity from the sixteenth to twenty-first centuries, it is relevant to develop the "Filipinization" of the various expressions of Euro-American Christianity among the diverse churches. Since the versions of Philippine Christianity have been closely identified with Western foreign expressions, contemporary churches need to overcome "the alienation or the lack of authentic appropriation and assimilation . . . making them appear to be no more than clones of foreign missionaries."[81]

The challenges for Philippine churches are to take into account the full spectrum of Filipino culture and indigenous religion, with its Malayan,

---

79. Christ Commission Fellowship was started by Peter Tan-Chi in 1982. Caesar "Butch" Conde started Bread of Life Ministries International in 1982. Eduardo "Ed" Lapiz started Day by Day Christian Ministries in 1985. David Sobrepena of the Assemblies of God started the Word of Hope Christian Church in 1988. Some megachurches were started by American missionaries but have taken root in the Philippines, like Greenhills Christian Fellowship started by David Yount in 1978 and Victory Christian Fellowship started by Rice Broocks and Steve Murrell in 1984.
80. The reference to a third wave of mission was less of "foreign missionaries sweeping over the country than a general religious revival." Keesler and Ruland, *Give Jesus a Hand*, 78. The first wave refers to the first foreign missionaries who came during the American colonial period; the second wave refers to the next groups of foreign missionaries who arrived after the Japanese Occupation. The third wave commenced near the end of martial law and after.
81. Miranda, *Buting Pinoy*, 6.

Spanish, American, and Muslim elements,[82] and to develop genuinely Filipino and Christian churches. Philippine churches can address these challenges by contextualizing from within rather than from without, using cultural themes or root metaphors by which the culture describes itself,[83] along with integral efforts toward incarnated communities among the masses who are poor, marginalized, and victims of social injustice.[84]

Phenomenon of the Filipino Diaspora Mission

Though the Philippines has been a consistent recipient of foreign missionaries over the centuries, the country has also experienced a robust sending of international and local missionaries. The United Methodist Church of America may have been the first to officially send Filipino missionaries overseas. In 1919, the denomination sent five missionaries to teach English in a Methodist school in Penang, and later to Okinawa and Sarawak.[85] A 1972 survey, the earliest research, revealed that the Philippines sent out 155 missionaries through thirteen mission agencies, which made the country the fourth highest among the new missionary-sending nations.[86] In 1988, another survey showed that the Philippines sent 1,814 missionaries through fifty-four mission groups,[87] mostly among the tribal minorities.[88] About two-thirds of mission agencies were started in the 1970s and the first half of the 1980s with main placements to Indonesia, Hong Kong, Singapore, the Middle East, Latin America, and

---

82. Missions to the Muslims also need to use principles of contextualization and indigenization, emphasizing reconciliation of Muslim and Christian communities, holistic ministry, and church-based movements of Muslim engagement. See Jonathan Fuller, "Kingdoms in Conflict: The History of Islam in the Philippines" (unpublished MA thesis, Fuller School of World Mission, 1999); and Frank M. C. Pardue, "The Philippines' Last Frontier" (unpublished DMin diss., Columbia International University, 2000).
83. Melba P. Maggay, "Early Protestant Missionary Efforts in the Philippines: Some Intercultural Issues," in *Asian Church and God's Mission*, eds. Wonsuk and Julie C. Ma (Mandaluyong City, Metro Manila: OMF Literature, 2003), 38; see also Andrea Roldan, "The Gospel in the Filipino Context: José M. de Mesa and Melba P. Maggay," *Mission Round Table* 13, no. 1 (2018), 24–30.
84. Maggay, "Crossing the Cultural Divide," 15.
85. Merlyn L. Guillermo and L. P. Verora, *Protestant Churches and Missions in the Philippines*, Vol. 1, *National Council of Churches in the Philippines* (Quezon City, Metro Manila: World Vision Philippines, 1982), 65.
86. Lawrence E. Keyes, *The Last Age of Missions: A Study of Third-World Mission Societies* (Pasadena, CA: William Carey Library, 1983), 58, 64.
87. Larry Pate, "The Dramatic Growth of Two-Thirds World Missions," in *Internationalizing Ministry Training: A Global Perspective*, ed. William Taylor (Grand Rapids, MI: Baker Books, 1991), 31–32.
88. The tribal minorities reached were the Mamanwa, the Atta/Ati, the Ifugao, the Ilongot, the Kankaney, the Ibaloi, the Manobo, the Bilaan, the Bagobo, and the T'boli.

Africa.[89] As of October 2006, the Status of Philippine Missions Research Report indicates that 1,900 missionaries were sent to seventy countries from 360 mission agencies and seventy-two missionary-sending churches.[90]

In 1983, the Philippine Missions Association (PMA) was launched to train, send, and receive missionaries. As PMA has expanded, the association has emphasized mobilization for doing mission in the Philippines and beyond through partnerships with mission-minded churches and mission agencies in the Philippines. The PCEC adopted PMA as their mission commission.[91] Shifting to a tentmaker missions approach, PMA collaborated with four mission networks – evangelical, charismatic, transformational, and diasporal – to adopt the Philippine Missions Mobilization Movement (PM3) in 2005.[92] As of 2009, PM3 had trained 8,924 tentmakers: 5,004 in the Philippines and 3,920 overseas.[93]

Along with sending career and tentmaker missionaries, the phenomenon of the Filipino diaspora (or scattering) has been a catalyst for global mission.[94] At least four waves of international Filipino migration prepared the Filipinos for diaspora mission.[95] As a result, Filipino missionary overseas networks

---

89. Eric Smith, Dean Wiebracht, and Thomas Wiseley, "Philippine Mission Boards and Societies," in *Evangelical Dictionary of World Missions*, ed. Scott Moreau (Grand Rapids, MI: Baker Academic, 2000), 752.
90. David S. Lim, "Indigenous Mission Movement of the Philippines" (unpublished paper, September 2015), 4.
91. Tereso C. Casiño, "The Rise of the Filipino Missionary Movement: A Preliminary Historical Assessment," in *Mission History of Asian Churches*, ed. Timothy K. Park (Pasadena, CA: William Carey Library, 2011), 208.
92. Lim, "Indigenous Mission Movement," 6.
93. Casiño, "Rise of the Filipino Missionary Movement," 211.
94. For the use of the word *diaspora* in the New Testament and its implications for missions, see Narry F. Santos, "Survey of the *Diaspora* Occurrences in the Bible and Their Contexts in Christian Missions," in *Scattered: The Filipino Global Presence*, eds. Luis Pantoja, Jr., Sadiri Joy Tira, and Enoch Wan (Manila: LifeChange, 2004), 53–66. See also Narry F. Santos, "Exploring the Major Dispersion Terms and Realities in the Bible," in *Diaspora Missiology: Theory, Methodology, and Practice*, ed. Enoch Wan (USA: CreateSpace Independent Publishing Platform, 2012), 21–38.
95. Casiño presents these four waves of Filipino migration this way: The first wave occurred between 1900 and 1945 when thousands of Filipinos went to Hawaii to work on pineapple plantations, later to California and Washington as agricultural workers, and then to Alaska to work in fish canneries. The second wave took place between 1946 and 1965, especially in the US where "war brides" (wives of US servicemen) moved to the US and later petitioned their families. The third wave happened in the 1960s when many Filipino professionals went to North America and Europe to work as medical doctors, nurses, and medical technicians. The fourth wave of migration occurred in the 1970s when many Filipino engineers, architects, caregivers, and construction workers were "exported" as Overseas Filipino Workers (OFWs) through a government program. Casiño, "Rise of the Filipino Missionary Movement," 205–6.

were formed, like the EURONET TRUST based in Europe and the Filipino International Network based in Canada.[96]

As of mid-2020, there are 109,581,078 Filipinos, giving the country 1.41 percent of the total world population and ranking it at thirteenth in countries by population. About 10 to 12 percent of the total population live or work abroad, which was estimated to be 10.2 million in 2013. In 2019, 2.2 million Filipino migrants worked abroad.[97] In light of this ongoing Filipino diaspora phenomenon, Catholic, evangelical, and other faiths in the Philippines have engaged in global outreach through their respective churches.[98]

Mission efforts to embrace and engage locally and internationally through the PMA, PM3, and Filipino diaspora mission can be considered to be "reverse mission" which refers to "sending of missionaries to Europe and North America by churches and Christians from the non-Western world, particularly Africa, Asia, and Latin America, which were at the receiving end of Catholic and Protestant missions as mission fields from the sixteenth to the late twentieth century."[99] This geographical inversion in the direction of missions has been described as "from the rest to the West"[100] and "from below."[101]

Through Filipino diaspora missions, Philippine Christians are able to actively participate in missions not by imperial or economic power but by powerlessness through the Overseas Filipino Workers (OFWs) program – a vulnerable community abroad that is becoming a "vital mission force in the world today."[102] From being a mission field, the Philippine Christians are now transitioning into a global mission force.

CONCLUSION

This chapter on the history of Philippine Christianity shows that it has been an interface between colonial forces, missionaries, and the local people. This

---

96. Casiño, 211–12.
97. For more details on 2019 and projected populations, see "World Population Prospects 2019," produced by the Department of Economic and Social Affairs of the United Nations.
98. Jayeel Cornelio, "The Philippines," in *Christianity in East and Southeast Asia*, eds. Kenneth R. Ross, Francis D. Alvararez, and Todd M. Johnson (Edinburgh, UK: Edinburgh University Press, 2020), 242–253.
99. Matthews Ojo, "Reverse Mission," in *Encyclopedia of Mission and Missionaries*, ed. Jonathan Bonk (London: Routledge, 2007), 380.
100. Rebecca Catto, "From the Rest to the West: Exploring Reversal in Christian Mission in Twenty-First Century Britain" (unpublished PhD thesis, University of Exeter, 2008).
101. Paul Freston, "Reverse Mission: A Discourse in Search of Reality," *Pentecost Studies* 9, no. 2 (2010): 155.
102. Maggay, "Early Protestant," 39.

religious interaction has brought about diverse expressions and streams of Philippine Christianity and Christian mission. For future decades of the country's history and Christian mission, the Philippines can serve as a "site and mediator of cultural traffic . . . a hybrid set and influx of cultures"[103] that can bridge the islands in the archipelago in contextualized and indigenous ways and that can engage and embrace the nations of the world with the transformative love and good news of Christ in community.

REFERENCES

Abinales, Patricio N., and Donna J. Amoroso. *State and Society in the Philippines*. Lanham, MD: Rowman and Littlefield, 2005.

Agoncillo, Teodoro A. *Introduction to Filipino History*. Quezon City, Metro Manila: Garotech, 1974.

Anderson, Gerald H. *A Short History of the Philippines*. New York: New American Library, 1969.

———. "Providence and Politics behind Protestant Missionary Beginnings in the Philippines." In *Studies in Philippine Church History*, edited by Gerald H. Anderson, 279–300. Ithaca: Cornell University Press, 1969.

Anderson, Gerald H., and Peter G. Gowing. "The Philippines: Bulwark of the Church in Asia." In *Church and Christ in Southeast Asia*, edited by Gerald H. Anderson, 135–62. New York: Friendship Press, 1968.

Apilado, Mariano C. *Revolutionary Spirituality: A Study of the Protestant Role in the American Colonial Rule of the Philippines, 1989–1928*. Quezon City, Metro Manila: New Day, 1999.

———. "The United Church of Christ in the Philippines." In *Chapters in Philippine Church History*, edited by Anne C. Kwantes, 335–58. Metro Manila: OMF Literature, 2001.

Aragon, Averell U. "The Philippine Council of Evangelical Churches." In *Chapters in Philippine Church History*, edited by Anne C. Kwantes, 369–89. Metro Manila: OMF Literature, 2001.

Balayo, Jun. "Historical Sketch of the DAWN 2000 Movement in the Philippines." In *Making Missions Practical: A Compendium of the Regional Consultation on Missions*, edited by Averell U. Aragon, 1–6. Davao, Mindanao: Mindanao Challenge, 1990.

Bautista, Lorenzo. "The Church in the Philippines." In *Church in Asia Today: Challenges and Opportunities*, edited by Saphir Athyal, 175–202. Singapore: Asia Lausanne Committee for World Evangelization, 1996.

---

103. Trevor Hogan, "In But Not of Asia: Reflections on Philippine Nationalism as Discourse, Project and Evaluation," *Thesis Eleven* 84 (2006): 115–32.

Bulatao, Jaime C. "A Socio-Psychological View of the Philippine Church." In *Phenomena and their Interpretation: Landmark Essays 1957–1989*, 12–21. Quezon City, Metro Manila: Ateneo de Manila University Press, 1992.

Casiño, Tereso C. "The Rise of the Filipino Missionary Movement: A Preliminary Historical Assessment." In *Mission History of Asian Churches*, edited by Timothy K. Park. Pasadena, CA: William Carey Library, 2011.

Catto, Rebecca. "From the Rest to the West: Exploring Reversal in Christian Mission in Twenty-First Century Britain." Unpublished PhD thesis, University of Exeter, 2008.

Constantino, Renato, and Leticia R. Constantino. *A History of the Philippines: From the Spanish Colonization to the Second World War*. New York: Monthly Review, 2008.

Cornelio, Jayeel. "Jesus Is Lord: The Indigenization of Megachurch Christianity in the Philippines." In *Pentecostal Megachurches in Asia: Negotiating Class, Consumption and the Nation*, 242–253. Singapore: ISEAS, 2019.

———. "The Philippines." In *Christianity in East and Southeast Asia*, edited by Kenneth R. Ross, Francis D. Alvararez, and Todd M. Johnson. Edinburgh, UK: Edinburgh University Press, 2020.

———. "Religious Worlding: Christianity and the New Production of Space in the Philippines." In *New Religiosities, Modern Capitalism and Moral Complexities in Southeast Asia*, edited by J. Koning and G. Njoto-Feillard, 169–97. New York: Palgrave Macmillan, 2017.

Cornelio, Jayeel, and Ia Maranon. "A 'Righteous Intervention': Megachurch Christianity and Duterte's War on Drugs in the Philippines." *International Journal of Asian Christianity* 2 (2019): 211–30.

Deats, Richard L. *Nationalism and Christianity in the Philippines*. Dallas, TX: Southern Methodist University Press, 1967.

De la Costa, Horacio. *Readings in Philippine History*. Makati, Metro Manila: Bookmark, 1992.

Del Castillo, Fides. "Gospel-Culture Relationship of Traditional Filipino Religion and Catholicism." *The International Journal of Religion and Spirituality in Society* 6, no. 2 (2015): 41–46.

Domingo, Eduardo. "Re-reading the Contexts of Historical Records." *Philippiniana Sacra* (2007): 417–32.

Elisha, Omni. "Moral Ambitions of Grace: The Paradox of Compassion and Accountability in Evangelical Faith-Based Activism." *Cultural Anthropology* 13, no. 1 (2008): 154–89.

Enriquez, Virgilio. *From Colonial to Liberation Psychology*. Manila: De La Salle University Press, 1992.

Fernandez, Pablo. *History of the Church of the Philippines*. Metro Manila: Navotas, 1979.
Francisco, Jose. "Tagalogs at the Spanish Contact." In *The Beginnings of Christianity in the Philippines*, edited by Christian Quirino, 176–200. Quezon City: Vertex, 1965.
Freston, Paul. "Reverse Mission: A Discourse in Search of Reality." *Pentecost Studies* 9, no. 2 (2010): 153–74.
Fuller, Jonathan. "Kingdoms in Conflict: The History of Islam in the Philippines." Unpublished MA thesis, Fuller School of World Mission, 1999.
Gardiner, David E. "Ecumenism among Philippine Protestants, 1945–1963." *Philippine Studies* 50, no. 1 (2002): 118–28.
Go, Raymundo. *The Philippine Council of Evangelical Churches*. Carlisle, UK: Langham Monographs, 2019.
Gorospe-Jamon, Grace. "The El Shaddai Prayer Movement: Political Socialization in a Religious Context." *Philippine Political Science Journal* 20 (1999): 83–126.
Gowing, Peter. *Islands Under the Cross*. Manila: National Council of Churches, 1967.
Guillermo, Merlyn L. and L. P. Verora. *Protestant Churches and Missions in the Philippines*, vol. 1: National Council of Churches in the Philippines. Quezon City, Metro Manila: World Vision Philippines, 1982.
Hofpe, Lewis. *Religions of the World*. New York: Macmillan, 1983.
Hogan, Trevor. "In But Not of Asia: Reflections on Philippine Nationalism as Discourse, Project and Evaluation." *Thesis Eleven* 84 (2006): 115–32.
Ileto, Reynaldo C. *Pasyon and Revolution: Popular Movements in the Philippines (1840–1910)*. Quezon City: Ateneo University Press, 1979.
Jocano, F. Lando. "Conversion and the Patterning of Christian Experience." In *Acculturation in the Philippines: Essays on Changing Societies*, edited by Peter G. Gowing and William Henry Scott. Quezon City, Metro Manila: New Day, 1971.
———. *Filipino Prehistory: Rediscovering Precolonial Heritage*. Quezon City, Metro Manila: Punlad Research House, 1998.
Kessler, Christl, and Jurgen Ruland. *Give Jesus a Hand! Charismatic Christians: Populist Religion and Politics in the Philippines*. Quezon City, Metro Manila: Ateneo de Manila University Press, 2008.
Keyes, Lawrence E. *The Last Age of Missions: A Study of Third World Mission Societies*. Pasadena: William Carey Library, 1983.
Kroeger, James H. "The Catholic Church in the Philippines: A Brief Historical and Contemporary Overview." *Philippinia Sacra* 37, no. 109 (2002): 79–100.
Kwantes, Anne C. *Presbyterian Missionaries in the Philippines*. Quezon City, Metro Manila: New Day, 1989.

Latourette, Kenneth. *A History of the Expansion of Christianity*, vol. 3. Milton Keynes, UK: Paternoster, 1971.

Lim, David S. "Consolidating Democracy: Filipino Evangelicals between People Power Events, 1986–2001." In *Evangelical Christianity and Democracy in Asia*, edited by D. Lumsdaine, 235–84. Oxford, UK: Oxford University Press, 2009.

———. "Indigenous Mission Movement of the Philippines," unpublished paper: https://www.academia.edu/12304593/Philippine_Misions_Mobilization_Movement.

Maggay, Melba P. "Crossing the Cultural Divide: Reflections from Down Under." *PATMOS* 11 (1995): 14–16, 21.

———. "Early Protestant Missionary Efforts in the Philippines: Some Intercultural Issues." In *Asian Church and God's Mission*, edited by Wonsuk and Julie C. Ma, 29–41. Mandaluyong City, Metro Manila: OMF Literature, 2003.

Majul, Cesar A. *Muslims in the Philippines*. Manila: St. Mary's, 1973.

———. "Succession in the Old Sulo Sultanate." In *The Muslim Filipinos*, edited by Peter G. Gowing and Robert D. McAmis, 61–73. Manila: Solidaridad, 1974.

Man, W. K. Che. *Muslim Separatism: The Moros of Southern Philippines and the Malays of South Thailand*. Manila: Ateneo de Manila University Press, 1990.

Marcouxm, Marcene. *Cursillo: Anatomy of a Movement; The Experience of Spiritual Renewal*. New York: Lambeth, 1982.

Mercado, Leonardo N. *El Shaddai: A Study*. Manila: Logos, 2001.

———. *Spirituality on Creation*. Manila: Logos, 1998.

Mesa, José M. de. "Nicolas Zamora: Religious Nationalist." In *Studies in Philippine Church History*, edited by Gerald H. Anderson, 325–36. Ithaca: Cornell University Press, 1969.

———. "Primal Religion and Popular Religiosity." *East Asian Pastoral Review* 37, no. 1 (2000): 73–82.

———. "Tuloy Po Kayo sa Loob: Some Guidelines in Understanding Filipino Culture." *East Asian Pastoral Review* 27 (1991): 141–64.

Mesa, José M. de, and Lode Wostyn. *Doing Theology: Basic Realities and Processes*. Quezon City: Claretian, 1990.

Miranda, Dionesio. *Buting Pinoy: Probe Essays on Value as Filipino*. Manila: Divine Word, 1992.

Montgomery, Jim. *DAWN 2000: 7 Million Churches to Go*. Pasadena, CA: William Carey Library, 1989.

Ojo, Matthews. "Reverse Mission." In *Encyclopedia of Mission and Missionaries*, edited by Jonathan Bonk, 380–82. London: Routledge, 2007.

Pardue, Frank M. C. "The Philippines' Last Frontier." Unpublished DMin diss., Columbia International University, 2000.

Pate, Larry. "The Dramatic Growth of Two-Thirds World Missions." In *Internationalizing Ministry Training: A Global Perspective*, edited by William Taylor. Grand Rapids: Baker Books, 1991.

Phelan, John L. *The Hispanization of the Philippines: Spanish Aims and Filipino Responses, 1565 – 1700*. Madison: University of Wisconsin Press, 1959.

———. "Prebaptismal Instruction and the Administration of Baptism in the Philippines during the Sixteenth Century." In *Studies in Philippine Church History*, edited by Gerald H. Anderson, 22–43. Ithaca, NY: Cornell University Press, 1969.

Rafael, Vicente L. *Contracting Colonialism: Translation and Christian Conversion in Tagalog Society Under Early Spanish Rule*. Durham, NC: Duke University Press, 1993.

Reyes, Ramon C. "Religious Experience in the Philippines: From Mythos through Logos to Kairos." *Philippine Studies* 33 (1985): 203–12.

Roldan, Andrea. "The Gospel in the Filipino Context: José M. de Mesa and Melba P. Maggay." *Mission Round Table* 13, no. 1 (2018): 24–30.

Sanders, Albert. "An Appraisal of the *Iglesia ni Cristo*." In *Studies in Philippine Church History*, edited by Gerald H. Anderson, 350–65. Ithaca: Cornell University Press, 1969.

Santos, Narry F. "Exploring the Major Dispersion Terms and Realities in the Bible." In *Diaspora Missiology: Theory, Methodology, and Practice*, edited by Enoch Wan, 21–38. USA: CreateSpace Independent Publishing Platform, 2012.

———. "Survey of the *Diaspora* Occurrences in the Bible and Their Contexts in Christian Missions." In *Scattered: The Filipino Global Presence*, edited by Luis Pantoja, Jr., Sadiri Joy Tira, and Enoch Wan, 53–66. Manila: LifeChange, 2004.

Schumacher, John N. *The Propaganda Movement 1880–1895: The Creation of Filipino Consciousness; The Making of the Revolution*. Quezon City, Metro Manila: Ateneo de Manila University Press, 1997.

Sitoy, Valentino. *A History of Christianity in the Philippines*. Quezon City: New Day, 1985.

Smith, Eric, Dean Wiebracht, and Thomas Wiseley. "Philippine Mission Boards and Societies." In *Evangelical Dictionary of World Missions*, edited by Scott Moreau, 752–753. Grand Rapids: Baker Academic, 2000.

Suarez, Oscar S. *Protestantism and Authoritarian Politics: The Politics of Repression and the Future of Ecumenical Witness in the Philippines*. Quezon City, Metro Manila: New Day, 1998.

Tizon, Al. *Transformation after Lausanne: Radical Evangelical Mission in Global-Local Perspective*. Eugene: Wipf and Stock, 2008.

Tuggy, Arthur. *The Philippine Church: Growth in a Changing Society*. Grand Rapids, MI: Eerdmans, 1971.

"World Population Prospects 2019." Department of Economic and Social Affairs of the United Nations (2019). https://population.un.org/wpp/Publications/Files/WPP2019_DataBooklet.pdf.

CHAPTER 7

HISTORY OF CHRISTIANITY IN SINGAPORE

Andrew Peh

INTRODUCTION

Located just north of the equator and at the southern tip of the Malay Peninsula, Singapore has been a trading post for visiting vessels for millennia. Chinese junks, Arab dhows, Portuguese carracks, Buginese schooners, and modern container ships have moved through its ports through the rise and fall of various kingdoms and powers in Southeast Asia. Accordingly, a third-century Chinese account described Singapore as "Pu-luo-chung" (蒲罗中), referring to "Pulau Ujong" which means the "island at the end of a peninsula" in the Malay language.[1] As settlements were established later in the thirteenth century, Singapore became known as "Temasek," meaning "Sea Town" in Malay, which attracted trade with India as well as Song China.[2]

In the fourteenth century the island was given a name that has become synonymous with the success of modern Singapore. Most Singaporeans are familiar with the legend of Sang Nila Utama, a prince from Palembang, the capital of Srivijaya in Sumatra, modern day Indonesia, who spotted what he thought was a lion, an animal he had never previously seen. Seizing the fortuitous moment, the prince established a new settlement on the island naming it Singapura meaning "lion city" from the Sanskrit words *simha* (lion) and *pura* (city). As a trading post, Singapura languished on the periphery with the subsequent arrival of the Portuguese and the Dutch colonial powers.

It is to the credit of Sir Stamford Raffles of the British East India Company who realized the significance of Singapore as a trading port. Raffles established

---

1. C. M. Turnbull, *A History of Modern Singapore, 1819–2005* (Singapore, NUS Press, 2009), 20.
2. Michael Barr, *Singapore: A Modern History* (London: I. B. Tauris, 2019), xxv-xxviii. Barr provides a timeline of premodern Singapore, highlighting the various flows of commerce and political development between Temasek and neighboring powers and European colonial empires.

a free port in Singapore in February 1819 and subsequently ensured British dominance of the Straits of Malacca, a vital link in the maritime trade route with China. In 2019, Singapore commemorated the bicentennial of the arrival of the British and the establishment of the trading port. Attendant to these mercantile endeavors, the arrival of the British East India Company simultaneously ushered in a turning point in Christianity in Singapore.

EARLY BEGINNINGS

Christian merchants on the Silk Road and the other trade routes of Central and South Asia possibly account for a Christian presence in Southeast Asia as early as the seventh century.[3] The paucity of historical data, however, lends credence to the view that this early advent "had no lasting impact in the early kingdoms and cultures of Southeast Asia."[4] It was with the later arrival of the European colonial powers of Portugal, Spain, France, Netherlands, and Britain that Christianity became increasingly transplanted in this corner of Asia.

The Portuguese were the first European colonial power to arrive in Southeast Asia in the sixteenth century, and Roman Catholic missionaries soon followed in establishing centers of faith in the various trading ports. The later arrival of Dutch and English trading companies eclipsed the initial impact of the Portuguese, particularly in the Indonesian Spice Islands and the Malay Peninsula, which includes both Malaysia and Singapore. A scramble for colonial trading supremacy between the Dutch East India Company and the British East India Company was the backdrop for the acquisition and development of the ports of Penang, Malacca, and Singapore, later referred to as the Straits Settlements. Eventually the British were able to wrest control of the Straits of Malacca, thereby establishing a very lucrative maritime trade route between London and the Far East, and Singapore became for the company the "emporium of the east."[5]

THE FIRST WAVE

The growth of Christianity in Singapore closely follows the founding of the island as a free port by Sir Stamford Raffles of the British East India Company. Penang and Malacca in Malaysia already had a significant Christian presence,

---

3. Ian Gillman and Hans-Joachim Klimkeit, *Christians in Asia Before 1500* (London: Routledge, 1999), 307–9.
4. Robbie G. H. Goh, *Christianity in Southeast Asia* (Singapore: ISEAS, 2005), 2.
5. Please refer to "The Bicentennial Experience," SG Bicentennial (2020), https://www.sg/sgbicentennial/the-bicentennial-experience/.

and from these ports the Roman Catholic and Protestant missionaries began to arrive in Singapore. With the establishment of the ports along the Straits of Malacca, the London Missionary Society (LMS) started pioneering missionary work first in Malacca and later in Singapore.[6] Bobby Sng refers to this as the first of three waves of missionary arrivals to Singapore.[7] It must be noted that in the early stages, most of these missionaries were bound for China, and their stay in Singapore served more as a stopover. Among them was Dr. William Milne who was sent by the LMS to China in 1813. Due to China's closed-door policy for Christian missionary work, setting up the Ultra-Ganges Mission by Milne in Malacca in 1815 was an expedient decision. Not only was the Ultra-Ganges Mission a staging ground to gather experience and establish contacts with the highly migrant Asian trading societies, but it also served as a prelude for the new mission field in China that these missionaries hoped to see open. It was in these tangential "new" places in Southeast Asia that Protestantism began to take root.

Sent by the LMS, missionaries such as William Milne and Robert Morrison initiated Christian ministry in Singapore as early as the 1820s. By coming overland from Malacca, these LMS missionaries were able to circumvent the British East India Company's strictly enforced rule of not mixing commerce with Christianity. Furthermore, the missionaries' presence was welcomed as they were able to minister to the spiritual needs of a steadily growing number of British merchants, and later an increasing number of European merchants, as they awaited China's opening to the West. Though the mission operated a printing press for the publication and distribution of tracts, song books, and portions of Scripture, the emphasis was evidently on chaplaincy rather than conversion. Goh rightly notes that "A large part of the mission's work in the first few decades after Singapore's founding was among the British community."[8]

Various communities of traders and immigrants were attracted to this new trading post, and in 1820, the first Armenians arrived. Part of the process of rooting this small but entrepreneurial community was their request to build their own church instead of being dependent on visiting clergy from Penang. They were given a land grant by the British governor, and the small community

---

6. Bobby Sng, *In His Good Time 1819–2002* (Singapore: Bible Society of Singapore, 2003), 22.
7. Bobby Sng, "On the Road to Somewhere: The Singapore Church in Historical Perspective," *Impact Magazine* (August–September 1982): 23.
8. Goh, *Christianity*, 36.

of about ten families raised the costs for building the church. In 1836, the Armenian Apostolic Church of St. Gregory the Illuminator was consecrated, and it stands today as the first and oldest church building in Singapore.[9] Similarly, the British plan to develop Singapore also attracted Roman Catholic settlers from neighboring ports and towns, notably Malacca, which had had a Roman Catholic presence under the Portuguese since the sixteenth century. The Roman Catholics were to have a more muted but sustained presence in Singapore under British colonial rule, and they were among the first to establish schools and medical missions for the immigrant population.

Within the first few decades of British rule, various missions were established in Singapore including the Roman Catholics in 1821, the American Board of Commissioners for Foreign Missions (ABCFM) in 1834, the Church Missionary Society (CMS) in 1837, and the Plymouth Brethren in 1857. While there were numerous Protestant missions, most were eagerly waiting for China to be opened for Christian missions. Singapore was in many ways merely a temporary holding area for missionaries to prepare for the mission field of China. Until access to China's vast interior was possible, the advance guard found places outside the Middle Kingdom, that is China, in order to make preparations for the work of evangelizing the Chinese. This mindset is evident in numerous reports such as the following from the Western Foreign Missionary Society:

> This great people, not more remarkable for the extent of their territory, and the number of their population than for their ignorance of the true God, have of late engaged the thoughts of professing Christians in all parts of our country.... In every island in the Eastern Archipelago, Chinese emigrants are to be found.... And only men of right spirit are wanted to carry to these accessible, perishing thousands the bread of life.[10]

One of the most important turning points for these missions was China's defeat in the Opium Wars, which forced China to sign the "unequal treaties,"

---

9. For more information, see "History," Armenian Church Singapore (2021).
10. Fifth Annual Report of Western Foreign Missionary Society (May 1837), 17–18. As quoted by Joseph Harry Haines, *A History of Protestant Missions in Malaya During the Nineteenth Century, 1815–1881* (Princeton, NJ: Princeton Theological Seminary, 1962), 197.

thereby opening China to foreign countries.[11] Hence from the 1842 signing of the Treaty of Nanking and its ratification in 1843 and the eventual opening of China, many missionary societies shifted gears. Missionaries were moved to the five "treaty" ports in China – Canton (Guangzhou), Amoy (Xiamen), Fuzhou, Ningpo, and Shanghai. Particularly by 1843, the Singapore "experiment" for the ABCFM, and for that matter most of the other missionary organizations, had come to a close, and all the remaining work was handed over to the LMS. Among the remaining LMS missionaries were John Stronach and Benjamin Keasberry. Keasberry had started a ministry among the Malays in Singapore.[12] But in 1846, both Stronach and Keasberry were ordered to close the work and move to Hong Kong. Keasberry, however, chose to remain, and he wrote to the LMS about his unwillingness to abandon the work he had established:

> I cannot reconcile myself to the thought of this station being given up, in view of the present prospect of usefulness which it holds among the Malays both in the school and in the preaching to the adults. My earnest request is that I be allowed to remain here and labour for the poor Malays. Can it be considered too much to have one missionary to break to them the bread of life?[13]

When his request was not granted, Keasberry resigned from the LMS and stayed on in Singapore. He started a school for Malay boys in 1848, founded a church ministering to Chinese laborers, and at the same time worked with the increasing influx of Scottish expatriates. Keasberry was to leave a lasting legacy in the work of establishing a Straits-Chinese church in Singapore. As Sng puts it, "The Straits Chinese Church is an ever-living memorial of the selfless devotion of Benjamin Keasberry."[14]

The departure of the LMS in 1846 exemplified the spirit of the time, for it demonstrated that China was the focus of not only the British East India Company but also of most, if not all, of the missionary-sending organizations or societies. It is not surprising then that the next forty years following the departure of the LMS missionaries are described as the "wilderness years" of

---

11. These were treaties that China was forced into signing with various colonial powers, including Great Britain, Portugal and France, as a result of China's defeat in the wars that were catalysed by the sale of opium which was prohibited in China. Refer to https://www.britannica.com/event/Unequal-Treaty.
12. See Gracie Lee, "Benjamin Keasberry," Singapore Infopedia (n.d.).
13. Benjamin Keasberry quoted in Haines, *History*, 233.
14. Sng, *In His Good Time*, 25.

Protestant missionary history in Malaya, which included Singapore.[15] These wilderness years perhaps mark the end of the first wave of missionary arrivals to Singapore; however, this period of dormancy was but a time of preparation for the second wave.

THE SECOND WAVE

A renewed impetus for missions in this fast-growing British colonial trading post developed at the end of the nineteenth century with the arrival in 1885 of the American Methodists from the South India Conference of the Methodist Episcopal Church, USA, which was led by Rev. Dr. James Mills Thoburn. After an intense ten days of ministry in Singapore, which resulted in the formation of the Methodist Church on Sunday, 22 February 1885, Thoburn returned to Calcutta. He left the work in Singapore to William Oldham, another American missionary who had come from India with him, giving him the charge, "Methodism appoints you an herald to a nation, and there must be continual overflow to your activities which will never end until you overtake all Malaysia."[16] Oldham took hold of Thoburn's charge to the extent that the advent and spread of Methodism in Singapore and Malaya was closely intertwined with church planting along ethno-linguistics lines, evangelism, education, publication, addressing social concerns, and outreach. Thus the model of Methodist mission work in Singapore has been called "a pluriform mission."[17] Oldham understood mission as more than just building churches, and that his mission was more than just evangelizing the migrant population, be they workers from India or China or the colonial officers of the British East India Company. Mission was all that together and more. The story of the arrival of the Methodists in Singapore reflects a mission that is "multidimensional in order to be credible and faithful to its origins and character."[18]

Within the short span of five years, the Methodist work grew to include the founding of three churches with services in three different languages: the Wesley Methodist Church (1885), the Tamil Methodist Church (1887), and

---

15. Haines, *History*, 245.
16. James Mills Thoburn quoted by Theodore Doraisamy, *The March of Methodism in Singapore and Malaysia 1885–1980* (Singapore: Methodist Book Room, 1982), 8.
17. The term "pluriform mission" is the title of chapter seven in the book on Oldham by Bishop Theodore Doraisamy, *Oldham Called of God* (Singapore: Methodist Book Room, 1979), 50–63. Among the various chroniclers of the history of Methodism, it seems likely that the term was first applied to Oldham's mission work and strategy by Doraisamy.
18. David J. Bosch, *Transforming Mission: Paradigm Shifts in Theology of Mission* (Maryknoll, NY: Orbis, 1994), 512.

the Chinese Church at Telok Ayer (1889). The Methodists also established three schools – the Anglo-Chinese School (1886), Tamil Girls' School (1887), and Telok Ayer Chinese Girls' School (1889) – as well as a printing press in 1890. What began as a mission in 1885 grew to be a mission conference in 1893 and later achieved autonomy as an independent annual conference in 1902. What began as a place where missionaries were received became increasingly the place from which missionaries were sent. The Methodist work grew northward up the Malaysia Peninsula to Penang in 1891 and spread toward Ipoh, Kuala Lumpur, and Malacca. Before the turn of the century the work grew eastward toward the Philippines and in 1901 toward Sarawak, a Malaysian state on Borneo. Beginning in 1905, the work grew westward to Sumatra (Indonesia) and southward when the Methodists began mission work in Java, Indonesia. Then in 1908 the work grew to southern Sumatra. In less than twenty years, the Methodist mission in Singapore had taken root and was growing toward becoming a center from which the good news was carried to the rest of Southeast Asia.

American Methodism was not the only missionary presence in Singapore at the end of the nineteenth century, but their arrival and growth sparked a renewed vigor. At the turn of the twentieth century, various other denominational churches and mission agencies began ministries in Singapore including "the Seventh-Day Adventists in 1908, the Assemblies of God in 1928, the Salvation Army in 1935, and in the 1950s the Church of Christ, Southern Baptists, Lutherans, Bible Presbyterians, Finnish Pentecostal Mission, and the Evangelical Free Church."[19] The arrival of these different agencies and denominations attest to the growing importance of Singapore as a free port. While each might have had varied emphases in their missionary focus, this was a period when educational mission became an increasingly important cornerstone.

Education had always been close to the heart of Sir Stamford Raffles. The port's founder generously supported the early LMS missionaries in setting up schools and colleges. In a letter dated 12 June 1819, he wrote that he had "just granted permission to the Extra Ganges Mission (of the London Missionary Society) to establish a college at Singapore, and for the study of the Chinese language and for the extension of Christianity."[20] It should be noted that the

---

19. Goh, *Christianity*, 37–38.
20. Stamford Raffles, *Memoirs of the Life and Public Services of Sir Thomas Stamford Raffles*, vol. 2 (London: John Murray, 1830), 37.

London Missionary Society pioneered the introduction of Western-style education in Singapore. As early as 1828, the society reported the establishment of Cantonese schools on Kampong Glam and Pekin Streets and a Hokkien school as well as an English school on Pekin Street. In 1842, the LMS missionary Maria Dyer, en route to China, saw the plight of the girls and established what is today the oldest girls' school in Singapore, St Margaret's Girls' School.[21] The LMS also founded the first Anglican school for boys in 1862, St. Andrew's School. The ABCFM reported setting up printing presses, medical clinics, and schools, as did the Roman Catholic missions: St Joseph's Institution was founded in 1852 and the girls' school Convent of the Holy Infant Jesus in 1842. These mission schools served the goals of the colonial administration to provide education without requiring the British to expend a significant portion of the colonial budget. The arrival of the Methodists and the establishment of the Methodist schools – Anglo-Chinese School (1886); Tamil Girls' School, now Methodist Girls' School in 1887; and Telok Ayer Chinese Girls' School, now Fairfield Methodist School in 1888 – in many ways challenged the colonial administration's educational budgeting and policies and provided an important educational alternative that included social and scriptural holiness.[22] In view of the multireligious and multiracial composition of the largely immigrant population in Singapore, there was inevitably a tacit unease with the mission schools which at various times were charged with using education as a means of evangelism. This unease was especially pronounced among the Chinese who harbored "fears of loss of cultural identity"[23] and resulted in a few public exchanges that are notably referred to as the "Isaiah Incident."[24] To their credit, the principal and the Methodist missionaries were able to clarify that there was never any deceit in offering religious instruction, nor was there ever any

---

21. See the video commemorating the founding of the school: "St Margaret's Story: Blessed to be a Blessing." St Margaret's Ex-Students Association (SMESA 1842). YouTube (20 November 2012).
22. A more detailed discussion of the educational mission of the Methodists may be found in chapter 4 of Andrew Peh, *Of Merchants and Missions: A Historical Study of the Impact of British Colonialism on American Methodism in Singapore from 1885 to 1910* (Eugene, OR: Pickwick, 2019), 103–69.
23. Robbie G. H. Goh, "The Mission School in Singapore: Colonialism, Moral Training, Pedagogy, and the Creation of Modernity," in *Asian Migrants and Education: The Tensions of Education in Immigrant Societies among Migrant Groups* (Dordrecht, Netherlands: Kluwer Academic, 2003), 31.
24. For an account of the Isaiah Incident, see Low Aik Lim, "Anglo-Chinese School, 1886–1941: Case Study of a Mission School," Academic Exercise, Department of History (Singapore: National University of Singapore, 1991/1992), 28–30.

compulsion for conversion. The mission's educational work perhaps received its most profound vindication when its most vocal critic, Dr. Lim Boon Keng, who was the "Isaiah" who had earlier written to the press, sent both his son and his grandson to be educated at Anglo-Chinese School where they both became distinguished scholars.[25] To date, this symbiotic relationship between the schools and missions forged in the vision of the missionaries in Singapore remains a monument of Christian legacy in the mission history of Singapore.

THE THIRD WAVE

Colonial policies notwithstanding, world and regional events were to exert certain influences on Christianity in Singapore. The Boxer Rebellion in various parts of China precipitated a mass exodus of missionaries and Chinese Christians from China to Singapore including Chinese pastors, Bible women, and merchants, all of whom helped "to further augment the Chinese churches in southeast Asia."[26] Churches across the denominations including Anglicans, Methodists, and Presbyterians with services in various dialects recorded an increase in their previously transient congregations, and these new migrant members facilitated the rapid growth of churches in Singapore.

In the mid-1930s in the wake of the Great Depression, the rise of a Chinese evangelist was significant for the Chinese churches in Singapore and various parts of Southeast Asia. Dr. John Sung's active ministry was only from 1928 to 1939, but his impact on the church in China and Southeast Asia can still be felt today. He has been variously referred to as the "Wesley of China," the "Billy Sunday of China," the "apostle of China," the "greatest evangelist China has ever known," and probably the greatest preacher of this century.[27] As an evangelist, John Sung was unequivocal against personal sins such as opium smoking, adultery, concubinage, gambling, cheating, and other behaviors which were often tolerated among the Chinese. Undaunted, John Sung rebuked pastors, leaders, and missionaries alike for their indolence and apathy. Sung was also explicit in emphasizing personal devotion and discipline in both prayer and evangelism. And for the brief period of his ministry in Singapore, John Sung left an inordinate legacy to the Chinese churches, inspiring many

---

25. Peh, *Of Merchants and Missions*, 146–47.
26. Sng, *In His Good Time*, 177.
27. Lim Ka-Tong, *The Life and Ministry of John Sung* (Singapore: Armour, 2011), 2.

to godly service, about which Sng rightly notes, "The spiritual legacy that he left behind in Singapore and elsewhere has never been surpassed since."[28]

THROUGH THE DARKEST DAYS

The spark that lit the fires of revival was soon eclipsed by the darkness of the Japanese Occupation of Singapore when the British surrendered to the Japanese forces on 15 February 1942. Singapore was ironically renamed *Syonan-To* meaning the "light of the southern island." However the unimaginable misery, the unthinkable brutality, and the unspeakable agony under the three years and seven months of Japanese Occupation did not break the spirit of the people, not least of all the Christians. For it was out of this crucible of suffering, within the walls of Changi Prison where church leaders of the different denominations were interned, that an idea was sparked that would give birth to an institution of theological learning that had as its ideal *Lux Mundi*, Light of the World.

Up to this time, Christian missions and ministry had been undertaken by various missionary societies backed by different denominations, largely without much cooperation or collaboration and generally without local leadership. The Pacific portion of World War II jolted the leaders of the denominational churches into the harsh realization that they had not only an unhealthy overdependence on Western leadership, they also had a shortage of indigenous leaders and pastors and little interdenominational cooperation.[29] Following the end of the war in January 1948 was the inauguration of the Malayan Christian Council[30] which was constituted on 24 July 1974 as the National Council of Churches of Singapore after Singapore's independence in 1965. More significantly, within the Changi Prison walls the heads of the Anglican, Methodist, and Presbyterian churches were interned, and they determined to establish a union college for the training and equipping of future pastors and leaders for the church. And it came to pass that Trinity Theological College, conceptualized in the darkness of prison, was officially instituted on 4 October 1948 as the first union theological college in Singapore.

Another significant event to affect Christianity in Singapore was the rise of communism in China under Chairman Mao Zedong, which led to the departure of many Western missionaries in the early 1950s. By July 1953,

---

28. Sng, *In His Good Time*, 180.
29. The National Council of Churches, *Many Faces, One Faith* (Singapore: Armour, 2004), 93.
30. The founding members of the Malayan Christian Council included the Anglican Diocese, the Methodist Church, the Presbyterian Church, the Bible Society, the Young Men's Christian Association, and the Young Women's Christian Association.

all of the missionary organizations had exited China. China Inland Mission, founded by Hudson Taylor in 1865, was then the largest missionary organization in China. They withdrew from China, established their new headquarters in Singapore, renamed the organization the Overseas Missionary Fellowship, and redirected missionary focus to Southeast Asia. The "closing" of China also resulted in the entrance of various other denominational churches to Southeast Asia, including Singapore. These included the Chinese Nationals' Evangelism Commission, the Lutheran Church of America as well as the Baptist.

The 1950s were a time of stability in the Christian presence in Singapore. However the significant growth in the numbers of conservative immigrant Christians resulted in stratifications in the churches, such as the formation of more conservative denominations, including the Bible Presbyterian Church in January 1955, as well as the establishment of training colleges that emphasized "solid biblical teaching and evangelistic efforts."[31] In response to liberalism, the Bible Presbyterian Church opened the Far Eastern Bible College in September 1962. Similarly in response to the then more Western-dominated Trinity Theological College, the Chinese leadership of the more conservative churches founded the Singapore Theological Seminary in 1952, which was later renamed Singapore Bible College.[32] These developments underscore the growth pangs of the indigenous leadership that Sng understands as representative of "a part of the subtle theological tension that existed between the theologically conservative Chinese churches and a liberal western leadership."[33]

THE "BIRTH" OF SINGAPORE

Singapore became an independent nation on 9 August 1965. With the separation from the Federation of Malaya and the subsequent announcement of the British withdrawal, Singapore's survival was in the balance because it was really a port to serve the rich hinterland of the Malay Peninsula. But under the capable leadership of Prime Minister Lee Kuan Yew and his pioneer team, Singapore's economic growth has been regarded as unparalleled. Amid these national changes, developments were also afoot due to a significant influx of parachurch organizations. The Inter-School Christian Fellowship, Asia Evangelistic Fellowship (AEF), Graduates' Christian Fellowship, Gideons Singapore, Singapore Every Home Crusade, Navigators, Singapore Campus

---

31. Sng, *In His Good Time*, 248.
32. Sng, 249.
33. Sng, 249.

Crusade for Christ, Scripture Union, Youth with a Mission (YWAM), and Eagles Evangelism are just some of the groups that started during this decade.[34] The AEF, founded by G. D. James in 1960, was the first Asian mission that was established at a time when all the mission organizations were exclusively for Western Christians, and the Asian Christians had no organized means of doing cross-cultural missions. The proliferation of these parachurch organizations was in part due to the growth of a new generation of youth and corresponded with an increased emphasis on evangelism in response to the general spiritual tepidity in the mainline denominational churches.

Yet God was also doing a work of reviving his church through a fresh outpouring of his Spirit, resulting in a series of revivals. The beginning may be traced to the Anglo-Chinese School Clock Tower Revival in 1972 when students had gathered to pray for the revival of the church along with revival in their own personal lives. Those who experienced this work of the Spirit described it as "a move of God" and "an outpouring of the Holy Spirit."[35] When detailing the Clock Tower Revival, Michael Poon makes the point that this was indeed the definitive event that has often been overlooked in various accounts of the charismatic revivals in the history of Singapore.[36] Spiritual renewal experiences such as speaking in tongues were also recorded at different churches and most notably in the personal experience of Chiu Ban It, the Bishop of the Anglican Diocese of Singapore. The charismatic movement received institutional backing from the Anglicans, from which sprang forth subsequent charismatic renewal movements and the growth of the Pentecostal-charismatic movement in Singapore.

These various revivals and renewals resulted in a concerted move to bring evangelical churches from different denominations and parachurch organizations together with an emphasis on evangelism that had never before been witnessed in the history of Singapore.[37] They all worked alongside each other for a combined national event – the Billy Graham Crusade. For five nights starting on 6 December 1978, Billy Graham shared the message of salvation

---

34. Sng, 282–88. See also Violet James, "The Church and the Missionary Movement in Singapore," in *Mission History of Asian Churches*, ed. T. K. H. Park (Pasadena, CA: William Carey Library, 2010), 182–85.
35. Michael Poon and Malcolm Tan, eds. *The Clock Tower Story: The Beginnings of the Charismatic Renewals in Singapore*, CSCA Occasional Paper No. 8 rev. ed. (Singapore: CSCA, 2012), 4.
36. Poon and Tan, *Clock Tower Story*, 9–13.
37. It should be noted that numerous other large-scale evangelistic events were held prior to the Billy Graham Crusade of 1978. Bobby Sng records these gospel rallies and evangelistic meetings. Sng, *In His Good Time*, 295–96.

with 337,000 at the National Stadium in Singapore.[38] Not unlike the John Sung revivals of about forty years earlier, this crusade was a watershed moment for the church in Singapore where the renewed passion for God would bring about the start of a church growth era. The Pentecostal-charismatic renewal and the evangelistic fervor fueled the growth of the Calvary Charismatic Centre in 1977 and the Trinity Christian Centre in 1978.

SINGAPORE IN THE TWENTY-FIRST CENTURY

The rapid economic growth of Singapore in the 1980s and 1990s earned it the distinction of being one of the "Asian Tigers."[39] In the relatively short span of time in which Singapore developed from "third world to first,"[40] Christianity gradually grew. The percentage of the population who identified themselves as Christians, including Roman Catholics, increased from 10.1 percent in 1980 to 14.6 percent in 2000,[41] and then grew to 18.8 percent in 2015.[42] Robbie Goh also comments that Christianity "is the religion with the strongest representation among the well-educated" and "has a strong association with middle-class status."[43] This upward economic mobility seems to have a direct correspondence with the phenomenon of megachurches in the city state, notably New Creation Church and City Harvest Church. Daniel Ahn notes that the "mega-churches express Christianity in the language of market practice and logic, converging with and appealing to the economic aspirations and consumer habits of many young, upwardly mobile Singaporeans."[44] In her assessment of the megachurch movement, Jeaney Yip and Susan Ainsworth note,

---

38. The personnel involved in the event included 5,500 counselors, 4,500 choir members, 8,000 ushers, and 1,800 follow-up leaders. Graham's message was simultaneously translated into Mandarin, Hokkien, Cantonese, Malay, and Tamil. For a fortieth anniversary interview with the men who planned this crusade, see Gabriel Ong, "Remembering the 1978 Billy Graham Crusade, Part 1: The men who planned the Crusade," Thir.st (5 December 2018).
39. See Bruno Marshall Shirley, "The Asian Tigers from Independence to Industrialisation," E-International Relations (16 October 2014), https://www.e-ir.info/2014/10/16/the-asian-tigers-from-independence-to-industrialisation/.
40. From the title of Lee Kuan Yew, *From Third World to First: The Singapore Story - 1965–2000* (New York: Harper, 2000).
41. "Religion," Singapore Statistics. Census 2000 (2021), 33.
42. "Marriage and Fertility," Singapore Statistics, Infographics on General Household Survey 2015, 4.
43. Goh, *Christianity*, 41–42.
44. Daniel S. H. Ahn, "Changing Profiles: The Historical Development of Christianity in Singapore," in *Religious Transformation in Modern Asia*, ed. David Kim (Leiden: Brill, 2015), 267.

Market-friendly ideologies associated with individualism and self-empowerment are often blended with **selective** Christian theologies to emphasize **positive living and blessing** while deflecting overtly negative Christian doctrines such as suffering, judgment, sacrifice, hell or death from sin . . . church services are scripted and "produced" with deliberate use of contemporary music, sound and lighting.[45]

Regionally as a trade, transportation and tourism hub, Singapore has become a key sending base for Christian missions to various parts of the Asia Pacific region and beyond. In Singapore are the local and regional bases of international mission organizations including Asia Evangelistic Fellowship (AEF), Operation Mobilization (OM), Overseas Mission Fellowship (OMF), Singapore Centre for Global Missions (SCGM), SIM International, World Evangelization for Christ, and Wycliffe Bible Translators. This concentration of missions agencies that have made Singapore their headquarters, as well as the relative ease of travel which encourages churches to embark on short-term mission trips, have contributed to the significant growth of missions awareness and cross-cultural ministry. Research conducted in 2010 by the Center for the Study of Global Christianity at Gordon-Conwell Theological Seminary found support for Singapore's significance in missions. The statistics placed Singapore among the highest missionary sending nations when measured by the number of missionaries per million church members.[46] Not surprisingly, this statistic has led some to refer to Singapore as the "Antioch of the East" (an appellation for which this writer has reservations). Yet the fact remains that Singapore continues to have a major part to play in missions in the Asia Pacific region, especially in the wake of more current developments such as trade wars and the COVID-19 pandemic.

CONCLUSION

This brief account of Christianity in Singapore illustrates that Singapore's success seems inexorably tied to commercial considerations. It is called the

---

45. Jeaney Yip and Susan Ainsworth, "We aim to provide excellent service to everyone who comes to church! Marketing mega-churches in Singapore," *Social Compass* 60, no. 4 (2013): 503–16, emphasis added. See also Jeaney Yip, *Branding Religion: The Inter-discursive Construction of a Mega-church's Corporate Identity Through Artefacts, Practice and Performance* (PhD diss., University of Sydney, 2010).
46. Cited in Todd Johnson and Kenneth Ross, *Atlas of Global Christianity* (Edinburgh, UK: Edinburgh University Press, 2009), 268–71.

emporium of the East and one of the Asian Tigers and has one of the world's busiest and best seaports and airports, the best-ranked airline, and other superlative distinctions. In a society that constantly emphasizes upward economic mobility – to update, upgrade, upsize, and upscale – the churches in Singapore must be cautious never to allow this preoccupation with affluence to distract their vision and to eclipse their mission. In telling the story of Christianity in Singapore, Brett McCracken aptly alludes to the movie *Crazy Rich Asians* (2018), which has for its opening scene a group of wealthy Singaporean *tai tais* (rich housewives) having a Bible study in a palatial home. He notes, "The dichotomous scene plays for laughs, but it captures one of the unique contours of Christianity in Singapore – a nation where affluence and piety often coexist, for good and for ill."[47] The Scriptures sound many reminders of the dangers of the love of money and that the pursuits of possession, power, prestige, preeminence, and privilege are all but a chasing after the wind. The churches in Singapore must take heed, for history will show if the substance of our richness is ultimately defined by the kingdoms of this world or the kingdom of God.

REFERENCES

Ahn, Daniel S. H. "Changing Profiles: The Historical Development of Christianity in Singapore." In *Religious Transformation in Modern Asia*, edited by David Kim, 250–273. Leiden: Brill, 2015.

Alvarez, Francis D., SJ. "Christianity in East and Southeast Asia." In *Christianity in East and Southeast Asia*, edited by Kenneth R. Ross, Francis Alvarez, and Todd M. Johnson, 15–36. Edinburgh, UK: Edinburgh University Press, 2020.

Barr, Michael. *Singapore: A Modern History*. London: I. B. Tauris, 2019.

Bosch, David J. *Transforming Mission: Paradigm Shifts in Theology of Mission*. Maryknoll: Orbis, 1994.

Doraisamy, Theodore R. *The March of Methodism in Singapore and Malaysia 1885–1980*. Singapore: Methodist Book Room, 1982.

———. *Oldham Called of God*, Singapore: Methodist Book Room, 1979.

Gillman, Ian, and Hans-Joachim Klimkeit. *Christians in Asia Before 1500*. London: Routledge, 1999.

Goh, Robbie. *Christianity in Southeast Asia*. Singapore: ISEAS, 2005.

———. "The Mission School in Singapore: Colonialism, Moral Training, Pedagogy, and the Creation of Modernity." In *Asian Migrants and Education:*

---

47. Brett McCracken, "How the Gospel Takes Root in 'Crazy Rich' Singapore," The Gospel Coalition (24 September 2018). For this article, McCracken interviewed three pastors from independent churches in Singapore. His choice is interesting in that he omits any pastors of mainline denominational churches or historians.

The Tensions of Education in Immigrant Societies among Migrant Groups, 27–37. Dordrecht, Netherlands: Kluwer Academic, 2003.

Haines, Joseph Harry. *A History of Protestant Missions in Malaya During the Nineteenth Century, 1815–1881*. Princeton: Princeton Theological Seminary, 1962.

"History." Armenian Church Singapore (2021). https://www.armeniansinasia.org/about-the-church.

Hull, Sophia. *Memoirs of the Life and Public Services of Sir Thomas Stamford Raffles*, reprint. Cambridge, UK: Cambridge University Press, 2014.

James, Violet. "The Church and the Missionary Movement in Singapore." In *Mission History of Asian Churches*, edited by T. K. H. Park, 175–194. Pasadena: William Carey Library, 2010.

———. "Singapore." In *Christianity in East and Southeast Asia*, edited by Kenneth R. Ross, Francis Alvarez, and Todd M. Johnson, 225–37. Edinburgh, UK: Edinburgh University Press, 2020.

Johnson, Todd, and Kenneth Ross. *Atlas of Global Christianity*. Edinburgh, UK: Edinburgh University Press, 2009.

Lee, Gracie. "Benjamin Keasberry." Singapore Infopedia (n.d.). https://eresources.nlb.gov.sg/infopedia/articles/SIP_781_2005-01-03.html.

Lee Kuan Yew. *From Third World to First: The Singapore Story – 1965–2000*. New York: Harper, 2000.

Lim Ka-Tong. *The Life and Ministry of John Sung*. Singapore: Armour, 2011.

Low Aik Lim. *Anglo-Chinese School, 1886–1941: Case Study of a Mission School*. Academic Exercise, Department of History. Singapore: National University of Singapore, 1991/1992.

"Marriage and Fertility." Singapore Statistics. Infographics on General Household Survey 2015. https://www.singstat.gov.sg/-/media/files/visualising_data/infographics/ghs/highlights-of-ghs2015.pdf.

McCracken, Brett. "How the Gospel Takes Root in 'Crazy Rich' Singapore." The Gospel Coalition (24 September 2018). https://www.thegospelcoalition.org/article/gospel-takes-root-crazy-rich-singapore/.

The National Council of Churches of Singapore. *Many Faces, One Faith*. Singapore: Armour, 2004.

Ong, Gabriel. "Remembering the 1978 Billy Graham Crusade, Part 1: The men who planned the Crusade." Thir.st (5 December 2018). https://thirst.sg/remembering-the-1978-billy-graham-crusade-part-1-the-men-who-planned-the-crusade/.

Peh, Andrew. *Of Merchants and Missions; A Historical Study of the Impact of British Colonialism on American Methodism in Singapore from 1885 to 1910*. Eugene, OR: Pickwick, 2019.

Poon, Michael, and Malcolm Tan, eds. *The Clock Tower Story: The Beginnings of the Charismatic Renewals in Singapore*. CSCA Occasional Paper No. 8 rev. ed. Singapore: CSCA, 2012.

Raffles, Stamford. *Memoirs of the Life and Public Services of Sir Thomas Stamford Raffles*, vol. 2. London: John Murray, 1830.

"Religion." Singapore Statistics. Census 2000 (2021). https://www.singstat.gov.sg/-/media/files/publications/cop2000/census_2000_advance_data_release/chap5.pdf.

Sng, Bobby. *In His Good Time 1819–2002*. Singapore: Bible Society of Singapore, 2003.

———. "On the Road to Somewhere: The Singapore Church in Historical Perspective." *Impact Magazine* (August–September 1982): 23–27.

"St Margaret's Story: Blessed to be a Blessing." St Margaret's Ex-Students Association (SMESA 1842). YouTube (20 November 2012). https://youtu.be/GjZ1x1SSObw.

Turnbull, C. M. *A History of Modern Singapore, 1819–2005*. Singapore: NUS Press, 2009.

Yip, Jeaney. "Branding Religion: The Inter-discursive Construction of a Megachurch's Corporate Identity Through Artefacts, Practice and Performance." PhD diss., University of Sydney, 2010.

Yip, Jeaney, and Susan Ainsworth. "'We aim to provide excellent service to everyone who comes to church!': Marketing mega-churches in Singapore." *Social Compass* 60, no. 4 (2013): 503–16.

CHAPTER 8

HISTORY OF CHRISTIANITY IN THAILAND

Karl Dahlfred

The entry of Christianity into Thailand (Siam until 1939) began with the arrival of Roman Catholic priests in 1511.¹ These priests accompanied the Portuguese diplomatic mission which established an embassy in the city of Ayutthaya, the capital of then Siam.² Two Dominican priests arrived in 1555 but were subsequently martyred within two decades. Jesuits came in 1607 and the Paris Foreign Missionary Society in 1662.³ In the 1680s, a Greek Roman Catholic adventurer named Constantine Phaulkon came to prominence in the court of King Narai. However, Phaulkon was arrested and executed in 1688 by Siamese political enemies who feared both the conversion of the ailing monarch to Catholicism and that French colonial ambitions would be enabled through Phaulkon's political power.⁴ Siamese suspicions of Catholics persisted through the end of the eighteenth century, and the small Catholic community in Siam experienced insignificant growth during this period. In the minds of the Siamese ruling powers, the Christian religion was associated with Western culture and politics, and therefore suspect. The kings of Thailand from the late eighteenth century through the middle of the nineteenth century were generally wary of Westerners, and it was only with the ascent of King Mongkut to the throne in 1851 that there was renewed openness to Westerners

---

1. Historical references to Siam and Siamese generally refer to the pre-World War II period, and references to Thailand and Thai predominate in the postwar period. Siam and Thailand will be used interchangeably in this chapter.
2. The Burmese army sacked Ayutthaya in 1767.
3. Alex G. Smith, *Siamese Gold: A History of Church Growth in Thailand: An Interpretive Analysis 1816–1982* (Bangkok: OMF Thailand, 1982), 9.
4. Smith, *Siamese Gold*, 9. See also Chris Baker and Pasuk Phongpaichit, *A History of Thailand*, 3rd ed. (Cambridge: Cambridge University Press, 2014), 13; Bantoon Boon-Itt, "A Study of the Dialogue between Christianity and Buddhism in Thailand as Represented by Buddhist and Christian Writings from Thailand in the Period 1950 – 2000" (PhD thesis, The Open University, St. John's College, 2007), 33–34; and Thanet Aphornsuvan, "The West and Siam's Quest for Modernity," *South East Asia Research* 17, no. 3 (2009): 405–6.

and their potential contributions to Thai society. Prior to this, the priests who came to Thailand largely ministered among the foreign community and made few converts among native Siamese.

PROTESTANT BEGINNINGS IN SIAM (1828–1840)

The first Protestant efforts to reach the Thai were those of the American Baptist missionary Ann Judson who reached out to Thai prisoners of war and their descendants in Burma. Though she never traveled to Siam, Ann Judson, with the support of her husband, Adoniram, learned the Thai language and translated into Thai a Burmese catechism, a tract, and the Gospel of Matthew.[5] The first recorded Siamese conversion to Protestant Christianity took place outside of Siam. Moung Shway-pwen, a young man who was likely a descendent of Siamese war captives relocated to Burma, came to faith in connection with the ministry of the Judsons.

The first resident Protestant missionaries in Thailand were Karl Gützlaff and Jacob Tomlin who arrived in Bangkok on 23 August 1828.[6] Gützlaff already spoke Chinese, and the pair set to learning Siamese. Gützlaff and Tomlin eventually translated the four Gospels and Romans into Siamese and produced an English-Siamese dictionary up to the letter R.[7] They engaged in distributing Christian books in Chinese, which attracted considerable interest from the locals, especially the Chinese, as well as opposition from Catholic priests. Though Tomlin's journal includes multiple accounts of people who read at least portions of the missionaries' books, it is probable that many eagerly received the free books because of their novelty since the printing press had not yet arrived in Siam and literacy was not widespread.[8] Protestant missionaries in Thailand from Gützlaff and Tomlin onward were strong proponents of literacy, but some were unsure about the evangelistic effectiveness of literature distribution. American Presbyterian missionary Stephen Mattoon commented on this in 1858, saying that "we fear it is only a desire to satisfy curiosity or the love of acquisition" that people received Christian books.[9]

---

5. Smith, *Siamese Gold*, 12–13.
6. Anthony Farrington, ed. *Early Missionaries in Bangkok: The Journals of Tomlin, Gutzlaff, and Abeel, 1828–1832* (Bangkok: White Lotus, 2001), 8–10.
7. Smith, *Siamese Gold*, 14–15.
8. Jacob Tomlin, *Journal of a Nine Months' Residence in Siam* (London: F. Westley and A. H. Davis, 1831), 53, 55.
9. Stephen Mattoon quoted in Maen Pongudom, "Apologetic and Missionary Proclamation: Exemplified by American Presbyterian Missionaries to Thailand (1828–1978), Early Church Apologists: Justin Martyr, Clement of Alexandria and Origen, and the Venerable Buddhadasa

Though the two men only remained in Thailand a few years, their efforts resulted in several inquirers and one baptized convert, a Chinese man named Boon Tee (Koë Bun Tai).[10] However, they sent letters to the American Board of Commissioners for Foreign Missions (ABCFM) and the American Baptist mission in Burma. In response, the ABCFM sent David Abeel, and the American Baptists in Burma sent John Taylor Jones and Eliza Grew Jones to Thailand.[11] Abeel arrived in 1831 but stayed little more than a year before leaving Siam due to poor health. The Joneses arrived in 1833 and set to work learning Siamese. John Jones translated the New Testament from Greek into Siamese, which was printed in 1843. John and Eliza Jones are noteworthy for being the first Protestant missionaries to come to Siam specifically to reach the Siamese, in contrast to those who came to evangelize the Chinese. After the arrival of the Joneses, a small number of other Baptist missionaries arrived in the following decades, and there were several conversions among the Chinese in Bangkok. In 1837, a small group of Chinese converts formed the Maitri Chit Church, which bears the distinction of being the first Chinese Protestant church in Asia. The first Siamese convert in Siam was reported in 1849, and by 1850 the congregation had increased to thirty-five members.[12] However, after several missionaries died and others relocated from Siam to China, the American Baptist mission officially ended their work in Siam in 1868.

The ABCFM sent several missionary couples, though many of them met tragic deaths, and others left after only a short time.[13] The ABCFM missionaries saw few conversions as the result of their work, but two of their missionaries are nonetheless of historical significance: Jesse Caswell and Daniel Beach Bradley. Caswell bears the distinction of having been the English language tutor to Prince Mongkut, the future King Rama IV of Siam, who ruled from 1851–1868.[14] In 1845 Prince Mongkut, who was then living in a Buddhist

---

Bhikkhu, a Thai Buddhist Monk-Apologist" (PhD diss., University of Otago, 1979), 110.
10. Smith, *Siamese Gold*, 15–16; Jessie Gregory Lutz, *Opening China: Karl F. A. Gützlaff and Sino-Western Relations, 1827–1852* (Grand Rapids, MI: Eerdmans, 2008), 52. For more on Chinese immigration and Chinese Protestant Christianity in Thailand, see Carl E. Blanford, *Chinese Churches in Thailand* (Bangkok: Suriyaban, 1974).
11. Lutz, *Opening China*, 52; George Bradley McFarland, ed. *Historical Sketch of Protestant Missions in Siam, 1828–1928* (Bangkok: White Lotus, 1999), 5–9, 27.
12. Smith, *Siamese Gold*, 21–22; The Maitrichit Chinese Baptist Church, "History of the Church."
13. Smith, *Siamese Gold*, 23–24.
14. Regarding the title "Rama," Baker and Phongphaichit note that
> in his lifetime, a king was simply called the king. At death, he was given a regnal name. The sequence Rama I, Rama II, and so on was invented retrospectively in 1916. The

temple as a monk, invited Caswell to instruct him in English. As an enticement to accept this invitation, Caswell was offered use of a room at the temple for preaching and tract distribution following the conclusion of lessons. This friendly and mutually beneficial relationship likely contributed to the future king's patronage of Christian missionaries in successive years.[15]

Daniel Beach Bradley may be the most well-known missionary in Thai history, having distinguished himself in the areas of medicine and printing.[16] A medical doctor by training, physician Bradley and his wife, Emilie, arrived in Bangkok in 1835, thus making Bradley one of the earliest Protestant medical missionaries and a contemporary of Peter Parker in China.[17] Bradley brought with him a printing press which was used to produce the first printed page in Thailand using Thai font.[18] The printing quality was deemed unsatisfactory, however, and both the American Baptist mission and the ABCFM obtained better presses. One of these presses printed the first printed document of the Thai government published in 1839, an edict banning opium.[19] Bradley spent substantial time over his thirty-eight years in Thailand printing various materials, including not only religious literature but also Siamese government documents and Siam's first newspaper, *The Bangkok Recorder*. Through their printing endeavors, Bradley and other missionaries facilitated the modernization of Siam by promoting the dissemination of both printing technology and a diversity of information published using that technology.

In addition to his printing accomplishments, Bradley became renowned for his contributions to modern medical practice in Siam. Shortly after arrival, Bradley opened a medical dispensary, treating patients and giving medicines for free. As he acquired the Siamese language and native helpers, Scripture

---

kings from Rama IV to Rama VII have become better known in English by the names given to them as princes (Mongkut, Chulalongkorn, Vajiravudh, Prajadhipok). Since King Rama VIII, the regnal name has been conferred at accession.
Baker and Phongpaichit, *History of Thailand*, 298.
For a list of the kings of Thailand from 1782 through 2014, see also Baker and Phongpaichit, 298.
15. McFarland, *Historical Sketch*, 19–21; Smith, *Siamese Gold*, 24.
16. Bradley is prominent in secular as well as Christian history in Thailand and was featured in a television documentary series. Thai PBS, "Medical Treatment Advances" (การแพทย์ก้าวหน้า), in *Stories from 9 Kingdoms* (เรื่องเล่า ๙ แผ่นดิน), aired 22 June 2009.
17. Gerald H. Anderson, "The Legacy of Peter Parker, M.D.," *International Bulletin of Missionary Research* 37, no. 3 (July 2013): 152–56.
18. As early as the seventeenth century, Catholic missionaries in Thailand were using the printing press to publish religious materials, albeit in transliterated Thai using Romanized script rather than Thai script. "Twenty Years Ago," *The Bangkok Times* (16 September 1933), SC-38, Box 227, Folder 13, Landon Papers, Wheaton College Special Collections, Wheaton, IL.
19. McFarland, *Historical Sketch*, 16.

verses and prayers were included in the free offerings of his clinics. Outbreaks of cholera and smallpox were common occurrences in Siam, and Bradley is credited with introducing vaccinations which reportedly greatly reduced the annual death rate due to preventable diseases. He performed the first modern surgery in Siam, amputating the arm of a Buddhist monk who was injured when a cannon exploded at a temple festival. His medical successes earned him favor with the Thai royalty, and he trained royal physicians in vaccination techniques during the reign of King Rama III.[20]

Thai royalty appreciated the contributions that missionaries such as Bradley and Caswell made to national development, but they only tolerated evangelization efforts up to a point. For example in 1851, Mrs. Sarah Bradley and two other missionary women were invited to teach English to the women in the royal palace. However, the palace was shut to them after they were found to be teaching more religion than English.[21] King Mongkut later found a more suitable replacement in Anna Leonowens, to whom he expressed his confidence that she would do her "best endeavor for knowledge of English language, science, and literature, and not for conversion to Christianity."[22] King Mongkut's sentiments, and those of successive Thai monarchs, are summarized in his reported statement to missionaries: "The sciences I receive, astronomy, geology, chemistry – these I receive; the Christian religion I do not receive."[23]

AMERICAN PRESBYTERIAN BEGINNINGS (1840–1860)

The first missionary of the American Presbyterian Mission arrived in 1840, and the Presbyterians initiated long-term work with the arrival of Stephen and Mary Mattoon and Samuel Reynolds House on 22 March 1847.[24] The American Presbyterians would be the dominant mission force in Thailand between 1850 and the outbreak of World War II in Thailand in 1941. On 31 August 1849, House, Mattoon, and Stephen Bush formally organized the first Presbyterian Church of Bangkok at Samray. The church was composed entirely of missionaries but shortly was joined by Qua Kieng, a Chinese convert who

---

20. King Rama III reigned from 1824–1851. Smith, *Siamese Gold*, 24–25; McFarland, *Historical Sketch*, 16–17.
21. Smith, *Siamese Gold*, 40–41.
22. Anna Harriette Leonowens, *The English Governess at the Siamese Court* (London: Trübner, 1870), v–vi.
23. King Mongkuk quoted in Presbyterian Board of Publication, *Siam and Laos as Seen by Our American Missionaries* (Philadelphia: Presbyterian Board of Publication, 1884), 391.
24. McFarland, *Historical Sketch*, 37.

transferred from the ABCFM and whose work closed in the same year.[25] The first female Siamese convert was Nang Esther Pradipasena who joined the church in 1860. During the initial years of the Presbyterian mission, the missionaries devoted themselves to medical work, preaching in a mission chapel, and book and tract distribution. Yet despite their dedication, the missionaries' work was not impressive to some outsiders. On a visit to Bangkok in 1855, the British diplomat and Unitarian Sir John Bowring commented on the lack of results from Christian mission work, pointing out that in regard to the Chinese, in twenty-seven years of Protestant missions the missionaries did not have even twenty-seven converts.[26]

PRESBYTERIAN EXPANSION OUTSIDE OF BANGKOK

Initially, all missionary activity in Siam was limited to Bangkok, but in 1861 the American Presbyterian Mission received permission to send Daniel and Sophia McGilvary and Samuel and Jane McFarland to Petchaburi province, seventy-five miles southwest of Bangkok.[27] Samuel McFarland preferred school work and taught the lieutenant governor's son while Daniel McGilvary focused on evangelistic work. In the 1870s, Jane McFarland opened an industrial school in Petchaburi for women and older girls, teaching them to sew, crochet, and knit. Around the same time, missionary Harriette House began an industrial school for girls in Bangkok, and when sewing machines were introduced to the country by missionaries, both women used them in their schools.[28] A church was established in Petchaburi in 1863, and a Siamese man was licensed to preach there in 1867.[29]

THE BEGINNING OF THE LAOS MISSION (1867)

In January 1867, McGilvary moved to Chiang Mai (Northern Thailand) to open a new mission station there. It took McGilvary forty-nine days to travel from Bangkok to Chiang Mai. At that time, the Lao states overlapped with Thailand and were ruled by feudal princes.[30] Five of those Lao states – Chiang

---

25. Smith, *Siamese Gold*, 26–27; McFarland, *Historical Sketch*, 36–42.
26. McFarland, *Historical Sketch*, 46–47; Smith, *Siamese Gold*, 26.
27. Smith, *Siamese Gold*, 57.
28. Runchana Suksod-Barger, "Religious Influences in Thai Female Education (1889–1931)" (PhD diss., Loyola University Chicago, 2010), 126–30; Bertha Blount McFarland, *McFarland of Siam* (New York: Vantage, 1958), 40–43.
29. McFarland, *Historical Sketch*, 52.
30. Daniel McGilvary, *A Half Century among the Siamese and the Lao: An Autobiography*, ed. Cornelius Beach Bradley (New York: Fleming H. Revell, 1912), 63.

Mai, Lampun, Lakawn, Prae, Nan – were later incorporated into present-day Thailand and the sixth, Luang Prabang, with modern Laos.[31] McGilvary founded the Laos Mission to reach these Lao states which were little known in Bangkok and almost another world. Before McGilvary, only one other foreigner had ever made it there. The missionaries were given a small plot of land in Chiang Mai in 1868, and they set down roots in the north. With their strong connections to Bangkok, McGilvary and other missionaries who followed came to play an important role in the eventual integration of the northern region into the kingdom of Siam, pioneering modern education, medical care, and printing in Chiang Mai and neighboring areas.

The first Lao converts were made in 1869 in connection with McGilvary's evangelization of conscripted laborers who came into Chiang Mai to work at building projects for the ruler of the city. As more converts were made, Chao Kawilorot, the ruler of Chiang Mai, felt threatened and sent a letter of accusation to Bangkok and asked the U.S. Consul to remove the missionaries. The prince was unhappy with the consul's negative reply and ordered that all Christians be arrested. Most Lao (Northern Thai) Christians fled, but two were captured. Because they refused to recant their faith, they were tortured and murdered. Acting U.S. Consul Noah McDonald, a Presbyterian missionary, and a royal commissioner appointed by the Siamese regent traveled together to Chiang Mai and informed Kawilorot that he could do whatever he wanted to his own servants – namely the Lao Christians – but the missionaries were not to be harmed. The prince consented to allow the missionaries to stay as long as they only distributed medicine and did not preach Christianity.[32]

After the death of Chao Kawilorot the following year, the new prince was friendlier to the missionaries. About three years later local Christians became confident enough to follow Christ openly. Some new converts were made, but these new believers were mostly older men who lived on the mission compound, working there or coming for medical attention. Church growth was slow in this period, and a number of converts returned to the spirit practices of Lao folk Buddhism. Still, a trickle of people continued to profess faith in Christ, increasingly those outside of the missionaries' employ.

---

31. It should be noted that what McGilvary calls Laoland became what is now Northern Thailand. The descendants of the people with whom McGilvary worked have linguistically and culturally assimilated into mainstream Thai culture.
32. Smith, *Siamese Gold*, 66–69.

In 1878 at the urging of the missionaries, the viceroy of the king of Siam issued an edict of religious toleration for three Northern Thai states. For the church, this edict meant that theoretically no person could be punished for becoming a Christian. The edict also opened the way for more people from the lower classes to publicly inquire about Christianity. During the final decades of the nineteenth century, Christianity grew in Northern Thailand, propelled by not only missionary evangelism, but more importantly by a growing number of Thai Christian evangelists, missionaries, and lay people.[33]

THE NEVIUS METHOD AND STUNTED LEADERSHIP DEVELOPMENT

In spite of positive church growth trends during the 1884 to 1914 period, largely in the North, there was also a retardation of leadership training and indigenization resulting from a botched implementation of the Nevius Method.[34] When the Laos Mission sought to make Northern Thai churches self-supporting by cutting funding, indigenous pastors and evangelists became resentful and reinstated a high pay rate at a Presbytery meeting when missionaries were in the minority. The missionaries viewed this act as rebellion and doubted whether these indigenous pastors and evangelists were truly ready for leadership.[35] Efforts to develop indigenous leaders floundered, and it would be nearly twenty years before the Laos Mission again organized formal theological training for Thai Christians, founding the Thailand Theological Seminary in 1912.[36] This institution would produce a modest number of Thai Christian leaders until its closure just before the outbreak of World War II. The school was reestablished in 1952 and today exists as McGilvary College of Divinity, a college of Payap University in Chiang Mai.

---

33. Austin Lee House, "An Ethnohistorical Study of Thai Christians and Their Participation in Cross-Cultural Missions from 1870–1940" (DMiss diss., Western Seminary, 2017).
34. The Nevius Method, popularized in Korea, theorizes that churches should be self-governing and self-supporting as quickly as possible for the benefit of their own growth and for evangelism. See John Nevius, *The Planting and Development of Missionary Churches* (Hancock, NH: Monadnock, 2003).
35. Herbert Swanson, "The Pastors' Revolt of 1895," in *Pastoral Care and the Church of Christ in Thailand: A Report on the State of Pastoral Care in the CCT Today* (Chiang Mai: Office of History, Church of Christ in Thailand, 1994).
36. McFarland, *Historical Sketch*, 229–31.

EDUCATIONAL WORK AND CHURCH GROWTH

During the latter part of the nineteenth and the early part of the twentieth centuries, there was a marked increase in the number of mission schools established both by the Laos Mission in Northern Thailand and the Siam Mission. Ostensibly, the goal of both missions was the same, namely to provide education for Christian youth, to win non-Christian children to the faith, to spread Christian values in society, and to train Christian leaders.[37] However in practice their goals and results were markedly different. Hugh Taylor, Presbyterian missionary to the Lao from 1888 to 1934, summarized and compared the philosophies and results of the Laos and Siam Missions, noting that the Laos Mission evangelized and then educated whereas the Siam Mission educated in order to evangelize. The Laos Mission sought to use their schools to retain the children of adult Christian converts whereas the Siam Mission centered in Bangkok sought to influence Buddhist children for Christ in order to plant the church of tomorrow. Taylor drew a correlation between strategy and results, concluding that the Laos Mission had many more converts though admittedly less educated, while the Siam Mission had fewer converts but "a few well-educated, outstanding leaders."[38] Although it is difficult to say with certainty whether the difference in educational philosophy between the two missions was as significant for church growth as Taylor believed, the difference in membership growth between the two missions up to 1913 was remarkable. In 1913, the church in Northern Thailand had over six thousand members compared to only six hundred in Bangkok and Southern Thailand. After 1914, growth continued through the start of the Japanese Occupation in December 1941, but at a slower pace. Throughout the whole period the majority of church membership remained in the Northern region.[39]

During the first part of the twentieth century, the American Presbyterians in the Siam and Laos Missions shifted away from prioritizing direct evangelism and church work, favoring instead educational and medical work, which paralleled the Siamese government's efforts toward universal education and expanding access to medical care. In 1899, the Laos Mission and Siam Mission together had seven schools educating 528 students. By 1938, mission schools were educating 5,500 students in sixty-five schools.[40] As the needs

---

37. McFarland, *Historical Sketch*, 209.
38. Hugh Taylor, "A Missionary in Siam" (unpublished manuscript: Payap University Archives, 1947), 162–64, 74–76; Smith, *Siamese Gold*, 94–95.
39. Smith, *Siamese Gold*, 92–93.
40. Smith, 159–60.

of the schools increased, an increasing proportion of missionary personnel were assigned to them. Though some missionaries believed that the schools were effective tools of evangelism, local church work and direct evangelism were neglected.[41] Even while the overall number of Presbyterian missionary personnel in Thailand was declining, the American Presbyterian Mission in Thailand increased the number and quality of their schools over the course of the early twentieth century.[42] The Mission was ostensibly hoping to develop indigenous churches and wanted to equip Thai Christians and churches to thrive in a rapidly modernizing world. However, their institutional commitments came at the expense of evangelism, leadership development, and pastoral care of Thai churches.

THE CHURCH OF CHRIST IN THAILAND (CCT)

In the 1930s, integration and modernization of the country was progressing rapidly, and the time was ripe for the formation of the first indigenous Thai church denomination. Following meetings in Bangkok led by John R. Mott, the Siam Christian Council was formed in 1930, the body which laid the groundwork for the formation of the Church of Christ in Siam (later Thailand) in 1934.[43] This new national church was composed of churches started by the American Presbyterians and American Baptists. Other smaller church bodies considered joining but remained separate from the new national church body, namely the British Churches of Christ, the Christian and Missionary Alliance, the Seventh Day Adventists, the Christian Brethren, and some independent Chinese churches.[44] Although the new denomination did not include all Protestant churches in the country, this organizational union of the majority of churches across the country contributed to a greater sense

---

41. By 1939 only 18 percent of national workers were employed in evangelistic work while the remaining 82 percent were engaged in educational, medical, or other work. Seung Ho Son, "Christian Revival in the Presbyterian Church of Thailand between 1900 and 1941: An Ecclesiological Analysis and Evaluation" (ThD diss., University of Stellenbosch, 2004), 70.

42. Smith, *Siamese Gold*, 179; Kenneth E. Wells, "Actions Taken by the Executive Committee at Chiengmai, December 15–21, 1936," American Presbyterian Mission (RG001/78), Box 14, Folder 2, Payap University Archives, Chiang Mai, Thailand.

43. Prasit Pongudom, *History of the Church of Christ in Thailand* (ประวัติศาสตร์สภาคริสตจักรใน ประเทศไทย) (Chiang Mai: Archives Unit, Church of Christ in Thailand, 1984), 51–57; Bertha Blount McFarland, *Our Garden Was So Fair: The Story of a Mission in Thailand* (Philadelphia: Blakiston, 1943), 73–79; Smith, *Siamese Gold*, 181–84; Boon-Itt, "Study of the Dialogue," 46–48; Charles Howard Hopkins, *John R. Mott, 1865–1955: A Biography* (Grand Rapids, MI: Eerdmans, 1979), 671.

44. Smith, *Siamese Gold*, 183.

of national consciousness among Thai Christians that was in line with the government's national integration efforts.

THAI NATIONALISM

Following the end of absolute monarchy in 1932 and the election of Plaek Phibulsongkram as prime minister in 1938, a new era of intensified nationalism began. The beginning of Phibulsongkram's militaristic rule witnessed arrests of people suspected of political opposition, and some were executed after trials of questionable legality. He banned displaying pictures of King Prajadhipok who abdicated 1935 and used mass media, press censorship, and the government radio monopoly to promote devotion to the nation. Phibulsongkram launched a military campaign to retake territory in Cambodia lost to France forty years earlier and sponsored persecution of Roman Catholics in Thailand who were associated with French missionaries. This persecution lasted from 1940 until 1944 when Phibulsongkram was ousted from power and an Allied victory seemed probable.[45] The persecution of Roman Catholics was accompanied by increased pressure on other religious minorities, including Protestants and Muslims, to "return to Buddhism" to express their national loyalty. Although there had been nationalistic pressure to be Buddhist during the reign of King Vajiravudh (1910–1925), Phibulsongkram ramped up the rhetoric, and civil servants and teachers felt the pressure to conform. In many cases their jobs were at stake if they failed to venerate a Buddha image. Lists of Thai people who had reconverted to Buddhism appeared in the daily newspapers.[46]

JOHN SUNG REVIVALS (1938–1939)

In the midst of rising nationalism that urged fidelity to Buddhism as a mark of patriotism, Thai Christians came under increasing social pressure to conform, and the Church of Christ in Thailand experienced a loss in overall numbers in the 1930s.[47] In the midst of these circumstances came Chinese evangelist John Sung who held evangelistic meetings in Thailand in the autumn of 1938 and

---

45. Baker and Phongpaichit, *History of Thailand*, 131–34. Bruce Reynolds, "Phibun Songkhram and Thai Nationalism in the Fascist Era," *European Journal of East Asian Studies* 3, no. 1 (2004): 107–10; David K. Wyatt, *Thailand: A Short History* (New Haven: Yale University Press, 1984), 255–56. For a detailed account of the Thai-France conflict and persecution of Catholics, see Shane Strate, "An Uncivil State of Affairs: Fascism and Anti-Catholicism in Thailand, 1940–1944," *Journal of Southeast Asian Studies* 42, no. 1 (2011): 59–87.
46. Smith, *Siamese Gold*, 171–78, 199–202.
47. Smith, 174–83.

again in early 1939.⁴⁸ His messages addressed the traditional Gospel themes of sin, repentance, redemption, and forgiveness, but did so in new and disconcerting ways. Sung's loud, direct style conflicted with the quiet decorum of Thai culture, but his meetings nevertheless made a great impact on many Thai and Chinese who attended. Hundreds of conversions or recommitments of nominal Christians, as well as open weeping and repentance, were reported at Sung's meetings.⁴⁹ Small groups called witness bands were formed for evangelism, and there was renewed desire for Bible teaching in some places.⁵⁰ Rising Thai church leaders Sook Pongsanoi and Boon Mark Gittisarn, both of whom interpreted for Sung at various times, reported being deeply impressed by the evangelist.⁵¹ In the years that John Sung visited Thailand, the number of communicant members in the CCT increased, breaking the previous multiyear slump.⁵²

CHRISTIANITY IN THAILAND DURING WORLD WAR II

As war broke out in Europe and Japan extended its reach into China, Japan invaded Thailand on 8 December 1941. With the beginning of Japanese Occupation, all missionary work in Thailand came to a halt. Missionaries living in the Bangkok area were interned and later repatriated. Missionaries in Northern Thailand fled into Burma. The missionaries were gone, and Thai Christians were now on their own to face nationalist and Japanese opposition through the end of the war.⁵³ Mission-owned schools, hospitals, and church buildings were seized by the Japanese, and public worship was prohibited. Christians were denied jobs, and believers scattered, many succumbing to nationalistic pressure to deny Christ. Boon Mark Gittsarn and other Christian leaders went house-to-house visiting and encouraging Christians to stay

---

48. For a detailed account of Sung's Thailand campaigns, see Son, "Christian Revival"; Shangjie Song, *The Diary of John Sung: Extracts from His Journals and Notes*, trans. Pheng Soon Thng (Singapore: Genesis Books, 2012), 330–41.
49. Song, *Diary of John Sung*, 330–44; Boon Mark Gittisarn, et. al., "Excerpts from Letters," *Siam Outlook* 10, no. 3 (July 1939): 114–18; "Trang – Personnel," *Siam Outlook* 10, no. 1 (January 1939): 61–62; Chinda Singhanetr, "Revival of the Heart Through Dr. John Sung [การฟื้นใจใหม่แห่ง ดร. โยฮัน ซง]," *Church News* [ข่าวคริสตจักร] 8, no. 5 (August 1939): 25–27; "Revival in the Nan Church [การฟื้นใจในคริสตจักร น่าน]," *Church News* [ข่าวคริสตจักร] 8, no. 5 (August 1939): 27–28.
50. Smith, *Siamese Gold*, 195–98.
51. Timothy Tow, *John Sung, My Teacher* (Singapore: Christian Life, 1985), 217–21; Son, "Christian Revival," 126; Suk Phongnoi, "Dr. John Sung Comes to Thailand (ดร. จอห์น ซง มาประเทศไทยโดย ศาสนาจารย์สุข พงศ์น้อย)," Tyrannus Centre.
52. Smith, *Siamese Gold*, 197.
53. Smith, 199, 207.

faithful. Yet by the end of the war, the overall membership of the Church of Christ in Thailand had dropped by 20–30 percent, though accurate numbers are impossible to determine.[54]

POSTWAR REVITALIZATION AND SHIFTING MISSION DYNAMICS

Following the end of the war, the Church of Christ in Thailand invited the American Presbyterian missionaries to return and assist in relief efforts, to help the churches secure buildings that had been seized during the war, and to resume ministry partnership with Thai Christians.[55] With the lifting of wartime restrictions, many of those who had bowed under pressure returned to the church during a flurry of postwar evangelism conducted by Thai Christians. As moderator of the Church of Christ in Thailand (CCT), Puang Akkapin spearheaded evangelistic efforts, and church growth swelled in the following decades, reaching over thirty-six thousand by 1970.[56] However, the relationship between Thai Christians and foreign missionaries had been forever changed by the war. For nearly five years, Thai Christians had been on their own without any missionary leadership or assistance, and they did not appreciate returning missionaries who presumed they would take up their former positions of leadership. The American Presbyterian Mission had long spoken of turning control of churches and mission institutions over to the Thai, and had made some initial efforts in that direction before the war. However, the reality often failed to keep pace with the rhetoric. Some Thai pastors left the CCT due to concerns about missionary paternalism and liberal theology. Among these was Boon Mark Gittisarn who joined forces with Finnish Pentecostal missionaries to launch the Pentecostal movement in Thailand.[57]

---

54. Smith, 208–13; Kenneth Wells, *History of Protestant Work in Thailand* (Bangkok: Church of Christ in Thailand, 1958), 160–61.
55. John L. Eakin, "Missions Work in Siam: A Post-War Picture," *International Review of Missions* 37, no. 145 (January 1948): 71–75.
56. Samuel I. Kim, *The Unfinished Mission in Thailand: The Uncertain Christian Impact on the Buddhist Heartland* (Seoul: East-West Center for Missions Research and Development, 1980), 152–53; Samrit Wongsan, *The Pastor without a Degree: Puang Akkapin* [อาจารย์ผู้ไร้ปริญญา พ่วง อรรณภิญญ์] (Bangkok: Urban Industrial Life Division, The Church of Christ in Thailand, 1970), 32–43.
57. Edwin Zehner, "Church Growth and Culturally Appropriate Leadership: Three Examples from the Thai Church," School of World Mission (unpublished manuscript: Fuller Theological Seminary, 5 November, 1987), 54–55; Boon Mark Gittisarn, *Modernism Takes Its Toll of Mission Work* (Collingswood, NJ: Christian Beacon, 1950); Herbert Swanson, "The Finnish Free Foreign Mission and the Origins of Pentecostalism in Thailand, 1946–1960," *Herb's Research Bulletin*, no. 6 (2003).

Despite the missionaries' good intentions for indigenous leadership of Thai churches, there were tensions between Thai leaders and American Presbyterian Mission missionaries over control and influence in the CCT. Although some of the postwar Presbyterian missionaries were united with Thai Christians in emphasizing evangelism and the spiritual vitality of church life, many of the missionaries in the 1950s and 1960s were more theologically liberal than their prewar counterparts and prioritized societal development projects, ecumenism, and interfaith dialogue.[58] In the view of Wichean Wattakeecharoen, general secretary of the CCT (1971–1977), the theological liberalism of the missionaries only caused spiritual damage to Thai churches.[59] The American Presbyterian Mission formally dissolved in 1957, and the "missionaries" became "fraternal workers," formally under the authority of CCT. However, their influence in the denomination continued through the 1970s until the Presbyterian Church USA (PCUSA) budget cuts and personnel departures changed the balance of power.[60] From the perspective of Thai leaders, the end of missionary influence was ultimately for the best.

During the decades following the war, the Protestant missionary and denominational landscape expanded well beyond the American Presbyterians and the CCT. From 1840 to 1941, the vast majority of missionaries in Thailand had been American Presbyterians. But between 1940 and 1960, sixteen new groups entered the country, and by 1980 that number had increased by an additional twenty-one. Overseas Missionary Fellowship (OMF), World Evangelization Crusade (WEC), Campus Crusade for Christ (now Cru), the Southern Baptists, the Korean Presbyterian Mission, and many other evangelical groups entered the country during this time.[61] Initially, the majority of these groups worked independently, many being wary of the Church of Christ in Thailand because of their connections with the World Council of Churches (WCC) and the PCUSA, both of whom were considered suspect because of theological liberalism and ecumenism.[62] In the early 1970s, these

---

58. Kim, *Unfinished Mission*, 56–59, 118–21; Patricia McLean, "Thai Protestant Christianity: A Study of Cultural and Theological Interactions between Western Missionaries (the American Presbyterian Mission and the Overseas Missionary Fellowship) and Indigenous Thai Churches (the Church of Christ in Thailand and the Associated Churches of Thailand-Central)" (PhD diss., University of Edinburgh, 2002), 100–12.
59. Kim, *Unfinished Mission*, 156–59, 75.
60. Wells, *History of Protestant Work*, 191; Kim, *Unfinished Mission*, 77–85.
61. Smith, *Siamese Gold*, 222–23; Kim, *Unfinished Mission*, 183–204.
62. David Anthony Huntley, "The Withdrawal of the China Inland Mission from China, and Their Redeployment to New Fields in East Asia" (PhD diss., University of Liverpool, 2002),

various evangelical groups began to talk together and to cooperate, resulting in the formation of the Evangelical Fellowship of Thailand (EFT) and interdenominational training institutions like Bangkok Bible Seminary.[63] Since the 1970s, there have been several interdenominational evangelical congresses in order to promote evangelism and interdenominational co-operation. An interdenominational Thailand Church Growth Committee eventually became a major sub-committee of the Thailand Protestant Churches Co-ordinating Committee (TPCCC), an interdenominational working group founded in 1988 and composed of the Church of Christ in Thailand, the Evangelical Fellowship of Thailand, and the Thailand Baptist Convention. Evangelical cooperative efforts begun in the twentieth century have continued and expanded in the first part of the twenty-first century.[64]

In addition to the influx and growth of various evangelical groups after the Second World War, the other major influence on twentieth-century Thai Christianity was Pentecostalism. The first Pentecostal missionaries to Thailand were Verner and Hanna Raassina of the Finnish Free Foreign Mission who arrived in 1946. They were soon joined by other Scandinavian missionaries and were helped by Boon Mark Gittisarn and his wife, Muan. Pentecostalism was given a boost forward in 1956 when healing evangelist T. L. Osborn held meetings in Bangkok. At those meetings, Saman Wannakiet (Presbyterian) and Chaiyong Wattanachan (Baptist) were reportedly healed, and the two men subsequently teamed up to hold Pentecostal evangelistic services throughout Thailand. Their efforts resulted in numerous new Pentecostal groups, especially in Northern Thailand, although the Church of Christ accused Pentecostals of stealing people from their congregations. At one meeting of Wannakiet and Wattanachan in Nakon Pathom in 1957, fifteen-year-old Wirachai Kowae responded to the message. Kowae would later become the founder of the Thailand Assemblies of God and chair of the Evangelical Fellowship in Thailand. Through the 1960s and 1970s, Pentecostalism continued to grow as

---

181–92; Neel Roberts, "Comity Agreements: The Not-So-Simple Art of Cooperation," *Mission Round Table* 10, no. 1 (2015): 34–35.
63. Kim, *Unfinished Mission*, 168–70; Averil Bennett and David Sheahan, *Beyond Ourselves: OMF in Thailand, the First 60 Years, 1951–2012* (Bangkok, Thailand: OMF Thailand, 2016), 60–61, 122–23, 233.
64. Smith, *Siamese Gold*, 223–26; Seree Lorgunpai and Sanurak Fongvarin, "Thailand," in *Christianity in East and South East Asia*, eds. Kenneth R. Ross, Francis Alvarez, and Todd M. Johnson (Edinburgh, UK: Edinburgh University Press, 2020), 163–65. Nantiya Petchgate, "Promoting Ecumenism between Catholic and Protestant Churches in Thailand," *CTC Bulletin: Commission on Theological Concerns (Christian Conference of Asia)* vol. 25, no. 1/2 (2009), 68–72.

numerous new Pentecostal missions entered Thailand.[65] In 1981, Dr. Kriengsak Charoenwongsak founded the Hope of Bangkok church which had grown to over thirty thousand members throughout Thailand by 2009, at which time the church association splintered, spawning numerous independent churches and smaller church networks.[66] By the early twenty-first century, Pentecostal and charismatic Christianity had become a major component of Protestant Christianity in Thailand, with significant influence flowing between charismatic and traditionally non-charismatic groups and denominations.

CHRISTIANITY IN THAILAND TODAY

At the end of the second decade of this century, there were five Christian groups recognized by the Thai government: the Church of Christ in Thailand, Evangelical Fellowship of Thailand, Thailand Baptist Convention, Seventh Day Adventist Church of Thailand, and Roman Catholic Church. All traditions of Christianity in Thailand total 1.6 million adherents of a national population of sixty-nine million. Protestants make up the largest Christian group (469,000), followed by Catholics (385,000) and Independents (89,000). Protestantism is growing at 5–6 percent per year, one third of that number coming from children born in Christian homes and two thirds from new converts. The growth rate varies by region, and new churches are growing more rapidly. Historically, the numbers of Christians have grown very slowly in Thailand compared to some neighboring countries, and strong Thai Buddhist identity continues to pose a challenge to conversion.

In the years ahead, the church in Thailand faces many challenges in a changing society, including post-Covid economic recovery, ongoing political tensions, and responding to increased advocacy for LGBTQ+ rights and loosening restrictions on abortion. The popularity of prosperity gospel teaching and the outreach of cult groups among Thai Christians are also putting Thai churches to the test. Nevertheless, the church in Thailand has shown strong growth in recent years, and half of all Protestant churches in Thailand have been started in the past twenty-five years. The legally protected religious

---

65. James Hosack, "The Arrival of Pentecostals and Charismatics in Thailand," *Asian Journal of Pentecostal Studies* 4, no. 1 (January 2001): 109–17; Swanson, "Finnish Free"; Alan R. Johnson and James Hosack, "Pentecostalism in Thailand," in *Global Renewal Christianity: Spirit Empowered Movements* (Lake Mary, FL: Charisma House, 2016), 196–212.

66. Narumol Plodtong, "A Case Study of Charismatic Leadership at the Hope of Bangkok Church, Thailand" (PhD diss., Assumption University, Thailand, 2010); Carolyn Boyd, *The Apostle of Hope: The Dr. Kriengsak Story* (West Sussex: Sovereign World, 1991).

freedom of the past will likely continue, and the prospects of Thai churches look bright as indigenous Thai Christians, assisted by foreign missionaries, pursue multifaceted efforts in evangelism, discipleship, church planting, and mercy ministries in order to reach their Thai neighbors for Christ. Christians have always been a tiny minority in Thailand, but many Thai believers are working hard and calling upon God to change that.[67]

REFERENCES

Anderson, Gerald H. "The Legacy of Peter Parker, M.D." *International Bulletin of Missionary Research* 37, no. 3 (July 2013): 152–56.

Baker, Chris, and Pasuk Phongpaichit. *A History of Thailand*, 3rd ed. Cambridge: Cambridge University Press, 2014.

Bennett, Averil, and David Sheahan. *Beyond Ourselves: OMF in Thailand, the First 60 Years, 1951–2012*. Bangkok, Thailand: OMF Thailand, 2016.

Boyd, Carolyn. *The Apostle of Hope: The Dr. Kriengsak Story*. West Sussex: Sovereign World, 1991.

Dahlfred, Karl. "A Bumpy Road to Indigenization: The American Presbyterian Mission and the Church of Christ in Thailand." *Journal of Presbyterian History* 99, no. 1 (Spring / Summer 2021): 35–47.

Eakin, John L. "Missions Work in Siam: A Post-War Picture." *International Review of Missions* 37, no. 145 (January 1948): 71–75.

Farrington, Anthony. ed. *Early Missionaries in Bangkok: The Journals of Tomlin, Gutzlaff, and Abeel*, 1828–1832. Bangkok: White Lotus Press, 2001.

Gittisarn, Boon Mark, et. al. "Excerpts from Letters." *Siam Outlook* 10, no. 3 (July 1939): 114–18.

———. *Modernism Takes Its Toll of Mission Work*. Collingswood: Christian Beacon, 1950.

———. "Trang - Personnel." *Siam Outlook* 10, no. 1 (January 1939): 61–62.

Hopkins, Charles Howard. *John R. Mott, 1865–1955: A Biography*. Grand Rapids, MI: Eerdmans, 1979.

Hosack, James. "The Arrival of Pentecostals and Charismatics in Thailand." *Asian Journal of Pentecostal Studies* 4, no. 1 (January 2001): 109–17.

House, Austin Lee. "An Ethnohistorical Study of Thai Christians and Their Participation in Cross-Cultural Missions from 1870–1940." PhD diss., Western Seminary, 2017.

---

67. "Thailand," in *World Christian Encyclopedia*, eds. Todd M. Johnson and Gina A. Zurlo (Edinburgh, UK: Edinburgh University Press, 2019), 789–93; Lorgunpai and Fongvarin, "Thailand," 155–56; Kate Shellnutt, "Making Missions Count: How a Major Database Tracked Thailand's Church-Planting Revival," *Christianity Today* (15 March 2019).

Huntley, David Anthony. "The Withdrawal of the China Inland Mission from China, and Their Redeployment to New Fields in East Asia." PhD diss., University of Liverpool, 2002.

Johnson, Alan R., and James Hosack. "Pentecostalism in Thailand." In *Global Renewal Christianity: Spirit Empowered Movements*, 196–212. Lake Mary, FL: Charisma House, 2016.

Kim, Samuel I. *The Unfinished Mission in Thailand*. Seoul: East-West Center for Missions Research and Development, 1980.

Leonowens, Anna Harriette. *The English Governess at the Siamese Court*. London: Trübner, 1870.

Lorgunpai, Seree, and Sanurak Fongvarin. "Thailand." In *Christianity in East and South East Asia*, edited by Kenneth R. Ross, Francis Alvarez, and Todd M. Johnson. Edinburgh, UK: Edinburgh University Press, 2020.

Lutz, Jessie Gregory. *Opening China: Karl F. A. Gützlaff and Sino-Western Relations, 1827–1852*. Grand Rapids, MI: Eerdmans, 2008.

The Maitrichit Chinese Baptist Church. "History of the Church," http://www.maitrichitchurch.org/about-us/. Accessed 18 July 2019.

McFarland, Bertha Blount. *Our Garden Was So Fair: The Story of a Mission in Thailand*. Philadelphia: Blakiston, 1943.

———. *McFarland of Siam*. New York: Vantage, 1958.

McFarland, George Bradley, ed. *Historical Sketch of Protestant Missions in Siam, 1828–1928*. Bangkok: White Lotus, 1999.

McGilvary, Daniel. *A Half Century among the Siamese and the Lao: An Autobiography*. Edited by Cornelius Beach Bradley. New York: Fleming H. Revell, 1912.

McLean, Patricia. "Thai Protestant Christianity: A Study of Cultural and Theological Interactions between Western Missionaries (the American Presbyterian Mission and the Overseas Missionary Fellowship) and Indigenous Thai Churches (the Church of Christ in Thailand and the Associated Churches of Thailand-Central)." PhD thesis, University of Edinburgh, 2002.

Petchgate, Nantiya. "Promoting Ecumenism between Catholic and Protestant Churches in Thailand." *CTC Bulletin: Commission on Theological Concerns (Christian Conference of Asia)* vol. 25, no. 1/2 (2009): 68–72.

Phongnoi, Suk. "Dr. John Sung Comes to Thailand (ดร. จอห์น ซง มาประเทศไทย โดย ศาสนาจารย์สุข พงศ์น้อย)." Tyrannus Centre. http://www.tyrannusthai.com/index.php?lay=boardshow&ac=webboard_show&No=83040. Accessed 27 November, 2017.

Plodtong, Narumol. "A Case Study of Charismatic Leadership at the Hope of Bangkok Church, Thailand." PhD diss., Assumption University, Thailand, 2010.

Pongudom, Maen. "Apologetic and Missionary Proclamation: Exemplified by American Presbyterian Missionaries to Thailand (1828–1978), Early Church Apologists: Justin Martyr, Clement of Alexandria and Origen, and the Venerable Buddhadasa Bhikkhu, a Thai Buddhist Monk-Apologist." PhD diss., University of Otago, 1979.

Pongudom, Prasit. *History of the Church of Christ in Thailand* [ประวัติศาสตร์สภาคริสตจักรในประเทศไทย]. Chiang Mai: Archives Unit, Church of Christ in Thailand, 1984.

Presbyterian Board of Publication. *Siam and Laos as Seen by Our American Missionaries*. Philadelphia: Presbyterian Board of Publication, 1884.

Reynolds, Bruce. "Phibun Songkhram and Thai Nationalism in the Fascist Era." *European Journal of East Asian Studies* 3, no. 1 (2004): 107–10.

Roberts, Neel. "Comity Agreements: The Not-So-Simple Art of Cooperation." *Mission Round Table* 10, no. 1 (2015): 34–35.

Shellnutt, Kate. "Making Missions Count: How a Major Database Tracked Thailand's Church-Planting Revival." *Christianity Today* (15 March 2019). www.christianitytoday.com/ct/2019/april/missions-data-thai-church-fjcca-reach-village.html.

Singhanetr, Chinda. "Revival of the Heart Through Dr. John Sung [การฟื้นใจใหม่แห่ง ดร.โยฮัน ซง]." *Church News* [ข่าวคริสตจักร] 8, no. 5 (August 1939): 25–27.

———. "Revival in the Nan Church [การฟื้นใจในคริสตจักร์ น่าน]." *Church News* [ข่าวคริสตจักร] 8, no. 5 (August 1939): 27–28.

Smith, Alex G. *Siamese Gold: A History of Church Growth in Thailand, 1816–1982*. Bangkok: OMF Thailand, 1982.

Son, Seung Ho. "Christian Revival in the Presbyterian Church of Thailand between 1900 and 1941." ThD diss., University of Stellenbosch, 2004.

Song, Shangjie. *The Diary of John Sung: Extracts from His Journals and Notes*. Translated by Pheng Soon Thng. Singapore: Genesis Books, 2012.

Suksod-Barger, Runchana. "Religious Influences in Thai Female Education (1889–1931)." PhD diss., Loyola University Chicago, 2010.

Swanson, Herbert. "The Finnish Free Foreign Mission and the Origins of Pentecostalism in Thailand, 1946–1960." Herb's Research Bulletin, no. 6 (2003). https://www.herbswanson.com/_files/ugd/4cfa9b_54cf820a72a24ba4b161f32a916250a5.pdf.

———. *Krischak Muang Nua: A Study in Northern Thai Church History*. Bangkok: Chuan Printing, 1984.

———. "The Pastors' Revolt of 1895." In *Pastoral Care and the Church of Christ in Thailand: A Report on the State of Pastoral Care in the CCT Today*. Chiang Mai: Office of History, Church of Christ in Thailand, 1994. http://www.herbswanson.com/_get.php?postid=70#c6.3. Accessed 27 November 2017.

"Thailand." In *World Christian Encyclopedia Online*, Todd M. Johnson, Gina A. Zurlo. Consulted online on 6 July 2022. http://dx.doi.org.dtl.idm.oclc.org/10.1163/2666-6855_WCEO_COM_02THA. First published online 2020.

Tomlin, Jacob. *Journal of a Nine Months' Residence in Siam*. London: F. Westley and A. H. Davis, 1831.

Tow, Timothy. *John Sung, My Teacher*. Singapore: Christian Life, 1985.

"Twenty Years Ago." *The Bangkok Times* (16 September 1933), SC-38, Box 227, Folder 13, Landon Papers, Wheaton College Special Collections, Wheaton, IL.

Wells, Kenneth. "Actions Taken by the Executive Committee at Chiengmai, December 15–21, 1936," American Presbyterian Mission (RG001/78), Box 14, Folder 2, Payap University Archives, Chiang Mai, Thailand.

———. *History of Protestant Work in Thailand*. Bangkok: Church of Christ in Thailand, 1958.

Wongsan, Samrit. *The Pastor without a Degree: Puang Akkapin* [อาจารย์ผู้ไร้ปริญญา พ่วง อรรฆภิญญ์]. Bangkok: Urban Industrial Life Division, The Church of Christ in Thailand, 1970.

Wyatt, David K. *Thailand: A Short History*. New Haven: Yale University Press, 1984.

Zehner, Edwin. "Church Growth and Culturally Appropriate Leadership: Three Examples from the Thai Church." Unpublished manuscript, Fuller Theological Seminary, 5 November 1987. http://www.thaimissions.info/gsdl/collect/thaimiss/index/assoc/HASHcbed.dir/doc.pdf.

CHAPTER 9

HISTORY OF CHRISTIANITY IN VIETNAM

EVANGELICAL CHURCHES IN VIETNAM IN THE EARLY TWENTY-FIRST CENTURY

KimSon Nguyen[1]

This chapter focuses on the history of Christianity in Vietnam after World War II, with particular emphasis on evangelical churches. But first a brief overview of Vietnam's history is provided to set the context of this late-twentieth century development.

A BRIEF HISTORY OF VIETNAM

The 1954 Geneva Accords were signed to bring about the end to the war in Indochina. France agreed to withdraw its troops from French Indochina, and the region was then split into three independent countries: Vietnam, Laos, and Cambodia.[2] However, these events did not end the warfare, and the Second Indochina war, known as the Vietnam War in the United States, engulfed the region for another two decades. In 1975, the northern communist army of the Democratic Republic of Vietnam (DRV) gained a final victory over the alliance between the United States and the Republic of Vietnam (RVN), respectively under the United States President Richard M. Nixon and South Vietnamese President Nguyễn Văn Thiệu.[3] Since then, the country has been united and renamed the Socialist Republic of Vietnam.

---

1. Adapted by Samuel K. Law from KimSon Nguyen, *Cultural Integration and the Gospel in Vietnamese Mission Theology: A Paradigm Shift* (Carlisle, UK: Langham Monographs, 2019).
2. Nicholas Tarling, *The Cambridge History of Southeast Asia*, Vol. 2, *The Nineteenth and Twentieth Centuries* (New York: Cambridge University Press, 1992), 365–74. See also Pierre Asselin, *Hanoi's Road to the Vietnam War, 1954–1965*, Series from Indochina to Vietnam 7 (Berkeley: University of California Press, 2013); and Jessica M. Chapman, *Cauldron of Resistance: Ngo Dinh Diem, the United States, and 1950s Southern Vietnam* (Ithaca, NY: Cornell University Press, 2013).
3. See David L. Anderson, *The Columbia History of the Vietnam War* (New York: Columbia University Press, 2011).

The history of modern *Việt Nam* (Vietnam in contemporary English) in terms of the people and culture started with Nguyễn Ánh (or Nguyễn Phúc Ánh), who later came to be known as Emperor Gia Long. He proclaimed Thăng Long (modern day Hanoi) as the capitol of the Kingdom of *Đại Việt* in the summer of 1802 and established the Nguyễn dynasty that ruled from 1802 to 1945. Nguyễn Ánh chose the name *Gia Long* for the Nguyễn imperial dynasty to reflect two significant geographic locations: *Gia Định* in the northern region and *Thăng Long* in the southern region of *Đại Việt*. Politically, the Nguyễn emperor united *Đại Việt*[4] for the first time after similar attempts by the Nguyễn Lord (Nguyễn Hoàng) and the *Tây Sơn* regimes earlier. Emperor Gia Long ruled *Đại Việt* after a long, brutal, and destructive century of civil war that "had drained the country's resources and exhausted its people."[5] The south, central, and north of *Đại Việt* were united into one nation for the first time which began a new chapter in Vietnam's history, drawing from the rich political, social, and cultural diversity of ethnic tribes like the Cham and Khmer and a number of Chinese immigrants. To accommodate this ambition for unity, Emperor Gia Long sought to deal with a significant element of Vietnamese national identity, naming the country *Việt Nam* through a 1804 edict.[6] This unity was a long-awaited moment after several regional conflicts before the colonial period. Nevertheless, Vietnam under the Nguyễn dynasty experienced relative independence from China despite being bombarded by rising European colonial threats as other Southeast Asian countries were also experiencing, particularly the threat of French colonization.[7]

Although sharing the social, cultural, and religious contexts of Eastern and Southeastern Asia – particularly Confucianism, Daoism, and Buddhism – Vietnamese culture has a unique identity in both philosophical beliefs and practices. These beliefs and practices have been reflected through Vietnamese literature in various ways. Understanding this context enables creating cultural approaches that can bridge the gap between the Christian faith and the culture

---

4. George E. Dutton, Jayne S. Werner, and John K. Whitmore, *Sources of Vietnamese Tradition* (New York: Columbia University Press, 2012), 258–59.
5. Dutton, Werner, and Whitmore, *Sources*, 253.
6. See *Dai Nam thuc luc [The veritable records of Đại Nam]*, 9 vols. (Tokyo: Keio Institute of Linguistic Studies, 1961); *Dai Nam thuc luc* [The veritable records of Dai Nam], trans. Nguyễn Ngọc Tỉnh, vol. 10 (Hà Nội: Nxb Khoa Học Xã Hội, 2004). For the Gia Long's edict of 1804 and the Minh Mạng's edicts in English, see Dutton, Werner, and Whitmore, *Sources*, 258–60.
7. Jacob Ramsay, *Mandarins and Martyrs: The Church and the Nguyen Dynasty in Early Nineteenth-Century Vietnam* (Stanford, CA: Stanford University Press, 2008).

of Vietnam, and thus enable Christian ministry in Vietnam to break from Western cultural hegemony to become a truly Vietnamese evangelical church.

THE EVANGELICAL VIETNAMESE CHURCHES OF THE EARLY TWENTY-FIRST CENTURY

The history of Christianity in Vietnam spans years, but the character of Vietnamese churches in the early twenty-first century is defined by developments over the last four hundred years. Though Vietnamese people may have encountered Christianity via the Syrian or Nestorian missionaries, there is no indication that they accomplished any significant evangelistic work during their visits.[8] It was not until the arrival of Jesuit priests in the seventeenth century that the Christian church was able to become somewhat established in Vietnam. They established the Catholic Church in Vietnam (*Công Giáo*),[9] and two centuries later, the Vietnamese evangelical church, or the *Tin Lành*, was formed.[10] Both Vietnamese Catholicism and Vietnamese evangelicalism are among the six largest religions recognized by the 2009 Population and Housing Census in Vietnam.[11]

Organizationally, Vietnamese evangelicals or the *Tin Lành*, that is, "Protestants," distinguish themselves into two main groups: the registered churches and the non- or pre-registered churches. The evangelical registered churches are those which received legal status in Vietnam after 2000 as they met

---

8. Phạm Văn Sơn's *Việt Sử Tân Biên* (1961) and J. Despon's *L'Eglise d'Indochine* (1964) cited in Hoàng Phu Lê, "A Short History of the Evangelical Church of Viet Nam (1911–1965)" (PhD diss., New York University, 1972), 97.
9. Kenneth Scott Latourette, *History of Christianity* (New York: Harper & Row, 1953), 853–54; Dale T. Irvin and Scott W. Sunquist, *History of the World Christian Movement*, 2 vols., vol. II: Modern Christianity from 1954–1800 (Maryknoll, NY: Orbis Books, 2012), 54.
10. For an extensive and notable history of Vietnamese Catholicism written in English, see Phan Phát Huồn, *History of the Catholic Church in Việt Nam*, vol. 1, 1533–1960 (Long Beach, CA: Cứu Thế Tùng Thư, 2000); Charles Patrick Keith, "Catholic Vietnam: Church, Colonialism and Revolution, 1887–1945" (PhD diss., Yale University, 2008); and Charles Patrick Keith, *Catholic Vietnam: A Church from Empire to Nation* (Berkeley: University of California Press, 2012). For Vietnamese evangelicalism, there are a number of notable sources in English, for instance, Hoàng Phu Lê, "Short History"; Violet B. James, "American Protestant Missions and the Vietnam War" (PhD diss., University of Aberdeen, 1989); Reginald Eugene Reimer, "The Protestant Movement in Vietnam: Church Growth in Peace and War among the Ethnic Vietnamese" (MA thesis, Fuller Theological Seminary, 1972); and Reginald Eugene Reimer, *Vietnam's Christians: A Century of Growth in Adversity* (Pasadena, CA: William Carey Library, 2011).
11. Tổng Cục Thống Kê, "The 2009 Vietnam Population and Housing Census: Completed Results" (Hanoi, Vietnam, 2009); and Nguyễn Cao Thanh, "Đạo Tin Lành ở Việt Nam từ 1975 đến nay, tư liệu và một số đánh giá ban đầu" [The Evangelicalism in Vietnam from 1975 to the present, sources and initial comments], Ban Tôn giáo Chính phủ.

certain legal criteria, for example being present in Vietnam before 1975 and continually after 1975. These registered churches include Vietnam Christian Mission (2007), United Christian Church (2007), Seventh Day Adventist (2008), Vietnam General Baptist (2008), Vietnam Southern Baptist (2008), Vietnam Presbyterian (2008), Vietnam Assemblies of God (2009), Jehovah's Witness (2009), and the Vietnam Mennonites (2009).[12] The Evangelical Church of Vietnam (ECVN) has two different denominational entities, the ECVN South and ECVN North.

In terms of beliefs, most Vietnamese evangelicals hold a high view of Scripture, evangelism, and devotion to a life of holiness. Moreover, they have inherited the foundational characteristics of the Christian & Missionary Alliance (CMA), including "The Fourfould Gospel" which is the preaching of Jesus Christ as Savior, sanctifier, healer, and coming king.[13] Vietnamese evangelicalism is generally influenced by Albert B. Simpson's works and John Drange Olsen's two-volume *Thần đạo học* (Theology), which was strongly influenced by the famous Baptist theologian Augustus Hopkins Strong's *Systematic Theology* (1907).

Initially under the name *Hội Tin Lành Đông Pháp* (Evangelical Church of [French] Indochina) (ECIC), the Evangelical Church of Vietnam (ECVN), or *Hội Thánh Tin Lành Việt Nam*, is the largest evangelical registered church and was established nationally in 1927. The church again changed its name to *Hội Thánh Tin Lành Việt Nam* (Evangelical Church of Vietnam) in 1950. This church was the offspring of the CMA missions started in the late nineteenth and early twentieth centuries in the Indochinese field, which includes the countries of Vietnam, Laos, and Cambodia today. Historically, the ECVN should be viewed through a few critical moments in its mission history: the early CMA mission in the 1900s; the efforts to indigenize evangelical practices modeled after the "three-self" movement during the 1920s; the institutionalizing process of giving the church an indigenous face as the national evangelical church

---

12. Nguyễn, "Đạo Tin Lành ở Việt Nam"; Đoàn Triệu Long, "Đạo Tin Lành buổi đầu vào Việt Nam," [Begining of Evangelicalism in Vietnam] *Nghiên Cứu Tôn Giáo [Journal of Religious Studies]*, no. 1 (2012): 43–49.

13. For more information on the CMA's history, see "Then and Now," sections The Founding Years (1887–1919), Sacrifice and Expansion (1919–1946), The Evangelical Era (1947–1974), and the Missionary Church Era (1974–Present), Christian Missionary Alliance (n.d.), https://legacy.cmalliance.org/about/history/. For the Vietnamese Pentecostal-oriented churches, see Vince Le, "The Pentecostal Movement in Vietnam," in *Global Renewal Christianity: Spirit-Empowered Movement Past, Present, and Future*, Vol. 1, *Asia and Oceania*, eds. Vinson Synan and Amos Yong (Lake Mary, FL: Charisma House, 2016), 181–95.

History of Christianity in Vietnam

in Vietnam and writing its first constitution; the departure of the Western missions in 1975; and the separation of the ECVN North and the ECVN South since 1955. The evangelical non- or pre-registered churches are usually called the Vietnamese House Churches (*Hội thánh Tư gia*). These churches have not been well researched in academic literature. Prior to receiving legal status in 2000, many evangelical registered churches had been gathering and conducting their religious activities in private houses, or sometimes in rented venues of the registered churches or of the Catholic Church in Vietnam. This "in house" phenomenon excludes evangelical churches who had their own church buildings before 1975. Churches that had their own buildings and were allowed to operate their religious activities with unofficial, though limited, permission include the Evangelical Church of Vietnam, both the North and the South; Vietnam Christian Mission in *Đà Nẵng* and *Quảng Ngãi* provinces in central Vietnam; United Christian Church in Hóc Môn district, *Hồ Chí Minh* City; Vietnam Southern Baptist Church / Grace Baptist Church in *Hồ Chí Minh* City; and Seventh Day Adventist Church in *Hồ Chí Minh* City.

The fast-growing Vietnamese house church phenomenon was the new ecclesiastical movement in the 1980s[14] which was characterized by and formed for various reasons. For instance, those who left or were forced to leave (excommunicated from) the ECVN due to conflicts regarding the understanding of various doctrines such as spiritual baptism, speaking in tongues, and organizational policy formed house churches. These ECVN pastors and members then joined other existing "in house" evangelical groups or churches such as the Assemblies of God or formed their own groups. In fact many of them, such as the Inter-Evangelistic Movement or United Gospel Outreach Church, have chosen to have their own church names or to affiliate with other international churches institutionally, though not necessarily in doctrine, such as with the Baptists, the Presbyterian Church (PCUSA), the Methodists, or the Anglicans. Nevertheless despite having denominational affiliation, a distinct characteristic of the Vietnamese house church movement is association with the Pentecostal phenomena of speaking in tongues, revival prayers, and other spiritual gifts manifestations.

Adding to this house church phenomenon is the influx of Vietnamese Christians returning from refugee camps in Asia, mainly from Hong Kong in the 1990s, from former communist countries in Eastern Europe including East Germany and the former Soviet Union, and from Asian countries such as

---
14. See Nguyễn, "Đạo Tin Lành ở Việt Nam."

South Korea, Taiwan, Malaysia, and Singapore. In addition, several missionary efforts from outside Vietnam in the 1990s to the 2000s have made the house church landscape more diverse and complex, including Korean missionary agencies and denominations such as the Methodists, the Anglicans, and the Free Churches, for example *Lời Sự Sống* (Living Word) church, to name a few. Today, most of these churches are associated with a few existing networks, such as two Vietnamese evangelical fellowships in the South and Hanoi Christian Fellowship in the North.

CHALLENGES FACING VIETNAMESE EVANGELICAL CHURCHES

There is no doubt about the impact of foreign missions on the formation of Vietnamese churches. On one hand, it is laudable for evangelicals to show their appreciation for the hearts and minds of the early Protestant missionaries in Vietnam. On the other hand, Vietnamese Christians cannot continually rely on foreign missions and the Euro-American theological heritage to form their own theology and practices. "Indigenous agency" is one of the necessary measures to ensure church growth.[15] The twenty-first century Vietnamese church, in obedience to the Holy Spirit, needs to adapt by observing continually "the signs of the times" in order to construct a theological framework that will make the church constantly relevant to the context.[16] While exploring these signs of the times, Vietnamese evangelicals must keep in mind that the process of making the church a "church" must be done in a way that brings people into being more like Christ, yet not less Vietnamese. Thus, the future of Vietnamese contextual ecclesiology, while learning from counterparts in East and Southeast Asia, depends on obedience to the prompting of the Holy Spirit while participating in the mission of the triune God working in every

---

15. Wilbert R. Shenk, ed. *Enlarging the Story: Perspectives on Writing World Christian History* (Maryknoll, NY: Orbis, 2002), xiv–xv.
16. Peter C. Phan, ed. *The Asian Synod: Texts and Commentaries* (Maryknoll, NY: Orbis, 2002), 301–2; Joseph Dinh Duc Dao, "The Christian Formation of the Laity and Lay Missionary Efforts in Asia," in *Proclaiming Jesus Christ in Asia Today*, ed. Pontificium Consilium Pro Laicis (Rome: Libreria Editrice Vaticana-Vatican Press, 2010), 105–6. Federation of Asian Bishops' Conferences Plenary Assembly, *FABC at Forty Years: Responding to the Challenges of Asia: A New Evangelization*, vol. 2014, FABC Plenary Assemblies Series 12/8 (Xuan Loc; Hồ Chí Minh City: FABC, 2012).

aspect of culture.¹⁷ Evangelicals can be seen as facing two particular challenges: namely ecumenical engagement and addressing of religiocultural realities.

First, ecumenically, evangelical churches should work together for the sake of Vietnamese Christians rather than for each church's own interests. Some collaborative initiatives, such as the Bible translation project pursued by the combined efforts of the Catholic Church and the evangelicals under the United Bible Society, were in place from 1974 to 1993.¹⁸ Evangelicals have also been in dialogue recently with the State of Vietnam.¹⁹ Furthermore in the past few years, some evangelical churches and theological educators have gathered for several discussions such as "Vietnamese Culture from an Evangelical Perspective."²⁰ Thus, it is very likely that there will be more dialogues in the near future among evangelicals, between the evangelicals and Catholics, and between the Christian church and the Vietnamese State.

Second, in participating in the mission of the triune God, evangelicals have an opportunity to be more serious in addressing the intertwined religiocultural realities of Vietnam. The future of the Catholic Church in Vietnam continues to be reshaped by the missiological approach of the Federation of Asian Bishops' Conferences (FABC), which is best described as *missio inter gentes* (mission *among* the nations) rather than traditional *missio ad gentes* (mission *to* the nations),²¹ and focused on various themes that were set at the 2012 Vietnam FABC Plenary Assembly, the "Mega-Trends in Asia and Ecclesial Realities."²² But the future of evangelicals is still unclear and perhaps complicated since they have not obligated themselves to speak in one theological voice or share in one ecumenical body. However, Vietnamese evangelicals may benefit from the work of their counterparts in East and Southeast Asia, considering in particular the "Guidelines for Doing Theologies in Asia."²³ The East and Southeast Asian contexts, for which this guideline was developed, share similarities with Vietnam. The guideline is designed to be used for constructing

---

17. See for instance Orrel N. Steinkamp, *The Holy Spirit in Vietnam* (Carol Stream, IL: Creation House, 1973).
18. See "About Us," Bible Society Vietnam, https://biblevietnam.org/en/.
19. Nguyễn, "Đạo Tin Lành ở Việt Nam."
20. See http://hoithanh.com/Home/tin-tuc/4151-hoi-thao-than-hoc-lan-thu-2.html, accessed December 11, 2014.
21. For an excellent study of the mission theology of the FABC's official documents, see Jonathan Y. Tan, "Missio Inter Gentes: Towards a New Paradigm in the Mission Theology of the Federation of Asian Bishops' Conferences (FABC)," *Mission Studies* 21, no. 1 (2004): 65–95.
22. Federation of Asian Bishops' Conferences Plenary Assembly, *FABC at Forty*, 7–13.
23. See Association for Theological Education in South East Asia, "Guidelines for Doing Theologies in Asia," *International Bulletin of Missionary Research* 32, no. 2 (2008): 77–80.

theological education and ultimately church theologies in the Asian context. The 2010 "Cape Town Commitment," in which many Vietnamese evangelical church leaders participated, continues to remind them to confess their faith as "For the Lord We Love" and of the call to action "For the Lord We Serve."[24]

Also evangelicals, and the ECVN in particular, need to revisit the motto that "*Tin Lành không tham gia chính trị*" (the evangelical church does not get involved in politics), which is often cited during political conflicts. Such an understanding of politics has been applied to the church for particular reasons, and yet it has paralyzed many Vietnamese evangelicals in responding to other needs of the people. Evangelical Christians in Vietnam must consider, for example, what it means for the church to engage people on issues of peace and reconciliation. Similarly, they must consider how they can be faithful to the truth while also seeking to maintain harmony when engaging particularly sensitive, potentially violent situations.

"The Cape Town Commitment" reminds us that "the task of the Christian church is to cooperate with God in shaping the society in light of the values of the coming kingdom of God, the kingdom of equality, justice, and peace."[25] The future of Vietnamese evangelicals should continue to be a "participatory ecclesiology"[26] – that is the "priesthood of all believers" in participation with the Trinity as opposed to mediative, "high church" ecclesiology (e.g. of the Catholic and Anglican churches) – at all levels as Miroslav Volf discussed in the charismatic structure of the church and follow the prompting of the Holy Spirit in the process of making the church an inwardly transformed agent that leads to an outward expression of faithful, contextual witness in Vietnam.[27]

REFERENCES

Anderson, David L. *The Columbia History of the Vietnam War*. New York: Columbia University Press, 2011.

---

24. "The Cape Town Commitment," Lausanne Movement (October 2011), www.lausanne.org/content/ctc/ctcommitment.
25. Veli-Matti Kärkkäinen, *Christ and Reconciliation: A Constructive Christian Theology for the Pluralistic World*, vol. 1 (Grand Rapids: Eerdmans, 2013), 377.
26. See Veli-Matti Kärkkäinen, *An Introduction to Ecclesiology: Ecumenical, Historical & Global Perspectives* (Downers Grove, IL: InterVarsity Press, 2002), 134–141.
27. Veli-Matti Kärkkäinen, "The Calling of the Whole People of God into Ministry: The Spirit, Church and Laity," *Studia Theologica* 54, no. 2 (2000): 153–155; See discussion on five principles of the charismatic structure of the church in Miroslav Volf, *After Our Likeness. The Church as the Image of the Trinity* (Grand Rapids: Eedmans, 1998), 222ff.

Association for Theological Education in South East Asia. "Guidelines for Doing Theologies in Asia." *International Bulletin of Missionary Research* 32, no. 2 (2008): 77–80.

Dao, Joseph Dinh Duc. "The Christian Formation of the Laity and Lay Missionary Efforts in Asia." In *Proclaiming Jesus Christ in Asia Today*, edited by Pontificium Consilium Pro Laicis. Rome: Libreria Editrice Vaticana-Vatican Press, 2010. http://www.laici.va/content/dam/laici/documenti/aamm/proclaiming-jesus-christ-in-asia/conferences/the-christian-formation-of-laity-and-lay-missionary-efforts.pdf.

Dutton, George E., Jayne S. Werner, and John K. Whitmore. *Sources of Vietnamese Tradition*. New York: Columbia University Press, 2012.

Federation of Asian Bishops' Conferences Plenary Assembly. *FABC at Forty Years: Responding to the Challenges of Asia: A New Evangelization*, vol. 2014. FABC Plenary Assemblies Series 12/8. Xuan Loc & Hồ Chí Minh City: FABC, 2012.

Huang, Po Ho. "Contextualization of Theological Education in South East Asia – Challenges and Responses: A Case Study of South East Asia Graduate School of Theology." IV International WOCATI Congress and Jubilee of the ETE of WCC (2008). https://www.oikoumene.org/sites/default/files/Document/WOCATI_2008_-_Lecture_of_Prof._Po_Ho__Taiwan__Contextualization_of_Theological_education.pdf.

Irvin, Dale T., and Scott W. Sunquist. *History of the World Christian Movement*. vol. II: Modern Christianity from 1954–1800. 2 vols. Maryknoll, NY: Orbis Books, 2012.

James, Violet B. "American Protestant Missions and the Vietnam War." PhD diss., University of Aberdeen, 1989. https://www.proquest.com/openview/55a0aabcf2c4a2700046ae0e086f2197/1?pq-origsite=gscholar&cbl=51922&diss=y.

Kärkkäinen, Veli-Matti. "The Calling of the Whole People of God into Ministry: The Spirit, Church and Laity." *Studia Theologica* 54, no. 2 (2000): 144–62.

———. *Christ and Reconciliation: A Constructive Christian Theology for the Pluralistic World*, vol. 1. Grand Rapids, MI: Eerdmans, 2013.

———. *An Introduction to Ecclesiology: Ecumenical, Historical & Global Perspectives*. Downers Grove, IL: InterVarsity Press, 2002.

Latourette, Kenneth Scott. *A History of Christianity*. New York: Harper & Row, 1953.

Lê, Hoàng Phu. "A Short History of the Evangelical Church of Viet Nam (1911–1965)." PhD diss., New York University, 1972. https://www.proquest.com/openview/09bf2bba9c4598d6f342afdf6fd26dc8/1?pq-origsite=gscholar&cbl=18750&diss=y.

Le, Vince. "The Pentecostal Movement in Vietnam." In *Global Renewal Christianity: Spirit-Empowered Movement Past, Present, and Future*. Vol. 1: Asia and Oceania, edited by Vinson Synan and Amos Yong, 181–95. Lake Mary, FL: Charisma House, 2016.

Martin, Luke S. *An Evaluation of a Generation of Mennonite Mission, Service and Peacemaking in Vietnam 1954–1976: Vietnam Study Project*. Akron, PA: Mennonite Central Committee, 1977.

Nguyễn, Cao Thanh. "Đạo Tin Lành ở Việt Nam từ 1975 đến nay, tư liệu và một số đánh giá ban đầu" [The evangelicalism in Vietnam from 1975 to the present, sources and initial comments]. Ban Tôn giáo Chính phủ. Ban Tôn giáo Chính Phủ - Cổng thông tin (btgcp.gov.vn).

Phan, Peter C. ed. *The Asian Synod: Texts and Commentaries*. Maryknoll, NY: Orbis, 2002.

Phan, Phát Huồn. *History of the Catholic Church in Việt Nam*, vol. 1, 1533–1960. Long Beach, CA: Cứu Thế Tùng Thư, 2000.

Ramsay, Jacob. *Mandarins and Martyrs: The Church and the Nguyen Dynasty in Early Nineteenth-Century Vietnam*. Stanford, CA: Stanford University Press, 2008.

Reimer, Reginald Eugene. "The Protestant Movement in Vietnam: Church Growth in Peace and War among the Ethnic Vietnamese." MA thesis, Fuller Theological Seminary, 1972.

———. *Vietnam's Christians: A Century of Growth in Adversity*. Pasadena, CA: William Carey Library, 2011.

Shenk, Wilbert R., ed. *Enlarging the Story: Perspectives on Writing World Christian History*. Maryknoll, NY: Orbis, 2002.

Steinkamp, Orrel N. *The Holy Spirit in Vietnam*. Carol Stream, IL: Creation House, 1973.

Tan, Jonathan Y. "Missio Inter Gentes: Towards a New Paradigm in the Mission Theology of the Federation of Asian Bishops' Conferences (FABC)." *Mission Studies* 21, no. 1 (2004): 65–95.

Tarling, Nicholas. *The Cambridge History of Southeast Asia*, vol. 2, The Nineteenth and Twentieth Centuries. New York: Cambridge University Press, 1992.

Tổng, Cục Thống Kê. "The 2009 Vietnam Population and Housing Census: Completed Results." Hanoi, Vietnam, 2009. https://www.gso.gov.vn/en/data-and-statistics/2019/03/the-2009-vietnam-population-and-housing-census-completed-results/.

PART II

A UNITY OF INTERWEAVING THEMES

CHAPTER 10

A COMPLEX SYSTEMS APPROACH TO PEDAGOGY AND RESEARCH FOR MULTICULTURAL CONTEXTS

Samuel K. Law

One of the first things I was introduced to when I moved to Singapore in 2016 from the United States was *Peranakan* culture. Drawing from the Malay word *anak* for "child," with appropriate prefixes and suffixes, *Peranakan* refers to Chinese people with mixed Chinese and Malay or Indonesian heritage. Later, I learned that there are also *Chittys* who are of mixed local and Indian heritage, *Kristangs* who are of mixed local and European heritage, and *Jawis* who are of mixed local and Arab heritage.

Unlike other cultures where those of mixed heritage are considered social outcasts, such as the children of American servicemen and local women in Southeast Asia, Peranakans are proud of their mixed heritage. Prominent citizens, such as Singapore's first Prime Minister, Lee Kuan Yew, are Peranakan. Indeed, the culture is celebrated with its own museum, and Peranakan food in Singapore is an Epicurean's delight.

As part of my acculturation to Singapore, I was also introduced to "Singlish," a patois reflective of Singapore's multicultural heritage. Singapore has four official languages: English, Mandarin Chinese, Malay, and Tamil. English is the *lingua franca* (common language) of education and business, and all school children must take one of the other languages as a second language. However, the "language of the street" is "Singlish," an amalgamation of these official languages.

These multicultural aspects of Singapore created dilemmas for me. I remember receiving my class roster at Singapore Bible College and finding it difficult to discern how to pronounce student names. For Chinese students, pronunciation required an understanding of both Pinying and Wade-Guiles romanization of names and guessing their dialect group. In the case of the Indian students, while many Singaporean Christians are Tamil, others are from Nagaland in Northeast India, and still others are Hindi from north India;

pronunciations also varied if the names were derived from Pali or Sanskrit. Finally, for Malaysians and Indonesians, it was difficult to ascertain their ethnicity as many had adopted a local name, either by force or to avoid racial prejudices. For example, Chinese with the surname "Lu" modified it to "Lukito" in Indonesian to blend in with the culture

I also created dilemmas for my students. In a course I was teaching on world religions, a student from Thailand said, "I realize I was never Buddhist!" She had always assumed she was Buddhist, for "to be Thai is to be Buddhist." By using the Western taxonomy of religions, it turned out that she was more a primal/folk ethnoreligionist with only a superficial veneer of formal Buddhist beliefs. Still, she was indeed a "Thai Buddhist" because the beliefs of most Thais are an amalgamation of Buddhism and Thai folk religion. But later this same student also informed me that the worldview of one of the books I had assigned, Kosuke Koyama's renowned *Water Buffalo Theology*, was now only limited to certain rural regions in Northern Thailand. In Bangkok and most urban centers, the worldviews were much more modern than what Koyama described.

I share these experiences to illustrate how understanding one another's cultural frameworks and resulting worldviews is becoming an increasingly complex endeavor, not only in Southeast Asia but throughout the world. My doctoral advisor, Michael Rynkiewich, repeatedly warned us against the dangers of reductionism and oversimplification. Even the assumption that a people group from a remote island in Indonesia were monocultural leads to incorrect conclusions.[1]

Southeast Asia is one of the most complex and diverse regions in the world. Singapore and Malaysia share similar historical experiences of colonialism and multiculturalism, yet critical inflection points have also resulted in their own divergent distinctives. For example to categorize the Vietnamese into one group would be to not only forget that the country was once politically divided into North and South Vietnam, but to also reveal one's ignorance that Vietnam's population is comprised not only of the Viet people group, but also a host of other tribal groups. Or to say that one will be working in Myanmar requires follow up questions to clarify with which of the eight major ethnic groups such as Bamar, Shan, Kayin, etc., and whether the work will be in an urban or rural setting. Or to say "I'm working in Indonesia" begs one to ask on which

---

1. Michael A. Rynkiewich, "The World in My Parish: Rethinking the Standard Missiological Model," *Missiology* 30 no. 3 (2002): 301–21.

of the six thousand inhabited islands in the archipelago, for that location will determine language, level of economic development, and whether the work is among a majority Muslim, Hindu, or Christian population.

These realities forced me to reevaluate how I taught my courses at Singapore Bible College and how I should carry out missiological research in Southeast Asia. I realized that much of what I had been trained in relied on traditional methods that were simple, linear, positivist, and reductionist and therefore woefully inadequate for both teaching and research in multicultural contexts. I had no framework by which to analyze even the multicultural context of a single diasporic, multicultural, Chinese church in North America. Because of this lack, I had to go outside of the seminary and the "Christian bubble" to find appropriate models for analysis.

Though my doctoral work was focused on applying complex adaptive systems (CAS), that is complex systems science (CSS) research methods for missiology – these terms will be defined below – it was more an academic exercise than an actual pedagogical approach. But by the end of my first semester, I realized that I needed to adapt my teaching to actively incorporate a CAS framework to help prepare my students for ministry and work in multicultural contexts.

Hence, the purpose of this chapter is twofold: first, to help us understand the shortcomings of the traditional missiological and intercultural studies frameworks taught in seminaries and Bible colleges during the late twentieth and early twenty-first centuries; and second, to introduce a CAS framework to equip missiology researchers and practitioners for the global, multicultural contexts of the twenty-first century. Numerous examples will be provided to help us understand how to integrate a CAS framework into missiological research and pedagogy. While this chapter focuses primarily on the social science aspect of missiology's interdisciplinary nature, a CSS framework has wide-ranging implications for theology and the historiography of missions. Some of these implications are mentioned in the conclusion.

Before we can understand why there are critical shortcomings in missiological research and pedagogy, it is important to understand these developments within the larger context of the social sciences, from which missiologists draw methods and models. Only when we recognize how far the social sciences have progressed since the late twentieth century can we realize how outdated missiological research and pedagogy have become.

THE SOCIAL SCIENCE TRANSITION TO COMPLEX SYSTEMS SCIENCE

Defining *traditional* science helps us understand why the shift to complex systems science (CSS) was so significant and why it is so critical for the twenty-first century. *Traditional* or *natural* science is defined as research approaches that are positivist, work from a static, reductionist, simple, and use a linear framework. Traditional science originated in the Enlightenment, and modern science development through viewing the universe mechanistically.[2] "Education in the natural sciences created the impression that linear and solvable systems were the only ones (or at least the only important ones) – an impression that came very close to being a prejudice of systems as regular and predictable as clockwork."[3]

In the same fashion, many of the social sciences – including missiology, as many research paradigms have been draw from anthropology and sociology – are grounded in what renowned sociologist Andrew Abbott calls *general linear reality*. This dominance of linear models led social scientists,

> to construe the social world in terms of a "general linear reality." This reality assumes (1) that the social world consists of fixed entities with variable attributes, (2) that cause cannot flow from "small" to "large" attributes/events, (3) that causal attributes have only one causal pattern at once, (4) that the sequence of events does not influence their outcome, (5) that the "careers" of entities are largely independent, and (6) that causal attributes are generally independent of each other.[4]

Consequently, complexity and change are generally dismissed in the formulations and representations of reality.[5]

But in the twenty-first century characterized by increasing globalization, urbanization, and global networking due to the acceleration of technological innovations, the avenues of change have been exponentially proliferating such that change has become more systemic, nearly continuous, and increasingly complex. Traditional science approaches increasingly prove inadequate to

---

2. Russ Marion, *The Edge of Organization: Chaos and Complexity Theories of Formal Social Systems* (Thousand Oaks, CA: Sage, 1998), xiii.
3. Stephen H. Kellert, *In the Wake of Chaos* (Chicago: University of Chicago Press, 1993), 134.
4. Andrew Abbott, "Transcending General Linear Reality," *Sociological Theory* 6, no 2 (Autumn 1998): 196.
5. Kellert, *Wake of Chaos*, 136.

represent realities in complex and fluid change. Abbott prophetically wrote at the turn of the century,

> The single most important challenge facing the empirical social sciences [including the field of missiology] in the next 50 years is the problem of finding patterns in such monumentally detailed data. And the blunt fact is that [the social sciences are] woefully unprepared to deal with this problem: We have neither the analytical tools nor the conceptual imagination necessary. Our stock-in-trade analytic methods were designed for investigating relations between small numbers of variables and are useless for large-scale pattern-recognition or, as we have pejoratively labeled it, data dredging. . . .
>
> Nor is it just a matter of ramping existing methods. We have to rethink data analysis from the ground up. . . . We have in the past simply ignored the vastness of data. We talk about "finding the right variable," but in reality we have always had thousands of variables to choose from and no sensible way to make the choice. There results in our literature the amusing spectacle of one indicator being used to indicate dozens of different things in dozens of different articles. In 50 years, people will view these activities the way we now view the people who paged through sheaves of two-way crosstabs.[6]

Hence, in response to the new complex realities of our contemporary era, researchers across many disciplines, in both the hard and soft sciences[7] and even the arts, have increasingly adapted CSS-framed approaches to collect, process, and analyze data in order to visualize and more accurately represent these new, increasingly fluid realities. This adaptation was made possible by the advent and now ubiquitous use of portable computing devices such as laptop computers and smartphones.

The essence of a CSS-framed paradigm shift is to expand the research boundaries of traditional scientific approaches to account for real-world, *in*

---

6. Andrew Abbott, "Reflections on the Future of Sociology," *Contemporary Sociology* 29, no. 2 (March 2000): 299.
7. Hard sciences generally refer to the natural sciences like physics, biology, astronomy, etc., while the soft sciences generally refer to the social sciences such as sociology, anthropology, psychology, etc.

vivo complexity, as opposed to laboratory, *in vitro* reductionism.[8] In other words, CSS-framed research does not replace traditional scientific approaches, but recognizes that such approaches are only valid in a single reality and a bounded context.

CSS-framed paradigms differ from traditional paradigms in three fundamental aspects that address the complex, changing nature of twenty-first century realities. First, CSS-framed paradigms are interdisciplinary to account for the expansion of the research horizon. Unlike what I was asked to do in my initial doctoral research proposal, which was to reduce my theoretical framework, CSS mandates an interdisciplinary, multidimensional framework to establish the systemic context of what is to be studied. Multiple theories and models are desired in the interdisciplinary nature of CSS, with the understanding that specific theories and models are not mutually exclusive, but each, more often than not, explains different realities of the same context.

Second, CSS-framed paradigms are dynamic to account for change. Boundaries are not fixed but are inherently "fuzzy"; that is, realities and contexts are recognized as being fluid and changing over time. Boundaries can expand, collapse, even disappear without the need to replace a model. Additionally, unlike traditional methods which are static and quickly become obsolete, the dynamic nature of CSS-framed approaches makes them inherently predictive. In other words CSS-framed approaches, because they must account for changing processes, enable research to be prescriptive, not just descriptive.

Third, CSS-framed paradigms require network definition and analysis to account for emergent relational contexts. They are not simple (dyadic) and linear (additive), but are networked and emergent. As such, CSS-framed paradigms

> offer a series of conceptual innovations to the concept of system that may be synthesized with selected traditions of social theory. . . . allow[ing] the transcendence of some of the old polarities of modernism and postmodernism. . . . The complexity notion of the system/environment distinction enables a more nimble conceptualization of systems and their interactions . . . It enables the rejection of the notion that parts must be nested within a whole, and thus a rejection of the reduction of one set of social

---

8. *In vivo* which means "in life" refers to the natural setting, while *in vitro* which means "in glass" refers to a laboratory setting.

relations of inequality into another. Complexity theory provides the theoretical flexibility to allow systematic analysis of social interconnections without the reductionism that so marred the old.[9]

According to renowned physicist Stephen Hawking, complexity systems is the science of the twenty-first century.[10] The adaptation to CSS first occurred in the hard sciences of mathematics and engineering,[11] but it is increasingly being applied to anthropology,[12] sociology,[13] and the study of religion.[14]

THE STATE OF MISSIOLOGY ADOPTION OF CSS

Unfortunately, the pace of adoption to CSS paradigms in missiology has lagged behind its hard and soft science siblings. This slow pace does not mean that missiologists do not recognize complexity and change. Rather, it is the ability to analyze complexity and change that are at issue as "Mission Studies is losing touch with the Social Sciences."[15]

---

9. Sylvia Walby, "Complexity Theory, Systems Theory, and Multiple Intersecting Social Inequalities," *Philosophy of the Social Sciences* 37 (2007): 466–67.
10. Ashutosh Jogalekar, "Stephen Hawking's advice for twenty-first century grads: Embrace complexity," *Scientific American*, April 23, 2013. https://blogs.scientificamerican.com/the-curious-wavefunction/stephen-hawkings-advice-for-twenty-first-century-grads-embrace-complexity/, accessed June 23, 2022.
11. Kellert, *Wake of Chaos*, 137.
12. Two following collections of case studies reveal the emergence of CSS approaches in anthropology: Mark S. Mosko and Frederick H. Damon, eds., *On the Order of Chaos: Social Anthropology and the Science of Chaos* (New York: Berhahn, 2005) and Stephen P. Reyna, *Connections: Brain, Mind and Culture in a Social Anthropology* (New York: Routledge, 2002).
13. Of all the social sciences, sociology has harnessed CSS approaches the most. The following works reveal both the origins, ubiquitous use, and continued adoption of CSS approaches in sociology: Raymond Eve, Sara Harsfall, and Mary E. Lee, eds., *Chaos, Complexity, and Sociology: Myths, Models, and Theories* (Thousand Oaks, CA: Sage, 1997); Marion, *Edge of Organization*; Stephen Johnson, *Emergence: The Connected Lives of Ants, Brains, Cities, and Software* (New York: Scribner, 1991); and Jeffrey Kluger, *Simplexity: Why Simple Things Become Complex (and How Complex Things Can be Made Simple)* (New York: Hyperion, 2008). The following provides examples of computational models in sociology: Uri Wilensky, "NetLogo" (1999), http://ccl.northwestern.edu/netlogo/. Center for Connected Learning and Computer-Based Modeling, Northwestern University, Evanston, IL.
14. Benjamin G. Purzycki, Omar S. Haque, and Richard Sosis, "Extending Evolutionary Accounts of Religion beyond the Mind: Religions as Adaptive Systems," in *The Evolution, Religion and Cognitive Science: Critical and Constructive Essays*, eds. Fraser Watts and Léon Turner (New York: Oxford University Press, 2014), 74–91; James V. Spickard, "Simulating Sects: A Computer Model of the Stark-Finke-Bainbridge-Iannaccone Theory of Religious Markets," paper presented at the Society for the Scientific Study of Religion: Kansas City, USA (October 2004).
15. Michael A. Rynkiewich, *Soul, Self, and Society: A Postmodern Anthropology for Mission in a Postcolonial World* (Eugene, OR: Cascade, 2011), 151.

At the dawn of CSS-framed paradigms in the 1980s, missiologist Paul Hiebert was most likely one of the first adopters. A follower of mathematical research trends,[16] Hiebert used the CSS-framework of centered set theory (from fuzzy logic)[17] to propose a new means of understanding conversion. Also, Hiebert's paradigm of critical realism draws heavily from the principles expressed in complexity theory and chaos theory. A CSS framework is nearly synonymous with "critical realism." For example, Hiebert writes,

> Critical realism offers an alternative that is more humble but also more proactive in its response to the human dilemma. . . . It affirms the presence of objective truth but recognizes that this is subjectively apprehended (68). . . . Critical realism draws on community hermeneutics, metacultural grids, and a broad range of rational analysis to test the validity of theories (74) . . . higher levels of knowledge involve logical processes – the mental abilities of forming abstract concepts, relating these in complex theories, and testing between competing theories. Critical realism accepts the validity of the formal algorithmic logic that is the basis for positivism and postpositivism, but it broadens the concept of rationality to include the other types of reasoning. It recognizes the role of metaphors, analogies, and other tropes in shaping human thought (86).[18]

But despite Hiebert's early adoption, the application of CSS-framed paradigms is sparse in mission studies. A recent review of three primary mission studies journals[19] from 2010 to 2014 gives evidence: *Missiology*, published by the American Society of Missiology; *Mission Studies*, published by the International Association for Mission Studies; and the *International Bulletin of Missionary Research*, published by the Overseas Ministries Study Center.[20] Of the 284 articles reviewed, *only two* applied metaphors, terminology, or

---

16. From a reflection on a personal conversation that Jay Moon had with Paul Hiebert at an Asbury Theological Seminary Graduate Seminar, Wilmore, KY, 10 February 2010.
17. Fuzzy logic is a variable process in contrast to discrete (yes/no or 0/1) logic.
18. Paul G. Hiebert, *Missiological Implications of Epistemological Shifts: Affirming Truth in a Modern/Postmodern World* (Harrisburg: Trinity Press International, 1999), 86.
19. These journals were selected from a review by Robert Priest of the most widely read mission studies journals to provide a representative spectrum of the field of missiology. See Robert Priest, "What is the Top Journal in the Discipline of Missiology" *Sapientia* (2012), https://henrycenter.tiu.edu/2012/03/topjournal/, accessed 23 June 2022.
20. Samuel K. Law, *Revitalizing Missions: Complex Systems Science Mazeways for Mission Theory amid Twenty-first Century Realities* (Lexington, KY: Emeth, 2016), 202.

research methodology directly from CSS.²¹ Of these, R. Daniel Shaw's article was the lone application of a complex systems science research paradigm; in the other article, Craig Van Gelder only used the complex systems-framed term, "adaptive leadership," as a call for the American Society of Missiology to respond to the changing realities of the twenty-first century.

The review of the three journals did find that most missiologists do recognize the complex nature of reality. Of the 284 articles reviewed, two-thirds or 189 articles were considered "complex" in nature even if the authors did not use CSS in their research methodology. Thus, this journal review confirms that, like their hard and soft science colleagues, missiologists were beginning to see complexity. Unfortunately, they had yet to adopt the metaphors, models, and methods that may enhance their ability to describe and analyze the complex, multicultural contexts of our twenty-first century realities.

One of the main reasons for not adopting CSS-framed paradigms could be that seminaries and Bible colleges now engage faculty from other seminaries and Bible colleges, compared to fifty years ago when they drew faculty from secular institutions. For example when Fuller Seminary, Trinity Evangelical Divinity School, and Asbury Theological Seminary started their schools of world missions, a significant portion of their faculty held degrees in anthropology, sociology, history, etc. from secular institutions.²² Thus much of what they taught was on the cutting edge of research theory. But as seminaries and Bible colleges began generating their own missiology or missions studies doctoral graduates, the level of competency diverged as the framework of missiology became fixed in the general linear reality of their post-World War II-trained faculty while the rest of the social sciences began the journey to adopt complex systems realities.²³ Rynkiewich shared that he used to take his seminary

---

21. Daniel R. Shaw, "Beyond Contextualization: Toward a Twenty-first Century Model for Enabling Mission," *International Review of Missionary Research* 34, no. 4 (2010): 208–14; Craig Van Gelder, "The future of the discipline of Missiology: Framing current realities and future possibilities," *Missiology* 42, no. 1 (2014): 39–56.
22. Michael A. Rynkiewich, "Do We Need a Postmodern Anthropology for Mission in a Postcolonial World?" *Mission Studies* 28 (2011): 152.
23. Dwight P. Baker, "Missiology as an Interested Discipline – and Where Is It Happening?" *International Bulletin of Missionary Research* 38, no. 1 (January 2014): 17–20; Wilbert R. Shenk, *Enlarging the Story: Perspectives on Writing World Christian History* (Maryknoll, NY: Orbis, 2002); Jonas A. Jorgensen, "Anthropology of Christianity and Missiology: Disciplinary Contexts, Converging Themes, and Future Tasks of Mission Studies," *Mission Studies* 28, no. 2 (2011): 186–208; Stefan Paas, "Post-Christian, Post-Christendom, and Post-Modern Europe: Towards the Interaction of Missiology and the Social Sciences," *Mission Studies* 28 (2011): 3–25; and Rynkiewich, "Do We Need."

students to anthropology and sociology conferences and that they could hold their own in dialogue with students from secular institutions. However, he laments that his students could not do so now.[24]

The failure of missiologists to incorporate CSS-frameworks can lead to devastating consequences since general linear reality can never adequately explain the complex, multicultural realities of the twenty-first century. Trying to do so would be akin to trying to use the equation of a straight line to define a Lorenz attractor, a three-dimensional, nonlinear but stable system which creates orbits around fixed points in space.[25] The failure of missiologists to incorporate appropriate frameworks to define the twenty-first century's complex, multicultural contexts creates a disconnect between mission strategy, policies, practice, and reality. As Dwight Baker concludes, "Missiology merits our close attention because the outcomes of good missiology, as of missiology poorly conceived, are so consequential . . . a missiology without internal development, one that resists change and growth, ossifies and fades into irrelevance."[26]

Hence, because of Southeast Asia's multicultural contexts, it is critical that any missiology pedagogy and research understand how to recognize and analyze the region's complex realities. Stefan Paas writes, "We cannot do without conceptual lenses. Without them it is impossible to understand what we see."[27] To rely on traditional methods would potentially do more harm than good.

A MISSIOLOGICAL COMPLEX ADAPTIVE SYSTEMS FRAMEWORK

This section seeks to provide a variety of examples of CAS pedagogy and how to frame research to account for multicultural complexity in missions studies. Here, because missiology deals with interaction across cultures, it is more appropriate to focus on a complex adaptive systems (CAS) framework within complex systems science (CSS). CAS can be understood as focusing on the agents in the complex system, their relationships and networks of the system, and the interactions between agents and the environment (context), rather than the context and environment (CSS).[28] Some of the examples are

---

24. Rynkiewich, "Do We Need," 163.
25. As an example, see https://en.wikipedia.org/wiki/Lorenz_system.
26. Baker, "Missiology," 17–18.
27. Paas, "Interaction," 5
28. See John H. Miller and Scott E. Page, *Complex Adaptive Systems: An Introduction to Computational Models of Social Life* (Princeton: Princeton University Press, 2007) which is an excellent primer on developing CAS models for social systems.

discussed in depth in a previous work,[29] and several others will be introduced here. Missiology is playing catch up, and there is already an abundance of texts to draw from in the social sciences. Missiology, especially those areas with origins in anthropology and sociology, can find a plethora of models and theories that can be readily adapted. If computational methods and models are to be pursued, missiologists also need not start from scratch, as they will find a host of developed programs and software by social scientists, and the vast majority of them are in the public domain (i.e. free).[30]

Any CAS framework requires three critical components: a systemic perspective, a historical trajectory, and an iterative process. A systemic perspective acknowledges that any context resides in a larger reality. The common missiological terms here are "holistic" and "integral." The historical trajectory considers the pathway to reaching a particular state and acknowledges that the state is not static, but is merely a single point in time of a larger story. To recognize historical trajectories is to acknowledge that all contexts are fluid and dynamic. Here, drawing from biblical studies, the common missiological term is "metanarrative." If so, then any proposed CAS model or theory must include a continuous iterative process to adapt to change. Common missiological processes are Paul Hiebert's "critical contextualization" and Gail Van Rheenan's "missional helix" (see definition and discussions below). These elements form the basis of CAS. Each of these components will be explored through the use of examples and a framework by which CAS can be integrated into pedagogy and research.

HOLISM: A SYSTEMS-BASED FRAMEWORK

Because of the increased complexities resulting from global networks and multicultural contexts, metaphors, models, and methodologies must now be framed into much larger complex realities to account for the host of different perspectives and worldviews. General linear reality is no longer adequate for twenty-first century *realities*.[31] It is crucial for missiologists to rapidly make the transition to a holistic CAS framework.

---

29. See Law, *Revitalizing Missions*.
30. See Wilensky, "Netlogo"; Cynthia Nikolai and Gregory Madey, "Tools of the Trade: A Survey of Various Agent Based Modeling Platforms," *Journal of Artificial Societies and Social Simulation* 12, no. 2 (2009): 1–2; and Steven F. Railsback and Volker Grimm, *Agent-Based and Individual-Based Modeling: A Practical Introduction* (Princeton: Princeton University Press, 2012).
31. Abbott, "General Linear Reality."

In fact, many missiologists have already voiced concerns over the lack of adequate foresight in missions due to the lack of both appropriate training and adequate models for the twenty-first century contexts.[32] Whether these deficiencies are called a "hole in the gospel"[33] or "when helping hurts"[34] or creating "split-level Christians,"[35] traditional, linear thinking and linear approaches have resulted in less than desired results and more often than not are accompanied with unanticipated and deleterious consequences.

These issues are why many missiologists have called for a more holistic approach to missions. For example, Bruce Bradshaw writes that the concept of holism

> seeks to restore the harmony of creation that reflects the glory of God. To this extent, distinctions between evangelism and development, or the physical and the spiritual aspects of creation are detrimental to our understanding and fulfilling the call of Christians to ministry. The visible, physical aspects of creation as well as the invisible, spiritual aspects must be harmonized to support the abundant life we have in Christ.[36]

Bradshaw terms this holism *shalom*, "the state of wholeness and holiness possessed by individuals and communities as they become part of the greater community of faith. . . . It does not see [things] as contradictory or competitive, but seeks their roles redemptively."[37] Rather than pursuing "peace" which can be linear and circumstantial, missiologists should pursue *shalom* as holistic and relationally integrative.

In the same vein, Tetsunao Yamamori uses the term "contextual holism."

> To effectively reach top-end and bottom-end population groups, "contextual holism" is necessary. This is a holistic ministry strategy that takes into account the needs, problems, opportunities, receptivity, and available resources of a particular area to determine

---

32. Jorgensen, "Anthropology"; Paas, "Post-Christian"; Rynkiewich, "Do We Need."
33. Richard Stearns, *The Hole in the Gospel: What Does God Expect of Us? The Answer That Changed My Life and Might Just Change the World* (Nashville: Thomas Nelson, 2010).
34. Steve Corbett and Brian Fikkert, *When Helping Hurts: How to Alleviate Poverty Without Hurting the Poor . . . and Yourself* (Chicago: Moody, 2014).
35. Paul G. Hiebert, R. Daniel Shaw, and Tite Tienou, *Understanding Folk Religion* (Grand Rapids, MI: Baker Books, 1999), 90.
36. Bruce Bradshaw, *Bridging the Gap: Evangelism, Development and Shalom* (Monrovia: MARC, 1993), 16.
37. Bradshaw, *Bridging the Gap*, 18.

A Complex Systems Approach to Pedagogy and Research

which aspect of holistic ministry should be underscored at any given time to fully accomplish God's work. The principle of contextual holism is sensible, practical, necessary and most important, biblical.[38]

Although complexity theory is not mentioned in the case studies in *Serving with the Poor in Africa*, CSS terminology, metaphors, and models are used throughout.

In another example, in his case study on community participation and holistic development, Samuel Voorhies writes about capacity building.

> Sustaining participation as well as project benefits will often depend on the community's capacity. Building the basic organizational capacity of communities must be an intentional part of the program strategy. This capacity should include the capability to forge links with other organizations, design and continue ways for local residents to participate in decision-making, collect information from local persons for decision-making and develop processes for solving problems and implementing decisions.[39]

Voorhies is essentially describing the identification and empowerment of positive deviants and enabling network resonance in order to sustain an organization within a CAS framework.

Interestingly, a "chaos-vision paradigm" is mentioned in Kweku Hutchful's case study. But instead of referring to CSS, he is referring to Genesis 1:2.

> While it is important to start with a clear description and understanding of chaos confronting communities, it is even more important that there is a crossover from chaos to vision, from a problem focus to a solution focus. Many communities in Africa are stuck in the problem analysis stage, needing help to move on to creative formulations of solutions.
>
> Holistic ministries should demonstrate the processes of creative thinking, envisioning and crossing over from problem to solution, and these ministries should train community leaders to

---

38. Tetsunao Yamamori, "Introduction," in *Serving with the Poor in Africa: Cases in Holistic Ministry*, eds. Tetsunao Yamamori, Bryant L. Myers, Kwame Bediako, and Larry Reed (Monrovia: MARC, 1996), 8.
39. Samuel J. Voorhies, "Community participation and holistic development," in *Serving with the Poor in Africa: Cases in Holistic Ministry*, eds. Tetsunao Yamamori, Bryant L. Myers, Kwame Bediako, and Larry Reed (Monrovia: MARC, 1996), 134.

do that for themselves. This will ensure a future and hope for the communities when they are finally left on their own to implement their own solutions to the problems confronting them.[40]

The similarities are not coincidental but are manifestations of concurrently emerging processes. This transition to CSS frameworks does not mean that traditional approaches are invalid; rather, as the boundaries of reality expand, traditional approaches are inadequate in the ever increasing number and diversity of realities. That is, "we need to develop both the ability to recognize the extent to which our mental models are correct and the ability to use different models simultaneously. This is not a case about making value judgements about simplicity or complexity, but instead to see the world as it really is: to have new eyes."[41]

One way to incorporate these multiple dimensionalities is through the use of a spreadsheet. Rather than a linear cause-and-effect dyad, a spreadsheet reminds the missiologist to capture all of the relationships that can influence the object of study.

One of the best examples is from Jean-Paul Heldt.[42]

	Holistic Mission			
	Social Gospel[43]			Evangelism
	Physical	Mental	Social	Spiritual
Individual				
Family				
Community				
Nation(s)				

---

40. Kweku Hutchful, "A biblical framework for management practice," in *Serving with the Poor in Africa: Cases in Holistic Ministry*, eds. Tetsunao Yamamori, Bryant L. Myers, Kwame Bediako, and Larry Reed (Monrovia: MARC, 1996), 152.
41. Ben Ramalingam, *Aid on the Edge of Chaos: Rethinking International Cooperation in a Complex World* (London: Oxford University Press, 2014), 234.
42. Adapted from Jean-Paul Heldt, "Revisiting the 'Whole Gospel': Toward a Biblical Model of Holistic Mission in the 21st Century," *Missiology* 32, no. 2 (April 2004): 161.
43. For further description of the term "social gospel" see Heldt who writes: "the 'social gospel' encompasses three distinct and yet fully integrated dimensions of human life: the physical, the mental (or economic) and the social (and political)." Heldt, "Revisiting the 'Whole Gospel'", 164.

A Complex Systems Approach to Pedagogy and Research

The chart requires one to appreciate the holistic nature of the gospel through considering its multiple dimensions. I have used this chart in several classes, and it trains students to think within a CAS framework. They realize that if they alter one parameter, the change inevitably impacts and changes relationships with other parameters. Students must then work until they are able to find a balanced solution across the entire grid. The use of a spreadsheet is perhaps the best way to incorporate a CSS framework in pedagogy and in designing research projects.

INCORPORATING THE TRAJECTORY OF THE METANARRATIVE

A second critical element of a CSS framework is the necessity to understand the concept of trajectories, which imply that change is actively occurring. In the twenty-first century, change has been continuous and multi-faceted. Sociologists responded at the end of the twentieth century by introducing new theories, models, and methods of analysis that are dynamic in nature. Andrew Abbott writes,

> A quiet revolution is underway in social science. We are turning from units to context, from attributes to connections, from causes to events. The change has many antecedents: the exhaustion of our old paradigm, our inherent desire for change, the new powers of computers. It also has many consequences: new areas for empirical work, new methodologies, rediscovery of important old theories.[44]

Any static model is doomed to fail. One may find an answer to a single problem for a particular context, but as a consequence, one fails to understand how the solution inevitably creates unintended consequences as time progresses and the context changes.

Unfortunately, much of missiological theory remains trapped in general linear reality.[45] Like being rear-ended when stopping on a highway, this theory oftentimes results in a cascade of compounding consequences. Andrew Walls argues that this thinking was characteristic of twentieth-century missions, particularly American mission efforts. He writes, "Here we see again

---

44. Andrew Abbott, "Sequence Analysis: New Methods for Old Ideas," *Annual Review of Sociology* 21 (1995): 93.
45. See Rynkiewich, "Do We Need"; Jorgensen, "Anthropology"; Paas, "Post-Christian"; and Baker, "Missiology."

the characteristically American problem-solving approach at work: identify the problem, apply the right tools, and a solution will appear. Then move on to the next problem."[46] Ben Ramalingam agrees, writing that

> As a result of the dominance of single-loop learning, which has only been reinforced by the formal movement, I would argue that an epidemic of 'bestpracticitis.' . . . The symptoms include the following: organizations spend all their time looking for the single right answer rather than diverse solutions; people spend more time trying to do things right than doing the right things; there is much more focus on knowledge transfer than on knowledge creation; the whole enterprise is underpinned by a search for efficiency and cost-based value-for-money measures that assume that what is known is needed (and should be cheap, although that is another issue).[47]

Looking at aid agencies, Ramalingam offers numerous case studies of how short-sighted practices only compounded problems, such as efforts to eradicate malaria in the 1950s with pesticides have now in the twenty-first century resulted in pesticide-resistant mosquitoes furthering the spread of malaria.[48] Ramalingam reaches the same conclusions as Corbett and Fikkert[49] – helping can hurt.

In another example, the failure to include the concept of trajectory has caused missiologists to fail in properly understanding guilt and shame because they lacked the framework to incorporate the temporal nature of personhood and identity. Christopher Flanders writes "The definition present in most contemporary missiological literature rests upon the unfortunate perpetuation of deficient notions regarding shame and guilt."[50]

As such, missions studies pedagogy and research design must include a framework that takes into account trajectories, both what happened in the past, what is transpiring in the present, and how it may evolve in the future. Jorgensen writes,

---

46. Andrew Walls, *The Missionary Movement in Christian History* (Maryknoll, NY: Orbis, 1996), 234.
47. Ramalingam, *Aid on the Edge*, 26.
48. Ramalingam, 30.
49. Corbett and Fikkert, *When Helping Hurts*.
50. Christopher L. Flanders, *About Face: Reorienting Thai Face for Soteriology and Mission* (Eugene, OR: Pickwick, 2016), 70.

A Complex Systems Approach to Pedagogy and Research

The way in which Christianity is studied depends not only on the observer and his or her categories and concepts, but also upon the time in which the study is done, because the larger theoretical background on which Christianity is studied shifts over time. . . . Christianity as well as our ways of studying it changes; that is, our categories as well as the phenomenon under study changes *simultaneously*.[51]

In order to account for trajectory, I again use a spreadsheet that factors in the longitudinal aspects of a certain context. The following chart is an example:

• Geographic • Social • Cultural • Metanarrative	Past	Present	Future
Macro – Global			
Meso – Regional		John 4: Jesus and the Samaritan Woman	
Micro – Local			

In a study using this chart, the geographic, social, cultural, and metanarrative elements would each be on separate sheets.

When studying the story of Jesus and the Samaritan woman in John 4, students fill in the chart from the perspective of Jesus, the Samaritan woman, and John as author and disciple, then chart the trajectory of each to understand the context of the John 4 narrative. This exercise teaches students how the past can impact the present and how transformation can impact the future.

If adding an additional level of complexity is desired, additional sheets may be added. Both Microsoft Excel and Google Sheets can rotate the axes so that we may remain on one sheet or go across sheets. Students not only come to understand the trajectory over time, but also how different dimensions

---

51. Jorgensen, "Anthropology," 205, emphasis original.

change and can interact with one another. Similarly, designing a research or missions project in this fashion forces researchers and practitioners to account for both longitudinal and latitudinal factors. The following chart explores the interaction of Singaporean short-term missions in Indonesia and is one of four sheets; the one shown represents the latitudinal and longitudinal sociopolitical aspects that must be considered to understand, evaluate, and develop an appropriate framework for discussion.

Systems Map

• Geographic • Social • Cultural • Metanarrative	**Past**	**Present**	**Future**
Macro – Global	Colonialism	Geopolitical and economic trajectories	Shifting global alliances
Meso – Regional	Early missionary work in both regions	**Interaction of Singaporean short-term missions in Indonesia**	Potential consequences on relationship
Micro – Local	Singaporean and Indonesian people groups	Singaporean and Indonesian cultural and sociological audit	Potential consequences on Indonesian society and culture

MISSIOLOGY AS TACIT KNOWLEDGE AND CONTEXTUALIZING

Following the dynamic analysis of contexts, the third aspect that any missiology pedagogy or research design should include is an iterative process. An iterative process intrinsically implies that models and theories are not static but must adapt to changing contexts. This process prevents the assumption that a case is closed when the "problem" is solved; in other words, it is a cure for Ramalingam's "bestpracticitis." An iterative process recognizes that change will occur and that some time down the road, we must revisit and adjust to the changes in context.

Moreover, in using the iterative process we must consider not just one dimension but understand the relationships and interactions across several dimensions, which is why any good missiology must be interdisciplinary in nature. Two examples of iterative processes are Paul Hiebert's critical contextualization and Gailyn Van Rheenan's missional helix.

Paul Hiebert developed the process of critical contextualization because he recognized that traditional, modern contextualization is a unidirectional, static-state process that often fails to account for the multiple realities of cross-cultural contexts. More importantly, he realized the dynamic nature of contextualization and that developing a process that incorporates growth is essential. Hiebert writes,

> From a theological point of view, contextualization is always an ongoing process. It is not a static state we can attain. This does not mean we can ignore the great insights of the church down through history. We have much to learn from the theological debates and resolutions of the past. But we must test theologies against the Scriptures and make them our own. And we must extend our theology to answer questions not yet asked by the churches in the west – questions that arise in new cultural settings. Theologizing must be a living, growing experience, and the use of critical contextualization in dealing with the problems faced in mission settings, and in dealing with different areas of our own lives can help make it so.[52]

Critical contextualization requires that different stakeholders come to Scripture with their different cultural perspectives and engage in dialogue to discern how to contextualize biblical principles into cultural practices. Its process is not a single cycle but an incorporation of continuous iterations that gradually expand the circle of stakeholders while incorporating growth factors and cultural shifts.

In similar fashion, the missional helix was proposed by Gailyn Van Rheenan in his study of the church growth movement. Van Rheenan writes, "The four limitations of Church Growth that we have discussed – anthropocentric focus, pragmatics and the segmentation of theology and praxis, theological level of inquiry, and focus on growth – suggest the need for a

---

52. Paul G. Hiebert, "Critical Contextualization," *Missiology* 12, no. 3 (July 1984): 295.

new model of missions."[53] In response, the *"missional helix* visualizes such an 'interdisciplinary and interactive' approach to the practice of ministry and provides a corrective to traditional Church Growth perspectives."[54]

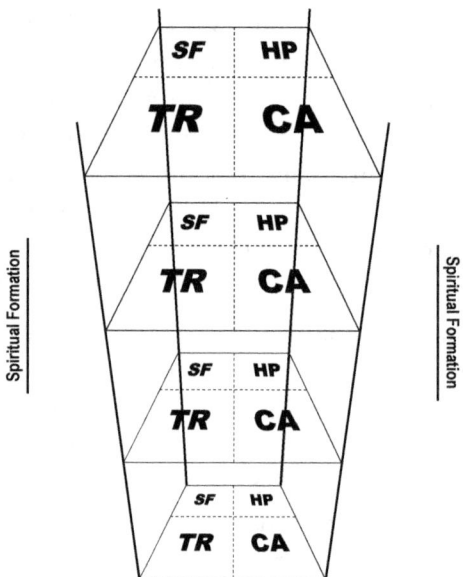

Figure 2: The Missional Helix[55]

Van Rheenan argues that

> Church Growth determines effective practice and then seeks to validate this practice by the use of Scripture. The movement emphasizes growth rather than faithful proclamation of the gospel and faithful living of the gospel. A missional model, on the other hand, begins with theological reflection (TR), while taking seriously [historical perspective (HP),] cultural analysis (CA) and strategy formation (SF).[56]

---

53. Gail Van Rheenen, "The Reformist View," in *Evaluating Church Growth: Five Views (Counter Points: Church Life)*, eds. Gary L. McIntosh, Elmer Towns, and Craig Van Gelder (Grand Rapids, MI: Zondervan, 2010), 186.
54. Van Rheenen, "Reformist View," 186.
55. Adapted from Van Rheenen, 186.
56. Van Rheenen, 189.

A Complex Systems Approach to Pedagogy and Research

Unlike traditional church growth theory, which tends to be linear, discrete, and static, only requiring scriptural validation, Van Rheenan's proposal is a fluid, dynamic, and most importantly, an iterative process. The process is continuous and is a spiral because all elements must interact with one and all the other elements and is also cyclical with each cycle building on the previous one.

In CAS literature, we find a similar metaphor in the Nonaka SECI (socialization, externalization, consolidation, internationalization) model of knowledge creation.[57] This CAS-framed model was developed for Japanese companies to bring the entire organization into the innovation process. The SECI model is also helical with multiple iterations in response to continuously changing market environments.

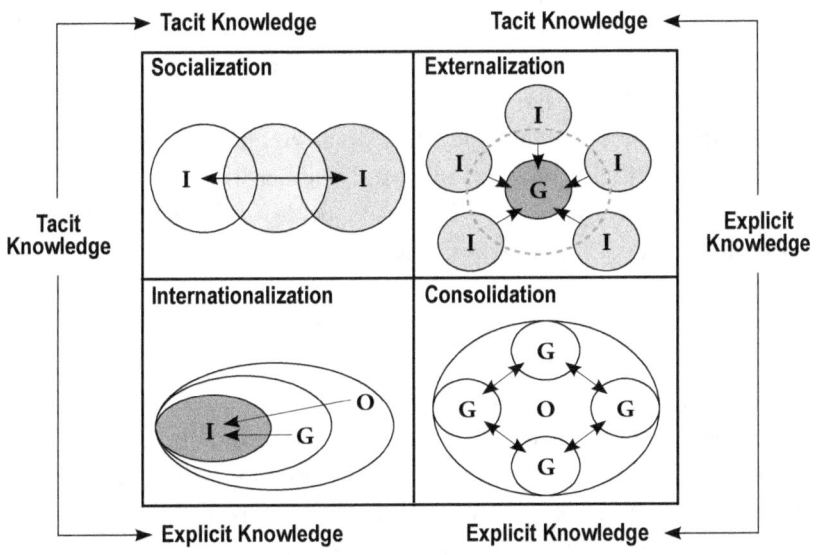

Figure 3: Nonaka's SECI Model of Knowledge Creation[58]

Here tacit knowledge derived through the more abstract avenues of personal experience and relationships is similar to Van Rheenan's theological reflection and cultural analysis, and explicit knowledge derived through tangible

---

57. Andrzej P. Wierzbicki and Yoshiteru Nakamori, *Creative Space: Models of Creative Processes for the Knowledge Civilization Age* (New York: Springer, 2006), 69.
58. Adapted from: Wierzbicki and Nakamori, *Creative Space*, 69.

communication avenues is similar to Van Rheenan's historical perspective and strategy formation.

However, Nonaka took the metaphor further by defining the contexts in which the processes should occur, whether they be individual (I), small group (G), or the entire organization. Nonaka's model reflects a combination of both Hiebert's critical contextualization groups and Van Rheenan's missional helix. For many missiological research studies, this approach is crucial in contexts that are relatively complex. Reaching this level of participatory integration would minimize the reductionist bias, empower the researcher to step back and consider the system as an integrated whole, and establish an iterative process that can respond to changes in the context.

One of the ways I teach the iterative process is by having students create a spreadsheet for a semester project and add to it on a regular basis. Students first create a skeletal framework, then "flesh it out" as they collect data throughout the semester. Since the course is one-on-one mentorship, as supervisor I help them to consider issues that they did not consider initially. Rather than just turning in a final assignment, they develop an iterative process of reflection and a communal dialogue with "another," whether it be for "critical contextualization" or "missional helix." Thus, students learn the necessity of seeking out a dialogue partner with whom they can engage to iteratively refine and modify their work.

CONCLUSION

We have seen that in the twenty-first century in Southeast Asia, traditional methodologies have reached their limits of validity and usefulness, thus requiring a paradigm shift as realities are integrally interconnected across multiple cultures and contexts. This need to shift is why so many fields have transitioned to complex systems science. Missiologists must also join this paradigm shift in order to navigate these new realities well.

This paradigm shift to complexity systems science, specifically a complex adaptive systems framework, in missiological analysis and pedagogy is even more critically necessary now as many mission agencies seek new mazeways, that is to say a revitalization or resynthesis of existing approaches, for the twenty-first century contexts such as business missions, development models, and the increasing use of short-term missions in place of career missionaries. Furthermore, as the COVID-19 pandemic has shown, flexibility and foresight in responding to rapid change is a matter of life and death. The concern is that without adequate supporting terminology, metaphors, models, and methodologies for analyses of networked, rapidly changing, complex systems, missiologists will be unprepared and unable to provide the necessary guidance for success, and worse, provide short-sighted, inaccurate, and detrimental guidance.

Further, beyond the revitalization, development, and aid, the application of CSS to a host of missiological issues holds great potential. Mission theory, ecclesiology, and mission theology and history all abound with a plethora of topics that can find greater illumination or solutions through CSS. Some that come to mind are the hermeneutical circle in biblical interpretation; resolving the polarities of the global and local, movement and institution, centripetal and centrifugal, evangelism and social justice, and church growth and the missional church; the art of preaching between two worlds; Bevans and Schroeder's constants and contexts; missions from everywhere to everywhere formed around multiple centers; inter-religious dialogue; the quest to better understand the C1–C6 contextualization spectrum; and explaining the Trinity as three-in-one. Ready-made parallels can be found in complex systems science. Hence, whether it be new theological models of the Trinity or missional models of *missio Dei* using attractors; historiographic integration of world Christianities using chaos theory; interreligious dialogue using dimensional integration; or reexamining conversion as a resonant interaction process, complex systems science can offer new insights, new questions, and new maze ways for twenty-first century contexts.

Case Study and Exercises

1. As an exercise, fill in the chart for the encounter of Jesus and the Samaritan woman in John 4.
2. Take any of the chapters in this book and choose one topic that is of interest to you. Use the chart and develop a systems map that includes the longitudinal (historical) and latitudinal aspects.
3. Take any of the issues raised in Kiem-Kiok Kwa's chapter and use Jean Paul Heldt's chart to develop a holistic response.

REFERENCES

Abbott, Andrew. "Reflections on the Future of Sociology." *Contemporary Sociology* 29, no. 2 (March 2000): 296–300.

———. "Sequence Analysis: New Methods for Old Ideas." *Annual Review of Sociology* 21 (1995): 93–113.

———. "Transcending General Linear Reality." *Sociological Theory* 6, no. 2 (Autumn 1998): 169–86.

Baker, Dwight P. "Missiology as an Interested Discipline – and Where Is It Happening?" *International Bulletin of Missionary Research* 38, no. 1 (January 2014): 17–20.

Bradshaw, Bruce. *Bridging the Gap: Evangelism, Development and* Shalom. Monrovia: MARC, 1993.

Corbett, Steve, and Brian Fikkert. *When Helping Hurts: How to Alleviate Poverty Without Hurting the Poor . . . and Yourself.* Chicago: Moody, 2014.

Eve, Raymond A., Sara Harsfall, and Mary E. Lee, eds. *Chaos, Complexity, and Sociology: Myths, Models, and Theories.* Thousand Oaks, CA: Sage, 1997.

Flanders, Christopher L. *About Face: Reorienting Thai Face for Soteriology and Mission.* Eugene, OR: Pickwick, 2016.

Goldstein, Jeffrey, James K. Hazy, and Benyamin B. Lichtenstein. *Complexity and the Nexus of Leadership: Leveraging Nonlinear Science to Create Ecologies of Innovation.* New York: Palgrave Macmillan, 2010.

Heldt, Jean-Paul. "Revisiting the 'Whole Gospel': Toward a Biblical Model of Holistic Mission in the 21st Century." *Missiology* 32, no. 2 (April 2004): 149–72.

Hiebert, Paul G. "Critical Contextualization." *Missiology* 12, no. 3 (July 1984): 287–96.

———. *Missiological Implications of Epistemological Shifts: Affirming Truth in a Modern/Postmodern World.* Harrisburg: Trinity Press International, 1999.

Hiebert, Paul G., R. Daniel Shaw, and Tite Tienou. *Understanding Folk Religion.* Grand Rapids, MI: Baker Books, 1999.

Hutchful, Kweku. "A biblical framework for management practice." In *Serving with the Poor in Africa: Cases in Holistic Ministry,* edited by Tetsunao Yamamori, Bryant L. Myers, Kwame Bediako, and Larry Reed, 149–68. Monrovia: MARC, 1996.

Jogalekar, Ashutush. "Stephen Hawking's advice for twenty-first century grads: Embrace complexity." *Scientific American*, April 23, 2013. https://blogs.scientificamerican.com/the-curious-wavefunction/stephen-hawkings-advice-for-twenty-first-century-grads-embrace-complexity/, accessed June 23, 2022.

Johnson, Stephen. *Emergence: The Connected Lives of Ants, Brains, Cities, and Software.* New York: Scribner, 1991.

Jorgensen, Jonas A. "Anthropology of Christianity and Missiology: Disciplinary Contexts, Converging Themes, and Future Tasks of Mission Studies." *Mission Studies* 28, no. 2 (2011): 186–208.

Kellert, Stephen H. *In the Wake of Chaos*. Chicago: University of Chicago Press, 1993.

Kluger, Jeffrey. *Simplexity: Why Simple Things Become Complex (and How Complex Things Can be Made Simple)*. New York: Hyperion, 2008.

Law, Samuel K. *Revitalizing Missions: Complex Systems Science Mazeways for Mission Theory amid Twenty-first Century Realities*. Lexington: Emeth, 2016.

Marion, Russ. *The Edge of Organization: Chaos and Complexity Theories of Formal Social Systems*. Thousand Oaks, CA: Sage, 1998.

Miller, John H., and Scott E. Page. *Complex Adaptive Systems: An Introduction to Computational Models of Social Life*. Princeton: Princeton University Press, 2007.

Mosko, Mark S., and Frederick H. Damon, eds. *On the Order of Chaos: Social Anthropology and the Science of Chaos*. New York: Berhahn, 2005.

Nikolai, Cynthia, and Gregory Madey. "Tools of the Trade: A Survey of Various Agent Based Modeling Platforms." *Journal of Artificial Societies and Social Simulation* 12, no. 2 (2009): 1–2.

Paas, Stefan. "Post-Christian, Post-Christendom, and Post-Modern Europe: Towards the Interaction of Missiology and the Social Sciences." *Mission Studies* 28 (2011): 3–25.

Priest, Robert J. "What is the Top Journal in the Discipline of Missiology." *Sapientia* (2012), https://henrycenter.tiu.edu/2012/03/topjournal/, accessed 23 June 2022.

Purzycki, Benjamin G., Omar S. Haque, and Richard Sosis. "Extending Evolutionary Accounts of Religion beyond the Mind: Religions as Adaptive Systems." In *The Evolution, Religion and Cognitive Science: Critical and Constructive Essays*, edited by Fraser Watts and Léon Turner, 74–91. New York: Oxford University Press, 2014.

Ramalingam, Ben. *Aid on the Edge of Chaos: Rethinking International Cooperation in a Complex World*. London: Oxford University Press, 2014.

Reyna, Stephen P. *Connections: Brain, Mind and Culture in a Social Anthropology*. New York: Routledge, 2002.

Rynkiewich, Michael A. "Do We Need a Postmodern Anthropology for Mission in a Postcolonial World?" *Mission Studies* 28 (2011): 151–69.

———. "Models and Myths of Revitalization: Wallace's Theory a Half Century On." In *Interpretive Trends in Christian Revitalization for the Early Twenty First Century*, edited by J. Steven O'Malley, 39–45. Lexington: Emeth, 2011.

———. *Soul, Self, and Society: A Postmodern Anthropology for Mission in a Postcolonial World*. Eugene: Cascade, 2011.

———. "The World in My Parish: Rethinking the Standard Missiological Model." *Missiology* 30, no. 3 (2002): 301–21.

Shaw, R. Daniel. "Beyond Contextualization: Toward a Twenty-first Century Model for Enabling Mission." *International Review of Missionary Research* 34, no. 4 (2010): 208–14.

Shenk, Wilbert R. *Enlarging the Story: Perspectives on Writing World Christian History*. Maryknoll: Orbis, 2002.

Spickard, James V. "Simulating Sects: A Computer Model of the Stark-Finke-Bainbridge-Iannoccone Theory of Religious Markets." Paper presented at the Society for the Scientific Study of Religion, Kansas City, October 2004. https://www.academia.edu/17211999/_Simulating_Sects_A_Computer_Simulation_of_the_Stark_Finke_Bainbridge_Iannaccone_Theory_of_Religious_Markets_Pp_131_152_in_Religion_in_Late_Modernity_Essays_in_Honor_of_P%C3%A5l_Repstad_edited_by_Inger_Furseth_and_Paul_Leer_Salveson_Trondheim_Tapir_Academic_Press_2007, accessed 23 June 2022.

Stearns, Richard. *The Hole in the Gospel: What Does God Expect of Us? The Answer That Changed My Life and Might Just Change the World*. Nashville: Thomas Nelson, 2010.

Van Gelder, Craig. "The future of the discipline of Missiology: Framing current realities and future possibilities." *Missiology* 42, no. 1 (2014): 39–56.

Van Rheenen, Gail. "The Reformist View." In *Evaluating Church Growth: Five Views*, edited by Gary L. McIntosh, Elmer Towns, and Craig Van Gelder, 186–230. Grand Rapids, MI: Zondervan, 2010.

Voorhies, Samuel J. "Community participation and holistic development." In *Serving with the Poor in Africa: Cases in Holistic Ministry*, edited by Tetsunao Yamamori, Bryant L. Myers, Kwame Bediako, and Larry Reed, 123–148. Monrovia: MARC, 1996.

Walby, Sylvia. "Complexity Theory, Systems Theory, and Multiple Intersecting Social Inequalities." *Philosophy of the Social Sciences* 37 (2007): 449–70.

Waldrop, Mitchell M. *Complexity: The Emerging Science at the Edge of Order and Chaos*. New York: Simon and Schuster, 1992.

Walls, Andrew. *The Missionary Movement in Christian History*. Maryknoll, NY: Orbis, 1996.

Wierzbicki, Andrzej P., and Yoshiteru Nakamori. *Creative Space: Models of Creative Processes for the Knowledge Civilization Age*. New York: Springer 2006.

Wilensky, Uri. "NetLogo." (1999) http://ccl.northwestern.edu/netlogo/. Center for Connected Learning and Computer-Based Modeling, Northwestern University, Evanston, IL.

Yamamori, Tetsunao. "Introduction." In *Serving with the Poor in Africa: Cases in Holistic Ministry*, edited by Tetsunao Yamamori, Bryant L. Myers, Kwame Bediako, and Larry Reed, 1–14. Monrovia: MARC, 1996.

CHAPTER 11
GLOCAL COMPLEXITIES

John Cheong

The term "glocal" is a combination of the words "global" and "local" and is derived from the study and phenomenon of globalization. To understand the meaning of glocal and glocalization requires us to first examine the character of globalization. As we survey the broader trends of globalization, we shall see that they play out in the local Southeast Asian contexts, thus bringing about the glocalization impacts and influences. This interplay between the global and the local raises challenges for Christian mission in the contexts of Southeast Asia. As we survey these global and glocal trends, we seek to provide guidance for critical thinking and wise service in today's world.

The chapter is divided into five sections. First, we examine the processes of globalization and see how modernization, human migration, and global networks drive the phenomenon. Second, we ask what glocalization is, a term which describes the relationship or interaction between global and local processes. Third, we see how globalization affects our perception and experience of time, space, distance, and types of flows or movements of people and things in today's world. Fourth, we consider the scale (or size) of globalization and the sets of actors involved in influencing those scales. In this section we also survey actors such as the nation-state, non-state (i.e. NGOs and other institutions), the city, and the internet. We then conclude with some thoughts on how glocalization helps but also hinders Christian missions in Southeast Asia.

Globalization is a complex phenomenon because it involves many sets of programs, processes, projects and people that interrelate in complex fashions.[1] Globalization requires us to imagine how these features relate to space

---

[1]. Key authors who have defined globalization are Immanuel Wallerstein, Anthony Giddens, Roland Robertson, Saskia Sassen, Arjun Apparudai, Michael Kearney, Ulf Hannerz, Jan Nederveen Pieterse, Ulrich Beck, Zygmunt Bauman, and Malcolm Waters. However, Appadurai, Hannerz, Kearney, Nederveen Pieterse (all anthropologists), Giddens, Robertson, and Sassen (all sociologists) were chosen for this article because they are most frequently cited in authoritative discussions.

and time in particular ways. Jan Nederveen Pieterse summarizes them in the following chart.[2]

Table 1: The Study of Globalization across Disciplines

Disciplines	Agency, domain	Keywords
Economics	MNCs, banks, technologies	Global corporation, world product, global capitalism, new economy, dot.com
Cultural studies	Mass media, international communication technology, advertising, consumption	Global village, CNN world, McDonaldization, hybridization
Political science, international relations	Internationalization of the state, social movements, international NGOs	Competitor states, post-international politics, global civil society
Geography	Space and place, relativization of distance	Global-local dialectics
Sociology	Modernity	Capitalism, nation states, industrialization
Philosophy	Global reflexivity	Planetary ethics, universal morality
Political economy	Capitalism	World market
History, anthropology	Cross-cultural trade, technologies, world religions, evolution	Global flows, global ecumene, widening scale of cooperation

To study global complexities, it is easier to begin by understanding people and their role in relation to it because globalization is not just about economics or giant institutions – it affects people and is also shaped by them.[3] Herein the glocal dynamics.

If globalization is examined as a *process*, we see how it drives people and society into ever-growing worldwide interconnectedness. For example, when migrants move from their home country to another, *how* do they stay in touch with their family? Do they call, e-mail, WhatsApp, or travel physically by bus,

---

2. Jan Nederveen Pieterse, *Globalization and Culture: Global Mélange*, 2nd ed. (Lanham, MD: Rowan and Littlefield, 2009), 16.
3. Robert J. Holton, *Global Networks* (New York: Palgrave Macmillan, 2008).

rail, or air? How do we know which of these options they prefer, and how do they decide? Is their preference determined by the cost (WhatsApp is free), proximity (they live just across the border), availability of travel amenities (roads, ferries, bridges, or airports), or technology (phone, wifi access)?

If globalization is examined as a *lens* through which to understand the sociocultural dynamics of how the world is organized, then we ask, other than physical amenities or infrastructure, what *cultural* choices influence people to opt for something to comprehend their world?[4] For example, do migrants choose to connect with family by flying more often to another country because being together physically to celebrate an event (birthday, wedding, funeral) is more significant than phone, e-mail, or social media? Or is religion more important in motivating people to connect with others, for example Christmas, Hari Raya,[5] or New Year's?

If globalization is examined as a *system*, we survey institutions, corporations, and empires and how they function in an interconnected world.[6] Such discussions usually center on economic institutions or multinational corporations (MNCs) with global reach. In this chapter as we study glocal complexities, we keep these three intersecting frames in mind, noting that they may sometimes overlap or affect one another.

THE PROCESSES OF GLOBALIZATION

Globalization was seen as the interconnected growth and processes of capitalism in the 1990s when the term became popularized in the media.[7] When globalization is understood in economics or capitalist terms, discussions center on global interconnections that are driven by the world capitalist economy. Generally, core centers such as the West, which are highly capitalist, relate to the periphery (i.e. two-thirds world) through this dominant mode.[8] The weakness of this globalization perspective is that it does not adequately explain how and why economic exchanges involve both the peripheries and other peripheries. Furthermore, economic centers and peripheries have shifted in world history. Although New York, London, and Tokyo are centers of finance

---

4. Nederveen Pieterse, *Globalization*, 18.
5. Also known as *Eid Al-Fitr*, which commemorates the end of Ramadan, Islam's fasting month.
6. Immanuel Wallerstein, *The Modern World System* (New York: Academic Press, 1974).
7. David Reynolds, "American Globalism: Mass, Motion and the Multiplier Effect," in *Globalization in World History*, ed. A. G. Hopkins (New York: W. W. Norton, 2002), 245.
8. Immanuel Wallerstein, *World-Systems Analysis* (Durham, NC: Duke University Press, 2004).

and capitalism today, Malacca was a center for world trade in the fifteenth century, as was Amsterdam in the sixteenth century.

At the grassroots level, the desire to improve or gain socioeconomic fortunes is one of the greatest factors that motivate globalization and its processes. This desire is found among both poor and rich people, small businesses and multinational corporations (MNCs). These MNCs from the banking or media sector are the primary actors. This desire to find or create more wealth motivates the crossing of national, cultural, and social borders in order to transact money, goods, and services. The end products are usually the internationalization of business and the assumption that such trade will bring about the better good of those on the other end.

Those who defend this view of globalization argue that the world is dominated, if not driven, by economics, a view typically favored by Western elites, the rich, and those with links to modern media and technology. Closely related is the belief, as reflected in Thomas Friedman's 1996 bestseller, *The World Is Flat*, that globalization brings irreversible homogenization.[9] The central weakness of this viewpoint is that it does not explain migrations or globalization due to war, religious persecution, or environmental catastrophes.

There is a *quantitative* aspect of globalization in which it is a "process that transforms economic, political, social, and cultural relationships across countries, regions and continents by spreading them more broadly, making them more intense, and increasing their velocity."[10] However, there is also a *qualitative* aspect, which asks if the kind of processes driving globalization and the changes it brings are, in principle, the same or different. For example, does cross-border communication or movements differ in *kind* from those in the past when we compare the telegraph versus the internet?[11] This discussion brings us to the next driver – modernization.

The Process of Modernization

The twentieth century witnessed the greatest technological developments in all eras of human history, among them the internet and satellite communications.

---

9. Nayan Chanda, *Bound Together: How Traders, Preachers, Adventurers, and Warriors Shaped Globalization* (New Haven, CT: Yale University Press, 2007), 251. He notes that it was Theodore Levitt's "seminal article entitled 'The Globalization of Markets'" in the *Harvard Business Review*, May 1983, that advanced a thesis that caught fire – the world's needs and desires have been irrevocably homogenized.
10. A. G. Hopkins, "The History of Globalization and the Globalization of History?" in *Globalization in World History*, ed. A. G. Hopkins (New York: W. W. Norton, 2002), 19.
11. Hopkins, "History," 20.

These two are seen to be central to globalization as both its structure and its driver.

From 1960 to 1970, early views of the media's effects on the world were positively framed as creating a "global village." With the emergence of satellite TV in the 1990s, almost instantaneous beaming of news and events around the world seemed to make the world smaller. As cable television and satellite TV proliferated, they opened fresh vistas for viewers to gaze into new worlds and sights, whetting people's appetites for travel and new experiences. The building of new airports and more efficient planes increased the accessibility and motivation for global tourism.

The Process of Natural Human Migration

This view is sometimes called globalization from below as it emphasizes the greater role of human agency rather than economics or modernization. Robert Holton, a sociologist, believed that social changes that have come to be called globalization at the heart are made by human actors rather than "fateful forces that are out of control."[12]

There are two main ways that people participate in globalization – (1) cross-border processes, for example trade, religion, diasporic connections, and work; and (2) the manipulation of "material or symbolic resources and repositories," for example technology, foodstuff, political institutions, or religious practices.[13] For example for cross-border processes, education is a great motivator for young people to travel in search of diplomas, knowledge, and self-advancement. Missionaries are a group who move abroad to spread their religion. When people move, they implicitly bring their own culture, ideas, and religion as well. Globalization is then not an "uncontrollable runaway world"[14] but mediated through global networks of human actors.

Migrants, for example, are one of the "penetrating" features of globalization into local and national space.[15] Besides the "traveling transnational classes or the new global civil society of international elites," lower working-class people also "construct and join even if they are not mobile."[16] Out of these

---

12. Robert J. Holton, *Making Globalization* (New York: Palgrave Macmillan, 2005), 2.
13. Holton, *Making*, 30.
14. Holton, *Global*, 9.
15. Arjun Appadurai, *Modernity at Large: Cultural Dimensions of Globalization* (Minneapolis: University of Minnesota Press, 1996), 4. It is important to note that discussions of deterritorialization in globalization should not overplay migrations and thus risk overshadowing the traditional rural-to-urban migrations within the nation state. Appadurai, *Modernity*, 61.
16. Saskia Sassen, *A Sociology of Globalization* (New York: W. W. Norton, 2007), 183.

engagements flow many transboundary issues such as immigration, asylum seeking, international women's agendas, and the anti-globalization struggle. Thus, even though local participation in interest-based organizations may not entail international travel, they materialize in the settings of global cities that allow local people to participate in translocal spaces.[17]

In all of the above scenarios, people also drive the globalization of culture. When migrations are temporary, manageable, or reversible, such as students, change to the host nations' culture is often small or negligible. But when migrations are large, fast, and uncontrollable, such as refugees, the migrants may be unable to return, and consequently, their temporary shelter in the host nation changes into a long-term stay. This residency can upset a host nation's culture, ethnic and religious composition, or population balance, and people who base their national identity on one of these characteristics.[18]

When migrants move, they "do not simply leave their 'homelands' nor culture behind [but] forge and maintain distantiated social relations . . . at a distance, across time and space – that link together their home and host societies."[19] These diasporic attachments require skills at being bi-cultural, learning to live, socialize, and communicate between both their host and home countries. This bi-citizenship mixes allegiance to home and host countries and challenges any nation-state's desire for their loyalty to a common government.[20] Instead of nations being permanent places of residence, they become a "transit depot" for passing, making the "ethnos and the territory no longer neatly coincide."[21] However, while human migration as a natural or bottom-up globalization process of personal motivations is compelling, we cannot overlook forced movements from above such as government pressures, expulsions, or denial of rights.[22]

---

17. Sassen, *Sociology*, 193.
18. Jonathan Xavier Inda and Renato Rosaldo, "Tracking Global Flows," in *The Anthropology of Globalization: A Reader*, eds. Jonathan Xavier Inda and Renato Rosaldo (Malden, MA: Blackwell, 2006), 24.
19. Inda and Rosaldo, *Tracking*, 21.
20. Inda and Rosaldo, 23.
21. Inda and Rosaldo, 23–24. Castles and Miller (cited by Holton, *Making*, 88) caution overplaying this impact as only about 2 percent of the world population can be considered migrants in the most liberal sense of the word.
22. Intimately related to the migrant argument are movements and activity of transnationals. Space does not permit a full examination of this topic, but for further discussions see Ulf Hannerz, "The Global Ecumene as a Network of Networks," in *Conceptualizing Society*, ed. A. Kuper (New York: Routledge, 1992), 6, 250; Holton, *Making*, 43–44, 145; Inda and Rosaldo, *Tracking*, 37–38; Michael Kearney, "The Local and the Global: The Anthropology

GLOCAL COMPLEXITIES

After seeing a number of processes and drivers of globalization, we now examine a case study to explore these dynamics.

> ### Case Study 1: Local Churches and Illegal Immigrants in Sabah, Malaysia
>
> Sabah is one of Malaysia's two eastern states on Borneo with the highest percentage population of Christians. When Sabah gained independence from the British in 1963, it joined Malaya to form Malaysia. From the late 1970s to the present, Malaysia's lax enforcement of its borders has facilitated the migration of illegal Muslim migrants from Indonesia and the south Philippine island of Mindanao. This migration has diluted Sabah's pre-independence Christian population of over 60 percent to around 25 percent. These migrants were given citizenship and thus incorporated into state census counts.
>
> Meanwhile internal strife in Mindanao created a desire among residents there to escape and seek a better life in nearby Sabah. A large population of these migrants have been concentrated in a nearby small island off Sabah's coast. There, they lack proper sanitation and public amenities. The net cumulative effect has hardened many local attitudes toward migrants, hindering Christian initiatives or outreach to them.
>
> Reflection questions:
> 1. Is this globalization (of migration) from above or below? What processes and drivers are causing it?
> 2. Among these options, what should the Sabah churches do first: (1) minister to poor, local indigenous Christians, (2) address the plight of the illegal migrants at their doorstep, or (3) petition Malaysia's Muslim-dominated government to rectify the situation?

---

of Globalization and Transnationalism," *Annual Review of Anthropology* 24 (1995): 548; Ted Lewellen, *The Anthropology of Globalization* (Westport, CT: Praeger, 2002), 150; and Anna Tsing, "The Global Situation," *Cultural Anthropology* 15, no. 3 (2000), 349.

Global Networks

A final element closely connected to bottom-up, grassroots globalization is global networks. If personal motivations are individualized expressions of globalization whose details may get lost in the vastness of this world, human networks are larger extensions of this and cannot be ignored. Global networks are extremely influential in today's interconnected world. They differ from personal, individual migrations because networks are larger and more complex relationships that link people and institutions in a flow of shared interest.[23] Global networks are the structures of the "human face of globalization"[24]

Not all networks are equal or open to everyone. For example, the scientific community has their own intellectual network that includes scientists but excludes non-scientists. However, the advantages of these networks are tremendous – by connecting and combining the knowledge, experience, and diversity of many people in a shared group, they create a multiplier force for innovation, information exchange, and investment of time and energy. Robert Holton identifies twelve existing global networks: advocacy, business/trading/commercial, friendship, imperial, information, knowledge/intellectual, migrant, policy, professional, religious, terrorist, and women's networks.[25] More could be listed. Such networks are "forms for multicentered social organization that are distinct from two other major organizational types, namely markets and hierarchies. Networks are more enduring forms of social commitment and trust than markets but are more flexible and less centralized than hierarchies."[26]

People are drawn into networks because they see benefits in connecting with people of similar interests, identity, ideas, or activity into a web of relationships that extends over space and time. They join networks for various reasons – to obtain or to confer social capital and status, to enjoy a shared emotional or intellectual bond to advocate or to push a cause, and so on. For example by joining Facebook, one enters into a global network of potential friends and obtains benefits. When people engage with a global network, their engagement can also strengthen *local* networks.[27]

Networks, however, are not static and may change over time, in frequency and intensity, reconfiguring relationships within the web. Relationships "wax and wane in intensity and may involve phases of conflict, or even breakdown,

---

23. Holton, *Global*, 81.
24. Holton, 3.
25. Holton, 81.
26. Holton, 4.
27. Sassen, *Sociology*, 211.

and this in turn may be connected to changes in the political and cultural context."[28] Because of context, networks do not operate in a vacuum – each network is different and needs to be studied contextually within each group. The study of networks will be the key to understanding twenty-first century society and culture. In addition, a network view of glocalization helps us understand how globalization functions between the power of big institutions versus individuals. In this sense, this view probes the "interstices" of the globalization structure.

GLOCALIZATION

Glocalization is the intermixing of the *global* and the *local* to make things glocal, that is to universalize the local things and conversely to localize things that seem universal. Sociologist Robert Holton lists seven types of global-local interactions: (1) The global predominates over the local. (2) The local awakes itself in a globalized or globalizing world. (3) The global, bringing opportunities, helps the local. (4) The global invents its own local. (5) The local struggles for a different global. (6) The interactions of the global and local build up a new synthesis, the glocal. (7) The local sets free the local.[29]

One example of global and local interaction is a global cultural form in which people around the world can both relate to and speak about with mutual understanding, for example Kentucky Fried Chicken (KFC). When American fast food was first introduced to Southeast Asia in the 1970s, a foreign concept soon became common. Ordering food quickly, with expectations of eating it in a clean and standardized, air-conditioned environment in any KFC outlet anywhere in any country soon became a commonly understood experience. Soon after whenever "KFC" was mentioned, these commonplace ideas were readily grasped and were different from other local eateries.

Global culture also emerges when spaces or places become more uniform in the global sameness in architecture, public spaces, or office buildings that convey a sense of the familiar yet unfamiliar at the same time. This is called hyperspace. For example, twenty-first century professional workplaces require a specialized physical infrastructure: state-of-the-art office buildings, residential districts, airports, and hotels[30] – the hyperspace of global business. As places and destinations begin to resemble one another, this resemblance

---

28. Holton, *Global*, 151.
29. Holton (citing Petralla), *Making*, 110.
30. Sassen, *Sociology*, 176.

produces a "curious sense of time and space: a feeling that they could literally be anywhere in the world and nowhere in particular," breeding a "familiarity and predictability within their life worlds [that] carries over to the people with whom they interact."[31] However, we easily assume that just because people work in similar looking environments, they also think and talk the same as we do, which is not always true. In this understanding of the globalizations of culture, cultural flows are "carried and extended by cosmopolitans who, of necessity, acknowledge and extend [Western] cultural frameworks even as they incorporate and remake non-Western cultures."[32]

In order for global events to affect the local, and vice versa, there must exist channels or pipelines for flows to occur. In globalizations, these channels or pipelines are sometimes called "scapes." There are at least seven scapes in a glocalized world:[33]

Table 2: The Scapes of Globalization

Scapes of Glocalization	Characteristics of the Scapes
Eduscapes	Flows of education
Ethnoscapes	Flows of migrants (ethnic and cultural groups)
Finanscapes	Flows of money and trade
Ideoscapes	Flows of ideology, ideas, and information
Materialscapes	Flows of material and goods
Mediascapes	Flows of media and images

Each of these scapes or channel flows are unpredictable because different people around the world use and interact with them in unique ways according to their own social, cultural, religious, or political priorities. In some cases, "each acts as a constraint and a parameter for movements in the others."[34] Let us consider one example of how the scapes function in the following case study.

---

31. James Davison Hunter and Joshua Yates, "In the Vanguard of Globalization: The World of American Globalizers," in *Many Globalizations: Cultural Diversity in the Contemporary World*, eds. Peter L. Berger and Samuel P. Huntington (New York: Oxford University Press, 2004), 333–34.
32. Tsing, "Global," 342.
33. Adapted from Appardurai, *Modernity*, 33. I have added two more of my own – eduscapes and materialscapes.
34. Appadurai, *Modernity*, 35.

Case Study 2: Short-term Mission Teams in a Glocal World

Husband and wife David and Sarah have been Christian missionaries in Thailand for over ten years. They know many locals, both Christians and non-Christians, and enjoy good friendships with many people, speaking their language and eating with them. They are also teachers in their community. Their work is supported by their church in the West. This church regularly sends short-term teams to Thailand, and David and Sarah are expected to lead and guide those teams. This includes arranging opportunities for the team to minister, to stay in a village, and to interact with the locals with David and Sarah translating. For one trip, without the missionaries' prior input or advice, the church team has decided to show a film, and the team plans to stay for a month, traveling around the area showing the film.

David and Sarah are concerned that using a film is an inappropriate method of evangelism. They prefer their way of sharing the gospel which is to record chanting the Psalms on CDs and then giving them away. However their supporting church insists on the film because they have heard that it has been effective in other parts of Asia. In addition, the team has spent a lot of time back home coordinating their evangelistic activities, including the invitation, meals, sermon, and follow up are planned around the film showing.

David and Sarah face a dilemma. If they allow this event to go on, they fear that the team will do long-term damage to the witness they have already established. Furthermore, time spent with the team would detract them from their work of teaching and strengthening relationships. If they disapprove of the team's plan, they fear that their church will be disappointed and may withdraw their support.

Reflection questions:
1. What scapes of globalization are operating here that seem to be in conflict?
2. What elements are global versus local, and how are they interacting?
3. What should David and Sarah do?

CHARACTERISTICS OF TIME, DISTANCE, AND FLOWS IN GLOCALIZATION

Distancing of Time-space

According to sociologist Anthony Giddens, globalization expresses the "fundamental aspects of time-space distanciation . . . the intersection of presence and absence, the interlacing of social events and social relations 'at distance' with local contextualities."[35] Distanciation means that distant things seem near and near things may seem "absent" or far. As a result social life is stretched across time and space when faraway people who connect online seem "near," but ironically we may be "far" from our next door neighbors who are also elsewhere in their own globalized time-space context.[36] In a way, it is "a dialectical phenomenon, in which events at one pole of a distanced relation often produce divergent or even contrary occurrences at another."[37]

Space-time Compression

Globalization also disturbs the idea of locality in society where traditional ideas of hierarchy and place are centered on the nation-state.[38] An example is the digital world – a "subnational within the global."[39] Subnational or local events, for example the terrorist attacks in the United States on 11 September 2001, can quickly spread virally online so that it becomes part of the global consciousness. The ability to then follow updates live on satellite TV or via a website also generates a sense of immediacy or closeness to the event. This sense of immediate closeness to something thousands of kilometers away is called space-time compression where the local becomes global. Conversely, this global event becomes local when people gather to view it, which soon becomes a local news topic that affects local perceptions and responses. Giddens summarizes space-time compression as "the intensification of world-wide social relations which link distant localities in such a way that local happenings are shaped by events occurring miles away and vice versa."[40]

---

35. Anthony Giddens, *Modernity and Self-Identity* (Stanford, CA: Stanford University Press, 1991), 21.
36. Anthony Giddens, *The Consequences of Modernity* (Stanford, CA: Stanford University Press, 1990), 16.
37. Giddens, *Modernity*, 22.
38. John D. Kelly, "Time and the Global," in *Globalization and Identity*, eds. Birgit Meyer and Peter Geschiere (Malden, MA: Wiley Blackwell, 1999), 240.
39. Sassen, *Sociology*, 13.
40. Giddens, *Consequences*, 64.

Reflexivity

If the internet and social media allow us to view events, places, and people immediately and feel close to them just as the locals do, it also enables reflexivity – the ability to communicate to another person and respond to these events instantaneously.

This process of increased intensification and reflexivity has been occurring since long-distance trade connections and the first migrations of people. However, the process accelerated during expansions of technologies, religions, literacy, empires, and trade.[41] A modern example of reflexivity is when a state censors local controversies, but locals circumvent that censor by recording the events on their smartphones and uploading material online.

Dislocation of Territory, Context, and Skills

Another aspect of time, distance, and flow in globalization is *disembedding* and *deskilling*. Disembedding is the encounter of "physical" people across space that becomes virtual (or digital) instead of physically near.[42] Deskilling is when production or work becomes detached from the actual person or transferred to a robot or program that can do it without an actual person present.

Furthermore there is dislocation or deterritorialization of culture and people.[43] Deterritorialization occurs when people move their workplace or residence, whether voluntarily or involuntarily, for example due to conflict or natural disasters. When people are emphasized, for example professional or lower-class migrant workers, refugees, or asylum-seekers in globalizations, one aspect focuses on their relocation or dislocation to other countries to work or to find safety for long, or possibly permanent, stretches of time. Deterritorialization then causes changes in social and cultural adjustments such as in identity, rituals, and language. When people move from one place to another, they also bring their skills, ideas, and materials along with them.

---

41. Jan Nederveen Pieterse, "Globalization as Hybridization," in *Global Modernities*, eds. Mike Featherstone, Scott Lash, and Roland Robertson (Thousand Oaks, CA: Sage, 1995), 48.
42. Giddens, *Consequences*, 18. Due to dislocation, the salience of home – for example homesickness, earth as a home, return to an imagined past, or nostalgia – in globalization discourse is a part of the deterritorialization of people and their increased mobility in the world. Robertson, *Globalization*, 159–62. Sufficed to say, the deterritorialization of people means the loss of place as a marker of identity and culture, prompting the search for fundamentals and essentials of an authentic self and identity in the (re)invention of traditions and the rise of imagined communities. Robertson, 166–67.
43. Giddens, *Consequences*.

In doing so, local practices or production that were once limited to their place and time become transported to another new space and time.

Table 3: Types of Local-global Flows in Today's Globalized World

Type of flows	Types of local	Types of global
People	Ethnic people, national citizens	Global tourists, business workers, refugees, students, missionaries, international workers
Material	Local food, craft, clothing, etc	Global products (iPhone, kimchee)
Money	Local currency	Global currencies (Euro, UK Sterling, US dollar, Yen)
Ideologies/Beliefs	Local beliefs	Communism, world religions and texts, yoga
Images	Local places and sights	Hollywood, Kung Fu, satellite TV/cable

If deterritorialization can affect people, it also touches all other things that flow in the streams of globalizations. In the diagram below, I sketch five elements that flow in a globalized world – migrants (people), money, materials, ideas, and images. All of them flow mainly through the global cities of the world, where the main channels are airports, banks, seaports, computers, and phone screens which are ubiquitous in global cities.

The idea of flows is tightly related to the notion of globalizations happening in a borderless world, a term popularized by Kenichi Ohmae.[44] According to Ohmae, the onset of the borderless world was when "the multinational corporation decentralized its headquarters and became a transnational corporation."[45] Thereafter, border crossing and borderlessness become prominent in cultural studies, sociology, politics, and international relations.[46] The concept later became entrenched in everyday conversation after Thomas Friedman's publication *The World Is Flat*.[47]

---

44. Kenichi Ohmae, *The Borderless World: Power and Strategy in the Interlinked Economy* (New York: Harper Collins, 1991).
45. Kenichi Ohmae quoted in Jan Nederveen Pieterse, "Fault Lines of Transnationalism: Borders Matter," *Bulletin of the Royal Institute for Inter-faith Studies* 4, no. 2 (2002): 38.
46. Nederveen Pieterse, "Fault Lines," 38.
47. Thomas Friedman, *The World Is Flat: A Brief History of the Twenty-first Century* (New York: Farrar, Straus, and Giroux, 2005).

GLOCAL COMPLEXITIES

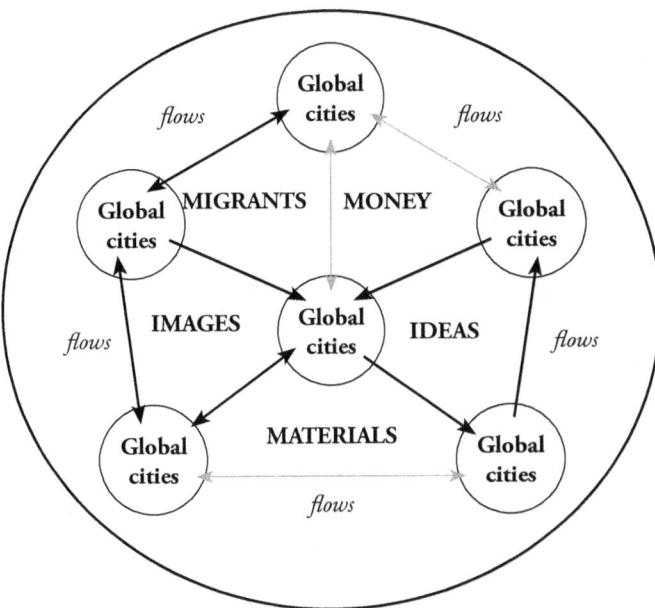

Diagram 1: Elements that Flow in Globalizations

Such global flows are not isolated but may have "parallel, crosscutting or overlapping connections."[48] Migrants often bring flows of money and materials. Information about educational opportunities may stimulate education migrants to come. And these streams flow through one of seven scapes of globalizations.

While flows imply movement and connectedness, things do not always "flow smoothly" – there are limits to the variety, volume, velocity, and vector of flows. For example, when someone wishes to relocate, governments may decide the kinds of people (variety), how many (volume), how quickly (velocity), and where they might go (vector) to stay or visit in their country. Other examples are money and images – each can also be forwarded, filtered, forced, or forbidden by governments. All nations today decide how much money can be transferred and reported, as well as imposing limits on images and information that might threaten their sociopolitical identity or national security. Thus, rather than a borderless world, the twenty-first century is becoming an

---

48. Ulf Hannerz, "The Global Ecumene as a Network of Networks," in *Conceptualizing Society*, ed. A. Kuper (New York: Routledge, 1992), 47.

unevenly open world. In some places flows are permitted, while in others they are forbidden because each nation decides how these flows will be "configured in particular places, for particular groups and for whose benefit."[49]

Smooth and Bumpy Flows

Flows may occur from above or from below. The poor migrate to richer countries, but their remittances will later flow back home. Flows also move at different rates and possess hierarchies,[50] have volume and can become a flood.[51] Money flows can move faster than people or materials. Movement becomes more difficult as we move from capital to labor and from intangible (finance) to tangible (goods, investments) assets.[52] The sharper the difference between these two – things that are digitizable versus those that are not – the "more abundant the business opportunities become" producing inequalities in wealth and power.[53] Where these occur, opportunities for holistic Christian mission arise. However, there are limits to global mobility and flow as the world is not shrinking for everyone and in all places. Anna Tsing states that when flows are

> valorized but not the carving of the channel [,] national and regional units are mapped as the baseline of change without attention to their shifting and contested ability to define the landscape. We lose sight of the coalitions of claimants as well as their partial and shifting claims. We lose touch with the material and institutional components through which powerful and central sites are constructed, from which convincing claims about units and scales can be made. We describe the landscape imagined within these claims rather than the culture and politics of scale-making.[54]

While studying the flows of glocalization helps us comprehend its processes (i.e. people movements, things, ideas, etc.), it does not show how these movements depend on defining tracks and grounds or scales and units of agency. Flow imagery can sideline the

---

49. Kristín Loftsdóttir, "Globalization and Modernity," in *Topographies of Globalization*, eds. Valur Ingimundarson, Kristín Loftsdóttir, and Irma Erlingsdóttir (Reykjavik: University of Iceland, 2004), 154.
50. Loftsdóttir, "Globlization," 158.
51. Tsing, "Global," 328.
52. Nederveen Pieterse, "Fault Lines," 45.
53. Saskia Sassen, "Spatialities and Temporalities of the Global: Elements for a Theorization," *Public Culture* 12, no. 1 (2000): 222.
54. Tsing, "Global," 330.

transformation of actors, objects, goals, perspectives and terrains that characterizes regional-to-global interaction. Instead, we might pay special attention to the roles of both cultural legacies and power inequalities in creating the institutional arenas and assumptions of world-making transitions.[55]

The reality is that in today's unevenly globalized world, "connection and disconnection seem to go hand in hand."[56] Flows are reversible. Deglobalization may occur as countries delink themselves from the global community as a "kind of active anti-globalization,"[57] as was seen in the COVID-19 pandemic in 2020 as nations shut their borders to protect their own residents. Besides deglobalization, another facet of flow is closure. In a globalized world, people desire "fixed orientation points and the re-affirmation of boundaries [as] a common element."[58] It should not be surprising if more countries in the twenty-first century erect more borders or stringent requirements for entry; the increased difficulties of obtaining passport visas for church or mission workers is one example and will require creative strategizing in the coming decades.

Hybridity – The Intermixing of Flows

When locality is deconstructed and culture becomes deterritorialized, there emerges room to examine mixed cultures, transnational movements, and diasporas. For example, when people become detached from their former culture and land and adopt new languages and customs, hybridization of culture and identity emerges. One way that hybridity[59] occurs is how media and migration jointly affect the "work of the imagination," offering "new resources and new disciplines for the construction of imagined selves and imagined worlds."[60]

The process of cultural hybridization is one aspect of globalizations that counters the global homogenization of culture. Even when people desire to

---

55. Tsing, 349.
56. Inda and Rosaldo, *Tracking*, 35.
57. Ulf Hannerz, *Transnational Connections: Culture, People, Places* (New York: Routledge, 1996), 18.
58. Birgit Meyer and Peter Geschiere, "Introduction," in *Globalization and Identity*, eds. Birgit Meyer and Peter Geschiere (Malden, MA: Wiley Blackwell, 1999), 3.
59. Hybridity is a key term in discussions of fluidity of identity and whether globalization is homogenizing or heterogenizing cultures. Space does not permit discussion on this topic, but see Néstor García Canclini, *Hybrid Cultures: Strategies for Entering and Leaving Modernity*, trans. Christopher L. Chiappari and Silvia L. López (Minneapolis: University of Minnesota Press, 2005); and Nederveen Pieterse, *Globalization*.
60. Appadurai, *Modernity*, 3.

hybridize or adopt new global elements into their local culture, their nation or society may try to limit change or flow. It is not easy to know when such limits may occur as they depend on the whims of nation-states and the fate of governments that may be replaced. Thus, the *"contingency* of boundaries is now a more common experience than ever before."[61] As

> some boundaries wane, others remain or come in. Thus, as national borders and governmental authority erode, ethnic or religious boundaries, or boundaries of consumption patterns and brand names emerge in their place [or] as some boundaries fade, people's differential capacities for border crossing and mobility come to the foreground.[62]

Cultures do not just float freely but are also reinserted into new and specific time-space contexts.[63] This means that culture "continues to have a territorialized existence, albeit a rather unstable one"[64] because globalizations remove barriers as new ones are erected.[65] Due to this fluctuation, flows are accompanied by attempts to control culture in a contest of power and control.[66] Let us now examine an example of material and religious flows.

---

61. Nederveen Pieterse, *Globalization*, 120, emphasis added.
62. Nederveen Pieterse, 121.
63. Inda and Rosaldo, *Tracking*, 14.
64. Inda and Rosaldo, 14.
65. Holton, *Global*, 140.
66. Meyer and Geschiere, "Introduction," 5.

GLOCAL COMPLEXITIES

> ### Case Study 3: "The Locals Just Don't Value It!"
>
> Susan is a missionary involved with Bible translation and literacy training among the indigenous Kimar people. The Kimar are smaller cousins of the Dak tribe, who are more well-known, having prominent religious and political leaders, their own newspaper, radio station, and a complete Bible. In the last five years, Susan's team has produced the first Kimar dictionary, some children's primary school-level reading books, and the Kimar New Testament. However, despite years of promotion, the Kimar still preferred to use the Dak language and books.
>
> Susan and her team are frustrated over this situation as they felt God called them to work among the Kimar to produce local resources that would benefit their local Christian culture. They don't understand why the Kimar are not proud of their local culture and language but prefer to use the Dak people's resources instead. Furthermore, many young Kimar people are migrating to the larger towns and cities for jobs and could potentially lose their local culture and language. The Kimar elders would like their young to keep their language and culture but are resigned over the situation.
>
> Reflection questions:
> 1. Why do you think the Kimar people prefer to use the Dak resources rather than their own?
> 2. If you were Susan, would you redouble your efforts to better educate and promote already existing Kimar resources with hopes the people will value it and agree to translate a completed Bible or stop the work and promote the Dak Bible and resources?

SCALES AND ACTORS (STRUCTURES AND PLAYERS) IN GLOCAL COMPLEXITY

The insertion or penetration of the global or universal, for example the priority of Bible translation, into the local or particular (pictured in the diagram below) may not result in local people responding to the global or universal in expected ways. The local people may seek another alternative to their own sociocultural or economic limitations and find a new scenario that better fits their own sense of priorities.

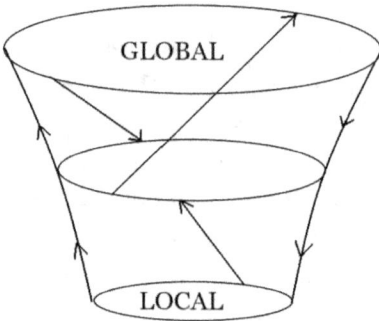

Figure 4: Interactions between the local and global

When penetration or flow occurs from the global into the local, it means that the nation-state's control as the container of local sociocultural aspects has loosened. Conversely, local settings, products, and ideas may escape national control or be easily influenced by outsiders. Because globalization produces these dynamics, it muddies traditional notions of the difference between what is "local" and "global." We thus need to look at actual structures and actors to understand what is happening.

The Nation-state in Glocalization

In the modern world, the nation-state determines our identity in the significance of place – where we were born and the local influences that shape us – and our citizenship. The nation-state can do this since it exercises control over territorial borders, identity cards, and media dissemination. When one or more of these control areas begin to deterritorialize or flow, globalizations challenge the power and autonomy of the nation-state to legitimize *one* people, *one* nation, and *one* country with *one* identity. For instance, political nationalism that was once contained within the nation-state has been loosened when its citizens become diasporas that exercise their rights to protest local events from overseas, exercising "long-distance nationalism."[67]

Another example of weakening nation-state power is when global cities with global influence on world culture or economics such as Beijing, Tokyo, or Singapore influence events independent of their country's interest in business

---

67. Appadurai, *Modernity*, 161.

or economic ties.⁶⁸ When either scenario occurs, three outcomes may occur: (1) the state is victimized and loses significance,⁶⁹ (2) the state continues functioning with little change, or (3) the state does not decline but adapts and may be transformed, becoming an actor with multidimensional and specialized functions.⁷⁰ Globalization produces "in-between spaces" where activities that take place in the national space are new in some of their features yet cannot be said to fully comply either.⁷¹ These are further extensions of what glocalization means.

Non-state Actors in Glocalization

Multinational corporations (MNCs) and non-governmental organizations (NGOs) are actors that play important roles in our glocalized world. They function independently of the nation-state and are connected to the globalization of business, private causes, or projects such as human rights or the environment. Whether they occupy offices around the world or exist as a virtual organization, they may be "non-state" and can benefit or threaten national interests. In Christianity, international megachurches such as Hillsong Church or Yoido Full Gospel Church function as examples of *de facto* non-state actors. When we study the characteristics of other non-state actors and compare them to megachurches, we can see how similar they are.

In positive scenarios, non-state (and non-Christian) actors such as The Asia Foundation, BRAC,⁷² or the Bill and Melinda Gates Foundation, all NGOs, have pursued causes to benefit the economics, health, or quality of human life worldwide. NGOs are typically non-territorial and non-state groups that operate in the "interstices" of globalization, or between the local and the global. If they are bottom-up initiatives, they are usually associated

---

68. Sassen, *Sociology*, 73.
69. Appadurai, *Modernity*, 19.
70. Lewellen, *Anthropology*, 194–99; Sassen, *Sociology*, 45; and Nederveen Pieterse, "Fault Lines," 38, see three different paradigms of globalization and the state: (1) a strong discourse of borders, as in Samuel Huntington, *Clash of Civilizations and the Remaking of World Order* (New York: Touchstone, 1997) and Benjamin Barber, *Jihad vs. McWorld: Terrorism's Challenge to Democracy* (New York: Ballentine, 1995); (2) a gradual erosion of borders due to increased modernization; or (3) ongoing mixing and hybridization resulting from neither strong borders nor uniformization.
71. Sassen, "Spatialities," 220.
72. Though little known, BRAC started in Bangladesh and operates in over a dozen Asian countries, specializing in starting social enterprises, development, and education. For details, see "Who We Are," BRAC (n.d.), http://www.brac.net/who-we-are.

with "networked organization among activists."[73] If they are top-down initiatives, they are non-state actors like intergovernmental bodies or "private, intermediary institutional arrangements [that] are . . . evolving into a parallel institutional world for the handling of crossborder operations."[74] In negative scenarios, intergovernmental bodies such as the World Bank and International Monetary Fund (IMF) have forced nations to accept macroeconomic demands that were unfavorable to local needs.

If globalization is economic-driven, global culture is "diffused through both elite and popular vehicles" such as the World Economic Forum, whose "basic engine is the international business" that also drives economic and technological globalization.[75] There are also other global business, fashion, and culture networks, but they are dominated by elites whose activities may lack transparency and accountability. Following behind them are the million others who desire a piece of this culture.

We could ask are international megachurches and large parachurch or mission organizations like Operation Mobilization or OMF International who operate with their own global networks also types of non-state actors, since they do possess many similar characteristics. If they are non-state actors, we must then ask how these international megachurches and large parachurch organizations can function responsibly in honoring God and being faithful in their call and mission in the world as "non-state actors." Consider the following scenarios in which international megachurches might operate under the radar of the nation-state:

- Sending short-term mission teams overseas to run projects in collaboration with the locals, without state knowledge or permission.
- Funding missionaries whose mission activities are considered illegal in that country.
- Introducing big or new programs, for example development projects like farms or roads, into an area without adhering to state laws or regulations.

---

73. Holton, *Global*, 16.
74. Sassen, "Spatialities," 229.
75. Peter L. Berger, "The Cultural Dynamics of Globalization," in *Many Globalizations: Cultural Diversity in the Contemporary World*, eds. Peter L. Berger and Samuel P. Huntington (New York: Oxford University Press, 2004), 3.

International megachurches and mission organizations are capable of doing these activities because of the influx of both Christians with professional skills and missionaries which "disrupt conventional hierarchies of scale."[76] What kind of ethics or guidelines should inform such organizations, whether Christian or non-Christian, so that their actions benefit the locals? Even with the best of intentions, Christian organizations that grow in size, power, and influence must grow responsibly in their actions so that they do not cause unintended harm.

We must realize that due to the various capabilities and resources of each actor in particular structures, organizations, and levels, different outcomes are produced, creating unevenness and hierarchies of relationships in globalized scales.[77] Depending on the actors and the opportunities that are opened, over time, these non-state actors can create a virtuous cycle with a multiplier effect, giving them an accumulation of advantage over others.[78] If their actions do indeed create mutual benefits for both parties, God is honored, and his kingdom grows healthily. If not, they can hurt people, waste resources, and tarnish Christian witness.

The City as an Actor in Glocalization

In globalization studies, cities are also considered actors because they not only *influence* economics, culture, and religion, but are *sites* of connection and exchange as well. For example, cities like Bangkok, Frankfurt, and Shanghai are "world cities" not only because economic and political transactions occur in them, but because they are also "transnational connections" since they order these structures.[79] They are "places in themselves and also nodes in networks; their cultural organization involves local as well as transnational relationships."[80]

According to Ulf Hannerz, world cities have four characteristics: (1) transnational businesses that are filled with highly-educated, skilled, and mobile white-collar professionals; (2) growing Majority World populations who live inside such cities or serve these professionals in that realm; (3) artistic and expressive workers who bring music, arts, and literature; and (4) tourists who visit these cities based on the cumulative effects of the previous three.[81] Such world

---

76. Sassen, "Spatialities."
77. Sassen, *Sociology*, 76.
78. Sassen, 148.
79. Hannerz, *Transnational*, 12.
80. Hannerz, 128–29.
81. Hannerz, 128–29.

cities provide for a positive and multidimensional convergence of workers who bring various combinations of skills, cultures, work, and desires. While these characteristics can and should work together to build a vibrant and flourishing city for all, often the net result is a global city but with large slums.

These cities have a vibe of their own and attract many elite professionals and also working-class migrants, creating new cultures along the way. The forces for cultural creativity in world cities are the (1) concentration of talent; (2) presence of international and legal supports; (3) self-belief as a vanguard of change; (4) the presence of diversity; and (5) daily experiences of "urban spectacle" and a market that feeds on it.[82] Glocalization happens when events in one city become news and influence others in another connected city to quickly respond reflexively. These world cities are "doubly creolizing" as they send and receive images from one site to another in a continuous relationship. In this way, they are "places of exchange, the switchboards of culture."[83]

The Internet as an Actor in Glocalization

The internet is not only a driver of globalization but also another structure and actor; it is the last but arguably the most important element of glocalization. Manuel Castell, the father of the sociology of the internet, in his seminal book, *Rise of the Network Society*, theorizes the emergence of a new social order based on the explosive growth of internet use in the last twenty years due to the following:[84]

- The internet reorders space-time configurations in human relationships, work, leisure, and almost every facet of life. In short, it creates a new globalized human-social-technological condition.
- The virtuality of the internet creates "timeless time" – an element that compresses everything into one time (i.e. "information economy time"), such as 24/7 trading, online banking, and telecommuting, all of which affect norms of immediacy and time in human relationships and communication.
- The internet creates a digital "space of flows" that network communities of people, finance, images, and information. These

---

82. Hannerz, 136.
83. Hannerz, 149. For an excellent example of how urban missions can look in this type of context, see Jared Looney, *Crossroads of the Nations: Diaspora, Globalization and Evangelism* (Portland, OR: Urban Loft), 2015.
84. Sassen, 73–74, 141–48.

flows are not just pipelines, but also by their very use, they reflexively reconfigure structures of relationship platforms.
- Due to these flows, the internet has a special form of scale that is under and over the national.[85] For example, when the internet or social media are used by the diaspora to practice online activism, we see both long-distance nationalism and electronic funding of projects. In this way, the global economy materializes within national territories, *between* digital space and state boundaries.

It is precisely because the internet is a human-mediated medium that it implicates human relations and creates new forms of social order.[86] The different actors who use it and create groups or networks online produce different digital outcomes. These outcomes eventually create and shape the context of their imagined social orders and objectives.[87] For example, social media tools such as Facebook and WhatsApp enable users to create specific groups that crisscross, if not bypass, social hierarchies and national borders by creating new online communities that are linked by specific interests.

Like a reflection of globalization, the internet also has asymmetry in its scale.[88] Not everyone, everywhere, and every time can operate at the same speed or access. These elements mitigate glocalization. Besides its structure, the internet has a social and cultural predisposition toward things American.[89] Dominant American values that implicitly operate and influence the internet are egalitarianism and the freedom of information. These values are illustrated when the internet creates decentralized hierarchical relationships through various apps, as well as by the posting and easy retrieval of information by individuals.

FUTURE TRAJECTORIES: WHERE DOES THE CHURCH GO FROM HERE?

According to anthropologist Anna Tsing, globalization produces

---

85. Sassen, *Sociology*, 81, 206.
86. Manuel Castells, *Rise of the Network Society*, 2nd ed. (Malden, MA: Wiley-Blackwell, 2010), xxxi.
87. Sassen, *Sociology*, 235–36.
88. Castells, *Rise*, 382.
89. Jean-Noël Jeanneney, *Google and the Myth of Universal Knowledge*, trans. Teresa Lavender Fagan (Chicago: University of Chicago Press, 2007); Sassen, *Sociology*, 234.

concreteness of "movements" in both senses of the word: social mobilizations in which new identities and interests are formed and travel from one place to another through which place-transcending interactions occur. These two senses of movement work together in remaking geographies and scales.[90]

Due to this remaking of geographies, scales, culture, and human identities in globalization, understanding *glocal* complexities requires a multidisciplinary examination. Globalization and glocalization cannot be reduced to -one explanatory system with a single unified logic. The following proposals for Christian mission should be considered.

Globalization is a complex and multidimensional phenomenon that requires the whole church to collaborate with others in order to best engage its complexities. At the same time, globalization is also liberating since it forces us to confront our limits, and it frees us to work with others in deeper partnerships. Thus perhaps the challenge of globalization brings the body of Christ together in a greater way.

Globalization is not only about economics but about people. This means we must know the specific promises and perils that confront people in a globalized world, including the dislocation and disembedding of their place and skills – both of which make people fear the loss of their culture or jobs. A vision for Christian ministry in the twenty-first century globalized world is to recognize "global nomads" who travel from one nation to another, bringing with them some local characteristics and cultures.

1. Globalization is not an unstoppable force – Christians have important roles to play to influence and shape it for better or for worse. The large movements of materials, migrants, money, ideas, and images can cause problems for nation-states if such flows are unregulated and unplanned. When these unplanned flows occur, this could be an opportune moment for the church as agents of the gospel of Christ to step in and play important roles to receive, resist, or reshape them.

2. Glocalization is where the local becomes the global and the global becomes the local, and Christian mindsets and ministries must change to reflect this reality. For example, most of us recognize

---

90. Tsing, "Global," 350.

and enjoy the benefits of the reflexive and time-compressed nature of globalization, such as watching a live English Premier League football game at *our* location in Kuala Lumpur or Manila.

3. Glocalization is a phenomenon that gives form, process, or expression to life; hence the church must critically evaluate what specific universal values, exchanges, and ideas should be derived from it and through it. In this light, churches must become agents of wisdom to know how to train their own ministers to use the elements of globalization critically – whether to adopt foreign cultural forms in worship and theology or to mimic non-indigenous ways of serving. In addition as the body of believers, the church is also called to be the salt of the earth and light of the world (Matt 5:13–14) to the citizens and policymakers of all nations. When governments struggle to balance the wellbeing of citizens against the desire to receive refugees, or to preserve local jobs against the offshoring of employment, the church can be a voice of conscience as well as an active agent of shalom and justice to address the inequalities and evils that are produced by globalization.

While globalization is one of the most powerful phenomena in the world because it reaches almost every sphere of human life and society, it is observed and experienced locally. Hence the way that Christians live and move and have our being within our local context, while being sensitive to the wider global forces, means that we can be a powerful witness for the kingdom of God, both locally and globally.

> ### Additional Case Studies
>
> 1. Select any country from Part I of this book. Using the systems mapping (ch 10, pg 168), fill in four tables that include the micro-, meso-, and macro-level influences with regard to culture, politics, and economics. Then ask (1) how do these influence the church, and (2) how can churches be influencers?
> 2. Consider something that has been discussed in the news recently. Do an internet search of the topic on global news media, for example CNN, CNA, and BBC, and compare their articles with those of local news media. How is the narrative similar or dissimilar? If you are able to, search the internet to see how churches have responded to the issue. What are the similarities and differences between Western and local perspectives?

REFERENCES

Appadurai, Arjun. *Modernity at Large: Cultural Dimensions of Globalization.* Minneapolis: University of Minnesota Press, 1996.

Berger, Peter L. "The Cultural Dynamics of Globalization." In *Many Globalizations: Cultural Diversity in the Contemporary World*, edited by Peter L. Berger and Samuel P. Huntington, 1–16. New York: Oxford University Press, 2004.

Castells, Manuel. *Rise of the Network Society.* 2nd ed. Malden, MA: Wiley-Blackwell, 2010.

Chanda, Nayan. *Bound Together: How Traders, Preachers, Adventurers, and Warriors Shaped Globalization.* New Haven, CT: Yale University Press, 2007.

García Canclini, Néstor. *Hybrid Cultures: Strategies for Entering and Leaving Modernity.* Translated by Christopher L. Chiappari and Silvia L. López. Minneapolis: University of Minnesota Press, 2005.

Giddens, Anthony. *The Consequences of Modernity.* Stanford, CA: Stanford University Press, 1990.

———. *Modernity and Self-Identity.* Stanford, CA: Stanford University Press, 1991.

Hannerz, Ulf. "The Global Ecumene as a Network of Networks." In *Conceptualizing Society*, edited by A. Kuper, 34–58. New York: Routledge, 1992.

———. *Transnational Connections: Culture, People, Places.* New York: Routledge, 1996.

Holton, Robert J. *Global Networks*. New York: Palgrave Macmillan, 2008.
———. *Making Globalization*. New York: Palgrave Macmillan, 2005.
Hopkins, A. G. "The History of Globalization and the Globalization of History?" In *Globalization in World History*, edited by A. G. Hopkins, 12–44. New York: W. W. Norton, 2002.
Hunter, James Davison, and Joshua Yates. "In the Vanguard of Globalization: The World of American Globalizers." In *Many Globalizations: Cultural Diversity in the Contemporary World*, edited by Peter L. Berger and Samuel P. Huntington, 323–57. New York: Oxford University Press, 2004.
Inda, Jonathan Xavier, and Renato Rosaldo. "Tracking Global Flows." In *The Anthropology of Globalization: A Reader*, edited by Jonathan Xavier Inda and Renato Rosaldo, 3–46. Malden: Blackwell, 2006.
Jeanneney, Jean-Noël. *Google and the Myth of Universal Knowledge*. Translated by Teresa Lavender Fagan. Chicago: University of Chicago Press, 2007.
Kearney, Michael, "The Local and the Global: The Anthropology of Globalization and Transnationalism." *Annual Review of Anthropology* 24 (1995): 547–65.
Kelly, John D. "Time and the Global." In *Globalization and Identity*, edited by Birgit Meyer and Peter Geschiere, 241–71. Malden, MA: Wiley Blackwell, 1999.
Lewellen, Ted. *The Anthropology of Globalization*. Westport, CT: Praeger, 2002.
Loftsdóttir, Kristín. "Globalization and Modernity." In *Topographies of Globalization*, edited by Valur Ingimundarson, Kristín Loftsdóttir, and Irma Erlingsdóttir, 151–62. Reykjavik: University of Iceland, 2004.
Metcalf, Peter. "Global 'Disjuncture' and the 'Sites' of Anthropology." *Cultural Anthropology* 16, no. 2 (2001): 175–77.
Meyer, Birgit, and Peter Geschiere. "Introduction." In *Globalization and Identity*, edited by Birgit Meyer and Peter Geschiere, 1–15. Malden, MA: Wiley Blackwell, 1999.
Nederveen Pieterse, Jan. "Fault Lines of Transnationalism: Borders Matter." *Bulletin of the Royal Institute for Inter-faith Studies* 4, no. 2 (2002): 33–48.
———. *Globalization and Culture: Global Mélange*. 2nd ed. Lanham, MD: Rowan and Littlefield, 2009.
———. "Globalization as Hybridization." in *Global Modernities*, edited by Mike Featherstone, Scott Lash, and Roland Robertson, 45–68. Thousand Oaks, CA: Sage, 1995.
Ohmae, Kenichi. *The Borderless World: Power and Strategy in the Interlinked Economy*. New York: Harper Collins, 1991.
Reynolds, David. "American Globalism: Mass, Motion and the Multiplier Effect." In *Globalization in World History*, edited by A. G. Hopkins, 244–263. New York: W. W. Norton, 2002.

Robertson, Roland. *Globalization: Social Theory and Global Culture.* Thousand Oaks, CA: Sage, 1992.
Sassen, Saskia. *A Sociology of Globalization.* New York: W. W. Norton, 2007.
———. "Spatialities and Temporalities of the Global: Elements for a Theorization." *Public Culture* 12, no. 1 (2000): 215–32.
Tomlinson, John. "Cultural Globalization and Cultural Imperialism." In *International Communication and Globalization: A Critical Introduction*, edited by Ali Mohammadi, 170–190. Thousand Oaks: Sage, 1997.
Tsing, Anna. "The Global Situation." *Cultural Anthropology* 15, no. 3 (2000): 327–360.
Wallerstein, Immanuel. *The Modern World System.* New York: Academic Press, 1974.
———. *World-Systems Analysis.* Durham, NC: Duke University Press, 2004.

CHAPTER 12

THE CHURCHES IN SOUTHEAST ASIA

Andrew Peh

In the study of the development of Christianity in the global south, there is growing attention to the impact of religions on politics at all levels – nationally, regionally, and internationally. In Southeast Asia, this attention is seen in considering religion's role in the people power movement in the Philippines and the plight of the Rohingyas in Myanmar, while in popular culture there is the tangential reference to a middle-class Christianity in Jon M. Chu's 2018 film, *Crazy Rich Asians*.

THE DEVELOPMENT OF SOUTHEAST ASIA

In earlier historical periods, Southeast Asia had been considered by its neighbors to be a region in its own right and not merely an extension of the neighboring empires or kingdoms. Thus, the early Indian navigators and merchants employed various terms, notably *Suvaranabhūmi* (golden land) or *Suvarnadvipa* (golden island)[1] to describe this area east of the Indian subcontinent. The seafaring Chinese referred to this region as *Nanyang* (南洋), literally translated as (regions in the) "southern ocean." Taking reference from the Chinese, the Japanese' term, *Nan'yō*, is similarly translated as "south ocean." Fifield stresses "that these expressions reflected the roles of the sea-minded people who used them and focused on seas with their adjacent lands rather than on lands with their adjacent sea."[2]

It was the Westerners who referred to this part of the world as "Asia" as well as "the Far East." The term "Asia" may be traced to the Greek plausible prototype, *Assuva*. Emmerson posits that "there is reason to believe that the Greeks took the word 'Assuva,' pronounced it more like the modern name 'Asia,' and

---

1. Anil Sakya, *Rethinking of Buddhism in Southeast Asia*, paper presented at the International Conference on Buddhism in Southeast Asia, Phnom Penh City, Cambodia (4–7 September 2018).
2. Russell H. Fifield, "Southeast Asia as a Regional Concept," *Southeast Asian Journal of Social Science* 11, no. 2 (1983): 2.

applied it to the eastern outskirts of their world, across the Aegean."[3] In the age of discovery, the European powers often took reference from the more "familiar shapes of India to the West and China to the north,"[4] for which the directional adjective "southeast" interestingly designates the location as south of China and east of India. Yet the term was not the common parlance in the early nineteenth century, as preference laid with references to either China or India, such as "Indochina" and "Indonesia."[5] For example, the London Missionary Society's work in Southeast Asia from the period between 1808 to 1842, as they awaited China's opening, was known as the Ultra Ganges (a river in India) Mission.

The phrase "Southeast Asia" was reportedly first used by the Baptist minister the Reverend Howard Malcom in the preface as well as the title of his two-volume book, *Travels in South-Eastern Asia embracing Hindustan, Malaya, Siam, and China; with notices of Numerous Missionary Stations and a full account of the Burman Empire*, published in 1850. Yet it was not until the period of World War II that usage of the term "Southeast Asia" became more common since this was the arena of the Japanese military conquests and the loci of the Pacific War. Prior to the bombing of Pearl Harbor in 1941, a good number of studies on the social, economic, and political problems of Southeast Asia had been undertaken by the Institute of Pacific Relations in Honolulu. These studies employed the term "Southeast Asia," which foreshadowed America's continued involvement in this region. World War II also provided the context for the appointment of Admiral Lord Louis Mountbatten as the Supreme Allied Commander of the South East Asia Command in August 1943. With the defeat of the Japanese, a British Defence Committee in South East Asia was established, reflecting the British concern for the region. The adoption of the term is important in its neutrality, in not asserting "one metropole over that of another,"[6] hence providing the fertile soil from which the concept of Southeast Asia developed.

The United States similarly set up a Division of Southeast Asian Affairs in 1945 for the formulation of policies in the Department of State, intentionally choosing to spell "'Southeast Asia' in place of 'South-East Asia' in order not

---

3. Donald Emmerson, "'Southeast Asia': What's in a Name?" *Journal of Southeast Asian Studies* 15, no. 1 (March 1984): 1–21.
4. Dennis Bloodworth, *An Eye for the Dragon: Southeast Asia Observed, 1954–1970* (New York: Farrar, 1970), xiii.
5. Emmerson, "Southeast Asia," 2.
6. Emmerson, 17.

to copy the British."[7] American interests in the region would spill over into another major conflict in the 1960s, escalating the Indochina wars. It is perhaps not an exaggeration to say that the Second Indochina War, also referred to as the Vietnam War – from about 1955 to 1975, brought Southeast Asia, at least continental Southeast Asia, into the homes of the Americans. This was the first war that was televised in the United States through which the words "Vietnam" and "Southeast Asia" were etched into the collective memories of almost all Americans. Correspondingly, perhaps the ubiquity in adopting "Southeast Asia" over "South East Asia" underscores the impact of American influence in modern Southeast Asia.

It may well be that World War II and the Second Indochina War thus provided the backdrop for the emergence of Southeast Asia as a region with increasing significance[8] which was further strengthened by corresponding developments in academia on both sides of the Atlantic.[9] These developments resulted in significant academic contributions in a wide number of disciplines related to the Southeast Asian context, though "American Southeast Asianists were disproportionately concentrated in political science, their European counterparts concentrated in anthropology, geography, and languages."[10] Yet one cannot ignore the fact that the term "Southeast Asia" was born out of geographical expediency. Hence the point of this introduction is to underscore the complexity – ethnic diversity, religious plurality, historical asymmetry, and political distinctions – of this geographical region that is presently composed of eleven countries: Brunei, Myanmar (Burma), Cambodia, Indonesia, Laos, Malaysia, Philippines, Singapore, Timor-Leste, Thailand, and Vietnam. Southeast Asia is "perhaps the most diverse region on Earth."[11]

LOOKING BACK – CHRISTIANITY IN SOUTHEAST ASIA

The religious mosaic of Southeast Asia underscores the layering of various cultural and religious influences. Most of the early history of the Southeast Asian kingdoms from 1000 BC onward was influenced by Indic culture and the Hindu religion – the Mon Kingdom in Myanmar, the Angkor Empire in

---

7. Fifield, "Southeast Asia," 5.
8. Fifield, 2–6.
9. Fifield records the establishment of the first American-integrated program in Southeast Asian studies at Yale University in 1947, which was very quickly followed by similar programs in the University of Cornell, University of California Berkeley, University of Michigan, and others. Fifield, 6–7.
10. Emmerson, "Southeast Asia," 12.
11. William Frederick, "Southeast Asia," *Encyclopedia Britannica online* (n.d.).

Cambodia, and the Majaphahit Empire in Java extending over to Bali. Over this veneer of Indianization was the influence of Theravada Buddhism in the third century BC through the missionary endeavors of Indian Emperor Ashoka in the Pagan Empire in Myanmar, Sukhothai Kingdom in Thailand, and the later Angkor Empire in Cambodia. Mahayana Buddhism significantly influenced the Nam Viet Kingdom in Vietnam, the Shailendra Dynasty in Java (Borobudur), and various coastal areas of Southeast Asia where Chinese diaspora communities took root. The later arrival of Arab and Indian Muslim traders[12] to the western tip of Sumatra, Aceh in the eighth to nineth centuries was to ignite an Islamic fervor across both sides of the Malacca Straits and across the Indonesian Archipelago, supplanting the earlier Hindu and Buddhist influences, with the exception of Bali, which until today retains Hindu religious roots. The spread of Islam across the archipelago resulted in the development of Indonesia as the country with the world's largest Muslim population.

In contrast, the record of significant Christian movements may be traced from the late nineteenth century onwards. The growth of the ancient Asian religions such as Hinduism, Buddhism, and Islam through trade and migration perhaps accounts for Christianity's minority status in most of Southeast Asia, with the exception of the Philippines and Timor Leste. The earliest signs of Christian presence in Southeast Asia predate the arrival of Islam, at about the seventh century.[13] Archaeological finds in the Malay Peninsula as well as Sumatra suggest the existence of Christian settlements originating from Central Asia. However, little is known about these early settlements and much less might be gleaned about their impact as they quickly disappeared from any historical records.

The Portuguese

A more substantial engagement of Christianity in Southeast Asia came with the colonial expansion of European maritime powers in Asia from the late fifteenth century onward, primarily the Portuguese and the Spanish. The maritime "conquest of the world" was made possible by the Treaty of Tordesillas in 1494, the agreement between Spain and Portugal with the Holy See dividing the rights to colonize all lands outside of Europe, the agreement in Spanish

---

12. Scholars are divided as to whether the first Islamic missionaries came directly from Saudi Arabia or were Sufi traders from Gujerat, India. But most are in agreement that Islam's spread in Indonesia was gradual and peaceful and through trade and exchanges instead of conquest.
13. Robbie G. H. Goh, *Christianity in Southeast Asia* (Singapore: ISEAS, 2005), 1–2.

called "Patronatus" and in Portuguese "Patroado." In principle the treaty followed the papal bull issued in 1493 by Pope Alexander VI which drew a line of demarcation from north to south poles in the Atlantic Ocean, about one hundred leagues (555 kilometers) west of the Cape Verde Islands (longitude 46 degrees, 37 minutes west). The treaty marked out that Portugal had access to all lands east of the line while Spain had access to lands west of the line.

Moving eastwards, the Portuguese established trading ports in Goa, India, as well as in Ceylon (Sri Lanka), and from these ports Portuguese merchants and missionaries entered Southeast Asia through the Straits of Malacca (Malaysia). Under Afonso de Albuquerque, the Portuguese program to gain control of all the main maritime trade routes of the East was further consolidated with the capture of the port of Malacca in 1511. From both the ports of Goa and Malacca, "Albuquerque permanently established the Portuguese presence in Asia and laid the foundation for further expansion into Southeast and East Asia."[14] It was from the port of Malacca that the Portuguese ventured further eastwards to Timor, Flores as well as Maluku, or Moluccas, an archipelago in Indonesia also known as the "spice islands," in 1512, establishing trading rights for the most sought after agricultural resources, nutmeg and cloves.[15] The Portuguese Roman Catholic orders directed their missionary activities toward the indigenous peoples who had not been brought under Buddhist, Hindu, or Islamic influence. This focus is particularly evident in Maluku, where the Portuguese concentrated their commercial and conversion efforts in Ambon (Kota Ambon in modern Indonesia), establishing it as a base from which they traded with other neighboring islands, notably with the Muslim rulers of Ternate.

Fernao de Magalhāis, better known as Ferdinand Magellan, a Portuguese who had participated in the conquest of Malacca in 1511, made several petitions to King Manuel I of Portugal to lead an expedition to reach the spice islands from the east, via the Atlantic. Repeatedly rejected by Manuel I, Magellan turned to Spain. News of the Portuguese, led by Francisco Serrao, arrival in Maluku (Ternate Island) in 1512, and the acquisition of the much sought after spices nutmeg and cloves spurred Magellan's westward voyage, resulting in the European naming of the Pacific Ocean (calm waters), the discovery of the Strait of Magellan in 1520, the arrival of Spanish powers in the Philippines in 1521, the Spanish competition in the spice trade in 1522,

---

14. Franz-Stefan Gady, "How Portugal Forged an Empire in Asia," *The Diplomat* (11 July 2019).
15. Gady, "How Portugal."

and most notably the first maritime circumnavigation of the globe.[16] Though Magellan died in the battle of Mactan (in modern day Philippines), his crew went on to establish trade with Tidore in Maluku in 1522. This series of events resulted in the confrontation between Portugal and Spain, since there was no line of demarcation in the East, hence leading to the Treaty of Zaragoza (Saragossa) of 1529.

The treaty designated the meridian 297.5 marine leagues (about 1,487 kilometers or 892 miles) east of the Maluku as the demarcation between Portuguese and Spanish territories. With this line, Portugal gained control of all of Asia as well as the islands, including Maluku, while Spain controlled westward from the meridian which included most of the Pacific Ocean. This treaty, *in toto*, placed all of the Philippine islands under Portuguese control since the islands are all west of the meridian. Various Spanish expeditions were dispatched, and the arrival of Miguel López de Legazpi in 1565 is regarded as the beginning of Spanish colonization of the Philippines as he wrested control of the island from Portuguese challenges.

The Roman Catholic Missionaries

It was through a "sustained engagement"[17] that Roman Catholicism began to take root in the Philippines. Based in Manila, the Roman Catholic orders, particularly the Augustinians, Dominican, and the Jesuits from 1596 onwards, fanned out across the islands on the Philippines, developing a network of educational and ecclesial establishments. By the middle of the seventeenth century, with the exception of the more remote mountainous tribes and the inhabitants of Mindanao and the Sulu Archipelago, most of the Philippines was brought into the fold (devoutly or otherwise) of the Roman Catholic Church.

The Portuguese brought commerce and Christianity beyond Maluku to other islands such as the eastern islands of Nusa Tenggara, which includes East Timor and Flores, establishing Roman Catholicism well beyond Portuguese colonial dominance. The fact that East Timor (Timor Leste) and the Philippines are the countries with the largest percentage of Roman Catholics in their population attests to the longevity of this missionary encounter.

---

16. Oskar Spate, *The Spanish Lake* (Canberra: Australia National University Press, 2010). See especially chapter 2, "Balboa, Magellan and the Moluccas," 25–37.
17. Robert Hunt, "Southeast Asian Christianity," in *The Encyclopedia of Christian Civilization* (London: Blackwell, 2012), 2221.

The Churches in Southeast Asia

On continental Southeast Asia, the dominance of both Sinic and Indic traditions are well attested by the various political, religious, and cultural traditions of the Indochinese region spanning Vietnam, Laos, Cambodia, Thailand, and Myanmar. Among the earliest arrivals of Christianity[18] were Portuguese traders in the early sixteenth century. The Portuguese influence was not limited to the western reaches of the Indonesian Archipelago, but from the base established in Malacca in 1511, they arrived in the courts of the king of Siam (Thailand) in 1511, and concluded a treaty in 1516. Similarly, they arrived in Tonkin (Northern Vietnam) and in Burma before the middle of the sixteenth century. Hrang Hlei writes, "The early Christian presence in Burma was brought by the Portuguese, who came seeking opportunities for political expansion and economic development."[19] Their arrival in Burma clearly preceded the British East India Company as well as the subsequent Baptist missionaries. But as Robbie Goh rightly notes, while the Portuguese should be credited with the introduction of Catholicism to Burma in the sixteenth century, this act, however, "did not have significant impact as the Portuguese did not establish any territorial control."[20]

Catholic Christianity arrived in the latter half of the sixteenth century in various parts of the Indochina region. Different orders from various bases participated in the propagation of the faith throughout the region. Franciscan, Augustinian, and Dominican missionaries from Portuguese Malacca and Macau and Spanish Manila arrived in Tonkin (Northern Vietnam) and Cochinchina (Southern Vietnam); Dominican missionaries and French Jesuits arrived in Ayutthia, Siam, in 1567 and 1664, respectively.

Catholicism took firm root in Vietnam with the arrival of the Jesuits in 1615, possible due to the establishment of a trading post with Chinese and Japanese merchants in Faifo (modern day Hoi An) as Portuguese merchant Fernandes da Costa obtained exclusive permission to trade there in 1614. These developments coincided with the Tokugawa Shogunate's persecution of Christians in Japan which led to an influx of Japanese Catholics who were seeking refuge from the persecution. On 18 January 1615, two Jesuit priests,

---

18. Thant Myint-U writes about the possibility of early Nestorian arrivals in Burma which correlates with the inference of Charles Duroiselle, *Report of the Superintendent: Archaeological Survey, Burma, for the Year Ending 31st March 1922*, 17–21, as quoted by Claudine Bautze-Picron, *Bagan Murals and the Sino-Tibetan World*, Hal open science (2014).
19. Hrang Hlei, "Myanmar," in *Christianity in East and Southeast Asia*, eds. Kenneth R. Ross, Francis Alvarez, Todd M. Johnson (Edinburgh, UK: Edinburgh University Press, 2020), 145.
20. Goh, *Christianity*, 66.

Francesco Buzomi and Diogo Carvalho, together with a few brothers arrived in Cửa Hàn (near present-day Hội An) to visit these displaced Japanese Catholics. Perceiving that the Vietnamese were responsive to the gospel, the Jesuits consequently established the first permanent mission in 1615 at Đà Nẵng in central Vietnam (Trung Việt). It may hence be surmised that "the Jesuit missions to Vietnam were an accident of history."[21] The arrival of another band of Jesuit brothers led by Alexandre de Rhodes, often referred to as the "Apostle to Vietnam," ushered in a more pronounced period of missionary activity. De Rhodes was excited with the missionary prospects in Vietnam and returned to Europe to petition the pope. What ensued was that in the spring of 1658, members of the Propaganda Fide took steps toward designating the Indochinese territories as apostolic vicariates – what George E. Dutton describes as "an act of geographical legerdemain designed to sidestep Padroado authority"[22] – and also to create an entirely new missionary apparatus, the Foreign Missions Society of Paris (*Missions Étrangerès de Paris*, MEP), to wrestle control of Asian missions from both Portuguese patronage and the Jesuits. These actions exacerbated the tensions that had existed between Padroado and papal authority as well as the rivalry between the ecclesiastical orders.

French, Dutch, and British Colonialism

French Catholic missionary endeavors preceded the arrival of French colonialism. The French colonization of Indochina began first with the conquest of Saigon in 1859, taking control of Northern Vietnam as a result of the Sino-French war (1884–1885) and forming French Indochina in 1887 with the inclusion of Annam, Tonkin, and Cochinchina, the inclusion of the kingdom of Cambodia as a French Protectorate, the addition of Laos following the Franco-Siamese War in 1893, and with a series of territorial annexations at the expense of Siam in 1907. The missionary efforts of the Portuguese and the Jesuits were likewise supplanted by the French missions in Siam (Thailand).

The total eclipse of the Portuguese was almost achieved with the rise of both the English and the Dutch trading companies – the British East India Company (EIC) in 1600 and the Dutch *Vereenigde Oostindische Compagnie*

---

21. Anh Q. Tran, SJ, "The Historiography of the Jesuits in Vietnam: 1615–1773 and 1957–2007," Brill (October 2018).
22. George E. Dutton, *A Vietnamese Moses: Philiphe Binh and the Geographies of Early Modern Catholicism* (Berkely: University of California Press, 2016), 28.

(VOC) in 1602.²³ The Portuguese had developed Malacca into a fort, the Fortaleza de Malaca, and were able to control access to the sea lanes in the Straits of Malacca, thereby securing a monopoly of the spice trade. In 1641, Malacca fell to the Dutch, and this takeover marked the beginning of the longest foreign rule of the port. The Dutch ruled for almost 183 years with intermittent British occupation during the Napoleonic Wars (1795–1818). The Dutch supplanted the Portuguese, being the only country that was allowed to trade with Japan from Dejima, off Nagasaki, as Japan closed all trade with all other European nations, notably Portugal and Spain. In ways not too divergent from the French MEP (*Missions etrangeres de Paris*), that is the Paris Foreign Missions Society, in Indochina, Dutch chaplains were also missionaries who sought to create a colonial Protestant community "whose ecclesial structures would parallel and eventually extend those of Dutch colonial interests."²⁴ Yet as a trading company, the VOC was primarily concerned with economic profit and understandably, "it was initially ineffectual in spreading the faith."²⁵

In the Indonesian Archipelago, the expanse and inaccessibility of the islands, the linguistic and cultural diversity of the people, the dominance of Islam which had arrived in the thirteenth century, and Christianity's proximity with colonialism were all factors that impeded its growth. This situation was further complicated by the Dutch suppression of Roman Catholicism and the prohibition of other Protestant missions. Internal structural problems, the low profitability of the company, and the fourth Anglo-Dutch War resulted in the weakening and eventual collapse of the VOC. The Napoleonic Wars brought the Netherlands under French control, and with the subsequent defeat of Napoleon, most of the VOC's Southeast Asian territories were ceded to the British East India Company.

For the British and especially for the East India Company, the growth in trade in Chinese tea "was the basic impulse that led to the expansion of British power in the Far East, and as a corollary, in Southeast Asia as well."²⁶ It became increasingly obvious, however, that the British had nothing that the Chinese did not already possess or was not quite prepared to do without. The Chinese

---

23. Portugal was able to retain colonial territories in Macau, which was returned to China in 1999, as well as the eastern islands of the Indonesian Archipelago, specifically Timor Leste, which gained independence from Portugal in 1975 and from Indonesia in 2002.
24. Hunt, "Southeast Asian Christianity," 2221.
25. Goh, *Christianity*, 58.
26. K. C. Tregonning, *The British in Malaya* (Tucson: University of Arizona Press, 1965), 5.

would have accepted payment in silver bullion, but Britain was hesitant to allow any silver to leave the country. Tregonning comments

> But if Britain itself produced nothing of value to China and if Indian cotton was insufficient, fortunately, there were a few other commodities Britain could secure in exchange for which the towkays of Canton would exchange their tea. Chief of these were tin and pepper. And it was largely for the acquisition of these two commodities that Britain doggedly continued its search for a Southeast Asian base.[27]

Operating from India, the EIC embarked on various mercantile missions into areas as Acheh, Bencoolen, Kedah, Perlis, and eastwards toward the island of Balambangan. The attempts of the British to establish trading posts in order to acquire tin and pepper, the two primary products, helped to facilitate an increasing volume of trade with China. The spice trade was very soon supplanted by the opium trade in the late eighteenth century, such that by 1773, the British became the leading suppliers of Indian opium to the Chinese market.[28] The EIC established a lucrative monopoly of opium cultivation in Bengal that resulted in the Opium Wars in China and that subsequently forced the opening of China to Western imperialism, including the ceding of Hong Kong to Britain on 20 January 1841, formalized by the Treaty of Nanking in 1842. Tregonning aptly sums up the situation,

> Of most importance was the acquisition of the British of a place to trade – a barren island off the mouth of the Canton River. Here in Hong Kong, the British were to establish what they had been seeking for over a hundred years. . . . in Hong Kong, at last, the British had secured a mart for trade with China. With the establishment of Hong Kong, the long move east from India has ended.[29]

---

27. Tregonning, *British in Malaya*, 5.
28. It is understood that opium was first introduced to China by Turkish and Arab traders in the late sixth or early seventh century AD. It was used as a drug for pain relief due to its limited quantities. In the early 1700s, the Portuguese introduced a new form of smokeable opium by mixing opium from India with tobacco, which became an addiction among the common folk in Chinese society and enabled the British East India Company to capitalize on China's growing demand. Refer to Sarah DeMing, "Economic Working Paper - No 25: The Economic Importance of Indian Opium and Trade with China on Britain's Economy, 1843–1890," Whitman College (Spring 2011).
29. Tregonning, *British in Malaya*, 158.

In seeking to supersede the Dutch and to gain the lion's share of trade with China, the EIC was relentless in out-maneuvering all European rivals. As a result, a series of additional ports were established between 1786 and 1824. Penang was acquired from the Sultan of Kedah in 1786, and in 1819, Sir Stamford Raffles established Singapore as a free port at the southern tip of the Straits with permission from the Sultan of Johor.

The EIC at the same time drew a clear distinction between their economic purposes and the zeal of those who sought to enter their territories as missionaries. Hence the EIC consistently resisted any missionary activities in its territories. Brian Harrison in his account of the missionary work of Robert Morrison, a pioneer missionary to China who was stationed in Malacca and Singapore, notes that while the EIC had "exclusive control of British shipping to China as well as India, was not in favor of introducing Christian missionaries into the eastern world at this time."[30]

Just as the European powers had partitioned Africa in the Berlin Conference of 1884–1885, there was a similar race to do the same in the Far East with the hopes of establishing trade with China. By the middle of the nineteenth century, Western imperialism became established in the region. Within the next century, the political map of the region was re-drawn by the arrival of these colonial powers: the Portuguese in Maluku (Timor Leste); the Spanish followed by the Americans in the Philippines; the French in Indo-China (Vietnam, Laos, and Cambodia); the Dutch in the East Indies (Indonesia); and the British in Burma (Myanmar), the Straits settlements, Malaya (West Malaysia and Singapore), and North Borneo (East Malaysia and Brunei). The exception was Thailand, which remained the only country in Southeast Asia to retain its sovereignty and was never colonized, successfully navigating between British and French threats under the successive kings Mongkut (1851–1868) and Chulalongkorn (1868–1910).[31]

Christianity and Colonialism

With the advent of each successive colonial power, not surprisingly Catholic and Protestant missions were initiated in each of the Southeast Asian colonies and Thailand. Colonialism thus opened the door for the advent of Christianity

---

30. Brian Harrison, *Waiting for China: The Anglo-Chinese College at Malacca, 1818–1843 and Early Nineteenth-Century Missions* (Hong Kong: Hong Kong University Press, 1979), 1.
31. In this book, it should noted that the Japanese invasion of Thailand is not considered colonization but an aspect of World War II.

in Southeast Asia, beginning with Portuguese and Spanish Roman Catholicism in the sixteenth century and increasing to the expansive range of Protestant denominations. Hunt summarizes the different strands of mission endeavors:

> Missions active in Southeast Asia by the 19th century included Baptists (1813) and Catholics (1850) in Burma, Catholics (renewed in 1834), Congregationalists (1835), Baptists (1833) and Presbyterians (1847) in Siam, and Anglicans (1813), Presbyterians (1841), and later Methodists (1885) in Malaya. In Indonesia, Dutch Reformed were present from the outset. Catholics returned in 1845, and then by 1900 Lutherans, Brethren, and Methodists arrived. The American defeat of Spain and its subsequent intervention in the Philippines in 1898 opened the way for Presbyterian, Methodist, Baptist, Anglican and Seventh-Day Adventist missions in the Philippines.[32]

Inopportunely, the same competition between rival colonial powers shaped the basis of a richly diverse Christianity in the nineteenth and twentieth centuries. The slow pace of growth and indigenization of the church in Southeast Asia continued in the early years of the twentieth century, only to be further decelerated by World War I followed by the Great Depression in the 1930s, both of which affected numbers and resources. Generally, Christian mission in Southeast Asia in the first half of the twentieth century was closely associated with education, medicine, and ministries that catered to socioeconomic progress. Bishop Doraisamy in chronicling the birth and spread of American Methodist missions in Malaya and Singapore employed the term "pluriform mission" in describing their work of church planting through evangelism, education, publications, medical ministries, and various social outreaches.[33] Avenues such as education and medical missions were also likewise prevalent among the missionaries ministering in the broader regions of Southeast Asia.

This season of growth was soon overtaken by the grave reality of growing international conflicts. Southeast Asia was in the context for war for almost half a decade. Most countries shared the common experience of invasion by the rising superpower Japan, seeking to supplant Western imperialism. Japan's

---

32. Hunt, "Southeast Asian Christianity," 2222.
33. Bishop Doraisamy uses the term "pluriform mission" in the title of chapter seven in his book on Oldham. Theodore Doraisamy, *Oldham Called of God* (Singapore: Methodist Book Room, 1979). Among the various chroniclers of the history of Methodism, it seems likely that the term was first applied to Oldham's mission work and strategy by Doraisamy.

military incursions into almost all of Southeast Asia resulted in a numerical decimation of Christians and of those aligned with the colonial powers. On the state of Christian missions in continental Southeast Asia in this time, Kane reported: "the Japanese occupation resulted not only in the destruction of church and mission property but also in the wanton slaying of many church leaders and the consequent falling off in church membership."[34]

This temporary setback, however, refined the church and reignited a renewed growth in the postwar period of nationalism. Roxborough observes that,

> the Japanese period of 1942 to 1945 forced issues of local church leadership and independence which had long been talked about but not always acted on. . . . The occupation demonstrated the ability of the churches to survive without European leadership, but the cost was high. The common experience of suffering was chastening and unifying.[35]

One of the results of World War II in the Pacific was the gradual exit of the colonial powers as over the next two decades, nations achieved political independence – Indonesia in 1945; the Philippines in 1946; Burma in 1948; Cambodia, Laos, and Vietnam in 1954; and Malaysia in 1963.[36] Formal independence provided the imperative for the development of national churches as well as the appointing and equipping of local indigenous leadership. Consequently, Christian participation in various movements across the region became more pronounced as indigenous leaders lent voice to social, political, and theological issues. Some examples include the participation of Roman Catholic leaders in the "people's power" movement in the Philippines that ousted President Ferdinand Marcos in 1986; the Baptist Karen Christians engagement in their struggle for autonomy against a military regime in Myanmar in 1976; and the legal challenges of Malaysian Christians against the 1991 ban of the use of "Allah" in the Bible in 2021.

The growth of Christianity during the formative years following the region's independence from Western powers was modest. The larger forces such

---

34. J. Herbert Kane, "Continental Southeast Asia" in *Christianity Today*, July 1965, available at https://www.christianitytoday.com/ct/1965/july-30/continental-southeast-asia.html (accessed 8 July 2020).
35. John Roxborogh, "Christianity in South-east Asia, 1914–2000," in *Christianity in East and Southeast Asia*, eds. Kenneth R. Ross, Francis Alvarez, Todd M. Johnson (Edinburgh, UK: Edinburgh University Press, 2020), 442.
36. Singapore was "kicked out" of the Federation of Malaya and became an independent country in 9 August 1965, while Brunei gained independence from Britain in 1984. Timor Leste is the "youngest" nation in Southeast Asia, becoming formally independent in 2002.

as the formation of People's Republic of China and subsequent closure to foreign missionaries, the rising conflicts on the Korean Peninsula and Indochina, and the propagation of Marxist ideology in various parts of the Southeast Asia all posed serious threats to the budding national church offshoots of the colonial stem. Yet every crisis was also a time of opportunity for the churches and missions. The expulsion of missionaries from China forced mission societies to relocate resources, both financial and personnel, and consider fresh mission fields in Southeast Asia. For example the China Inland Mission relocated their headquarters to Singapore and renamed themselves the Overseas Missionary Fellowship as they repositioned their focus to include new fields of missionary work all over Southeast Asia. Various parachurch organizations including Campus Crusade for Christ (Cru) and the International Fellowship of Evangelical Students (IFES) took root and were instrumental in revitalizing Christianity, especially among the youth in the various cities which were emerging as centers of trade, commerce, and education all across the region.

At the turn of the twenty-first century, a wave of renewed growth swept through Asia and Southeast Asia through Pentecostalism,[37] both in the Catholic and the evangelical traditions where many "have been influenced by the Pentecostal immediacy and intimacy of the Holy Spirit."[38] More recently one of the features of Pentecostal renewal has been the rise of megachurch movements all across Southeast Asia which are not limited to the urban centers inhabited by "crazy rich Asians" but has spread across the growing cities and suburbs of Indonesia, Malaysia, the Philippines, and Singapore. Terence Chong comments, "The Pentecostal megachurch, especially if it is of the independent variety, is known for its close association to the so-called prosperity gospel."[39] It cannot be ignored that "Pentecostalism has reconfigured church growth in South-east Asia."[40]

As we survey the history of Christianity in Southeast Asia, undoubtedly Christianity is the "new kid on the block," where the "block" is already home to various religious tenants. Waves of Indianization, Sinicization, and Islamization

---

37. For a summary of this growth in the Southeast Asian region, refer to Vinson Synan and Amos Yong, eds., *Global Renewal Christianity: Asia and Oceania Spirit-Empowered Movements: Past, Present, and Future*, vol. 1 (Lake Mary, FL: Charisma House, 2016), 181–282.
38. Scott Sunquist, *Explorations in Asian Christianity* (Downers Grove, IL: IVP Academic, 2017), 73.
39. Terence Chong, ed., *Pentecostal Megachurches in Southeast Asia: Negotiating Class, Consumption and the Nation* (Singapore: ISEAS, 2018), 5.
40. Terence Chong and Evelyn Tan, "Why Christian Expansionism is a Quiet Storm in Southeast Asia," *South China Morning Post* (21 November 2019).

The Churches in Southeast Asia

have given rise to the religious diversity of the region. Yet Christianity has been able to make some significant inroads, thereby adding to the richness as well as the potential fragility of this religious diversity.

Country	Religion (% of population)							
	Buddhist	Christian	Hindu	Jewish	Muslim	Traditional	Other Religions	Unaffiliated
Brunei	8.6	9.4	0.3	< 0.1	75.1	6.2	0.1	0.4
Cambodia	96.9	0.4	< 0.1	< 0.1	2.0	0.6	< 0.1	0.2
Indonesia	0.7	9.9	1.7	< 0.1	87.2	0.3	0.1	< 0.1
Laos	66.0	1.5	< 0.1	< 0.1	< 0.1	30.7	0.7	0.9
Malaysia	17.7	9.4	6.0	< 0.1	63.7	2.3	0.2	0.7
Myanmar	80.1	7.8	1.7	< 0.1	4.0	5.8	0.2	0.5
Philippines	< 0.1	92.6	< 0.1	< 0.1	5.5	1.5	0.1	0.1
Singapore	33.9	18.2	5.2	< 0.1	14.3	2.3	9.7	16.4
Thailand	93.2	0.9	0.1	< 0.1	5.5	< 0.1	< 0.1	0.3
Timor-Leste	< 0.1	99.6	< 0.1	< 0.1	0.1	0.1	< 0.1	< 0.1
Vietnam	16.4	8.2	< 0.1	< 0.1	0.2	45.3	0.4	29.6

Figure 5: Religious Diversity in Southeast Asia

The chart "Religious Diversity in Southeast Asia" well shows the religious diversity in Southeast Asia.[41] "Thus from missionary beginnings, Christianity in Southeast Asia has emerged in the twenty-first century as highly variegated, frequently conflicted, and intensely dynamic."[42] The plurality and diversity within Southeast Asian Christianity lends credence to Peter Phan's "Asian Christianities."[43]

---

41. Data from https://www.pewresearch.org/religion/2014/04/04/religious-diversity-index-scores-by-country/.
42. Hunt, "Southeast Asian Christianity," 2224.
43. Peter Phan, *Asian Christianities: History, Theology and Practice* (New York: Orbis, 2018).

LOOKING FORWARD – CHRISTIANITY IN SOUTHEAST ASIA

Having surveyed in broad strokes the history of Christianity in Southeast Asia, what may we say of the future prospects? Some have reflected on this question such as Charles Farhadian in his missiological discussion on Christian movements in Southeast Asia[44] and Mary Ho in her insightful record of twelve trends that will potentially shape the future of Christianity in East and Southeast Asia.[45] The following proposition builds on these perspectives with a particular appeal to the churches in Southeast Asia to be more collaborative, more contextual, and more compassionate.

Collaboration

Looking at the trajectory of Christianity in Southeast Asia, we cannot ignore the checkered contributions of the colonial past.[46] The motives that drove European colonial expansion and conquests have been described as "God, gold, and glory," and the reality is that missions was often obscured by economics or politics. Not uncommon is the perspective among postcolonial historians that the missionary expansion from the sixteenth century on was but one arm of Western aggressive imperialism. The general tenor of most colonial studies is that the Christian missions were coconspirators in connivance with the exploitative activities of colonial rule through conquest, commerce, code of law, and "civilizing mission." The church is still seen as a part of the colonial enterprise, and not surprisingly many today are skeptical of the church's missionary efforts. Yet in an assessment of Christian missions in Southeast Asia, the issue at stake is whether or not the missionaries contributed intentionally and purposefully or otherwise as colonial agents to the processes of subjugation, exploitation, and devastation of the land and the people. There needs to be more robust study and accounting of the mission history in each of the countries in the region. The significance of these historical studies is further underscored by the disproportionate social effect that Christianity as a minority faith has exerted

---

44. Charles Farhadian, "A Missiological Reflection on Present-day Christian Movements in Southeast Asia," in *Christian Movements in Southeast Asia: A Theological Exploration*, ed. Michael Nai-Chiu Poon (Singapore: Genesis Books, 2010), 101–19.
45. Mary Ho, "The Future of Christianity in East and Southeast Asia," in *Christianity in East and Southeast Asia*, eds. Kenneth R. Ross, Francis D. Alvararez, and Todd M. Johnson (Edinburgh, UK: Edinburgh University Press, 2020), 479–92.
46. Though Thailand remains the only Southeast Asian country that has never been occupied by a European colonial power, that situation did not proscribe Catholic and Protestant missionaries from bringing the gospel to the Thais.

on each of the different countries. In his perceptive assessment of the impact of colonial Christianity, Roxborogh grants that

> If even at its best its collective personality could not easily avoid being patronising, it also brought social change which was not all bad, and provided windows into a wider and more hopeful world. Many individuals made the interests of the people of south-east Asia their life's work. In its late phase colonialism also provided infrastructures that facilitated communication, movement and mission and a demand for medical and educational services which churches with international contacts were often the only institutions capable of providing.[47]

Scott Sunquist contends that the study of Christian history is much more complex in the twenty-first century because "three issues – the global nature of the faith, the collapse of Christendom, and the shift from western to non-western dominance – demand the exploration of new historiographies."[48] Thus there is a heightened need for studies that are more collaborative, in which indigenous Christian scholars contribute toward a deeper appreciation of the history of Southeast Asia.

While there are centers for Southeast Asia Studies in Kyoto University[49] and in the ASEAN Studies Centre located in the Institute of Southeast Asian Studies (ISEAS)[50] in Singapore, to date there have been few collaborative scholarly exchanges among indigenous Christian scholars of a similar vein. In the late 1990s, Trinity Theological College in Singapore initiated the development of such an effort in the study of Asian church history. The need for wider collaboration resulted in the launching of the Centre for the Study of Christianity in Asia (CSCA) in 2001, in order "to deepen the research and knowledge of the Church in Asia and to provide training for leaders in the Asian Church."[51] Regrettably, the Centre was shuttered in recent years,

---

47. Roxborogh, "Christianity in South-east Asia," 441.
48. Scott Sunquist, "Asian Christianity and Christian History: Reflections after Thirty Years," *Catalyst* (13 December 2017).
49. The Centre for Southeast Asian Studies was established in January 1963 on the campus of Kyoto University for coordinating Southeast Asian studies. See https://kyoto.cseas.kyoto-u.ac.jp/.
50. The Institute of Southeast Asian Studies was established by an Act of Parliament in 1968 and renamed ISEAS – Yusof Ishak Institute in August 2015. See https://www.iseas.edu.sg/.
51. Trinity Theological College, *At the Crossroads: The History of Trinity Theological College, 1948–2005* (Singapore: Trinity Theological College, 2006), 177.

but the residual momentum is being maintained through the *Asia Journal of Theology* (AJT), the journal of the Association for Theological Education in Southeast Asia (ATESEA).[52] One of the significant distinctives of this journal is the contributions of scholars and practitioners who are native to or located and ministering within the region.[53] Given the significance of these multidisciplinary studies, more attention and resources will hopefully be channeled to effect a resuscitation of such a center. Emmersen's appeal for Christian collaborative scholarship is prophetic:

> to help indigenous scholars increase understanding and reduce mistrust by getting out from under the imprint of the nation-state – for example, through collaborative research on Southeast Asian topics that are non-political, cross-cultural, and sub- or supra-national.[54]

Context

As highlighted earlier, Southeast Asia is one of the world's most ethnically and religiously diverse regions. Yet the Association of Southeast Asian Nations (ASEAN)[55] is perhaps the most cohesive transnational bloc, for "apart from the EU, no other regional organization comes close to matching ASEAN's record in delivering five decades without any major conflicts."[56] Yet this is a fragile peace that is threatened by the posturing of global powers including China,

---

52. ATESEA was founded in 1967 at Trinity Theological College in Singapore and is the first accreditation body set up in the region. See "ATESEA History," ATESEA (n.d.), http://atesea.net/about/history/.
53. Besides ATESEA, Asia Theological Association is another accreditation organization that was established in 1970 that extends beyond Southeast Asia, covering Asia. It has two regular journals: the *Journal of Asian Evangelical Theology* and the *Journal of Asian Mission*.
54. Emmerson, "Southeast Asia," 21.
55. ASEAN was formed on 8 August 1967 with the five founding member nations: Indonesia, Malaysia, the Philippines, Singapore, and Thailand. ASEAN has since grown to include the rest of the countries in the region except for Timor Leste, which was pending at the time of this publication. As a regional intergovernmental organization, ASEAN promotes intergovernmental cooperation and facilitates economic, political, security, military, educational, and sociocultural integration among its members and other countries in Asia. See "What We Do," ASEAN, https://asean.org/what-we-do.
56. Kishore Mahbubani and Jeffrey Sng, *The ASEAN Miracle: A Catalyst for Peace* (Singapore: Ridge Books, 2016), 209. Mahbubani and Sng continue, "Yet, even though the EU was awarded a Nobel Peace Prize in 2012, ASEAN has not even been considered for one." This Mahbubani and Sng understand as "the global ignorance about ASEAN."

the United States, Japan, India, Australia, and others, since the geoeconomics power play situated in Southeast Asia straddles the Indo-Pacific.[57]

Churches in Southeast Asia need to work within the nexus of the geopolitical context of the region. Despite their varied colonial history, churches cannot afford to ignore the cultural religious context – the bedrock of Indic and Sinic influences upon which the strata of Islamic influence is layered on. David Henley writes "the history of those precursor states – their rise, and more particularly their fall – may nevertheless greatly influence how new nations are imagined and constructed."[58] This tapestry of influences may well provide a deeper appreciation for the apparent "contradiction," as seen for example in the adoption of the *garuda*, a bird creature from Hindu mythical origins (for example, the *Rig Veda)* as the symbol of the national airline of Indonesia, the world's most populous Muslim country.

Amidst this religiously plural context in which Theravada Buddhism dominates continental Southeast Asia and Islam dominates maritime Southeast Asia, churches simply cannot ignore these other faiths – Hinduism, Buddhism, and Islam. And in an increasingly global context driven by economics and technology, churches cannot pursue the "Lexus" and ignore the "olive tree."[59] In a post-Tiananmen-Square world, a post-September-11 world, and (hopefully) in a post-coronavirus-pandemic world, the church can neither afford to feign ignorance or apathy, nor be myopic. Consequently, how can churches be holistically, missionally, and theologically relevant without deeply understanding their religiously plural, ethnically diverse, and economically disparate contexts?

It is crucial that churches in Southeast Asia be able to appreciate the immediate contexts from which arise mission and ministry issues, to think critically and confidently, and to craft a mission praxis that is coherent within the context. Singaporean diplomat Kishore Mahbubani's provocative and seminal work *Can Asians Think?* should challenge and inspire Southeast Asian

---

57. Rory Medcalf, *Indo-Pacific Empire: China, America and the Context for the World's Pivotal Region* (Manchester: Manchester University Press, 2020). See also Enze Han, *Asymmetrical Neighbors: Borderland State Building between China and Southeast Asia* (Oxford: Oxford University Press, 2019); and Sebastian Strangio, *In the Dragon's Shadow: Southeast Asia in the Chinese Century* (New Haven, CT: Yale University Press, 2020).
58. David Henley, "The Origins of Southeast Asian Nations: A Question of Timing," in *The Oxford Handbook of the History of Nationalism* (Oxford: Oxford University Press, 2013), 271.
59. Thomas Friedman, *The Lexus and the Olive Tree* (New York: Picador, 1999). Friedman explains globalization as the integration of capital, technology, and information across national borders. Finding the right balance between the drive for economic prosperity and development, symbolized by the Lexus, and the desire to retain identity and traditions, symbolized by the olive tree, is the great drama of this era.

Christians to not uncritically adopt Western or other foreign perspectives but to sagaciously engage the diverse contexts within their neighborhoods.

Compassion

Through more than five decades of collaboration, ASEAN has done much to improve the livelihoods of more than six hundred million people living in the region.[60] Yet a lot more still needs to be done in addressing the issues of poverty, inequality, food and water shortages, and various other social issues in the region. Sadly, the progress made since 2000 has been decimated by the coronavirus pandemic. In July 2020, the World Bank warned that "Southeast Asia is on the brink of a 'socio-economic crisis' caused by the COVID-19 pandemic that could reverse decades of poverty reduction."[61] At a time when the world is looking for ways to navigate the challenges of a world stricken by a viral pandemic, the onus is on the church to demonstrate "prophetic compassion" like that of Jesus Christ. "What Asia likes in Jesus is His compassion. This compassion can make the church in Asia weak and powerless with those who are weak and powerless. But it is a compassion that stands against injustices and exploitation. It is compassion that works to restore human wholeness."[62] In the urban contexts of Southeast Asia where Christianity tends to be middle class, one might also ask – will Christians continue to care for the poor, the marginalized, and the disenfranchised? Will those suffering in Southeast Asia find solace in those who claim to be followers of the Suffering Servant?

CONCLUSION

At the time of writing this chapter in 2021, there is news of political protests in Thailand and Indonesia, and conflict in Myanmar. There are also rising tensions in Malaysian politics. The growth of religious fundamentalism and the potential threat of religious persecution and terrorism remain realities that those who live in this region cannot take lightly, whether they are in the southern islands of the Philippines, southwestern Myanmar, the highlands of Vietnam, or the cosmopolitan cities of Bangkok, Jakarta, or Singapore. There are a myriad of issues about which Christians cannot afford to be apathetic – issues of

---

60. Mahbubani and Sng, *ASEAN Miracle*, 209–10.
61. Tom Allard, "Southeast Asia poverty to surge in 'socio-economic crisis': U.N.," *Reuters* (31 July 2020).
62. Jacob Kavunkal, SVD, "A Missionary Vision for Asia in the Twenty-First Century," in *Mission for the Twenty-First Century,* eds. S. Bevans SVD and R. Schroeder SVD (Chicago: CCGM, 2001), 174.

poverty, social inequality, and injustice, and all of these amidst the crushing weight of the coronavirus pandemic. There is no denying that the peace and prosperity of the region rests on a razor-thin balancing of ethnic and religious diversity. Yet the optimism of Mahbubani and Sng is not misplaced: "As the world moves away from two centuries of dominance by western civilizations and towards a multi-civilizational world, ASEAN provides a valuable model for how different civilizations can live and work together in close proximity."[63] It may well be that Southeast Asia is indeed a "living laboratory of cultural diversity" as well as an arena for the economic and political jousting of the emergent superpowers of the twenty-first century.[64] These multidimensional factors provide the intriguing context in which Christians and churches must navigate, and the potential crises create opportunities for them to shine as *lux mundi* (lights of the world).

Case Study 1

Christians from Sunrise Church in Country A have been going to Grace Church in Country B about twice a year for the past five years. Recently the leaders of Sunrise Church feel that those at Grace Church have become passive. They take little initiative to help plan and organize the visits and passively accept whatever program Sunrise Church suggests. Country B had been colonized by Country A for about one hundred years before this time.

1. Unpack the historical and cultural issues that could be affecting the relationship between Sunrise Church and Grace Church.
2. What suggestions can you give for Grace Church to grow in maturity?

---

63. Mahbubani and Sng, *ASEAN Miracle*, 230.
64. Mahbubani and Sng, 230.

Missions in Southeast Asia

> **Case Study 2**
>
> New Life Church is located in a Southeast Asia city. The members feel that their church is young and immature, and they want to grow. The church leaders have found a lot of "useful" worship and discipleship resources on the internet, and they want to use these resources to help their members grow spiritually. They have asked you, a missionary in their city, since you are fluent in English and their local language, to translate the internet materials (mainly American) from English to their local language.
>
> 1. Would you do what they ask you to do? Why or why not?
> 2. What are some other suggestions or proposals you would make to help New Life Church grow in maturity?

> **Additional Case Studies**
>
> 1. Using the systems mapping chart (ch 10, pg 168), choose a particular country and fill in the longitudinal influences on the micro-, meso-, and macro- levels. You may find the information in the country chapter in Part I to be helpful.
> 2. According to Peh, Christianity has been identified with colonialism in Southeast Asia. But which colonial powers have left indelible traits on national churches? Choose two different Southeast Asian countries that were ruled by different colonial powers, for example Britain and Holland, and explore how the differences in culture and colonial rule shaped each country's churches.
> 3. Peh notes that Pentecostalism will most likely be a primary influence as we move into the future. With an understanding of the historical trajectory of churches established on denominational lines in the region, explore how Pentecostalism's non-denominational, ecumenical approach may alter the forward trajectory. Will it be a bridge or a barrier to contextualization efforts in the region?
> 4. Apply Peh's narrative of church history in Southeast Asia to KimSon Nguyen's chapter 9 on the Vietnamese church and explore how the influence of Chinese, French, and American colonial eras have impacted the Vietnamese church.

REFERENCES

Allard, Tom. "Southeast Asia poverty to surge in 'socio-economic crisis': U.N." Reuters (31 July 2020). https://www.reuters.com/article/us-health-coronavirus-un-southeast-asia-idUSKCN24W071.

Alvarez, Francis D., SJ. "Christianity in East and Southeast Asia." In *Christianity in East and Southeast Asia*, edited by Kenneth R. Ross, Francis Alvarez, and Todd M. Johnson, 15–36. Edinburgh, UK: Edinburgh University Press, 2020.

Anh Q. Tran, SJ. "*The Historiography of the Jesuits in Vietnam: 1615–1773 and 1957–2007*." Brill (October 2018). https://referenceworks.brillonline.com/entries/jesuit-historiography-online/the-historiography-of-the-jesuits-in-vietnam-16151773-and-19572007-COM_210470.

Bautze-Picron, Claudine. *Bagan Murals and the Sino-Tibetan World*. Hal open science (2014). https://hal.archives-ouvertes.fr/hal-01099967/.

Bloodworth, Dennis. *An Eye for the Dragon: Southeast Asia Observed, 1954–1970*. New York: Farrar, 1970.

Brennan, Elliot. "Religion in Southeast Asia: Diversity and the threat of extremes." *The Interpreter* (19 September 2014). https://www.lowyinstitute.org/the-interpreter/religion-southeast-asia-diversity-and-threat-extremes.

Chong, Terence, ed. *Pentecostal Megachurches in Southeast Asia: Negotiating Class, Consumption and the Nation*. Singapore: ISEAS, 2018.

Chong, Terence, and Evelyn Tan. "Why Christian Expansionism Is a Quiet Storm in Southeast Asia." *South China Morning Post* (21 November 2019). https://www.scmp.com/week-asia/politics/article/3038665/why-christian-expansionism-quiet-storm-southeast-asia.

DeMing, Sarah. "Economic Working Paper - No 25: The Economic Importance of Indian Opium and Trade with China on Britain's Economy, 1843–1890." Whitman College (Spring 2011). https://www.whitman.edu/economics/Workingpapers/content/WP_25.pdf.

Doraisamy, Theodore R. *Oldham Called of God*. Singapore: Methodist Book Room, 1979.

Dutton, George E. *A Vietnamese Moses: Philiphe Binh and the Geographies of Early Modern Catholicism*. Berkeley: University of California Press, 2016.

Emmerson, Donald. "'Southeast Asia': What's in a Name?" *Journal of Southeast Asian Studies* 15, no. 1 (March, 1984): 1–21.

Farhadian, Charles. "A Missiological Reflection on Present-day Christian Movements in Southeast Asia." In *Christian Movements in Southeast Asia: A Theological Exploration*, edited by Poon Nai-Chiu Michael, 101–19. Singapore: Genesis Books, 2010.

Fifield, Russell H. "Southeast Asia as a Regional Concept." *Southeast Asian Journal of Social Science* 11, no. 2 (1983): 1–14.

Frederick, William. "Southeast Asia." *Encyclopedia Britannica online* (n.d.). https://www.britannica.com/place/Southeast-Asia.

Friedman, Thomas. *The Lexus and the Olive Tree*. New York: Picador, 1999.

Gady, Franz-Stefan. "How Portugal Forged an Empire in Asia." *The Diplomat* (11 July 2019). https://thediplomat.com/2019/07/how-portugal-forged-an-empire-in-asia/.

Goh, Robbie G. H. *Christianity in Southeast Asia*. Singapore: ISEAS, 2005.

Han, Enze. *Assymmetrical Neighbors: Borderland State Building between China and Southeast Asia*. Oxford: Oxford University Press, 2019.

Harrison, Brian. *Waiting for China: The Anglo-Chinese College at Malacca, 1818–1843 and Early Nineteenth-Century Missions*. Hong Kong: Hong Kong University Press, 1979.

Henley, David. "The Origins of Southeast Asian Nations: A Question of Timing." In *The Oxford Handbook of the History of Nationalism*, edited by John Breuilly, 263–286. Oxford: Oxford University Press, 2013.

Ho, Mary. "The Future of Christianity in East and Southeast Asia." In *Christianity in East and Southeast Asia*, edited by Kenneth R. Ross, Francis Alvarez, and Todd M. Johnson, 479–92. Edinburgh, UK: Edinburgh University Press, 2020.

Hrang Hlei. "Myanmar." In *Christianity in East and Southeast Asia*, edited by Kenneth R. Ross, Francis Alvarez, and Todd M. Johnson, 145–54. Edinburgh, UK: Edinburgh University Press, 2020.

Hunt, Robert. "Southeast Asian Christianity." In *The Encyclopedia of Christian Civilization*, 2220–224. London: Blackwell, 2012.

Kane, J. Herbert. "Continental Southeast Asia." *Christianity Today* (30 July 1965). https://www.christianitytoday.com/ct/1965/july-30/continental-southeast-asia.html.

Kavunkal, Jacob, SVD. "A Missionary Vision for Asia in the Twenty-First Century." In *Mission for the Twenty-First Century*, edited by S. Bevans SVD and R. Schroeder SVD, 162–175. Chicago: CCGM, 2001.

Mahbubani, Kishore, and Jeffrey Sng. *The ASEAN Miracle: A Catalyst for Peace*. Singapore: Ridge Books, 2016.

Medcalf, Rory. *Indo-Pacific Empire: China, America and the Context for the World's Pivotal Region*. Manchester: Manchester University Press, 2020.

Phan, Peter. *Asian Christianities: History, Theology and Practice*. New York: Orbis, 2018.

Roxborogh, John. "Christianity in South-east Asia, 1914–2000." In *Christianity in East and Southeast Asia*, edited by Kenneth R. Ross, Francis Alvarez, and Todd M. Johnson, 436–49. Edinburgh, UK: Edinburgh University Press, 2020.

Sakya, Anil. "Rethinking of Buddhism in Southeast Asia." Paper presented at International Conference on Buddhism is Southeast Asia, Phnom Penh City, Cambodia, 4–7 September 2018. https://www.academia.edu/37362751/Rethinking_of_Buddhism_in_Southeast_Asia.

Spate, Oskar. *The Spanish Lake*. Canberra: Australia National University Press, 2010.

Strangio, Sebastian. *In the Dragon's Shadow: Southeast Asia in the Chinese Century*. New Haven, CT: Yale University Press, 2020.

Sunquist, Scott. "Asian Christianity and Christian History: Reflections after Thirty Years." *Catalyst* (13 December, 2017). https://www.catalystresources.org/asian-christianity-and-christian-history-reflections-after-thirty-years/.

———. *Explorations in Asian Christianity*. Downers Grove, IL: IVP Academic, 2017.

Synan, Vinson, and Amos Yong, eds. *Global Renewal Christianity: Asia and Oceania Spirit-Empowered Movements: Past, Present, and Future*, vol. 1. Lake Mary, FL: Charisma House, 2016.

Tregonning, K. C. *The British in Malaya*. Tucson: University of Arizona Press, 1965.

Trinity Theological College. *At the Crossroads: The History of Trinity Theological College, 1948–2005*. Singapore: Trinity Theological College, 2006.

CHAPTER 13

SOUTHEAST ASIAN CHURCHES AT THE GLOBAL CHURCH ROUNDTABLE

Robert M. Solomon

With a population of 660 million, Southeast Asia is the third most populous geographical area in the world, after South Asia and East Asia.[1]

As far as the church and missions are concerned, consider the following facts:

- The nation with the largest population of Muslims in the world is Indonesia, which is in Southeast Asia.
- There are more Roman Catholics in the Philippines than in any European country, for example Italy, France, and Spain.
- Muslims are the largest religious group in Southeast Asia with 240 million adherents.
- Large and dense urban centers are located in Southeast Asia including Manila (13 million), Jakarta (10.3 million), Bangkok (9.3 million), Ho Chi Minh City (7.3 million), Kuala Lumpur (6.8 million), Singapore (5.6 million), and Yangon (4.8 million).[2]

THE CHURCH'S GLOBAL CONNECTIONS

In this essay we explore how Southeast Asian churches relate with other churches and global Christian networks and organizations in theologizing, missions, worship and theological education. Depending on their own histories and traditions, the churches have developed their own theological and ecclesial hues. In large churches that are organized according to ethnic identity, such as the Batak or Minahasa churches in Indonesia which resulted historically from mass tribal conversions,[3] the expression of Christianity tends to be

---
[1]. "Infographic: top cities and urbanization in ASEAN," ASEAN Up (5 July 2017). The population is expected to rise to 720 million by 2030.
[2]. "Infographic."
[3]. Robbie G. H. Goh, *Christianity in Southeast Asia* (Singapore: ISEAS, 2005), 59.

nominal, ritualistic, or strongly cultural and traditional. There are also more recently planted churches through the advent of megachurches that have an evangelical or Pentecostal identity and focus on personal discipleship and vibrant worship styles.

This diversity of church expressions can be seen in the way Southeast Asian churches are connected with global ecclesial bodies. Many of the older, mainline denominations churches are members of the World Council of Churches (WCC) and national councils of churches. There are exceptions, however. For example in Singapore, many key denominations are not connected with the WCC and consider WCC membership to be a compromise to their commitment to biblical teachings. The National Council of Churches of Singapore (NCCS) have no formal relations with the WCC or the Christian Conference of Asia. However, membership in the NCCS is not confined to mainline Protestant denominations, but is also open to other denominations such as the Brethren, Evangelical Free Churches, and independent churches. In other countries, churches organize themselves into a national evangelical fellowship of churches which are often affiliated with organizations such as World Evangelical Fellowship. How closely the national councils of churches and the evangelical fellowships work together varies from country to country. In some countries, there is a warm, even cooperative relationship while in others, there is little dialogue or cooperation.

The Lausanne Movement has also had significant influence in Southeast Asian churches. Many churches participate in Lausanne congresses and regional meetings and committees. With its current emphasis on evangelical Christianity along with holistic and integral mission, the movement continues to have a growing influence. The Lausanne Movement has developed scholarships for seminaries and churches through bursaries given for higher theological education and faculty development as well as providing pastor training for leadership and preaching.

DENOMINATIONAL CONNECTIONS

Many mainline churches in Southeast Asia are connected with sister churches worldwide. Through these connections some have made significant contributions to the life and witness of their connectional communities. For instance, the Anglican Province of Southeast Asia, created in 1996 by bringing together the dioceses of Singapore, West Malaysia, Kuching, and Sabah, was a significant player when the worldwide Anglican communion went through a crisis following the consecration of a practicing gay clergyman as a bishop in the Episcopal Church in the United States (ECUSA). At that time, the Southeast Asia province, together with other provinces and dioceses outside the Western world, refused to accept the presence of ECUSA delegates at the Anglican Communion's official meetings. They pressed for statements to be made condemning the actions of ECUSA as going against the teachings of Scripture and the traditions of the church. Even in the West, some parts of the Anglican Communion asked for similar actions to be taken.

In the United States, amid the debates and chaos, some churches and dioceses eventually took the step of separating from ECUSA to form their own Anglican church structure. The Right Reverend Moses Tay, then archbishop of the Province of Southeast Asia, was involved in helping to form this breakaway group, The Anglican Mission in America. In January 2000, Tay, with the bishop of Rwanda, conducted in Singapore the consecration of two American clergy as bishops for this orthodox Anglican group. These actions produced much debate among Anglicans worldwide.

Since then, the Province of Southeast Asia has been a strong advocate within the broader Anglican Communion for faithfulness to biblical teaching and orthodox historical Christianity in matters related to human sexuality, in stark contrast to some of their counterparts in the West who are pro-gay and accepting of same-sex marriage. The Fellowship of Confessing Anglicans was formed to preserve the historical traditions of the Communion. The Anglicans in Southeast Asia provided a strong voice and support to this realignment movement, and the Southeast Asian leaders played significant roles in the leadership of this global movement. In 2003, the Province of Southeast Asia declared that relations with ECUSA were "impaired" and said the same about the Scottish Episcopal Church in 2018 and the Episcopal Church of Brazil in 2019, both of which had accepted same-sex marriage.[4] The Province also formally recognized and is in full communion with the Anglican Church in North America (ACNA), a denomination formed by Anglicans who broke away from ECUSA.

The Methodist Churches in Southeast Asia illustrate another example of how regional churches have exerted global influence. The Federation of Asian Bishops (FAMB) with bishops from Southeast Asia from Singapore, Malaysia, Indonesia, the Philippines, and Myanmar together with bishops from other parts of Asia including Sri Lanka, Hong Kong, Taiwan, South Korea, and

---

4. Datuk Ng Moon Hing, Rennis Ponniah, Datuk Melter Jiki Tais, Danald Jute, "Statement from the Province of Southeast Asia," The Diocese of Singapore (21 February 2019).

India began annual meetings in the 1980s and formed the Asian Methodist Council. Meanwhile, within the United Methodist Church (UMC, USA) there are on-going attempts during their quadrennial general conferences to accept homosexual practice and same-sex marriage as an official position. In 2007 the FAMB sent a letter to the Council of Bishops of the UMC urging them to remain faithful to the historical teachings of the church.

In the letter the FAMB bishops wrote:

> Our Asian Methodist churches and communities have held, and continue to hold to the teachings of Scripture and our historic Christian faith on the issues of marriage and sexuality. Sexual relationships outside marriage are against the teachings of Scripture. The marital relationship is also between a man and a woman. We have also held that the practice of homosexuality is incompatible with Christian teachings. We expect our clergy and lay to abide by these teachings and standards.
>
> We appreciate that The United Methodist Church has taken a position [on homosexuality] similar to that of the Asian Methodist churches and pray that the UMC will continue to make a clear stand. The unity of the global Methodist family will be seriously affected if any member of this family moves away from the biblical and historical position on the issues of marriage and sexuality. Connectional relationships and mission partnerships will be affected.
>
> We therefore pray that together, we will be committed to maintain the teaching of Scripture and the historical and unanimous tradition of our global Methodist, and wider Christian, family.[5]

The UMC continues to hold on to its traditional position at the time of this writing despite moves to the contrary by certain factions within it. A similar letter was sent about the same time to the British Methodist Church (BMC).[6] The FAMB then sent another letter to the BMC, urging it to reconsider its present direction.

---

5. FAMB bishops, "Letter from the Fellowship of Asian Methodist Bishops to the Council of Bishops of the United Methodist Church" (10 September 2007). Private correspondence.
6. In June 2021, the British Methodist Conference voted to recognize same sex marriage. See "Marriage and Relationships," The Methodist Church (20 September 2021), https://www.methodist.org.uk/about-us/the-methodist-church/marriage-and-relationships/.

In general, churches in Southeast Asia seek to be biblically faithful and hold an evangelical and conservative view on many issues, and they will continue to make their views known in the global church.

SEMINARIES AND BIBLE COLLEGES

There are numerous seminaries in Southeast Asian nations. Some have been established by denominations or as collaborative ventures, and many of these have become well-established over the years. Others have been established by local churches or enterprising individuals. The quality of these theological training establishments varies. There are two major accrediting bodies for seminaries and Bible colleges in Southeast Asia: the Association for Theological Education of Southeast Asia (ATESEA) and the Asia Theological Association (ATA).

The Association for Theological Education in Southeast Asia

ATESEA, originally known as the Association of Theological Schools in South East Asia (ATSSEA), was established at Trinity Theological College in Singapore in 1957 with sixteen schools as members.[7] ATESEA has since expanded operations to include members in Southeast, East, and South Asia. Currently, the association has ninety-two member schools located in thirteen Asian countries.

ATESEA's office has been shifting between Singapore and the Philippines, and as of 2021 is located at Central Philippine University in Iloilo City. In 1966, ATESEA established an educational arm, the Southeast Asia Graduate School of Theology (SEAGST), which offered masters and doctoral level degrees.

ATESEA publishes the *Asia Journal of Theology*, which encourages Asian theologians to reflect on relating the gospel to the contextual situations found in Asia. For example in 1971, Filipino theologian Emerito P. Nacpil, then president of Union Theological Seminary, set out the Critical Asian Principle (CAP) as the framework for theological reflection using Asian thought and experience.[8]

The CAP highlights the contextual situations of Asian churches.

---

7. This and the related information on ATESEA can be found on the ATESEA website http://atesea.net/.
8. *Handbook: The Association for Theological Education in Southeast Asia and the South East Asia Graduate School of Theology* (Iloilo City, Philippines: ATESEA, 2005), 84.

First, plurality and diversity in races, peoples, cultures, social institutions, religions, ideologies, etc., characterize this region. Second, most of the countries in this region have had a colonial experience. Third, most of the countries in this region are now in the process of nation building, development, and modernization. They want to modernize through the use of science and technology. They want to develop and achieve economic growth, social-justice, and self-reliance.

Fourth, the people of this region want to achieve authentic self-identity and cultural integrity in the context of the modern world. Fifth, Asia is the home of some of the world's living and renascent religions, and these religions have shaped both the culture and consciousness of the vast majority of Asians. They represent alternative ways of life and experience of reality. Six, Asian peoples are in search for a form of social order beyond the current alternatives. Seven, and finally, the Christian community is a minority in the vast Asian complex.[9]

These seven characteristics of Asian contexts were then said to have four implications having to do with contextual, hermeneutical, missiological, and educational principles.[10]

While the CAP has guided ATESEA and SEAGST, further reflection on it has led to a reformulation and renaming to Guidelines for Doing Theologies in Asia, as ATESEA marked its fiftieth anniversary in 2007. The Guidelines identify eight areas of concern for theological construction and theological education in Asia: Asian contexts, indigenous cultures and wisdom, suffering experiences of the weaker parties, the interconnection of the whole creation, interfaith relations, challenges from natural impacts and social dynamics, economic imperialism, and the Christian responsibility to missions and evangelism.

Asia Theological Association

Following the Asia-South Pacific Congress of Evangelism held in Singapore in 1968, the Asia Theological Association (ATA) was established in 1970. The aim of ATA was to counter the growing influence of Western liberal theology

---

9. *Handbook*, 84.
10. *Handbook*, 86.

among Asian church leaders by encouraging and nurturing "evangelical scholars, thinkers and teachers."[11]

Today, ATA has 361 member theological institutions in thirty-eight countries in South, East, Southeast, and West Asia and beyond. To provide advanced theological degrees, ATA established the Asia Graduate School of Theology (AGST) in 1984 through a consortium of several member institutions. This graduate school has enabled ATA to train Asian theologians and faculties.

ATA publishes two journals, the *Journal of Asian Evangelical Theology* and the *Journal of Asian Mission*, both of which are produced twice annually. In addition, ATA is also producing a series of Bible commentaries in partnership with Langham Global Library. These commentaries are primarily written by Asian scholars for the purpose of encouraging sound, biblical exegesis coupled with good application, all of which take into consideration the social and cultural contexts in Asia. These commentaries complement those produced in the West, which often do not pay sufficient attention to contexts particular to Asia and to the concerns of Asian Christians.

Like SEAGST, the ATA was formed in response to a call to develop theological thinking that is relevant for Asia. One of the seminal influences was Indian theologian Saphir Athyal, whose paper "Towards an Asian Christian Theology" was one of two key papers presented at the 1974 ATA meeting in Hong Kong. This paper would become a key document to guide this exploration. Athyal calls for the development of an indigenous theology for Asian contexts drawn from biblical teaching, paying particular attention to the situations in Asia and to break free from over reliance on Western forms of theology, which have been greatly influenced by Greek philosophy and modern, secular Western thought.

According to Athyal, an Asian contextual theology should have the following characteristics:

1. Reflect a biblical basis and character. The Bible's authority, the proximity of its original context to many Asian contexts, and its modelling of an indigenous theology are factors that must be noted carefully.
2. Be systematized around contextual issues in Asia. The priorities of Asian theologies may differ from those in the West, and new areas

---

11. Hwa Yung, *Mangoes or Bananas?: The Quest for an Authentic Asian Christian Theology*, 2nd ed. (Maryknoll, NY: Orbis, 2015), 191.

not dealt with or emphasized in Western theologies may have to be explored in Asian contexts.

3. Be orientation to the cultures and religions of Asia. Rather than taking an anti-cultural view, there is a need to explore the relevance and fit between biblical teachings and Asian culture. Interreligious dialogue is also needed if churches are to be relevant to their religious contexts.

4. Directed to practical life and mission. Theology must become a "living theology" for the church that makes sense to Christians in their daily living and challenges. It must also be mission-oriented, not just of theoretical interest among a few elite.[12]

There are certainly some similarities and overlaps between the approaches by SEAGST and ATA.

DOING THEOLOGY IN SOUTHEAST ASIA

While the CAP, adopted by ATESEA, and Athyal's work have directed the thinking of ATA and its evangelical member institutions, there is still more extensive work to be done. Some of this work, especially among evangelicals, has been produced by Southeast Asian theologians such as Filipinos José de Mesa and Timoteo Gener, Malaysian Hwa Yung, and Singaporean Simon Chan.

Chan notes that a lot of implicit theology has been going on as "found in sermons, hymns, poetry, testimonies, etc. of the practitioners of the faith . . . , often placed within the category of 'devotion' or 'spirituality' but . . . no less theological."[13] However, what is lacking is explicit theology. This is the theology found in textbooks and in the writings of well-trained systematic theologians arising from specific Asian contexts. There is a need to draw into systematic theologizing and writing the ecclesial issues, congregational experiences, and cultural concerns faced by Asian Christians.[14]

---

12. Saphir F. Athyal, "Toward an Asian Christian Theology," in *What Asian Christians Are Thinking: A Theological Source Book*, ed. Douglas J. Elwood (Quezon City, Philippines: New Day, 1976), 68–84.
13. Simon Chan, "Evangelical Theology in Asian Contexts," in *The Cambridge Companion to Evangelical Theology*, eds. Timothy Larsen and Daniel J. Treier (Cambridge: Cambridge University Press, 2007), 226.
14. W. John Roxborogh, "Situating Southeast Asian Christian Movements in the History of World Christianity," in *Christian Movements in Southeast Asia: A Theological Exploration*, ed. Michael Nai-Chiu Poon (Singapore: Trinity Theological College, 2010), 26–27.

For his part, Chan has written to emphasize exploring the affinity between biblical Christianity and the primal religions and worldviews which are predominant in many parts of Asia.[15] Even where world religions such as Buddhism and Islam dominate, we can find underlying primal worldviews forming foundational cultural and religious bedrocks of how people think, believe, and live. For instance among Batak Christians in Indonesia, there is a deep underlying layer of *adat* (ancient cultural tradition) that is characterized not only by long-held social customs but also religious beliefs, including ideas of the spirit world. Chan claims that conversions in Asia are largely among those who hold primal worldviews, like tribal peoples.[16]

One critique of CAP by Filipino Timoteo Gener is that while it emphasizes developing indigenous theologies, it "has often been joined to a liberationist social agenda and identified more with liberal Western theologians who are both skeptical of the supernatural and lacking in any critical engagement with Asian congregational experience and leadership."[17] Chan comments that CAP represents "elitist theology" that "does not take seriously the church's living tradition." Theologians must be deeply connected with the life of the church; otherwise, they will have very little that is helpful or significant to say to the church.

Indeed, many Southeast Asian contexts emphasize and recognize the importance of the supernatural spirit world, while many Western theologies are more skeptical of such views and as a result tend to dismiss these beliefs as mere superstitions. However, the Bible has much to say about spiritual beings, both benign and malignant. Granted, while many local superstitions need to be corrected by a truly biblical worldview, dismissing the existence and importance of the spirit world will result in a schizophrenic form of Christianity, what missiologists Hiebert, Shaw, and Tienou term "split-level Christianity."[18] In writing about the Filipino worldview of spirits, missionary Rodney Henry

---

15. Simon Chan, "Folk Christianity and Primal Spirituality: Prospects for Theological Development," in *Christian Movements in Southeast Asia: A Theological Exploration*, ed. Michael Nai-Chiu Poon (Singapore: Trinity Theological College, 2010), 1–17. Chan asserts that Southeast Asian churches may be on the threshold of a Copernican revolution when theologizing takes seriously the ground-level experiences of the churches.
16. Simon Chan, "Evangelical Theology in Asian Contexts," in *The Cambridge Companion to Evangelical Theology*, eds. Timothy Larsen and Daniel J. Treier (Cambridge: Cambridge University Press, 2007), 226–27.
17. Timoteo D. Gener, "Doing Contextual Systematic Theology in Asia," *Journal of Asian Evangelical Theology* 22 nos. 1–2 (March-September 2018): 57.
18. Paul G. Hiebert, R. Daniel Shaw, and Tite Tienou, "Responding to Split-level Christianity and Folk Religion," *International Journal of Frontier Missions* 16, no. 4 (Winter 1999/2000): 173–82.

highlights the danger of a split-level Christian life in which Christians attend churches to deal with their eternal security and things to come, but visit shamans to deal with present difficulties which they believe are influenced by the activity of spirits.[19] Such disconnects need to be addressed.

Elsewhere I have written on the importance of the spirit world in Asian contexts and the need to reflect theologically and pastorally on how to respond properly to such cultural realities without adopting a position that either rejects the spirit world outright or embraces it uncritically.[20] There is an ongoing need to explore a Southeast Asian theology that takes into cognizance such abiding worldviews that are not necessarily antithetical to what we read in the Bible. A study in this area would turn out many interesting features. For example, Thai literary scholar Suradech Chotiudompant refers to Thai "magical realism" as a genre that represents the tensions between modern, rational global forces and traditional local cultures.[21]

Another theme that Chan explores is the importance of the family and ancestors in Asian cultures. He suggests that the Trinity can be seen in familial terms as the Divine Family, and that the importance of ancestors can be a biblical emphasis in contrast with the tendency toward a highly individualistic view of the Christian life and the future.[22]

Filipino theologian de Mesa has explored Filipino vocabulary and concepts such as *ganda* (good, goodness) for use as a cultural lens by which to view the Christian faith so that key elements of the Christian faith can be "seen, felt, and shared" with Filipinos in meaningful ways.[23]

---

19. Rodney Henry, *Filipino Spirit World: A Challenge to the Church* (Manila: OMF Publishers, 1986). For a similar situation in the Indonesian context, see Emanuel Gerrit Singgih, "Competing or Complementing Social Imaginaries? Lessons from Two Case Studies," in *Visions of a Good Society in Southeast Asia: Social Imageries and Inter-religious Dialogue*, ed. Chiang Ming Shun (Singapore: Trinity Theological College, 2017), 97–108.
20. See Robert M. Solomon, *Living in Two Worlds: Pastoral Responses to Possession in Singapore* (Frankfurt am Main: Peter Lang, 1994); and Robert M. Solomon, "Traveling the Supernatural Highways: A framework for understanding the spirit worlds in Asia," *Mission Round Table* (The Occasional Bulletin of OMF Mission Research) 7, no. 1 (January 2012): 2–8. See also, Robert M. Solomon, "Healing and Deliverance," in *Global Dictionary of Theology*, eds. William A. Dyrness et al. (Downers Grove, IL: InterVarsity, 2008), 361–368.
21. Suradech Chotiudompant, "Thai Magical Realism and Globalization," in *Globalization and Its Counter-forces in Southeast Asia*, ed. Terence Chong (Singapore: Institute of Southeast Asian Studies, 2008), 380–95.
22. Simon Chan, *Grassroots Asian Theology: Thinking the Faith from the Ground Up* (Downers Grove, IL: IVP Academic, 2014), 42–44.
23. José de Mesa, "Kapag ang 'Ganda' ang Pag-Uusapan: Mungkahi para sa Dulog at Paraan ng Mabathalang Pag-Aaral," in *Ang Maganda sa Teolohiya* (Quezon City, Philippines: Claretian, 2017), 1–22.

These promising attempts at developing a theology rooted in Southeast Asia require ongoing work. Malaysian theologian Hwa Yung has observed that

> Asian Christians need a framework within which to think about God's revelation of himself and his activity in the world, in the context of their own cultures and the missiological tasks they face. Unfortunately, there is not one single adequate text in this field written from within Asia at the time of this writing. Thus, almost every Asian seminary still uses systematic theology texts written in the West.[24]

GROWING MISSIONS INVOLVEMENT OF SOUTHEAST ASIAN CHURCHES

For much of their history, churches in Southeast Asia have been on the receiving end of missionary activity. Many were founded by missionaries from the West who came to the region to plant churches. Not only were churches planted, but educational institutions were also established, which in turn strengthened the outreach and witness of the churches. Funding also continued to be provided by churches in the West.

Although the percentage of Christians in the world population has changed little, with a slight decline from 34.5 percent in 1900 to 31 percent in 2010, the proportion of Christians in Africa, Asia, and Latin America has changed dramatically.[25] Since the 1980s, there have been more Christians in the Global South than in the Global North.

Theological education and pastoral training are increasingly provided to raise new generations of local leadership in churches and Christian institutions. Within the last twenty to thirty years, more Southeast Asian churches are sending out cross-cultural missionaries, both through mission agencies and directly sending churches. Indeed as early as 1956, it was noted that Southeast Asian churches began to be interested in sending out missionaries, and the churches in Malaysia and the Philippines sent missionaries to Thailand, Indonesia, and Okinawa in Japan, while Cambodians and Karens from Myanmar were sent to

---

24. Hwa Yung, *Mangoes or Bananas?*, 228.
25. See "Christians," Pew-Templeton Global Religious Futures Project, http://www.globalreligiousfutures.org/religions/christians.

work among their fellows in Thailand.[26] However, it is only in recent decades that this sending has become a significant movement.

Some statistics would help us note this trend. In 2019, it is estimated that Singapore churches sent more than five hundred cross-cultural missionaries to serve largely in Asia, but also in other parts of the world. They primarily served as church planters, educators, and leadership trainers, but also reached out to the socially needy and forgotten.[27] In addition, more than seven hundred people served as tent-makers, professionals, and business people who assisted in church planting and discipleship training in the places where they work.[28] Local churches have formed about five hundred partnerships with overseas churches and Christian organizations. Furthermore, numerous mission trips are organized to enable church members to be exposed to and to engage in mission fields.[29]

In major international mission agencies such as Overseas Missionary Fellowship (OMF) and SIM,[30] the number of missionaries from Southeast Asia has been steadily increasing and is expected to continue to do so. Furthermore, Southeast Asians have also started taking on global leadership in these organizations.

In 1978, American evangelist Billy Graham held a crusade in Singapore that galvanized churches to work together and to recognize the importance of evangelism and missions. Graham is said to have called Singapore the "Antioch of the East," suggesting that just as the New Testament church in Antioch began ground-breaking missionary activity, sending the apostles Paul and Barnabas and others to preach and reach many parts of the ancient world (Acts 13), the churches in Singapore have the potential and responsibility to reach out with a similar missionary fervor. This challenge has been taken

---

26. Rajah B. Manikam and Winburn T. Thomas, *The Church in Southeast Asia* (New York: Friendship, 1956), 167.
27. "National Missions Study Report," Singapore Centre for Global Missions, 2019. This figure was derived from a survey of 155 churches, and the actual number from all churches would likely be more. There are also 256 people serving as staff in mission agencies, 138 serving as missional professionals (tent-makers), and 335 serving in missions in other ways, for example as itinerant evangelists and non-resident missionaries serving in Singapore in "missions at our doorstep." https://www.scgm.org.sg/nms/.
28. See Robert Solomon, "A Southeast Asian Perspective on Mission and Transformation in The Post-Cold War Era," in *Mission and Transformation in a Changing World* (New York: General Board of Global Ministries, The United Methodist Church, 1998), 55–62.
29. "National Missions Study Report."
30. SIM was originally Sudan Interior Mission, then in 1992 the name was changed to Society for International Ministries.

seriously by many churches in Singapore, and a growing stream of Singaporean missionaries have been and are being sent out all over the world.

Initially, this sending was done mainly by established mission agencies such as OMF, OM (Operation Mobilization), and SIM. But over the years, churches began to directly send out missionaries to plant churches, to work in collaboration with overseas churches to train Christians, and to set up educational and social outreach ministries, among other endeavors.

Along with these types of sending, denominations have established their own mission agencies to work in line with their denominational strategies in activities including church planting and supporting ministries such as educational and social outreach. An example is how the Anglican Diocese in Singapore, together with Malaysian partners in the Province of Southeast Asia, has set up deaneries in Southeast Asian countries such as Indonesia and Cambodia in order to establish Anglican churches. Another example is the Methodist Church in Singapore which established the Methodist Missions Society (MMS) in 1991 to be directly involved in missionary outreach in the region. In the early years, MMS focused on countries such as Cambodia, Thailand, and Nepal where they established Methodist churches, as well as on Vietnam and China. This process cannot be rushed, and much patience, wisdom, and perseverance are needed to give rise to healthy and thriving churches. The following account provides a case study on how MMS worked with other mission agencies to establish the Methodist Church in Cambodia.

THE METHODIST CHURCH IN CAMBODIA: A CASE STUDY

During the terrifying days of the Khmer Rouge regime under Pol Pot, many Cambodians escaped the country to settle in the United States and French-speaking Europe. There they established Cambodian churches and Christian associations. With the reopening of the country to Christian missionary work, growing interest among the diaspora Cambodian community led to the beginning of missionary work carried out with the support of Methodist churches in the United States and Europe.

In the early 1990s, a handful of Cambodian Methodist congregations were planted by the missionary efforts of United Methodists from the United States, France, and Switzerland.[31] Meanwhile missionaries from the Korean Methodist

---

31. The information given here and in what follows is taken from the Bishops' Advisory Committee, "Provisional Book of Discipline of the Methodist Church in Cambodia and Its Predecessors" (The People Called Methodists and the Mission Conference of the People Called

Church (KMC) also began planting congregations, and by 1995, there were seven congregations along with facilities to train Cambodian pastors.[32] The Methodist Church in Singapore, through the Methodist Missions Society (MMS), sent their first missionary in 1996.[33] The World Federation of Chinese Methodist Churches, comprised of Methodist churches in Singapore, Malaysia, Taiwan, Hong Kong, and Australia, also began to be interested in missionary work in Cambodia and appointed their first missionaries from the Sarawak Chinese Annual Conference of the Methodist Church in Malaysia in 1998.[34]

Because of the global Methodist connections, all of these different entities met in Singapore in May 1996 with the intention of setting up a joint mission in Cambodia. After a leadership visit to Phnom Penh in May that year, the need to create one Methodist entity in Cambodia instead of working separately became clearer. The generous donation of a Singaporean Methodist enabled MMS to acquire a piece of land and build the Methodist Center in which a school was established. In 1997, a coordinating board was set in place comprised of members of all the various participating churches working in Cambodia through their mission agencies.[35]

A Joint-Pastors' School for Khmer pastors from the Methodist congregations was held in February 1998 with one hundred lay pastors and interested persons in attendance. More schools were conducted in 1999 and 2000. The Cambodia Christian Methodist Bible School (CMBS) was established in 2000 to train Cambodian pastors, and the first class graduated in 2003.[36]

In 2001, a hymn and worship book was produced for the Methodist churches in Cambodia.[37] Also in that year, the bishops of the participating churches were involved in consultations, and in January 2002, four bishops representing the four entities involved in church planting work signed a document to establish the Methodist Mission in Cambodia and to form a Board of Ordained Ministry to oversee the training, licensing, and ordination of pastors

---

Methodists), presented to the Annual Meeting of the Methodist Mission in Cambodia in Phnom Penh, Cambodia in March 8–9, 2006. This document was updated and adopted in 2018 at the first session of the Provisional Annual Conference of the Methodist Church in Cambodia.
32. "Provisional Book of Discipline," 4.
33. "Provisional Book of Discipline," 4. See Robbie B. H. Goh, *Blessed to be a Blessing: The Methodist Missions Society Singapore* (Singapore: Methodist Missions Society, 2014), 81–86.
34. "Provisional Book of Discipline," 4–5.
35. "Provisional Book of Discipline," 5–7.
36. "Provisional Book of Discipline," 8.
37. "Provisional Book of Discipline," 8.

for the Mission.[38] In January 2003, the first Annual Meeting of the Methodist Mission in Cambodia was held in Phnom Penh, and there ten Cambodian pastors were ordained as deacons.[39]

All of these meetings and events show that establishing an indigenous national denominational church is a challenging and long process that requires much patience, wisdom, and understanding. Because the formation of the Methodist Church in Cambodia was the result of the collaborative efforts of an international coordinating board, the process caused much rejoicing at the deep level of cooperation but also a recognition of challenges caused by differences in cultures and values. Decisions were made jointly and involved much discussion about unity of purpose and methods. Annual meetings were conducted with the participation of the partner mission churches. Ordinations were conducted jointly with the bishops from all the churches laying on hands. Finances for the work were provided by contributions from the various partners. All of these activities provided reason to be grateful for the cooperative spirit, and this missionary enterprise remains as a model for how churches in the East and West can join hands in cooperative mission.

Lessons were also learned on how differences can cause difficulties in working together across cultures and church traditions. The Western mission partners tended to operate on an egalitarian principle, seeking to empower the indigenous partners as early as possible. Each mission partner church paid the pastors in their own groups of churches, though the churches were under the joint authority of the united mission. The Asian churches tended to be more careful in their choices of pastors and leaders, being more aware of cultural cues and signs of the candidates' character strengths or weaknesses of which the Westerners may not have been aware. As a result, the Asian churches tended to delay the process of handing over responsibilities to local leadership because they wanted to give more time for leaders to be tested and proven reliable. The Western churches may have viewed this process as too patronizing or condescending, while the Asian churches may have viewed the actions of the Western churches as too naïve.

At the beginning, leadership of the mission was in the hands of the missionary agencies. The presiding bishop was from Singapore, and the mission superintendent was appointed from among the missionaries, the UMC or

---

38. "Provisional Book of Discipline," 9–11.
39. I was appointed the presiding bishop of this entity until 2012, and I witnessed the burgeoning mission grow to eventually become the national Methodist Church in Cambodia.

KMC. As more Cambodian pastors were ordained, there was also a growing number of ordained elders. Some of these elders became district superintendents as the Methodist Mission in Cambodia was organized into several districts. Eventually, a Cambodian pastor was appointed as the mission superintendent in 2018, and a Provisional Annual Conference was organized with a Cambodian as the president. In time this position would be changed into episcopal leadership.

This is an interesting case study on how a national denominational church was established in a Southeast Asian country by Southeast Asian churches in Singapore and Malaysia working together with mission partners from the United States, Europe, and South Korea. Working together in an international partnership like this is not easy, but it can be very rewarding and satisfying. In other countries such as Thailand and Nepal, the MMS embarked on planting Methodist denominations on their own, while other Methodists from the United States and Korea are also doing so. How the ecclesial entities that will eventually result will relate with one another and whether they will remain separate entities or unite together as national churches is yet to be seen.

Planting churches separately and independently is easier. Yet Southeast Asian churches who seek to do so must be aware of certain dangers. For when the process is not carefully thought through, a Singapore church may plant a church in Thailand or Nepal that resembles Singaporean culture and ways of doing things, with strong emphasis on efficiency, productivity, contractual expectations, and governance. This way may not sit well in contexts where processes may be slower and trust is based on relationships rather than on paper contracts, where saving face is of great importance, and where inefficiencies and corruption may be accepted realities. Taking a cookie-cutter approach to church planting is not helpful.

Southeast Asian churches, whether in their theologizing or mission enterprises, should not isolate themselves in reaction to the strong influence of Western models. They should avoid both uncritical acceptance of Western methods, ideologies, and models and the reactive anti-Western stance. The church universal is a multicultural reality, and we can learn from one another. The church in the West has many valuable things to teach the Southeast Asian churches. The patristic, Reformation, and evangelical heritage that has come to Southeast Asia is to be treasured even as we learn to read the Bible in our own contexts and as we explore the relevance of the Christian faith in these contexts.

In missions and church planting, learning from others has great value. Everyone has blind spots, but as we learn together, we can do things better, correct cultural deficiencies that may impede mission work, and use cultural strengths that may enhance our efforts. As the Cambodian example shows, Southeast Asian churches have the closest affinity culturally and contextually to other Southeast Asian mission fields and therefore have a significant role to play in missionary efforts in this part of the world.

WORSHIP AND LITURGY

Southeast Asian theologians such as Simon Chan and José de Mesa have shown the importance of liturgy in theology as well as developing contextual expressions of the Christian faith.[40] Much of the liturgy practiced in Southeast Asian churches has come from the West, such as older hymns written in Europe and the United States and more recent worship songs. Many of these hymns and songs have been translated into local languages, but the lyrics and music remain close to the original forms. Worship styles also follow forms that are largely imported from the West. However, we can find small indications of meaningful contextualization. On one occasion, I attended a worship service in Malaysia, and one of the songs sung had a beautifully gentle Malay tune and matched very well with the local context.

The East Asia Christian Conference (EACC), later the Christian Conference of Asia (CCA), attempted to produce more contextualized hymns for Asian churches, and in 1963, Ceylonese theologian D. T. Niles prepared a hymnal. This hymnal was well received in ecumenical circles in the West but remains largely unused in Asian churches. In 1990, the CCA produced a new hymnal, *Sound the Bamboo*, with 280 hymns written by Asian Christians from the "grassroots" of Asian churches. The editor, I-to Loh, a leading ethnomusicologist in Asia, suggests musical accompaniment to the hymns that is more Asian in flavor – such as flutes, lutes, and drums. In the hymnal are many indigenous Asian tunes, harmonization, and modes of song forms and performance practice. The hymnal states that the contents are a "haphazard garden of many flowers, with each bloom adding its own color to the whole glory of the garden." A revised edition was produced in 2000 with 315 pieces in over forty languages from twenty-one countries.

---

40. Simon Chan, *Liturgical Theology: The Church as Worshiping Community*, rev. ed. (Downers Grove, IL: InterVarsity, 2006); José de Mesa, *The Prayer Our Lord Taught Us* (San Juan City, Philippines: Center for Collaborative and Creative Ministry, 2005); José de Mesa, *Isang Maiksing Katekismo para sa mga Bata: A Study in Indigenous Catechetics* (Manila, Philippines: Wellspring, 1988).

In 2015, the Methodist School of Music and Trinity Theological College in Singapore jointly published the hymnal *Let the Asian Church Rejoice* (LACR) which contains 135 hymns written by mainly Southeast Asian Christians and in languages spoken in the region.[41] In his brief theological reflection on this collection of hymns, theologian Michael Nai-Chiu Poon, who was the director of the Centre for the Study of Christianity in Asia at the Trinity Theological College, makes a few pertinent observations. He notes that traditional Western hymnals are usually structured in ways that reflect a stable Christendom setting, the structure adopted by *Hymns of Universal Praise* published in 1933 by mainline churches in China which is still used by many churches in Southeast Asia. However, the LACR makes a clean break from this structure and instead adopts a five-part liturgical structure: (1) "We Meet God and One Another," (2) "We Encounter God's Story," (3) "We are One Body in Christ," (4) "We Enact Christ's Story," and (5) "We are Sent into the World."[42] Poon highlights that the headings in the hymnal "are all expressed in relational and connectional terms. This structure underscores the gift of presence in Christian life. God places those who come to worship into His holy and hope-filled presence. In so doing, He makes them able to confront what is real about themselves, one another and the world."[43]

In commenting on the section "We are One Body of Christ," which has the largest selection of thirty-nine hymns, Poon writes that this

> is in itself a conversation with God on real life in Asia. Like the psalmist, the lyricists neither offer tidy description nor give triumphalist solution to the human situation. Rather, they bring to God their confusing, messy and raw situations, while pleading for Him to act. These hymns should unsettle some in their complacency, while alerting others to re-examine the character of their public witness.[44]

These are hymns and liturgical pieces arising from mainly the Southeast Asian context and are a significant contribution to the hymnology and liturgy that can be used by all churches. Unfortunately, the forces of globalization on worship songs and forms are largely dominated by the West. Hence, additional

---

41. Mary Y. T. Gan, I-to Loh, and Judith Laoyan-Mosomos, eds., *Let the Asian Church Rejoice* (Singapore: Methodist School of Music and Trinity Theological College, 2015).
42. Michael Nai-Chiu Poon in Gan, Loh, and Laoyan-Mosomos, eds., *Let the Asian*, x, xi.
43. Poon in Gan, Loh, and Laoyan-Mosomos, eds. *Let the Asian*, x, xi.
44. Poon in Gan, Loh, and Laoyan-Mosomos, eds. *Let the Asian*, xi.

efforts need to be made to encourage Southeast Asian churches to sing songs with lyrics, musical cadences, and rhythms which express their culture and context in more relevant and powerful ways. If they do so, not only will Southeast Asian churches connect better with their own souls and communities – and thus deepen their spirituality and witness – but they will also bless the global church by offering a perspective that could enrich others.

POTENTIAL CONTRIBUTIONS OF SOUTHEAST ASIAN CHURCHES

Christianity is considered a Western religion in many parts of Southeast Asia, especially where other religions such as Islam and Buddhism are considered to be more native religious traditions.[45] The popular narrative is that the way Christianity is lived and practiced is a mirror image of Western expressions of the religion. There is some truth in this as the books we read, the songs we sing, and the preachers we listen to are predominantly from the West. In light of this situation, Southeast Asian theologians, along with others in Asia, have been called to contextualize theology and develop ecclesial and liturgical forms that are congruent with cultural and social realities in the region. We have reviewed how this process has developed in theologizing and theological education, liturgy, and missionary outreach.

We will conclude by exploring some of the developing churches in Southeast Asia who are faithful to Scripture and squarely rooted in their own contexts. As contextualizing is done, care should be taken that we do not end up with a parochial or isolated and insulated form of Christianity that fails to recognize the globalization process that is so much a part of modern life.

Globalization

In today's world, globalization is keenly observed as a significant reality. We all face the effects of climate change and environmental pollution, and many face the effects of highly urbanized cities in which overcrowding, lifestyle changes, and the fast pace affect how individuals, families, and communities experience everyday life.

In the 1970s, Japanese missionary and theologian Kosuke Koyama wrote books such as *Water Buffalo Theology* and *Three Mile an Hour God*.[46] Serving

---

45. Goh, *Christianity in Southeast Asia*, 5.
46. Kosuke Koyama, *Water Buffalo Theology* (London: SCM, 1974); Kosuke Koyama, *Three Mile an Hour God* (London: SCM-Canterbury, 1979).

as a missionary in rural Thailand, Koyama found Western theology to be irrelevant to the context and felt that theology and spirituality had to fit with the lifestyles of farmers in the rural hinterlands, which was the dominant reality in Southeast Asia at that time. Today, while a significant part of Southeast Asia is still rural, the burgeoning cities and modernization that is taking place means that we cannot rely on water buffalo theology alone to make sense to the masses in Southeast Asia. Globalization means that we must interact with what other theologians, Christian leaders, and congregations elsewhere are doing to meet the challenges of both modernization and globalization. To be truly contextual, we cannot just produce a disconnected theology, or we will end up in a frog-in-the-well syndrome, living in our own local silos.

We have already noted how we must interact with and learn from others, and that our attempts to produce a Southeast Asian form of Christianity cannot be divorced from historical Christianity. What is needed is to break free from the predominant influence of Western Christianity that tends to be globalized to such an extent that it diminishes local cultures and contexts. As historian John Roxborough has noted, Southeast Asian attempts to contextualize Christianity cannot ignore the commonalities of Christian expressions shared in global and historical Christianity. In finding particularities in their contexts, Southeast Asian churches must also be aware of the need to differentiate between contextualization and syncretism. Contextualize they must, remembering that "world Christianity is incomplete without the sharing of Southeast Asian narratives."[47] While the potential is great and there are many possible explorations, the following are some suggestions.

Exploring Shame

In his classic book *Pastoral Counseling Across Cultures*, pastoral theologian David Augsburger points out that Asian cultures are largely shame-oriented as compared to Western cultures which are guilt-oriented.[48] Augsburger highlights a cultural bias in Western thought that is "a direct descendent of Enlightenment thought and the individualism, privatism, rationalism, and egocentrism it has offered us."[49] This same thinking can also be seen in much of Western theology and pastoral practice. While much of Christian theology deals with our guilt

---

47. Roxborogh, "Situating," 38.
48. David W. Augsburger, *Pastoral Counseling Across Cultures* (Philadelphia: Westminster, 1986), chapter 4.
49. Augsburger, *Pastoral Counseling*, 115.

as sinners, there is a need to explore more deeply the shame that comes from having broken our promises or not measured up to expectations. For example, the first emotion that Adam and Eve faced after sinning was shame. They felt ashamed and hid from each other and from God. Shame is connected to the relational aspects of life.

In an Asian setting where face is important and the loss of face and shame has serious effects, the gospel may be better presented in terms of the shame of unhealthy and broken relationships. Grace then removes disgrace when God accepts us as we are and gives us face so that we can face him and others. The Christian life can be seen as gaining the face of Jesus, growing into his likeness, and being given dignity as the children of God. This approach has implications for theology, evangelism, and discipleship.

There is potential to explore shame in this way. Sri Lankan theologian Ajith Fernando has written on the rubrics of shame and dishonor in many Asian societies and their implications for discipleship.[50] More work can be done to explore the subject in holistic and comprehensive ways.[51] For example in Filipino culture, the concepts of *hiya* (shame), *pakikisama* (yielding to the leader or the majority), and *utang na loob* (gratitude) are all based on the core cultural value of *kapwa* (shared identity with others).[52] Mature Filipino people are those who share their identity with others. The most mature people are those who belong, not those who are independent. Many Western psychologies are based on views of maturity linked with growing independence. By implication what is seen as healthy behavior in one culture, say in California, may be seen as unhealthy in another, say in the Philippines.

Community

The traditional sense of community is still strong in many parts of Southeast Asia, especially in rural settings. The term *gotong royong* is of Malay-Indonesian origin and refers to the cooperation in a community or communal helping of one another. It is this "*kampong* spirit" that enables local communities to build bridges and roads or clear rubbish to improve communal life. This

---

50. Ajith Fernando, *Discipling in a Multicultural World* (Wheaton, IL: Crossway, 2019).
51. See for example David A. de Silva, *Honor, Patronage, Kinship and Purity: Unlocking New Testament Culture* (Downers Grove, IL: InterVarsity, 2000) in which he relooks at the New Testament using the lens of honor and dishonor that characterized ancient Mediterranean culture.
52. As noted by Virgilio G. Enriquez, "Developing a Filipino Psychology," in *Indigenous Psychologies: Research and Experience in Cultural Context* (London: SAGE, 1993), 152–169.

sense of volunteerism and mutual aid is a needed corrective to the increasingly individualistic and emotionally isolated lives of many people, especially in urban settings.

This sense of community fits in well with both Old and New Testament teachings on how communities can thrive when people look after each other's needs. In the New Testament the phrase "one another" is frequently used to describe how life in community should look. The New Testament church was a community in which deep sharing took place to the extent that "there were no needy persons among them" (Acts 4:34 NIV). Throughout history, churches have often reached out to needy societies with Christian love, ministering to the poor and marginalized.

The Lord Jesus distilled biblical teaching as the call to love God and neighbor (Matt 22:37–40). What does this teaching mean in our societies in which the majority of people do not share our faith and where there is much need? What does it mean to be good neighbors to those around us? The challenge amid globalized economic and social structures is to resist self-centered individualism by learning how to practice Christian love and generosity in the global *kampong* (village).[53]

Religious Dialogue in a Multi-Religious Context

Southeast Asia has many religions. Several countries have a dominant religion, such as Islam in Malaysia, Indonesia, and Brunei and Buddhism in Thailand. But these countries also have minority religions, of which Christianity is one, except in the Philippines and Timor Leste where it is the majority religion. These multireligious contexts have created a spectrum of realities, from persecution and restrictions on the church to fostering interreligious dialogue and religious harmony. The presence of Christianity in some countries creates political tensions. For example, many tribal groups in Thailand, Myanmar, and East Malaysia have significant numbers of Christians, but this Christian identification has caused the tendency in the majority population to marginalize tribal Christians.[54]

Within these realities, churches need to develop pathways that allow them to relate to people of other faiths in constructive ways while managing religious

---

53. See Ha Tung Chiew, "Hosting Versus Hoarding of Wealth: Reading James in the Global Kampong," in *Contextual Reflections from Asia*, ed. Cheong Weng Kit (Kota Kinabalu, Sabah: Sabah Theological Seminary, 2013), 298–315.
54. Goh, *Christianity in Southeast Asia*, 76.

conflicts and persecution by authorities. In the West other religions have tended to be viewed either in negative terms or through naïve perspectives. Southeast Asians must adopt their own approach that is faithful to the gospel as well as winsome when living among peoples of other faiths.

The experience of the church as a minority in Southeast Asia is to be taken seriously. Much of Western theology reflects Christendom perspectives, or Christianity as the dominant or significant religion – though this situation is changing with the rise of alternative humanistic and scientific perspectives. The churches in Southeast Asia can contribute to the theologizing of the minority status of the Christian community, which is not far removed from the New Testament church who also experienced being a persecuted minority. In this respect, Southeast Asian churches can learn much from the New Testament.

Suffering, Poverty, and Social Inequalities

While Southeast Asian nations are feeding into globalization, trade, modernization with the rise of technology, growing affluence among elites, and a burgeoning middle class, chronic poverty still remains a major problem.[55] This issue can be seen in both rural areas and highly urbanized settings where the poor are left behind by the rapid social and economic changes. They live in squatter huts and shanty towns trying to survive as best as they can.

In many places, Christians attending church tend to be better off and may not relate to the poor around them. This disconnect needs to be addressed so that churches can live out their mission and character in meeting the needs of the poor and marginalized. Where churches engage in social outreach and action, they receive a better hearing and can make better connections with their neighbors. There is a need to engage in contextualized theology and mission to address the causes of marginalization and chronic poverty and how they can be alleviated. Churches need to produce theologians who are well-versed in economics, public policy, and social enterprises and can provide some answers. As missiologist Roger Hedlund asserts, mission in Southeast Asia "must give attention to the growing disparity between rich and poor."[56]

---

55. See Maizura Ismail, "Southeast Asia's Widening Inequalities," The ASEAN Post (17 July 2018), https://theaseanpost.com/article/southeast-asias-widening-inequalities.
56. Roger Hedlund, "Understanding Southeast Asian Christianity," in *Christian Movements in Southeast Asia: A Theological Exploration*, ed. Michael Nai-Chiu Poon (Singapore: Trinity Theological College, 2010), 88.

Corruption

Many Southeast Asian societies are troubled by endemic corruption at all levels of society. How can Christians live as disciples of Christ where corruption appears in many forms and is often institutionalized? Malaysian theologian Hwa Yung wrote on the subject in his book *Bribery and Corruption*.[57] Hwa adopts an incarnational model that recognizes some of the ambiguities that Christians face in societies with endemic corruption that is socially accepted. He attempts to show that the Bible recognizes some of these ambiguities. For example, the book of Proverbs contains six verses on bribery: three verses condemn it (Prov 15:27; 17:23; 22:16), and another three seem to describe it in positive terms (17:8; 18:16; 21:14).[58] Hwa points out that we need to differentiate between a gift, which may be a social custom, and a bribe. He offers some guidelines that will help us avoid participation in both active and passive corruption, always keeping in mind the Christian vocation of transforming society.

More work needs to be done on this issue that will help Christians in Southeast Asia handle life in societies where corruption is deeply embedded, and that will go beyond – to help transform their societies to be righteous and transparent.

Migrant and Diaspora Ministries

Many Southeast Asian countries have large migrant and expatriate communities and the potential opportunities and problems they pose.[59] In Singapore, about a third of the workforce are foreigners, including professional, construction, domestic, nursing, and hospitality workers. Many churches have developed ministries to reach out to these communities, offering fellowship, worship services, and forms of legal and medical help. Missions at our doorstep is an important ministry in such contexts. Given the large number of migrants in Southeast Asia, a theology of migration and ministry need to be developed.[60]

Moreover, Singaporean and other Southeast Asian Christians have become involved in diaspora ministries by helping Chinese, Indian, Vietnamese,

---

57. Hwa Yung, *Bribery and Corruption: Biblical Reflections and Case Studies for the Marketplace in Asia* (Singapore: Graceworks, 2010).
58. Hwa Yung, *Bribery and Corruption*, 26.
59. Amarjit Kaur, "Labour Migration in Southeast Asia: Migration Policies, Labour Exploitation and Regulation," *Journal of the Asia Pacific Economy* 15, no. 1 (February 2010): 6–19.
60. See Fabio Baggio and Agnes M. Brazal, eds., *Faith on the Move: Toward a Theology of Migration in Asia* (Manila: Ateneo de Manila UP, 2008).

Filipino, and other communities. Some have also seen the need to reach out to the Western church. For example, some Methodist pastors from Singapore and Malaysia have gone to assist the Methodist Church in Britain which is aware of their shrinking numbers and need for help from thriving churches overseas. This help is a significant contribution that Southeast Asian churches can make to Western churches.[61]

CONCLUSION

Looking ahead, the Southeast Asian church can grow and develop in many areas. Contextualized theology, liturgy, missiology, and spirituality are good starting points for such growth. What I have presented here are examples of what has been done and how it has been done. Moving forward, such contextualization efforts must continue not only for the growth of the Southeast Asian church but also to inform and enrich other Christian churches elsewhere.

QUESTIONS FOR FURTHER RESEARCH

1. What are the patterns of church growth in Southeast Asia? Where is church growth taking place, and in what forms? What does this growth say about how effective the churches are in evangelism and discipleship?
2. What strategies have the churches employed when they are a religious minority and often marginalized or sometimes persecuted? Are there better strategies that can be explored?
3. What are some emerging, local Southeast Asian theologies that can contribute to global discussions on biblical studies, theology, and missiology? Is there any possible development of a "theology of shame" in Southeast Asian churches that can significantly contribute to global theologizing?
4. How are Southeast Asian churches dealing with injustice, suffering, inequalities, poverty, and corruption? Can such responses, if any, be improved and made more effective and biblically informed?
5. To what degree is Western Christian material, such as theology, popular Christian literature, and various forms of media, relevant

---

61. See "Missionaries from the global south try to save the godless West," *The Economist* (12 January 2019), https://www.economist.com/international/2019/01/12/missionaries-from-the-global-south-try-to-save-the-godless-west.

or irrelevant in Southeast Asia? To what extent is it important to develop local material that speaks to the needs and aspirations of the Southeast Asian churches?

Additional Case Studies

Robert Solomon – SEA Churches Roundtable
1. Using the systems mapping chart (ch 10, pg 168), choose a local or national church and fill in the various micro-, meso-, and macro-level partnerships the church has in the region. In the twenty-first century, how might each of these partnerships impact the forward trajectory of Southeast Asian? Which partner do you think will have the greatest influence, and why?
2. From Part 1, compare a country where the church has a major role in society, for example Singapore or the Philippines, with a country where the church has a minority role, for example Myanmar or Cambodia. How would partnerships be different in these two countries?

REFERENCES

Adeney-Risakotta, Bernard. *Visions of a Good Society in Southeast Asia: Social Imageries and Inter-religious Dialogue*, edited by Chiang Ming Shun. Singapore: Trinity Theological College, 2017.

Athyal, Saphir F. "Toward and Asian Christian Theology." In What Asian Christians are Thinking: A Theological Source Book, edited by Douglas J. Elwood, 68–84. Quezon City, Philippines: New Day, 1976.

Augsburger, David W. *Pastoral Counseling Across Cultures*. Philadelphia: Westminster, 1986.

Baggio, Fabio, and Agnes M. Brazal, eds. *Faith on the Move: Toward a Theology of Migration in Asia*. Manila: Ateneo de Manila UP, 2008.

Cariño, Feliciano V., and Marina True, eds. *Faith and Life in Contemporary Asian Realities*. Hong Kong: Christian Conference of Asia, 2000.

Chan, Simon. "Evangelical Theology in Asian Contexts." In *The Cambridge Companion to Evangelical Theology*, edited by Timothy Larsen and Daniel J. Treier, 225–240. Cambridge: Cambridge University Press, 2007.

———. "Folk Christianity and Primal Spirituality: Prospects for Theological Development," in *Christian Movements in Southeast Asia: A Theological*

Exploration, edited by Michael Nai-Chiu Poon, 1–17. Singapore: Trinity Theological College, 2010.

———. *Grassroots Asian Theology: Thinking the Faith from the Ground Up*. Downers Grove: IVP Academic, 2014.

———. *Liturgical Theology: The Church as Worshiping Community*, rev. ed. Downers Grove: InterVarsity, 2006.

Cheong Weng Kit, ed., *Contextual Reflections from Asia*. Kota Kinabalu, Sabah: Sabah Theological Seminary, 2013.

Chong, Terence, ed., *Globalization and Its Counter-forces in Southeast Asia*. Singapore: Institute of Southeast Asian Studies, 2008.

———. ed. *Pentecostal Megachurches in Southeast Asia: Negotiating Class, Consumption and the Nation*. Singapore: ISEAS, 2018.

Chotiudompant, Suradech. "Thai Magical Realism and Globalization." In *Globalization and Its Counter-forces in Southeast Asia*, edited by Terence Chong, 380–95. Singapore: Institute of Southeast Asian Studies, 2008.

Elwood, Douglas J., ed. *What Asian Christians Are Thinking: A Theological Source Book*. Quezon City, Philippines: New Day, 1976.

Enriquez, Virgilio G. "Developing a Filipino Psychology." In *Indigenous Psychologies: Research and Experience in Cultural Context*, 152–169. London: SAGE, 1993.

FAMB bishops, "Letter from the Fellowship of Asian Methodist Bishops to the Council of Bishops of the United Methodist Church" (10 September 2007). Personal Correspondence.

Fernando, Ajith. *Discipling in a Multicultural World*. Wheaton, IL: Crossway, 2019.

Gan, Mary Y. T., I-to Loh, and Judith Laoyan-Mosomos, eds. *Let the Asian Church Rejoice*. Singapore: Methodist School of Music and Trinity Theological College, 2015.

Gener, Timoteo D. "Doing Contextual Systematic Theology in Asia." *Journal of Asian Evangelical Theology* 22 nos. 1–2 (March-September 2018): 49–68.

Goh, Robbie B. H. *Christianity in Southeast Asia*. Singapore: Institute of Southeast Asian Studies, 2005.

Hedlund, Roger. "Understanding Southeast Asian Christianity." In *Christian Movements in Southeast Asia: A Theological Exploration*, edited by Michael Nai-Chiu Poon, 59–100. Singapore: Trinity Theological College, 2010.

Henry, Rodney. *Filipino Spirit World: A Challenge to the Church*. Manila: OMF Publishers, 1986.

Hiebert, Paul G., R. Daniel Shaw, and Tite Tienou. "Responding to Split-level Christianity and Folk Religion." *International Journal of Frontier Missions* 16, no. 4 (Winter 1999/2000): 173–82.

Hing, Datuk Ng Moon, Rennis Ponniah, Datuk Melter Jiki Tais, and Danald Jute. "Statement from the Province of Southeast Asia." The Diocese of Singapore (21 February 2019). https://www.anglican.org.sg/page/statement-from-the-province-of-south-east-asia.

Hwa Yung. *Bribery and Corruption: Biblical Reflections and Case Studies for the Marketplace in Asia*. Singapore: Graceworks, 2010.

———. *Mangoes or Bananas?: The Quest for an Authentic Asian Christian Theology*, 2nd ed. Maryknoll, NY: Orbis, 2015.

"Infographic: top cities and urbanization in ASEAN." ASEAN Up (5 July 2017). https://aseanup.com/infographic-top-cities-urbanization-asean/.

Kaur, Amarjit. "Labour Migration in Southeast Asia: Migration Policies, Labour Exploitation and Regulation." *Journal of the Asia Pacific Economy* 15, no. 1 (February 2010): 6–19.

Koyama, Kosuke. *Water Buffalo Theology*. London: SCM, 1974.

Manikam, Rajah B., and Winburn T. Thomas. *The Church in Southeast Asia*. New York: Friendship, 1956.

Mesa, José de. *Isang Maiksing Katekismo para sa mga Bata: A Study in Indigenous Catechetics*. Manila, Philippines: Wellspring, 1988.

———. "Kapag ang 'Ganda' ang Pag-Uusapan: Mungkahi para sa Dulog at Paraan ng Mabathalang Pag-Aaral." In *Ang Maganda sa Teolohiya*, 1–22. Quezon City, Philippines: Claretian, 2017.

———. *The Prayer Our Lord Taught Us*. San Juan City, Philippines: Center for Collaborative and Creative Ministry, 2005.

Poon, Michael Nai-Chiu, ed. *Christian Movements in Southeast Asia: Theological Exploration*. Singapore: Trinity Theological College, 2010.

Ross, Kenneth R., Francis Alvarez, and Todd M. Johnson, eds. *Christianity in East and Southeast Asia*. Edinburgh: Edinburgh University Press, 2020.

Roxborogh, W. John. "Situating Southeast Asian Christian Movements in the History of World Christianity." In *Christian Movements in Southeast Asia: A Theological Exploration*, edited by Michael Nai-Chiu Poon, 19–38. Singapore: Trinity Theological College, 2010.

Solomon, Robert M. *Living in Two Worlds: Pastoral Responses to Possession in Singapore*. Frankfurt am Main: Peter Lang, 1994.

Willford, Andrew C., and Kenneth M. George, eds. *Spirited Politics: Religion and Public Life in Contemporary Southeast Asia*. Ithaca, NY: Southeast Asia Program, 2004.

CHAPTER 14

A HOLISTIC RESPONSE TO SOCIAL JUSTICE

Kiem-Kiok Kwa

Southeast Asia is economically, culturally, and religiously diverse. Diversity of economic status results in the rich and poor living almost side by side in cities like Manila and Jakarta. The urban and rural divide means not only a difference in income for those who live in these places but also different worldviews and resources available for socioeconomic growth. People of all the major world religions reside here. Some groups are in the majority, such as Muslims in Brunei, Malaysia, and Indonesia; Buddhists in Thailand; and Christians in the Philippines. As a region, Southeast Asia is probably not more problematic than other parts of the world with despotic rulers, unjust governments, unequal societies, and environmental degradation.

It is in this combination of injustices and religious diversity that questions arise about how Christian missions should be carried out. Surely Christian missions must engage with people of different religions and worldviews not just with the truth claims of the gospel but also by displaying real and spiritual manifestations of the gospel in transformed lives and communities and spiritual signs and wonders. Because the gospel is a message of hope for all peoples, the church can and should respond holistically in all of these situations and in some ways to the injustices in society.

Much of Christian missions in the region has been more focused on saving souls and setting up churches, with engaging the issues of the context carried on by the way. There are various reasons for this focus. For example, a theological worldview prevailing in the nineteenth and early twentieth centuries of Christian missions was that souls and the spiritual are much more important than physical bodies or environs. That thinking continues to prevail today, and evangelism often has a *higher priority* in Christian missions than holistic mission.

In this chapter, we first unpack the context. We then suggest a theology of missions based on justice and transformation that enables Christian missions to be more holistic in internal foundations as well as external perceptions. We end this chapter with some suggestions on how such missions could look.

THE CHURCH IN ASEAN TODAY

Looking around today, churches are visible in many places in Southeast Asia, whether a small building with a cross, a cathedral built several hundred years ago, or a shiny, brand-new, modern building. In other places a church building cannot be seen, either because no church has yet been planted or because it is safer for believers not to be so visible. Both the buildings and the lack of visible presence reflect the various ways the church started and has grown in the region.

Portuguese Catholics arrived as early as the fourteenth century and established a port in Malacca on the west coast of the Malay Peninsula, while Protestant Christians came to the region in the eighteenth and nineteenth centuries. Generally, Protestant Christian missionaries came with the colonial expansion of that time. Because of this connection with the colonial powers, many perceive Christianity to be a foreign and Western religion as it was expressed in *foreign languages* and was culturally alien.

For example, tensions between the more communally oriented Asian cultures and the more individualistic "Christian" and Western cultures have led to the perception that when people become Christians, they lose their cultural identity.[1] While this change in cultural orientation may be more easily accepted or tolerated in some urban contexts, it may not be so in rural areas, or where families are more conservative. This perceived loss of cultural identity of Christians is a stumbling block to conversion. Today there are still cultural barriers to receiving the Christian message, and thus the need for sound and sensitive contextualization and to develop an Asian theology remains.[2] Furthermore, the gospel should not be preached in words only but should also be seen as holistic and as engaging with the spiritual powers, since many Asians have a holistic and integrated worldview. Thus to make further inroads into Southeast Asia, Christians need to present a message which not only touches people's daily lives, but is also culturally sensitive and contextually appropriate.

---

1. Darrell Whiteman, "Contextualization: The Theory, The Gap, The Challenge," *International Bulletin of Missionary Research* 21, nos. 1, 2 (January 1997): 2–7.
2. See Hwa Yung, *Mangoes or Bananas* (Carlisle, UK: Regnum 1997).

A Holistic Response to Social Justice

In the early years as reflective of Christian missions of that time, many of the missionaries who came were more interested in saving souls.³ That is, Christian missionaries did not see their primary role to be addressing social ills such as opium addiction or the unhealthy working conditions of migrant workers. To their credit though, these missionaries did seek to educate girls, a revolutionary concept in those days, and set up girls' schools. Today many of these schools still stand, and mission schools are well-regarded educational institutions.

After more than two hundred years of missions, the church in Southeast Asia remains numerically small. Christians are a minority in most countries in Southeast Asia, except in the Philippines which is majority Catholic.

While the history of missions and the church is discussed elsewhere in this volume, significant geopolitical developments in the twentieth century have made positive impacts in the region. In 1967, the countries in the region organized themselves into The Association of Southeast Asian Nations (ASEAN), which is similar to the European Union, for both economic cooperation and to increase the region's clout on the world stage.⁴ On ASEAN's fiftieth anniversary in 2017, Singapore ambassador-at-large Tommy Koh said that ASEAN has helped to build a new regional order.⁵ Within the bloc, member countries try to strike a balance between noninterference and allowing each country to exercise sovereignty over their own affairs while presenting a united economic and sociocultural community. Over the years ASEAN has matured, and there is now a more confident regional identity and greater cooperation at various levels, such as visa-free entry for citizens within the region, among other things. This greater ease of movement and openness to citizens of the bloc could be harnessed for missions.

However, some seemingly intractable issues within the region reflect the complex intertwining of history, religion, the environment, and human rights. We shall mention just three. First, the plight and status of about one million Rohingya people, Muslims who live in the Rakhine state in Buddhist-majority

---

3. In the early twentieth century, Methodist missionaries in Singapore wrote to the press in protest of the official supplies of opium to which many coolies were addicted, but such engagement with authorities was rare. See Andrew Peh, *Of Merchants and Missions* (Eugene, OR: Wipf & Stock, 2019).
4. ASEAN started in 1967 with five countries – Indonesia, Malaysia, the Philippines, Singapore, and Thailand – and the other countries joined later to form the ten nation bloc that ASEAN is today.
5. Tommy Koh, "Why I Believe in ASEAN," in *ASEAN@50*, vol. 1, The ASEAN Journey: Reflections of ASEAN Leaders and Officials (2017).

Myanmar, where they have an undocumented status despite having lived there for generations.⁶ A brutal military-led crackdown in 2017 led to hundreds killed and an exodus of thousands of Rohingyas into Bangladesh, creating a refugee crisis there and raising questions about finding a viable long-term solution for them.⁷ While the government has stoically defended their actions, within ASEAN Indonesia and Malaysia have expressed grave concerns about the treatment and fate of these Muslims. Christians should refrain from providing simplistic answers to these complex issues, but rather seek a nuanced understanding of the issues.

The second issue is the regular smoky haze that blankets the region in various degrees of intensity, especially in the dry months of July to October. This haze is a result of burning peat, of farmers and large corporations in Indonesia using slash and burn techniques to clear land to grow the cash crop palm oil, and of the dry inter-monsoon weather which does not dispel the smoke. The burning happens in some parts of Indonesia such as Kalimantan and Sumatra, and the people there suffer the brunt of the smoke because of the winds. However people in Malaysia and Singapore also suffer from this haze. Related concerns include global warming and climate change. To counter this issue, Christian doctrines of caring for and being faithful stewards of the earth, combined with changes in personal consumer habits and living more simply have to be lived out.

The third issue is one of the most insidious in the region: corruption. From the petty bribes that government officials expect to the millions of dollars which are siphoned off by political leaders, bribery, which is illegal in most countries, is extremely common in Southeast Asia.⁸ As Adeney points out, "Bribery undermines the cause of justice in society by making it difficult for the poor to be treated fairly."⁹ In many Southeast Asian societies, there are wide socioeconomic reasons for bribery, such as poorly paid civil servants

---

6. This Rohingya issue has since been overshadowed by the military coup and crackdown of January 2020 and the civil disobedience, including the rise of ethnic-based armies within the country.
7. "Myanmar Rohingya: What you need to know about the crisis," *BBC News* (23 January 2020).
8. For example, in 2018, Singapore was ranked three out of 180 countries in Transparency International's annual Corruption Perceptions Index. However this ranking does not mean that there is no corruption in the country. Over the years there have been cases of corruption both by public servants and employees in a government-linked company, Keppel Offshore and Marine Company, which came to light in 2018.
9. Bernard T. Adeney, *Strange Virtues: Ethics in a Multicultural World* (Leicester: Apollos, 1995), 155.

who resort to supplementing their income with some forms of gifts or tips from the public. Furthermore in these cultures, relationships are maintained by a finely balanced system of reciprocal gift giving, a practice which neither party would consider to be giving bribes.[10]

In various ways, these three issues are all matters of justice. They raise questions such as, how can minority groups within society experience justice? When the tangled matters of history, culture, religion, and political rights intertwine, what are some just solutions?

For example, the land often bears the brunt of human activity, and global warming is now an ever-present issue of deep concern to individuals and societies around the world. Christians who view themselves as stewards and not exploiters of the earth can take steps within their community to show care for the created world. Perhaps there is little that Christians in Malaysia or Thailand can do about peat burning in Indonesia, but they can certainly carry out the mandate to care for the earth where they are. All Christians everywhere should become more aware of the many facets of earth stewardship – such as the need to maintain a healthy ecological balance. Indeed within evangelical theology and praxis, Christians have methods and frameworks to begin to engage in these issues missionally.

JUSTICE: BIBLICAL AND THEOLOGICAL

Yahweh is a God of justice, and his justice is reflected in the natural world, in the worship of his people, and in the ways he deals with humanity. "And the heavens proclaim his righteousness, for he is a God of justice" (Ps 50:6).[11] The Psalmist declares, "The LORD loves righteousness and justice; the earth is full of his unfailing love" (33:5), and in contrast to prideful human beings who will be brought low, Isaiah the prophet says, "But the LORD Almighty will be exalted by his justice, and the holy God will be proved holy by his righteous acts" (Isa 5:16). God shows his concern for the vulnerable and those who cannot defend themselves, like widows, orphans, and foreigners, and commands his people to show them justice (Deut 24:17; 27:19). God also hates that which perverts justice, like bribes (Deut 16:19).

This character of God is also seen in the Servant of the Lord (Isa 42:1–4), a passage which the Gospel writer Matthew quotes as fulfilled in Jesus Christ

---

10. Adeney, *Strange Virtues*, 155.
11. All Scripture references are from the New International Version (NIV) 2011 unless otherwise stated.

who will bring justice to the nations (Matt 12:15–21). This is the Messiah, an ideal Israel, and "[through] his obedient service to God, Israel will be enabled to perform the service of blessing the nations."[12] One especially tender characteristic of justice is portrayed here:

> A bruised reed he will not break,
> > and a smoldering wick he will not snuff out.
> In faithfulness he will bring forth justice;
> > and he will not falter or be discouraged
> till he establishes justice on earth.
> > In his law the islands will put their hope. (Isa 42:3–4)

Jesus Christ portrayed such love and justice in his earthly ministry. He demanded that religious leaders live up to their teaching and stop exploiting ordinary folk, including the marginalized. He touched lepers, ate with the socially outcast, welcomed women to learn from him, and portrayed Samaritans as heroes. Those who follow Christ should also express the same tenderness and justice.

Indeed justice is what God expects of his people as can be seen in the laws that God put in place in Israel, such as the gleaning laws in Leviticus 19:9–10 which reflect God's care for the poor. This justice is also seen in the sacrificial system which includes avenues for the poor to participate, laws which many years later the parents of Jesus followed (Luke 2:24).

> [I]t is not an abstract entity *justice as such* that God loves. What God loves is the *presence* of justice in society. And God loves the presence of justice in society not because it makes for a society whose excellence God admires, but because God loves the members of society – loves them, too, not with the love of admiration but with the love of benevolent desire. God desires that each and every human being shall flourish, that each and every shall experience what the Old Testament writers call *shalom*. Injustice is perforce the impairment of *shalom*. That is why God loves justice. God desires the flourishing of each and every one of God's creatures; justice is indispensable to that. Love and justice are not pitted against each other but intertwined.[13]

---

12. John N. Oswalt, *Isaiah Chapters 40–66*, New International Commentary on the Old Testament (Grand Rapids, MI: Eerdmans, 1998), 108.
13. Nicholas Wolterstorff, *Justice: Rights and Wrongs* (Princeton: Princeton University Press, 2010), 82, emphasis original.

A Holistic Response to Social Justice

Herein is the theological warrant for Christians to be involved in acts of justice, for in bringing about God's justice and thus shalom in the world, we are showing God to the world. Indeed, God has a broad vision for the world, as can be seen for example, in Isaiah 11. This vision will be brought about by a shoot from the root of David on whom will be the Spirit of the Lord, the spirit of wisdom, understanding, counsel and might. This one will bring about a world where

> The wolf will live with the lamb,
> > the leopard will lie down with the goat,
> the calf and the lion and the yearling together;
> > and a little child will lead them. . . .
> They will neither harm nor destroy
> > on all my holy mountain,
> for the earth will be filled with the knowledge of the Lord
> > as the waters cover the sea. (Isa 11:6, 9)

This vision will be fulfilled, as Wolterstorff points out, when there are three right, harmonious relationships in the kingdom – right relationships to God, the human community, and the lived physical surroundings.[14] This three-fold understanding of justice provides a holistic framework for Christian missions which seek to build harmony with God, with others in the community, and with the physical world. According to Isaiah 11:6–8, shalom is not merely the absence of hostility, but is being in right relationships.[15] All three dimensions – self, others, and nature or land – are necessary for shalom. When there is justice, there should be flourishing of lives. Wolterstorff goes on to emphasize that such justice brings about God's shalom, peace, in which people are in right relationships with each other. He concludes his argument by reminding Christians that shalom too is the task of missions:

> Can the conclusion be avoided that not only is shalom God's cause in the world but that all who believe in Jesus will, along with him, engage in the works of shalom? Shalom is both God's cause in the world and our human calling. Even though the full incursion of shalom into our history will be divine gift and not

---

14. Nicholas Wolterstorff, *Hearing the Call: Liturgy, Justice, Church, and World* (Grand Rapids, MI: Eerdmans, 2011), 70.
15. Nicholas Wolterstorff, *Until Justice and Peace Embrace* (Grand Rapids, MI: Eerdmans, 1983), 69.

merely human achievement . . . nonetheless it is shalom that we are to work and struggle for. . . . We are workers in God's cause, his peace-workers. The mission Dei *is* our mission.[16]

God's mission is about bringing people into right relationship with him, and this comes through belief in Jesus Christ. Thus while the evangelism element of missions remains strong, to present Jesus is more than just to save souls; it is also to introduce the person who brings and gives the fullness of life (John 10:10). When people know and experience that their sins have been forgiven by a merciful God, in Christ, they can also do his work. Salvation is much broader than simply resting on the assurance and waiting to go to heaven; it is also actively seeking to bring about God's kingdom on earth.

While missions involve evangelism, telling people about the good news of Jesus Christ, this aspect does not mean that the other two relationships – with other people and with the physical environment – are only consequential. All three relationships should always be growing and improving, and Christian missions is finding ways to improve all these dimensions of life. For example, when Christians serve a community by improving the sanitation system, their work can have a positive impact on relationships within the community and present opportunities to tell people about the God who cares about all aspects of life. Even in an urban setting, the built environment has an impact on human relationships and activities, and Christians can find creative ways of providing for the community, for example through building or maintaining a park or community garden. This type of working together is common within Southeast Asian cultures, and Christians can and should be part of such initiatives and efforts.

The apostle Paul did not seem to have taken steps to actively change social structures. For example, he did not seek to upend the Roman slave system. Indeed, he asked the runaway slave Onesimus to obey the law and return to his owner, Philemon. Yet the way Paul asked believing slaves and masters to treat each other with love and respect would have undermined the very structures of that institution.[17] Likewise, Peter wrote to believers who were scattered in the Roman Empire to "Live such good lives among the pagans that, though they accuse you of doing wrong, they may see your good deeds and glorify God on the day he visits us" (1 Pet 2:12). By doing good in their

---

16. Wolterstorff, *Until Justice*, 72, emphasis original.
17. William Webb, *Slaves, Women and Homosexuals: Exploring the Hermeneutics of Cultural Analysis* (Downers Grove, IL: InterVarsity 2001).

communities, they would be living up to the call of Jesus to be the salt of the earth and the light of the world (Matt 5:13–16). Thus, Christians are to be active and live out their faith and beliefs in the world.

Mission and Missions

There is a general consensus among scholars that mission (singular) is God's sending activity, the "very sending mandate of the church as a whole."[18] This is the *missio Dei*, "all that God is doing in his great purpose for the whole of creation and all that he calls us to do in cooperation with that purpose."[19] Missions (plural) is narrower and refers to the specific tasks and "multitude of activities that God's people engage in, by means of which they participate in God's mission."[20] Thus mission is God's self-revelation, while missions is the human activity and participation of God's people, the church, in that mission.[21] Since the people of God are doing God's mission, the church on earth is, by its very nature, missionary.[22] Thus God's mission (singular) shapes and informs how God's people do missions (plural) in the world. There is an on-going cycle of theological reflection on who God is and what he is doing in the world and the state of the world.

It is in this missional task then, as the church engages in the world, that brings God's justice and shalom into the world. Beyond "saving souls for heaven," missions challenges and inspires Christians to be involved and bring in God's values in all areas of life, including his justice. Missions transforms individuals as well as societies as people begin to live out God's reign in their lives.

In his seminal work, *Transforming Mission*, Bosch does not wish to define missions too sharply or self-confidently, but he helpfully presents thirteen emerging missionary paradigms which guide the church in the task of missions.[23] He masterfully combines biblical, theological, and practical insights for missions. For example, in his suggestions for religious dialogue and mission, an area which needs to be developed in the Southeast Asian context, he urges Christians to recognize that "religions are worlds in themselves, with their own

---

18. Craig Ott and Stephen Strauss, *Encountering Theology of Missions: Biblical Foundations, Historical Developments, and Contemporary Issues* (Grand Rapids, MI: Baker Academic 2010), xv.
19. Christopher J. H. Wright, *The Mission of the People of God* (Grand Rapids, MI: Zondervan, 2010), 25.
20. Wright, *Mission*, 25.
21. David J. Bosch, *Transforming Mission: Paradigm Shifts in Theology of Mission* (Maryknoll, NY: Orbis, 1991), 10.
22. Bosch, *Transforming*, 10.
23. Bosch, 349–510.

axes and structures; they face in different directions and ask fundamentally different questions. This means, among other things, that the Christian gospel relates differently to Islam, than it does to Hinduism, Buddhism, etc."[24] This humble posture is necessary to maintain in the religiously diverse Southeast Asian context. Doing God's missions entails a constant evolving of what Christians do, through constant theological reflection, and as they meet the challenges of the context. We explore what Christians in Southeast Asia can do in missions later in the chapter.

The Lausanne Movement, formerly known as the Lausanne Committee for World Evangelization, influences and guides much of the evangelical world's missions strategies. From the first Congress in 1974 and subsequent growth and diversification of this movement into the Lausanne Occasional Papers and gatherings on a variety of missional issues such as the environment, business as mission, and the arts, the Lausanne Movement has provided evangelical reflection and thinking as well as suggested best practices for doing missions today. This breadth of vision recognizes God's rule and reign over all aspects of life, both physical and cultural, and is a guide for how the church can do missions.

This broad approach is relevant and applicable in the Southeast Asian context where, in the people's minds, all of life is one interrelated and connected whole. Hence the bifurcation of the religious and secular or the physical and spiritual is false in this worldview. For example, to be Thai is to be Buddhist, as the culture and religion are so deeply intertwined.[25] Furthermore as we have seen, the problems of injustice are a result of the complex intertwining of many factors. Therefore, the fullness of the gospel needs to be brought to bear in this context. For it is only when the whole gospel is brought by the whole people of God into the context that we can begin to make inroads with the good news of Jesus Christ.

Holistic Missions

As various authors like Bosch have traced, there was a time when the main task of missions was to bring people out of the world and into the church, and such sentiments still prevail in some sectors of the church today. But such withdrawal from the world was at the expense of Christians engaging holistically in the community and doing acts of justice. However, over time scholars have moved toward a more theologically holistic view of missions. After Bosch's

---

24. Bosch, 485.
25. Whiteman, "Contextualization," 2.

Transforming Mission published in 1994 came Christopher Wright's *The Mission of God* in 2006 and Timothy Tennent's *Invitation to World Missions* in 2010 in which he suggests a trinitarian model for missions.[26] More recently Al Tizon has proposed that reconciliation could be a theme in holistic missions.[27] There are theological hurdles to be overcome, for as Bosch says, "[t]he relationship between the evangelistic and the societal dimensions of the Christian mission constitutes one of the thorniest areas in the theology and practice of mission."[28] But missiology as a discipline has taken a definite turn toward being more holistic, which also means that there is greater awareness of different aspects of individual life such as the physical and the economic and of attending to concerns of life such as the environment and social concerns.

Thus grassroots movements have sprung up, like Micah Global which began in 1982 and whose guiding principle is Micah 6:8: "He has shown you, O mortal, what is good, and what does the LORD require of you? To act justly and to love mercy and to walk humbly with your God." It is noteworthy that some of the prime movers of this movement came from the Global South, for there the issues of injustice are keenly felt. Today, Micah Global has grown to be a network of ministries across the world who meet regularly at conferences held at both the regional and global levels to discuss how to do integral missions and live justly in the face of the complex issues faced today.[29]

Another example of a grassroots movement is A Rocha, "The Rock" in Portuguese, which began in 1983 when some Christians started to reflect on how to be good stewards of the environment. Soon diverse conservation and scientific research projects were being done in parts of Europe. Today, they encourage the appreciation of nature and participation in conservation through environmental education and outreach, and they provide a forum for understanding the relevance of Christian faith to environmental issues.[30] These are two fine examples of global, ground-up initiatives which do holistic missions and who have related organizations in Southeast Asia.

Holistic missions requires a firm theological grounding to not only be true to the whole counsel of God as revealed in Scripture, but also that missions

---

26. Wright, *Mission of God*; Timothy Tennent, *Invitation to World Missions: A Trinitarian Missiology for the Twenty-First Century* (Grand Rapids, MI: Kregel Academic, 2010).
27. Al Tizon, *Whole and Reconciled* (Grand Rapids, MI: Baker Academic, 2018).
28. Bosch, *Transforming*, 401.
29. For more information, see Micah Global, www.micahnetwork.org.
30. For more information, see "Welcome to A Rocha," A Rocha International, www.arocha.org.

may be sustained in the long haul. This breadth in missions areas is explored in *Mission as Transformation* by Samuel and Sugden.[31] They suggest that the practice of holistic missions transformation include ministry in such diverse areas as children at risk, economics, the political mission of the church, nation building, and establishing the kingdom of God. There are certainly adequate grounds, both theologically and in practice, for Christian missions today to embrace a wide range of activities which can bring justice and God's shalom to the world.

It should not be presumed that this theological thinking comes only from the West, for as Beattie traces, Asian theologians echo many of these same ideas.[32] Indeed, missiologists from the Global South influenced the thinking at the first Lausanne Committee on World Evangelization in 1974 to take a more holistic approach to missions. Coming from contexts which were more obviously more unjust than those of the Global North, missiologists like René Padilla and Samuel Escobar exerted a positive influence toward a more holistic practice of missions.

While there may be shades of difference between these terms – holistic missions, integral missions, and missions as transformation – at heart they all capture the sense that God's people are to reflect the fullness of God's character in the world. Indeed, Beattie's suggestion for a transformational missiology captures this well, because it would result in "engagement in nation-building in terms of developing civil society, promoting justice and participating in wider social structures as well as the proclamation of the gospel" and "is a response to the multi-religious nature of Asian societies interacting with pluralism, engaging in dialogue and finding appropriate ways to witness to, and defend the place of Christian faith in Asian societies."[33]

Contextualization

Since Christianity came with Western colonial powers to Southeast Asia, it is often perceived as a Western and alien religion. When Christian life and ministry is carried out in English instead of the local languages, it is already one

---

31. Vinay Samuel and Chris Sugden, eds. *Mission as Transformation: A Theology of the Whole Gospel* (Oxford: Regnum, 1999).
32. Warren Beattie, "Transformational missiology: An emerging trend in evangelical missiology in Asia: an analysis with reference to selected Asian writers" (PhD diss, University of Edinburgh, 2006).
33. Beattie, "Transformational Missiology," 159.

step removed from the local culture.[34] There is an urgent need in Southeast Asia to present the gospel in culturally appropriate terms, not only in the heart language of the audience, but also in the cultural forms, for indeed the gospel is incarnational. Hiebert's critical contextualization model is helpful here.[35] He suggests that in doing the task of contextualization, we should exegete culture and Scripture thoroughly, build hermeneutical bridges between the two, and then be open for people in the local community to make a critical response to these attempts.

When contextualization is not critical, there can be syncretism, which is an inappropriate mix of cultures or religions and thus a dilution of the gospel. For example, Hindus can happily pray to Jesus, alongside all their other gods, for they will not see the necessity to worship Jesus Christ as the one true God. Split-level Christianity can also occur.[36] For example, some Chinese Christians will not take part in the Taoist funeral rites of their parents because they see such participation as worshipping ancestors. By this stance, they are perceived by the extended family to be unfilial, a heavy offence within that culture. These are tensions that must be managed in the Southeast Asian context where religion and culture are so closely intertwined and to the extent that some forms of contextualization may seem like a compromise.

Therefore, critical contextualization as Hiebert proposes requires holding a deep understanding of the culture with a close study of the Scriptures. In Southeast Asia various work has been done in this area, for example in theological seminaries in the region which train pastors in the local language and publications such as *Family and Faith in Asia* which highlight the importance of family networks for conversation, conversion, and social transformation.[37] These are some known examples in English, but other efforts and examples can be found in Bahasa Indonesia, Thai, Vietnamese, and Khmer which are suitable for believers in those communities.

Because of this close relationship between religion and culture, people on the street or in the pew may not reflect deeply whether their actions are cultural or religious. For example, Chinese people show their filial piety in a variety of

---

34. Certainly sectors of residents, mainly in Southeast Asian cities, are comfortable in English. But most Southeast Asian residents are most comfortable in their mother tongue.
35. Paul Hiebert, "Critical Contextualization," *International Bulletin of Missionary Research* (July 1987): 104–12.
36. See Paul G. Hiebert, R. Daniel Shaw, and Tite Tienou, "Responding to Split-level Christianity and Folk Religion," *International Journal of Frontier Missions* 16, no. 4 (Winter 1999/2000): 173–82.
37. Paul De Neui, *Family and Faith in Asia* (Pasadena, CA: William Carey Library, 2010).

ways, such as caring for their parents when they are alive, carrying out funeral traditions upon their death, and regularly offering food for them thereafter. However, some Christians see those actions after death as ancestor worship or veneration which Scripture prohibits. In this regard, David Lim from the Philippines has suggested that just as the Chinese have an interconnectedness that maintains relationships with the ancestral dead, so the Christian view of "a great cloud of witnesses" (Heb 12:1) is the Christian faiths' continuation with the faith of ancestral heroes.[38] By adopting this posture of cultural continuity, he suggests, Christians can show filial piety to their ancestors in culturally appropriate ways.

There are many aspects of culture which can and still need to be contextualized, as Christian missions involves engaging with people of other religions within their cultural expressions. Apologetics, presenting reasoned arguments of the truth claims of Christianity, can and has been effective in reaching out to educated, secular urbanites. However, when approaching people from a rural or suburban setting, or those who are oral learners, or those who hold on to more folk expressions of their religion, missions and evangelism may need to be shown in signs and wonders and in trading stories. Chan has pointed out this form of grassroots Asian theology is certainly a valid and vibrant form of Asian Christianity.[39]

Missionaries

Traditionally missions, especially cross-cultural missions, has been carried out by full-time missionaries, both singles and families. They would go often at great personal cost to set up a church and live in another culture, and in this way fulfilled the Great Commission to go and preach the gospel. Their lives continue to be an inspiration to believers today. While there are such missionaries working now, there is a shift in the kinds of people who do missions. As Wright points out, missions today are to be carried out everywhere by all of God's people.[40] The breadth and scope of the task now requires this involvement of all of God's people. No longer is missions the purview of just a few in a "full-time" capacity, but the whole church has to be mobilized – the whole people of God bringing the whole word to the whole world, as is the tagline

---

38. David S. Lim, "Contextualizing the Gospel in Ancestor-Venerating Cultures," in *The Gospel in Culture*, ed. Melba Padilla Maggay (Manila: OMF Literature, 2013), 400.
39. Simon Chan, *Grassroots Asian Theology: Thinking the Faith from the Ground Up* (Downers Grove, IL: IVP Academic, 2014).
40. Wright, *Mission*.

A Holistic Response to Social Justice

for the Lausanne Movement. Such an approach is particularly relevant today because several countries like Indonesia and Brunei do not issue missionary visas to Christians but do welcome professionals who will bring their specialized skills. Since all believers are sent out into the world, the church thus needs to teach a theology of work which does not separate sacred work from secular work, but which values all work done unto the Lord. Such good work can be a witness for the Lord because Christians who do their work well, in whatever sphere God has placed them, will be God's witnesses to those around them.

When the task of missions is broadly defined, there can and should be different types of missionaries with varied skills. Apart from the ability to plant a church, missionaries may need to be able to set up or work in businesses or in good educational or health care institutions. As Christians seek to serve the community, whether providing counselling services, setting up a missional business that will provide jobs and teach skills to the locals, or running environmentally sustainable businesses – all these require a wide variety of skills and talents. Few individuals can do this work by themselves; hence doing missions today requires Christian missionaries to work in teams and in partnerships.

Cities such as Bangkok and Singapore are open to foreigners for work and business, conferences, education, and tourism; hence, there are many opportunities for churches in the city to reach out in creative ways to the foreigners in their midst. In a world in which traveling abroad is relatively cheap and easy, especially around a small geographical region such as Southeast Asia, all Christians can and should be trained to be missionaries – to share their stories and to do acts of justice and mercy where they are. Missions is no longer the task of a chosen few but is the role of every believer.[41]

A greater awareness of issues such as corruption should lead Christians to search the Scriptures and find solutions befitting their context. Indeed, corruption is one area where many citizens, not only Christians, are deeply concerned about in their societies. In Malaysia, the civil society group *Bersih* ("Clean" in the Malay language) was launched in 2006 to call for a reform of the electoral process which had been plagued by allegations of corruption and discrepancies.[42] Many Christians also participate in this movement. When addressing the issues of bribery, theologians can provide sound biblical and

---

41. Since the COVID-19 pandemic swept the world in 2020, cheap and convenient travel is no longer possible, and this practice will need to be reexamined and adjusted.
42. See http://www.bersih.org.

theological thinking, while business people and civil servants from different societies can give suggestions for how to deal with the problem.[43]

MISSIONS AND PUBLIC THEOLOGY

To be able to engage well with social and justice issues, Christians need a public theology which will provide the theological framework they need to identify the issues they could be addressing, as well as the posture and language with which to communicate a Christian point of view to those who are outside Christian circles. The term "public theology" may have been first coined by historian Martin Marty in 1974 and has been used to describe "religious engagement with social issues and questions of public morality."[44] Recognized as a theological discipline, public theology is also missiological because it is the framework by which the church engages in public. While Wright's *The Mission of God's People* has a section on "Missional Engagement in the Public Square,"[45] there is no entry for public theology in the *Dictionary of Mission Theology*,[46] which illustrates how new and uncharted this field is in missiology. Only in 2020 was *Public Missiology* by Gregg Okesson published.[47] In doing public theology, churches engage in their specific context to bring the gospel to bear on the issues and concerns in local, regional, and global communities. Such engagement should fit each context in terms of the language used, how issues are framed, and even who to engage with. For example, Malaysian Christians in *Bersih* were engaging with the government to agitate for clean and fair elections through public demonstrations, while in Singapore in 2006, Christians took part in a public debate carried out in the press and other public forums on whether or not to introduce casinos into the country.

Hence Christians should find ways to engage graciously and positively outside the church in discourse as well as in providing services. A well-rounded public theology, suited for the context, will help churches to engage in this discourse. As the Lausanne Cape Town Commitment puts it, the role of the church is to articulate and defend biblical truth in the public arena, as well as for believers to have "the tools to relate the truth with prophetic relevance

---

43. For example see Hwa Yung, *Bribery and Corruption: Biblical Reflections and Case Studies for the Marketplace in Asia* (Singapore: Graceworks, 2010).
44. E. Harold Breitenberg, Jr., "To Tell the Truth: Will the Real Public Theology Please Stand up?" *Journal of the Society of Christian Ethics* 23, no. 2 (2003): 64.
45. Wright, *Mission*, 222–242.
46. John Corrie, *Dictionary of Mission Theology* (Downers Grove, IVP Academic, 2007).
47. Gregg Okesson, *Public Missiology: How Local Churches Witness to A Complex World* (Grand Rapids, MI: Baker Academic, 2020).

to everyday public conversation, and so to engage every aspect of the culture we live in."[48] This public engagement can be both official – that is carried out by a national council of churches or equivalent which can be the Christian voice in the public square, especially with the state – or at the grassroots level by individuals or local Christian communities engaging with social needs and ills where they live.

Public theology rests on the assumption that the Christian worldview and belief is true not just for Christians in their spiritual lives but for all people. Since Christians believe that Jesus is Lord of all, then surely he is Lord not only of the church but of the world, and not only in religious life but in all of life.[49] This worldview is part of the story that Christians should tell, and these public engagements and conversations show this reality to others.

As mentioned, God is concerned for justice and for the marginalized, and many Christians are compassionate and would happily serve to alleviate the sufferings of others. However, Christians should also be concerned about the structures within society and the community which cause inequalities and poverty and seek to find ways to change those structures to rectify the injustices and break poverty cycles. This service could include not only being involved in the lives of the community, for example in providing education or a means of livelihood, but also speaking up to those in power. Thus, public theology is not just about solving problems but also seeing society as a whole and seeking justice and shalom for the community.

Communication in Public

Since public theology is about engaging the wider public, communication is key. Both the posture of Christians and the language they use have to be appropriately contextual. With regard to speech, for example, Christians could use the language of natural law, or appeal to common sense and good reason, even if the primary reasoning is drawn from Scripture. They should not quote the Bible for it is not authoritative for those who are not Christians. The acts employed should also be appropriate; in many countries, people may demonstrate on the streets, but such demonstrations are illegal in Singapore. Christians there have learned to engage by using more subdued means such as writing letters to their members of parliament.

---

48. The Cape Town Commitment, Part IIA, 1 and 2, see https://lausanne.org/content/ctc/ctcommitment#capetown.
49. Lesslie Newbigin, *Truth to Tell: Gospel as Public Truth* (London: SPCK, 1991), 34–35.

Engaging the LGBT Lobby[50]

The issue of the rights of homosexuals in society has become a hotly contested public issue in many Southeast Asian societies and is often a testbed for how the church engages in the public square. Generally, more liberal elements within society want to allow for the LGBT community to have greater rights and freedom of expression, while those who are more conservative wish to limit those rights. In Southeast Asia, churches and Christians often identify with the latter group.[51] The issues are complex and contextual; for example Indonesia laws criminalize homosexual behavior and prohibit greater rights for this community.

Then there are Christians and others who may struggle with same-sex attraction and who seek solace and pastoral care within the Christian community. But when they see that churches are against homosexuals, however perceived, they turn away from the church. Christians also face the issues of biblical hermeneutics and the tensions between traditionalist and revisionist interpretations of Scripture. The many facets of this issue will probably continue to be hotly contested in many Asian societies for some time.

Thus, evangelical churches have to engage with different groups within churches and in the broader society while maintaining a biblical stance. In particular, engaging in the public square with the lobby groups requires that Christians communicate their views truthfully and with gentleness and respect (1 Pet 3:15). The language used should be accessible to their audience. In Singapore where there is a well-formed gay lobby, Christians have learned that it is counterproductive to contend with them directly. Instead one church began to tell stories of how Christians with same-sex attraction have found acceptance within the church. In this way, they began to change public perceptions that the church is antigay and homophobic.[52] However, when engaging with the authorities, the church has taken a more uncompromising stance.[53] It is not my intention to present solutions here, but rather to illustrate how this issue requires Christians to have much wisdom and flexibility to engage

---

50. Lesbian, gay, bisexual, and transgender.
51. For example in 2021, the Asia Theological Association held a seminar on gender equality and homosexuality. See Shang-Jen Chen, presenter, "Gender Equality and Homosexuality," YouTube (27 September 2021). https://www.youtube.com/watch?v=Lm8xXLtl4mE.
52. See for example "What Is TrueLove.is" at www.truelove.is/about, a ministry of 3:16 Church, www.316-church.com.
53. See National Council of Churches Singapore (NCCS), https://nccs.org.sg/statements/official-statements/.

with different groups and use different language while maintaining a consistent Christian posture.

Social Media

Engaging in the public square also requires engagement in the social media space, which is now vibrant and active and reaches beyond geographic and political boundaries. Christians must be adept in using social media and post well-thought, thorough, pithy, and winsome comments on social media accounts, as well as respond well to criticisms and opposing points of view.

SPECIFIC ACTIONS

As I have suggested above, *missio Dei* is among other things to live out the kingdom of God in society today, and that includes showing and living out God's justice. That justice includes care for the marginalized and vulnerable.

Acts of Justice

To act justly in the community, missions must not then merely give people a monetary handout, but must also give them the dignity of labor as well as improving structures so that there will be greater justice within the community.[54] While it may be difficult to make an impact on the broad global economic forces, small acts are like a mustard seed, and we can make a difference in one community or through one business project. While humanitarian work is sometimes necessary, for example immediately after a natural calamity like a devastating typhoon, such relief work often depends on sponsorship and is often not sustainable in the long term. Missions practitioners are now concerned with sustainability and the growth of communities and on giving communities the means of upward lift, such as can come from starting businesses.

The principles which govern business as missions are helpful here. The Lausanne Movement has done much work in thinking through issues such as wealth creation, justice, and stewardship.[55] An early Lausanne Occasional Paper on business as missions helpfully sets out the biblical basis for this work as well as providing ten guiding principles for carrying out such businesses.[56]

---

54. For example see Steve Corbett and Brian Fikkert, *When Helping Hurts* (Chicago: Moody, 2012).
55. See for example BAM Global: Business as Missions, https://bamglobal.org/.
56. Lausanne Occasional Paper No. 59, https://businessasmission.com/resources/bam-lausanne-occasional/.

These principles can be well encapsulated in the need for such businesses to address four areas or bottom lines: purpose, people, profits, and the planet.

The purpose of the business should be missional, and popular examples include restaurants and cafés and motorcycle repair or other services which not only provide employment and teach skills to the local community but are also beneficial for them in other ways. Some start a business to provide new Christians with employment, and others do so as an opportunity to witness to staff and the community. A business should also generate healthy profits, for indeed such profits are necessary to enable the business to grow. A poorly run business does not grow and is a poor witness to the community. Finally, a missional business should reflect care and stewardship of the physical environment. An example could be a restaurant that uses locally sourced ingredients, tries to use the whole animal, and composts food waste.

Dialogue with People of Other Faiths

As mentioned, the Southeast Asian region is religiously diverse. Many people are deeply religious in the sense that their religion gives them identity and forms their values. Apologetics, presenting the truths of the Christian faith in a logical and persuasive manner, may be suitable for educated and urbanized people who are familiar with this type of exchange and discourse. However, for rural folk and oral learners, that style of argumentation may not be persuasive. Instead, they may need more engagement and dialogue at different levels and different types. The aim of such dialogue is not direct conversion *per se*, but rather opportunities for interacting with people of other faiths in meaningful and holistic ways.

> Dialogue *is*, of course, the only option in today's globalized and polycentric world; it *does* and *must* include a moment of proclamation – of each partner to the other. In no way does dialogue *replace* proclamation or the necessity of an invitation to Christian conversion. . . . [It is] the "norm and necessary manner of every form of Christian mission" because Christian mission is participation in the mission of *God*, and God's being and action is dialogical.[57]

---

57. S. Bevans SVD and R. Schroeder SVD, *Constants in Context* (Maryknoll, NY: Orbis, 2004), 378. emphasis original. Quoted text with block text cited from: Address of the Pope

A Holistic Response to Social Justice

Christians often shy away from the concept of dialogue because they perceive it to be a compromise of Christian belief, or a place to find the lowest common denominator of belief. That need not be so because interreligious dialogue requires attentive listening, conversation skills, empathy, study, and respect. Indeed, Jesus himself engaged in such conversations, for example with the Samaritan woman at the well (John 4:4–42) and with the Canaanite woman in the region of Tyre and Sidon (Matt 15:21–28). These dialogues are good models for Christians today.

Bevans and Schroeder have helpfully identified four types of dialogue which can be used as ways for Christians to engage in dialogue.[58] First is the dialogue of life through which people get to know each other as human beings, neighbors, and fellow citizens. This interaction forms the foundation of every kind of dialogue as people begin to see one another as faces and personalities. Life dialogue is simply having conversations with neighbors and friends about everyday matters and where appropriate introducing a Christian perspective. Second is the dialogue of action through which people of different faiths can work together for justice, peace, and the integrity of creation without minimizing their different faiths but holding on to a common goal of social, political, or ecological justice. For example in Singapore, interreligious confidence circles are organized, grassroots groups where religious leaders gather for activities to build relationships and understanding. During Christmas, some churches in a neighborhood were asked to organize a carnival for the community and to share the story of Christmas. Third is the dialogue of theological exchange which should be carried out by officials or experts of the religion and be about a common and particular religious subject; for example, how the different religions view the current environmental crisis. Fourth is the interreligious dialogue of religious experience which should also be done by religious experts, though the dialogue should be accessible to ordinary religious practitioners.

Apart from the last two forms of dialogue which Bevans and Schroeder suggest should be carried out by theological experts, the other two can occur naturally as Christians interact daily with non-Christians at home, work, and in the marketplace. After all in the Southeast Asian context, Christians are often in the company of people of other faiths. Rather than teaching rote methods

---

at the Secretariat for Non-Christians, "The Attitude of the Church towards the Followers of Other Religions: Reflections and Orientations on Dialogue and Mission," see https://www.dicasteryinterreligious.va/dialogue-and-mission-1984/.
58. Bevans and Schroeder, 383–85.

of evangelism, churches can equip believers to listen for these opportunities and to find ways of engaging naturally with their neighbors.

In the multicultural contexts of Southeast Asia, communities celebrate various cultural festivals such as the New Year, harvest festivals, or the end of the Muslim fasting month. These are excellent opportunities for Christians to be involved in these festivities with their neighbors. Some Christians have chosen to withdraw from such celebrations because they view such festivals as demonic. However while some festivals have some spiritual elements, others, for example New Year festivities, are often joyful opportunities for the community to celebrate together. By participating, Christians show that they are part of the wider community and do not hold themselves aloof.

Developing Artistic Expressions

As a legacy of missions from the West, many Christian missions tend to be word based and propositional, which can be ways of reaching those who have been exposed to these forms of communication. However, many cultures use a variety of oral and artistic expressions because people respond better to stories, music, and song. Evangelism can use various artistic expressions because they have the ability to connect with people at the emotional and not merely the cognitive level. A well-told story which incorporates elements from the local culture and is told in their heart language can be a powerful outreach method. In the same vein, Christian discipleship should use more artistic expressions, such as encouraging believers to write songs about their faith or to draw their beliefs.

CONCLUSION

Missions is an evolving practice. As Christians reflect theologically on what they see and experience in the world, they engage missionally. The church in Southeast Asia is in the minority, and Christians may not even be well regarded in some communities. Even so, with sound theological reflection, in particular on concepts of justice and public theology, churches can serve the community and fulfil their calling to be salt and light in the world. To do this, their missions must be holistic – addressing whole people in their physical and spiritual context. When Christians do so, they reflect God's righteousness in the world.

A Holistic Response to Social Justice

Case Study 1

You and your family are full-time missionaries doing church planting work in a city in another country. You are introduced to Abraham, a local Christian who ministers in a slum community of about twenty-thousand people. Those who can work look for whatever money they can make each day, and even the children scavenge in rubbish dumps for items they can sell. You have visited this slum with Abraham several times, and what strikes you is the strong smell of waste since there are no toilets. Abraham suggests that with about US $10,000, he could build a simple sanitation system within the slum that can pipe sewage out of each household.

1. Would you help to finance his project? Why or why not? If you decided to do so, would you give him the money or lend it to him?
2. As you go into this slum community, how can you do holistic missions there? With limited financial and human resources, how would you prioritize your work?

Case Study 2

Your job in human resources of a transnational company means that you travel regularly to the different cities in Southeast Asia. On each trip, you have the opportunity to interact with the locals which gives you insight into their culture and worldview. Also you often have several hours during the day between your work meetings when you are free to do other things. As you walk around the streets of the city, you do not always see a visible church, but there are several social service agencies which help the poor in the community.

1. You ask your home church for prayer support as you make these trips, but your church leaders say that what you do isn't missions. What Scriptures will you use to explain to them that what you seek to do is missions?
2. What are some areas in which you think you could be involved, bearing in mind your professional work situation?

Additional Case Study
1. Take any of the issues raised by Kiem-Kiok Kwa in this chapter and use Jean Paul Heldt's chart (pg 164) to develop a holistic response.

REFERENCES

Adeney, Bernard T. *Strange Virtues: Ethics in a Multicultural World*. Leicester: Apollos, 1995.

Beattie, Warren. "Transformational Missiology: An emerging trend in evangelical missiology in Asia: an analysis with reference to selected Asian writers." PhD diss., University of Edinburgh, 2006. http://hdl.handle.net/1842/18710.

Bevans, S., SVD, and R. Schroeder SVD, eds. *Constants in Context*. Maryknoll, NY: Orbis, 2004.

Bosch, David J. *Transforming Mission: Paradigm Shifts in Theology of Mission*. Maryknoll, NY: Orbis, 1991.

Breitenberg, E. Harold, Jr. "To Tell the Truth: Will the Real Public Theology Please Stand up?" *Journal of the Society of Christian Ethics* 23, no. 2 (2003): 55–96.

Chan, Simon. *Grassroots Asian Theology: Thinking the Faith from the Ground Up*. Downers Grove, IL: IVP Academic, 2014.

Corbett, Steve, and Brian Fikkert. *When Helping Hurts*. Chicago: Moody, 2012.

De Neui, Paul. *Family and Faith in Asia*. Pasadena, CA: William Carey Library, 2010.

Hiebert, Paul. "Critical Contextualization." *International Bulletin of Missionary Research* (July 1987): 104–12.

Hor, Joanna, Ng Zhi-Wen, Bernice Tan, Tan Soo-Inn, Ronald J. J. Wong, and Raphael Zhang. *Bruised Reeds, Walking with Same-Sex Attracted Friends*. Singapore: Graceworks, 2018.

Hwa Yung, *Mangoes or Bananas*. Carlisle, UK: Regnum 1997.

Koh, Tommy. "Why I Believe in ASEAN." In *ASEAN@50*, vol. 1, The ASEAN Journey: Reflections of ASEAN Leaders and Officials, 177–80 (2017). https://www.eria.org/asean50-vol.1-30.tommy-koh.pdf.

Lim, David S. "Contextualizing the Gospel in Ancestor-Venerating Cultures." In *The Gospel in Culture*, edited by Melba Padilla Maggay, 377–415. Manila: OMF Literature, 2013.

"Myanmar Rohingya: What you need to know about the crisis." BBC News (23 January 2020). https://www.bbc.com/news/world-asia-41566561.

Newbigin, Lesslie. *Truth to Tell: Gospel as Public Truth*. London: SPCK, 1991.

Okesson, Greg. *Public Missiology: How Local Churches Witness to a Complex World.* Grand Rapids, MI: Baker Academic, 2020.
Oswalt, John N. *Isaiah Chapters 40–66.* New International Commentary on the Old Testament. Grand Rapids, MI: Eerdmans, 1998.
Ott, Craig, and Stephen Strauss. *Encountering Theology of Missions: Biblical Foundations, Historical Developments, and Contemporary Issues.* Grand Rapids, MI: Baker Academic 2010.
Peh, Andrew. *Of Merchants and Missions.* Eugene, OR: Wipf & Stock, 2019.
Samuel, Vinay, and Chris Sugden, eds. *Mission as Transformation: A Theology of the Whole Gospel.* Oxford: Regnum, 1999.
https://www.straitstimes.com/asia/se-asia/what-you-need-to-know-about-malaysias-bersih-movement.
Tizon, Al. *Whole and Reconciled.* Grand Rapids, MI: Baker Academic, 2018.
Webb, William. *Slaves, Women and Homosexuals: Exploring the Hermeneutics of Cultural Analysis.* Downers Grove, IL: InterVarsity 2001.
Whiteman, Darrell. "Contextualization: The Theory, The Gap, The Challenge." *International Bulletin of Missionary Research* 21, no. 1 (January 1997): 2–7.
Wolterstorff, Nicholas. *Hearing the Call: Liturgy, Justice, Church, and World.* Grand Rapids, MI: Eerdmans, 2011.
———. *Justice: Rights and Wrongs.* Princeton: Princeton University Press, 2010.
———. *Until Justice and Peace Embrace.* Grand Rapids, MI: Eerdmans, 1983.
Wright, Christopher J. H. *The Mission of the People of God.* Grand Rapids, MI: Zondervan, 2010.

CHAPTER 15

CASE STUDY OF CULTURAL INTEGRATION FOR SELF-THEOLOGIZING IN THE EVANGELICAL CHURCH OF VIETNAM

KimSon Nguyen[1]

The Evangelical Church of Vietnam (ECVN)[2] has long sought to develop an indigenous church in Vietnam modeled after the "three-self" concept: self-governing, self-supporting, and self-propagating. The concept reached Vietnam in the early twentieth century as reflected in the early missionary work of the Christian and Missionary Alliance (CMA) and ECVN. Rev Lê Hoàng Phu concluded in his findings that "a large number of local churches of the Evangelical Church of Vietnam were actually organized" on these "three principles of self-support, self-government, and self-propagation."[3]

The "three-self" concept, coined initially by Henry Venn, is a reflection of the manner in which national Christians can govern, give, and evangelize in ways that address the sociological aspects of the evangelization process, but the concept does not relate to the cultural aspects. There is a fourth self, "self-theologizing," but the church has shown little evidence of having a specific Vietnamese contextual theology.[4] In other words, the church has not "nurtured" or "expressed" themselves theologically in their own cultural

---

[1]. Adapted by Samuel K. Law from KimSon Nguyen, *Cultural Integration and the Gospel in Vietnamese Mission Theology: A Paradigm Shift* (Carlisle, UK: Langham Monographs, 2019).
[2]. The Evangelical Church of Vietnam or *Hội Thánh Tin Lành Việt Nam* in Vietnamese (ECVN), the former Christian and Missionary Alliance (CMA) church in Vietnam, is the evangelical church with the longest history and the largest membership of any evangelical church in Vietnam. *Vietnamese evangelicalism* (*Tin Lành*, in Vietnamese) is the term used in this study to discuss Vietnamese evangelical Christianity and to differentiate it from Vietnamese Catholicism (*Công Giáo*, in Vietnamese). Also by Vietnamese evangelicals, the writer means both the evangelical registered and the non- and pre-registered churches in Vietnam.
[3]. Lê Hoàng Phu, "A Short History of the Evangelical Church of Viet Nam (1911–1965)" (PhD diss., New York University, 1972), iii.
[4]. Paul G. Hiebert, *Anthropological Insights for Missionaries* (Grand Rapids, MI: Baker, 1985), 193–224. This fourth self was proposed and articulated first by Hiebert.

context: their architecture, liturgy, music, homiletical style, and organizational structure have all reflected the foreign culture of the missionaries, thus remaining discontinuous from Vietnamese cultural patterns. The church remains to this day, for the most part, a Western CMA church in Vietnam rather than a contextualized and culturally appropriate ECVN, as Violet James states in her doctoral dissertation, "the ECVN was but another American denomination."[5]

Like other Asian people, the Vietnamese are devout and religious. The major world religions of Hinduism, Buddhism, Islam, and Christianity, with Confucianism and Daoism have greatly influenced the religiocultural traditions of East Asians, including the Vietnamese. But early Christian missionaries hardly understood the people's complex worldview which intertwines sacred and secular aspects. In other words, the missionaries seldom appreciated the syncretistic spirituality of the Asian people and their holistic worldview that integrates and synthesizes religious aspects with secular life.

The vision of a contextualized evangelical theology in Vietnam – had past efforts not failed as will be illustrated later – was the initial thought and driving force behind this chapter. This is a vision for churches which have their own form or style of expression rooted in the culture where they exist. Christian faith, then, should be both relevant and indigenous in Vietnamese form, style, language, and so forth. The church should present Christian faith in such a way that it meets Vietnamese people's deepest needs and penetrates their worldview, allowing them to follow Christ while remaining rooted in their Vietnamese culture.[6] For instance, incorporating the Vietnamese way of venerating ancestors into Christian theology and liturgical practices is one aspect which could be contextualized.

Efforts to contextualize were made in Asia in the sixteenth and seventeenth centuries by the Jesuits Francis Xavier in Japan and Matteo Ricci and Alexander de Rhodes in China, including today's Vietnam. They put great effort into learning local languages and cultures to contextualize Christian faith in these Asian societies as a way for Christianity to "re-encounter" Asia in the seventeenth century. In fact, "what the Jesuits had done in contextualization, particularly in Vietnam, and generally in Asia in the previous centuries, became

---

5. Violet B. James, "American Protestant Missions and the Vietnam War" (PhD diss., University of Aberdeen, 1989), 354.
6. A similar effort has been done among Thai Christians. See for instance, Ubolwan Mejudhon, "The Way of Meekness: Being Christian and Thai in the Thai Way"(DMiss diss., Asbury Theological Seminary, 1998).

a foundational premise for a better picture of holistic contextualization for the Vietnamese Catholic Church (*Công Giáo*) in the twentieth century."⁷

In contrast, the French and American Protestant missionaries in early twentieth-century Vietnam seemed to be intent on making the native Vietnamese look more like Western Christians, overlooking perhaps that in the process, they were also making them less Vietnamese.⁸ Should not a genuine Vietnamese evangelical Christian be expected to be a good Vietnamese as well? Nguyễn Ái Quốc (Ho Chi Minh) in his letter to a French pastor in 1921 laments,

> Whether students of illiterate peasants, they are Annamites [the older word for Vietnamese], and Annamites they should remain. Being good Annamites does not stop them from being good Christians . . . and thus if you want to find a true Christian in Indochina [Vietnam], look for him in a good Indochinese [Vietnamese] man, but nowhere else.⁹

Mr Nguyễn Ái Quốc was living in Paris at the time this letter was written, arguing that French Christian missions and colonization should not go together, as he said, "every civilizing mission – whether it is in the Antilles, Madagascar, Indochina, or Tahiti – is always towed by a so-called evangelizing mission."¹⁰ Rather, he believed there is "goodness" for Vietnamese people if Buddhism, Confucianism (Vietnamese or "Orientals" value), and Christianity ("Occidentals" value) work in harmony because only "one Truth" exists

---

7. Nguyen KimSon, "The Catholic Church in Vietnam: An Example of Contextualization," *Asia Journal of Theology* 29, no. 1 (2015): 74.
8. "History will help us evaluate the critique of missions and empires, of missionaries creating 'rice Christians,' and of missionaries 'making one more Christian and thus one less Chinese.'" See Scott W. Sunquist, *Understanding Christian Mission: Participation in Suffering and Glory* (Grand Rapids, MI: Baker Academic, 2013), 14.
9. Known as Hồ Chí Minh, the former president of North Vietnam and considered to be the founding father of modern Vietnam, Nguyễn Ái Quốc's original writing was, "Etudiants ou paysans illettrés, annamites ils sont annamites ils doivent le rester. Etre bons annamites n'empêche pas d'être bon chrétiens . . . si vous voulez trouver un vrai chrétien en Indochine, cherchez le chez le bon Indochinois, mais pas ailleurs." See Hồ Chí Minh, "Unpublished Letter by Hồ Chí Minh to a French Pastor (September 8, 1921)," trans. Kareem James Abu-Zeid, *Journal of Vietnamese Studies* 7, no. 2 (2012): 3; and Pascal Bourdeaux, "Notes on an Unpublished Letter by Hồ Chí Minh to a French Pastor (September 8, 1921) or the Art of Dissenting Evangelization," *Journal of Vietnamese Studies* 7, no. 2 (2012): 14.
10. Nguyen Ai Quoc, *Le procès de la colonisation francaise [The process of French colonization]* (Paris: Imprimerie et Librairie du Travail, Première Série, Mœurs Coloniales, 1926), 142.

regardless "whatever side we find ourselves on."[11] His statement reflects the struggle of the Protestant missionaries to communicate the gospel in a manner that was both relevant and indigenous to Vietnamese people. Because of their lack of cultural sensitivity, the Protestant missions and missions fruit, the Evangelical Church of Vietnam have not yet found the optimal solution for contextualizing the gospel relevantly to the diverse cultural and religious contexts of Vietnam.

How then can the Vietnamese follow Christ and yet remain within their Vietnamese culture? The purpose of this chapter is three-fold: (1) to situate the Vietnamese evangelical theology and critically evaluate its cultural integration within the larger context of East Asia and the context of Vietnamese spirituality; (2) to show how the present paradigm of Vietnamese theology has developed through the missionary movement of Protestant Christian missions by raising the issue of indigenous acceptance or rejection of Protestant Christianity in the colonial and postcolonial Vietnamese context; and (3) to propose a paradigm shift toward a more integrative Vietnamese evangelical theology, specifically to redeem the Vietnamese concept of God and the extended family, toward the trinitarian relationship and the Vietnamese Christian community of both the living people and the legacy and place of their ancestors. Just as God describes himself as "the God of Abraham, Isaac and Jacob" (see Gen 20:13; Exod 3:6; Acts 7:32), the place of ancestors in the identity of Vietnamese Christians needs to be addressed in the self-theologizing process. In addition to navigating ancestor veneration practices, a Vietnamese theological perspective contributes to contemporary conversations on the notion of "God in our midst" and "God with us."

The proposals offered are not new, having been theologized in other contexts. But it is important to recognize that although similarities may exist in similar cultures, one should nevertheless recognize that disparities also exist. Jesus had a reason for differentiating Jerusalem from Judea to Samaria in Acts 1:8. For example, the use of *Đạo*, in Vietnamese phonetics to differentiate from the Chinese "Dao," in Vietnamese Bible translations and in theological textbooks is akin to the use of "Dao" in Chinese Bible translations and Chinese theological textbooks. However as will be argued, the two terms are not interchangeable. The Vietnamese concept of God in the *Đạo* must be redefined in

---

11. Hồ Chí Minh, "Unpublished Letter," 2. More regarding Hồ Chí Minh's criticism of the French mission is discussed in Nguyen, *Cultural Integration*, chapter 4.

the Vietnamese context which will enable Vietnamese Christians to provide a theology that is more conducive to their specific worldview.

EVANGELICAL THEOLOGY AND VIETNAM'S SYNCRETISTIC SPIRITUALITY

Vietnamese spirituality is "glocal." Since the introduction of Confucianism (*Nho*), Daoism (*Đạo* or *Lão*), and Buddhism (*Phật*) – all of which came from outside Vietnamese culture – there has been an ongoing process of assimilation of sociopolitical and religiocultural dimensions (a form of contextualization?) with Vietnamese folk beliefs. This process of assimilation has influenced the philosophical thoughts, religious beliefs, and sociopolitical ideas at all levels of Vietnamese society. Such a syncretistic contextualizing process appears visibly in the sociopolitical realm in the three teachings examinations and in the religiocultural realm in the stele inscriptions in village temples.[12] This syncretistic or accommodating nature had a critical impact that went far beyond the borders of China, shaping the worldviews of diverse East Asian societies.

When Confucianism, along with Buddhism and Daoism, arrived in Vietnam, the Vietnamese literati adapted and transformed it to create an indigenized Vietnamese Confucian scholastic tradition.[13] As village intellectuals, these Vietnamese Confucian scholars played a central role in both uniting and leading people in various public affairs through their presence and offering inscriptions on new or renovated temples, pagodas, and other significant village structures. And as villagers themselves, they shared in the community's multidimensional spiritual life.[14] "These orthodox Neo-Confucian ideals had strongly affected the intellectual and cultural patterns of the Vietnamese elite and, through them, began to change the way of life of the population at large."[15] Trần Trọng Kim, a Vietnamese scholar and public leader who lived in the early twentieth century, concluded that this trinity of foreign beliefs had become the "national essence" of Vietnam,

---

12. Nguyen Nam, "Writing as Response and as Translation: 'Jiandeng Xinhua' and the Evolution of the Chuanqi Genre in East Asia, Particularly in Vietnam" (PhD diss., Harvard University, 2005), 300.
13. Xinzhong Yao, *An Introduction to Confucianism* (New York: Cambridge University Press, 2000), 7–9.
14. Nguyen Nam, "Writing as Response," 296–97.
15. John K. Whitmore, "Social Organization and Confucian Thought in Vietnam," *Journal of Southeast Asian Studies* 2, no. 15 (1984): 296.

> If humans adopt the middle course [that is, *Đạo*], behave according to the Way of Heaven (*Đạo*), and nurture their feelings, they will acquire benevolence (*nhân*). If, by means of self-cultivation, a person acquires benevolence, he will have a lively spirit, be able to distinguish right from wrong, and will always act in accordance with the law of Heaven and Earth. . . . All other notions, such as filial piety, righteousness, rites, wisdom, loyalty to the emperor, and trust, derive from this.[16]

Hence, the teachings of Confucianism, Daoism, and Buddhism are now fully intertwined with the life and spirituality of the Vietnamese.

We may hypothesize that a *resisting* and *assimilating* nature exists in Vietnamese culture where the integration of the Confucianism, Daoism, and Buddhism with each other and the encounter with the local religiocultural traditions resulted in a unique belief system. This integration took place because of the philosophical thought of the people at that time, when they accommodated the three teachings, a spiritual need, and the limited doctrinal content of each of the three teachings.[17] This means that although the people were governed by Confucian principles, which provided their understanding of political-social responsibility and morality, the people also needed spiritual values, found in Daoism and Buddhism, to understand their origins, life, and death. When the outside religions and ideologies of Confucianism, Daoism, and Buddhism arrived in Vietnam, the dual forces of resistance and assimilation allowed them to become unified with each other in a unique harmonious and balanced way that was specific to the political, social, and religiocultural needs in the context of Vietnam. This is the nature of Vietnamese religious belief.

Later in the late nineteenth and early twentieth centuries, the Vietnamese were challenged by French modernization and began to lose their traditional and cultural systems. The French colonial masters systematically replaced traditional Vietnamese education and *nôm*, using Chinese characters to represent

---

16. Trần Trọng Kim, *Nho giáo* [Confucianism], trans. Luu Doan Huynh, Jayne Werner, and John Whitemore (Sàigòn: Nxb Tân Việt, n.d.), 389, quoted in George E. Dutton, Jayne S. Werner, and John K. Whitmore, *Sources of Vietnamese Tradition* (New York: Columbia University Press, 2012), 414.
17. Nguyễn Tài Thư, "'Tam Giáo Đồng Nguyên': Hiện Tượng Tư Tưởng Chung của Các Nước Đông Á" [Unified source of the Three Teachings: A common ideological phenomenon of East Asian countries]. *Tạp Chí Hán Nôm (Journal of Han-Nom Studies)* 3, no. 40 (1999): 17.

the Vietnamese language, with their models of schools and universities[18] and *quốc ngữ*, the Romanized phonetic writing system, as the means of disseminating French policies of society, culture, and religion to make traditional Vietnam into another France in Asia.[19]

Quốc ngữ played the most important role in popularizing Vietnamese cultural traditions and the continual process of decolonization of French imperialism. Seeing how *quốc ngữ* had become popular in the early twentieth century, Đào Duy Anh comments, "from now on, the Europeanization of our society will deepen."[20] One of the first results of the French colonial conquest was to deprive the Vietnamese of the right to call their country by its proper name and of the right to think of themselves as "Vietnamese." Instead, they had to use the names Tonkin, Annam, and later on Cochinchina.[21] Vietnam was then under a new name, French Indochina (1884–1945), with the territory expanded to include Laos and Cambodia. By the 1930s, French colonialism had fully imprinted itself in every aspect of Vietnamese life.[22]

As this history demonstrates, Vietnamese spirituality has witnessed several crucial historical moments that have shown the resistance and assimilation nature in every aspect of Vietnamese life. Thus, the system of beliefs which has become the Vietnamese spirituality of today is a complex and integrated matrix of local beliefs in God(s), spirits, and the Confucianist-Daoist-Buddhist faith. Two insights are noted. First, the core or actual Vietnamese spirituality is the *Đạo*, the Way, a Vietnamese term used to differentiate it from the Chinese understanding of *Dao*, in which the process of syncretism has created and integrated a unique form of spirituality specific to the Vietnamese. Centuries before encountering the Christian God, this *Đạo* had been important to the Vietnamese people, leading them to believe that there is only "one true God"

---

18. Pierre Brocheux and Daniel Hémery, *Indochina: An Ambiguous Colonization, 1858–1954*, trans. Ly Lan Dill-Klein et al. (Berkeley: University of California Press, 2009), 227–29.
19. Although *quốc ngữ* was not popular in Vietnam until the early twentieth century, the early *quốc ngữ* developed by the Jesuits, that is, Alexandre de Rhodes (1591–1660) and other local Vietnamese Christians who were with them, was a historical beginning of the modern writing script of the Vietnamese. Further discussion on the role of *quốc ngữ*, see Nguyen KimSon, "The Catholic Church in Vietnam: An Example of Contextualization," *Asia Journal of Theology* 29, no. 1 (2015): 74–87.
20. Đào Duy Anh, *Việt Nam văn hóa sử cương* [An outline of Vietnamese culture] (Hà Nội: Nxb Văn học, 2010), quoted in Dutton, Werner, and Whitmore, *Sources of Vietnamese Tradition*, 424.
21. Hue-Tam Ho Tai, *Radicalism and the Origins of the Vietnamese Revolution* (Cambridge, MA: Harvard University Press, 1992), 7.
22. Hue-Tam Ho Tai, *Radicalism*.

(*Thiên, Thượng Đế*, or *Ông Trời* in common language) in the pantheon of divine spirits. However upon their arrival in Vietnam, early Christian missionaries saw several beliefs and practices including belief in spirits, common ritual ceremonies such as venerating heaven and ancestors, and oral folklore traditions, for example *The Tale of Kieu*, all of which had been transmitted from generation to generation over many centuries. These beliefs and practices seemed strange to the missionaries, and yet each story or ritual carried something of the essence of Vietnamese spirituality.

But the missionaries were ignorant of these religiocultural aspects, not knowing the essence underlying these manifestations; hence they failed to find ways to meaningfully contextualize the gospel. They didn't have the intuitive insight to see that these people held a monotheistic belief that could parallel the God of the Bible. The opportunity to contextualize did exist but was missed due to ignorance. For instance, it seems that Alexander de Rhodes did not know the full meaning underlying the concept called *Đạo* or *Đàng*, translated "way," nor the doctrinal spirituality behind the traditions, practices, and beliefs shaping the *Đạo* when he encountered it.[23] Rhodes assumed that Vietnamese spirituality was the physical practices of honoring certain realities in daily encounters with nature, respecting the living saints or heroes when they were alive and venerating them as spirits or deities after death, and venerating heaven (*Thiên, Ông Trời*, the Sacrifice to Heaven). However, he did not recognize that the root concept of Vietnamese spirituality was the *Đạo*; all other beliefs and practices were just satellites orbiting this concept.

Second, the development of Vietnamese spirituality was an interactive process of resistance to and assimilation of outside religious influences. This "dual force" demonstrates how Vietnamese spirituality is both able to resist the religiocultural influences from the outside and assimilate moderately, not absorbing completely all of one single religious doctrine, the essentials of the outside influences that are of specific interest to them. For example, the new religious movement of *Cao Dai* that began in 1926 was an attempt to integrate

---

23. "Having heard of the Law which they call *đạo* in scholarly language and *đàng* in popular tongue, which means *way* . . . I decided to announce it to them under the name of the Lord of heaven and earth, finding no proper word in their language to refer to God . . . I decided to employ the name used by the apostle Saint Paul when he preached to the Athenians who had set up an altar to an unknown God." *Histoire du Royaume*, 129–30, quoted in Peter C. Phan, *In Our Own Tongues: Perspectives from Asia on Mission and Inculturation* (Maryknoll, NY: Orbis, 2003), 163.

Cultural Integration for Self-Theologizing

Christianity with Confucian, Daoist, and Buddhist beliefs.[24] Understanding this dual force dynamic can help contextualization efforts that more systematically integrate external and local worldviews to maintain the integrity of Vietnamese Christianity rather than an adulterated and syncretized form.

A PARADIGM SHIFT IN VIETNAMESE MISSION THEOLOGY

If we understand this journey of spirituality, we can then integrate culture for a renewed contextual theology in Vietnam. Specifically, this understanding can help us cultivate a new perspective on how indigenous and Christian concepts and their practices can merge and create the paradigm shift necessary for a renewed evangelical theology.

The fact is that Christianity is still not at home in Vietnam, despite the "outward assimilation" of Christianity that could be seen as early as the Syrian Christian visitors and settlers in Asia.[25] Asian Christianity, and more specifically Vietnamese evangelicalism, has several Western characteristics that have been blended within it. Perhaps these Western characteristics of Vietnamese Christianity began because Christian missionary movements coincided with Western colonial expansion. Vietnamese Christians have been considered as having betrayed their own culture and way of life to embrace a foreign faith.

If it is to be successful in making Christianity more at home in Vietnam, "Vietnamese evangelical theology" must embrace three imperatives. First, historically and biblically, such a theology must be faithful in continuity with the larger Christian tradition. Such theology must both "embrace rightly oriented belief and confession and rightly oriented action and affection, and resist any bifurcation of head and heart, mind and soul, spirit and body."[26] That means such evangelical theology, while shaped by the Christian faith received from the missionaries, must be expressed locally and authentically and must have substantial continuity with the wider church.

Second, this theological perspective must be willing to see God's action in the religiocultural context of Vietnam but cannot ignore the spirituality of

---

24. The *Cao Dai* in Vietnam was among some "newer Asian religions" developed in Asia which had been "inspired" or "shaped" by their encounter with Christianity in the twentieth century. See Scott W. Sunquist, *The Unexpected Christian Century: The Reversal and Transformation of Global Christianity, 1900–2000* (Grand Rapids, MI: Baker Academic, 2015), 164–67. For a more detail discussion, see the original monograph: Nguyen, *Cultural Integration*.
25. Hans Küng and Julia Ching, *Christianity and Chinese Religions* (New York: Doubleday, 1989), 233–56.
26. Amos Yong, "Whither Asian American Evangelical Theology?" *Evangelical Review of Theology* 32, no. 1 (2008): 36–37.

the people. This spirituality is a complex, integrated matrix of local beliefs in God(s), spirits, and the Confucianist-Daoist-Buddhist faiths and a hybrid assimilation of both Asian and Western philosophical and socioreligious aspects. Theology ought to be done while observing God's intent and God's desire for the Vietnamese, while having the Bible continue to speak God's truth in fresh ways to them. Such theology is grounded not only by the view of God's speech in the Scripture (what God said), but also by the view of "God's act of speech" (the world of the scriptural text) which can be heard in classics of Vietnamese philosophy and religions.[27]

Here, the Asian concept(s) of God, learned from the wisdom of the Vietnamese philosophy and religions, can provide a voice to help construct theology.[28] Although constructing theology from Vietnamese philosophical-religio perspective may sound "irregular" to Western theologians, it offers a helpful nuance for theology from the Asian perspective. Such an argument has recently emerged to provide a "both-and" approach to core doctrines of Christianity.

Therefore, to create a Vietnamese theology in which the Bible continues to speak God's truth in "fresh ways" to the Vietnamese, it must begin with their ways or forms. That theology will work when it is able to "prophetically critique the accommodations of previous formulations of evangelical theology to any kind of ideological captivity."[29] This proposed paradigm shift provides a hope which can answer the following questions: (1) Do the Vietnamese need to escape their cultural concept of God to become Christians according to the ways of the missionaries? and (2) Can the Vietnamese become followers of Christ and still maintain their cultural identity?

Third, evangelical theology must be organized according to Vietnamese forms of thinking, that is from the assimilation-resistance characteristics of Vietnamese spirituality. Two critical aspects that must be addressed are (1) the concept of God, and (2) the extended family narrative.

---

27. Peter C. Phan, "An Asian Christian? Or a Christian Asian? Or an Asian-Christian? A Roman Catholic Experiment on Christian Identity," in *Asian and Oceanic Christianities in Conversation: Exploring Theological Identities at Home and in Diaspora*, ed. Heup Yong Kim, Fumitaka Matsuoka, and Anri Morimoto, *Studies in World Christianity and Interreligious Relations* 47. Church and Theology in Context Series (Amsterdam: Editions Rodopi B. V., 2011).
28. Allen Yeh, "Asian Perspectives on Twenty-First-Century Pluralism," in *The Gospel and Pluralism Today: Reassessing Lesslie Newbigin in the 21st Century*, ed. Scott W. Sunquist and Amos Yong (Downers Grove, IL: IVP Academic, 2015), 215–32.
29. Yong, "Whither Asian," 36.

Cultural Integration for Self-Theologizing

When the Western conception of God is seen through Vietnamese spirituality, it seems disconnected from the other two loci of theology: the Trinity, the relationship among God, Jesus Christ, and the Holy Spirit, and the church including the place of ancestors in the Christian community. The Christian paradigm introduced a strange, alien understanding of God to the Vietnamese. Although such a theology of God, despite being historically, culturally, and linguistically conditioned and shaped, was from the early missionary period, this theology had not connected to the God that was known in the hearts and minds of the people.[30] This "foreign" God was one of the biggest barriers, besides forbidding ancestral practices, to the Vietnamese acceptance of the Christian faith. It is important to construct a theology of God that not only carries on the historic tradition, the nature of "translatability" of Christians who have lived and witnessed the gospel in different times and places throughout the centuries, but which is also understood by the people culturally and linguistically.

But if we re-envision God through the core of Vietnamese spirituality, the *Đạo* (the way), an integrated, unique form of indigenous yet evangelical spirituality is possible. The Vietnamese spirituality of honoring certain realities in daily encounters with nature (that is, creation care), respecting the living saints or heroes when they are alive and venerating (as opposed to worshipping) their legacies after death, and venerating the heavenly realities (*Thiên, Ông Trời*) as seen in the Sacrifice to Heaven (not unlike the throne room of Revelation 7) can enable a robust Vietnamese Christian spirituality.

The Vietnamese family perspective can also become a framework for developing an understanding of both the relations of the three persons of the Trinity and addressing the issue of ancestor veneration. Within the context of Confucian teaching on family relationships, especially regarding the role of the eldest son, Jesus is viewed as "the eldest son and ancestor," or "the

---

30. For instance, Phan Khôi, a Vietnamese scholar who was part of the Vietnamese Bible translation from 1920 to 1925, argued that God could be known to humanity (God's image), not as an abstract perception (power). See Phan Khôi, "Giới Thiệu và Phê Bình Thánh Kinh Báo" [Introduction and critique of Bible magazine], *Phụ Nữ Tân Văn* 74 (16 October 1930), http://www.thuvientinlanh.org/phan-khoi-gioi-thieu-va-phe-binh-thanh-kinh-bao/. In one place in the first issue of *Thánh Kinh Báo* published on January 1931 he writes: "*Thế gian không phải tự nhiên mà có. Nhưng phải nhờ có một quyền phép lớn lắm mà đã dựng nên trời đất, và quyền phép lớn ấy tức là Đức Chúa Trời*" [This world is not created from nowhere. The earth and heaven were created by a massive power, and such power is God]. Mr Phan argued that equating God with such massive power is not biblically accurate and is not God's intention to be known by humanity.

ancestor-mediator."[31] When the Trinity is viewed according to the Vietnamese concept of God, whose being is connected within the "family relationship" of Father and Son, the issue of ancestor veneration may be treated as participation in an "extended family" in which the church is a community for both the physically living and the dead though alive in the spirit. This "communion" is large enough to encompass beings in both the physical and spiritual realms.

This proposal is similar to the argument advanced by Simon Chan who contends that a more adequate way of organizing an Asian theology is to center it in the doctrine of the triune God as the divine family. He believes that this approach reflects faithfully the fundamental way in which the first two persons of the triune God are revealed, namely as Father and Son.[32] Moreover, "in much of Asia a person's foremost identity is defined in relation to his or her family, and not just the immediate family but also the extended family, which may include an entire clan, and the linear family, which includes deceased ancestors."[33]

With these three suggestions in mind, perhaps theology should then begin with "God in our midst," a concept of God and the extended family perspective for both the trinitarian relationship – God the Father, God the Son, and God the Holy Spirit – and the Christian community of both the living and the deceased ancestors. This approach is not the only way to construct a Vietnamese theology, but it underscores the meaning of Vietnamese-ness when developing such a theology.[34]

God in Our Midst: A Vietnamese Concept of God

The Vietnamese concept of God is the most critical point to be redeemed in this new paradigm shift, namely the identity and nature of the *Đạo*. David J. Bosch argues that the old theological paradigm is a monolithic approach and that such a paradigm has to shift to a "critical hermeneutic" in which the

---

31. See for instance, "Jesus the Christ with Asian Face," and "Jesus as the Eldest Son and Ancestor" in Peter C. Phan, *Christianity with an Asian Face: Asian American Theology in the Making* (Maryknoll, NY: Orbis, 2003), 98–145. A similar argument views Jesus as "the ancestor-mediator" (priest). Simon Chan, *Grassroots Asian Theology: Thinking the Faith from the Ground Up* (Downers Grove, IL: InterVarsity, 2014), 91–127.
32. Chan, *Grassroots*, 42–43.
33. Chan, *Grassroots*, 66.
34. Hans Küng, "Focal Points of Chinese Theology: Understanding of God, Christ, and Spirit," in Hans Küng and Julia Ching, *Christianity and Chinese Religions* (New York: Doubleday, 1989), 261–68. See also Xinzhong Yao, "Confucian Christ: A Chinese Image of Christianity," in *Identity and Marginality: Rethinking Christianity in North East Asia*, ed. Werner Ustorf and Toshiko Murayama (Frankfurt am Main: P. Lang, 2000).

biblical text is recognized as contextual in its very nature.[35] Thus, God has interacted with human beings through time and space and in multiple contexts so as to communicate his intent and desire to be in relationship with human beings wherever they are found.

Can the Vietnamese concept of God, the *Đạo*, aid in making sense of the Western concept of God? Long before the arrival of Christian missionaries, the Vietnamese acknowledged the notion of monotheism, whether in forms of the *Đạo* (Way) as in Daoism, or of the *Trời* (*T'ien*/Heaven) as in Confucianism or even *Shang-ti* (Lord on High). Such forms of the *Đạo* (Way) and obeying the will of the Way do not diminish the visibility of seeing or knowing God. Certainly, such divine forms do not equate pagan unknown gods with the Christian God. But these divine phenomena and understandings of "God" may indicate that the people in East Asia are open to God's intent to be known.[36] Perhaps these divine phenomena and understandings also indicate that the people are ready to come into the full knowledge of God incarnate, Jesus the Christ. This is God, the Word, who incarnated himself into the world (John 1:10) and became flesh and lived among humanity. Jesus Christ living among humanity in local culture is God's revelation of who God is so that human beings can be reconciled with the Creator God. Just as "logos" was redeemed for Greek Christians and used in John 1:1, the concept of *Đạo* that is used for "logos" in the Vietnamese translation of John 1:1 must also be redeemed for Vietnamese theology.

Theologically, that the One True God came (incarnated) into the midst of the Vietnamese means that the *Đạo*, *Thiên*, *Đức Cao Đài* or *Đấng Cao Cả* is the One and Only One, and yet in the form of a human being. The Godman Jesus Christ has revealed the fullness of the One and the fulfillment of the "God in our midst" concept. Methodologically, the Vietnamese then can understand the nature of God's incarnation better in their perception of family, the relationship between God, Jesus Christ, and the Spirit in the concept of divine family.

---

35. David Jacobus Bosch, *Transforming Mission: Paradigm Shifts in Theology of Mission*, American Society of Missiology Series 16 (Maryknoll, NY: Orbis, 1991), 421–25.
36. For instance, Chinese scholars have recently attempted to make ancient understandings of the divine nuanced to the Chinese Christian God. See Chan Kei Thong and Charlene L. Fu, *Finding God in Ancient China: How the Ancient Chinese Worshiped the God of the Bible* (Grand Rapids, MI: Zondervan, 2009).

God with Us: A Vietnamese Hermeneutic

We turn now to provide a hermeneutical interpretation of the meaning of Jesus and the Christian church. From the perspective of the extended family, understanding Jesus the Immanuel is "God with us" by the power of the Spirit in a continual and relational way, the relationships between God and Jesus as Father and Son and the church as a community of believers can be integrated with Vietnamese spirituality. To explain this concept further, for the Vietnamese, Christ is seen as both high priest and ancestor; he is our "greatest ancestor" in the household of faith. Salvation is the restoration of a right position in the family of God where people can come to be called "holy brothers."[37] It is, however, the understanding of the larger framework of Vietnamese communal spirituality through the lens of *Đạo* that can help to bridge the gap in the mind of the Vietnamese that Jesus is not a distant God but the Incarnate God who came down to be with them as with any other people in the world. Thus, "the Word became flesh and lived among us" (John 1:14 NRSV) is a critical statement for the Vietnamese. The incarnation is also the "massive act of translation" as Andrew Walls believed.[38] In sum, the Word is God (the *Đạo*) who came in the flesh.[39]

Thus, Jesus is the way to God the Father (John 14:1–14) because "No one has ever seen God. It is God the only Son, who is close to the Father's heart, who has made him known" (John 1:18 NRSV). Jesus is also the enlightened light, the revealer of who God is and what God is doing through his church (Ps 119:105; John 1:9).

The trinitarian relationship is better understood from the Vietnamese perspective as the father and son relationship within a hierarchical structure of society, since their family structure is also hierarchical. A community built upon a hierarchical social structure would automatically embrace and reflect a familial model and a dynamic in which elders are respected and members

---

37. See Chan, *Grassroots*, 91–127. See also Nguyen KimSon, "Grassroots Asian Theology: Thinking the Faith from the Ground Up," *International Bulletin of Missionary Research* 39, no. 1 (2015): 46.
38. Andrew F. Walls, *The Cross-Cultural Process in Christian History: Studies in the Transmission and Appropriation of Faith* (Maryknoll, NY: Orbis, 2002), 29. See also chapter 3: "The Translation Principle in Christian History," in Andrew Walls, *The Missionary Movement in Christian History* (Maryknoll, NY: Orbis, 1996), 26–42; Lamin O. Sanneh, *Translating The Message: The Missionary Impact on Culture*, 2nd ed., American Society of Missiology Series 42. (Maryknoll, NY: Orbis Books, 2009).
39. Darrell L. Bock, *Jesus According to Scripture: Restoring the Portrait from the Gospels* (Grand Rapids, MI: Baker Academic, 2002), 410–16.

Cultural Integration for Self-Theologizing

within the community, as within the family, adopt a hierarchically ordered position in relationships.

The triune God's relationship should therefore be viewed from the perspective of both a relational and reciprocal relationship of Father and Son, as seen in the relational mode of being, rather than the perspective of an equal mode of being which is much stressed by egalitarians in the West.[40] When this relational perception is comprehended, the Vietnamese will understand that Jesus is the Logos or the *Đạo* (Way) and will see no contradiction with the concept of God. Again, since the Vietnamese like many Asians value the concept of family, this narrative nuances the continuity and relationship between the One True God called the Father God and the Son Jesus Christ, and the Spirit as well as the place of ancestors in the church as a community.

In the end, it is necessary to read and interpret Scripture through the lens of philosophical thoughts (Daoist and Confucianist), though the omnipotence of God is not conditioned by a historical period or ideology but by history as a whole. "The Mysteries of the Most Holy Trinity and of the Incarnate God were anciently known to the Chinese nation."[41] This statement appears in the translation of *Dao De Jing* (*Tao Te Ching*) presented to the British Royal Society in 1788.[42] A triune God can be seen, as it were, darkly through Chinese and Vietnamese traditions.

From this ordered and hierarchical relationship between the Father God and Jesus the Son, the Vietnamese can see the continuity of God with us (Immanuel) in the world. The meaning can be gleaned in John's prologue "In the beginning was the Word, and the Word was with God, and the Word was God" (John 1:1 NRSV) and the declaration of Jesus, "I am the way, and the truth, and the life. No one comes to the Father except through me" (John 14:6 NRSV); therefore, Father and Son are connected. Jesus the Son was in the beginning with God but was incarnated into the world to show the way to the Father God (the *Đạo*). In other words, the Incarnate God in Jesus is profoundly understood by the Vietnamese when associating God with the *Đạo* and Jesus with the *Đạo* (Way).

---

40. Elaine Storkey, "Evangelical Theology and Gender," in *The Cambridge Companion to Evangelical Theology*, ed. Timothy Larsen and Daniel J. Treier (Cambridge, MA: Cambridge University Press, 2007), 161–76.
41. Quoted in Paul S. Chung, *Constructing Irregular Theology: Bamboo and Minjung in East Asian Perspective*. Studies in Systematic Theology 1 (Leiden: Brill, 2009), 49.
42. James Legge, *The Sacred Books of China: The Texts of Taoism*, vol. 1 (New York: Dover, 1962), xiii.

But we have only spoken about Father and Son in the Trinity. What about the Holy Spirit? Theologically speaking, the family narrative in Scripture helps to clarify the "interrelatedness" of the triune relationship of God, Jesus Christ, and the Holy Spirit. From this family perspective, the Holy Spirit is the bond of unity of the Father and the Son. Principally, the Spirit is the bond of love and unity between the Father and the Son, and the church (believers).[43]

The Holy Spirit is the "condition and medium" of the fellowship between the Father and the Son and "only on this basis may the imparting of the Spirit to believers be seen as their incorporation into the fellowship of the Son with the Father."[44] The Spirit is the bond of love and unity between the church and its head, Christ, and access is by "one Spirit to the Father" (Eph 2:18 NRSV). "Through the Spirit's indwelling the church, the church is united to Christ as his body and ultimately to the Father, the source of all things. . . . Thus only in and through the church does creation find its true meaning and fulfilment."[45] The church as the Spirit-indwelled community to manifest "God with us" is further explored below.

The church is first then a Christian community who lives out the presence of God, a place which manifests "God with us" (Immanuel) or more specifically, to show that God is in our midst. That means as Jesus Christ is the head of the church, the purpose of God in the world is manifested through the community of all Christians, both the living and the deceased.

Second, the church is a relational community of the living where members are considered to be brothers and sisters. But this community includes the deceased ancestors, as seen from the Vietnamese perspective, the extended family. As an extended family, the church also reaches to the people who have gone before us. They are the ancestors, the respected people of the Bible, the saints. This thinking does not mean the living worship the dead or their spirits; rather they venerate or honor them in ways that uphold their lives and teachings as still of significant value for our present time. They are part of our community. A Vietnamese relational community as an extended family, therefore, is comprised of both the living and the deceased.[46] As an extended family, the church is not only for the living, but also the place where the ancestors are remembered and revered.

---

43. Chan, *Grassroots*, 129–56.
44. Wolfhart Pannenberg, *Systematic Theology*, vol. 1 (Grand Rapids, MI: Eerdmans, 1991), 316.
45. Chan, *Grassroots*, 156.
46. This perspective has also been called "a communion of saints" as in Chan, *Grassroots*.

In the final analysis, the Vietnamese concept of God and the extended family perspective need to be redeemed for a theology that is relevant in the specific context of Vietnam. The processes of theologizing these concepts will promote a paradigm shift in theology that will enable the church in Vietnam to be a church which is constantly relevant to the context, an essentially Vietnamese church.

REFLECTIONS ON THE FUTURE OF VIETNAMESE EVANGELICAL THEOLOGY

Within the larger East Asian context, the Vietnamese have shown throughout their long history their ability to syncretize and to integrate their animist beliefs with outside religiocultural influences, whether the process was simply osmotic or because of centuries of foreign rule. As a result, Vietnamese spirituality is a complex, integrated matrix of local beliefs in God(s), spirits, Confucianist-Daoist-Buddhist concepts, and Christian faith, forming a hybrid of both Oriental and Western philosophical and socioreligious aspects. This study has identified that within this long process of assimilation, the dialectic interplay of dual forces – resistance and assimilation – has shaped how the Vietnamese were able to both resist religiocultural influences from the outside and to assimilate moderately the essentials of the outside influences that were of specific interest to them.

The unintentional inability of the Christian missionaries to identify this resisting and assimilating interplay and their tendency to rationalize the essentials and unify them with local popular animistic beliefs into a single religious doctrine to be discarded were the major reasons why contextualization goals were not fully realized. However it seems promising that contextualization efforts in Vietnam are possible once the dual-force nature is recognized. We see what needs to be resisted and the crucial religiocultural elements or concepts that need to be or can be assimilated. This identification and acknowledgement should serve as a lens through which a contextualization process can review the essential elements or concepts of Vietnamese spirituality which can be redeemed for evangelical Christian beliefs and practices.

Contextualization efforts then remain ongoing and necessary for the Vietnamese church to make known God's intention to the Vietnamese people. The current study has identified the unique cultural and spiritual premises that indicate why Christian contextualization efforts have failed and at the same time has strongly suggested that any attempt at Christian contextualization in Vietnam cannot overlook the "dual force" and the nature of the *Đạo* of Vietnamese spirituality.

As a concluding remark, Christian faith is expected to be both relevant and indigenous in Vietnamese form, style, language, and meaning, not only at one point in time but constantly in the present and the future. Such Christian faith must reflect God the *Đạo* at the fundamental and ontological level at all times. That faith will then meet the deepest needs of the Vietnamese and will penetrate their worldview of the One True and Only God, the *Đạo* who is the source of all things. The vision of a fully evangelical Vietnamese contextual community was the initial thought and driving force behind the present study. A strong hope is that the church of Christ in Vietnam, which is built on Christ and against which the gates of hell shall not prevail (Matt 16:18), will continually be the catalyst for the spiritual awakening of the Vietnamese till the day of Christ's second coming.

Case Studies

1. Nguyen has proposed a trajectory for contextualization in Vietnam. You are tasked with a five-year project to take two additional steps forward in the arc. What would you propose? Consider what areas you will need to research and additional collaborators you will need, such as ideas from history or other cultures or religions, and the partners you will need locally, regionally, and globally. Will the Vietnamese diaspora be helpful or obstructive? You may wish to draw from Robert Solomon's chapter 13 on church networks to guide you as you develop this project.

2. Nguyen argues using the concept of *Đạo* to contextualize Christianity for the Vietnamese church. But the Vietnamese church would not be the first to use *Dao* as the bridge. Chinese and Korean churches have also explored this avenue. Research their conclusions and explore the bridges and barriers that were raised. Would these hold true for the Vietnamese church?

3. Nguyen's approach is a generalization for the evangelical Vietnamese church. Consider the Catholic Church in Vietnam and the regional variations, for example North and South, urban and rural, Viet and tribal and explore whether or not this approach would be viable for these different groups.
4. Do an internet search to explore the difference between Malaysian and Indonesian Islam, Cambodian and Indonesian Hinduism, or other regional variations. How might these variations impact the barriers and bridges Christianity might face in these regions?

REFERENCES

Bock, Darrell L. *Jesus According to Scripture: Restoring the Portrait from the Gospels.* Grand Rapids, MI: Baker Academic, 2002.

Bosch, David Jacobus. *Transforming Mission: Paradigm Shifts in Theology of Mission.* American Society of Missiology Series 16. Maryknoll, NY: Orbis, 1991.

Bourdeaux, Pascal. "Notes on an Unpublished Letter by Hồ Chí Minh to a French Pastor (8 September 1921) or the Art of Dissenting Evangelization." *Journal of Vietnamese Studies* 7, no. 2 (2012): 8–28.

Brocheux, Pierre, and Daniel Hémery. *Indochina: An Ambiguous Colonization, 1858–1954.* Translated by Ly Lan Dill-Klein with Eric Jennings, Nora Taylor, and Noémi Tousignant. Berkeley: University of California Press, 2009.

Chan, Simon. *Grassroots Asian Theology: Thinking the Faith from the Ground Up.* Downers Grove, IL: IVP Academic, 2014.

Chung, Paul S. *Constructing Irregular Theology: Bamboo and Minjung in East Asian Perspective.* Studies in Systematic Theology 1. Leiden: Brill, 2009.

Đào Duy Anh. *Việt Nam văn hóa sử cương* [An outline of Vietnamese culture]. Hà Nội: Nxb Văn học, 2010.

Dutton, George E., Jayne S. Werner, and John K. Whitmore. *Sources of Vietnamese Tradition.* New York: Columbia University Press, 2012.

Hiebert, Paul G. *Anthropological Insights for Missionaries.* Grand Rapids, MI: Baker Book House, 1985.

Hồ, Chí Minh. "Unpublished Letter by Hồ Chí Minh to a French Pastor (8 September 1921)." Translated by Kareem James Abu-Zeid, *Journal of Vietnamese Studies* 7, no. 2 (2012): 1–7.

Hue-Tam Ho Tai. *Radicalism and the Origins of the Vietnamese Revolution.* Cambridge, MA: Harvard University Press, 1992.

James, Violet B. "American Protestant Missions and the Vietnam War." PhD diss., University of Aberdeen, 1989. https://www.proquest.com/openview/55a0aabcf2c4a2700046ae0e086f2197/1?pq-origsite=gscholar&cbl=51922&diss=y.

Küng, Hans, and Julia Ching. *Christianity and Chinese Religions*. New York: Doubleday, 1989.

Legge, James. *The Sacred Books of China: The Texts of Taoism*, vol. 1. New York: Dover, 1962.

Lê, Hoàng Phu. "A Short History of the Evangelical Church of Viet Nam (1911–1965)." PhD diss., New York University, 1972. https://www.proquest.com/openview/09bf2bba9c4598d6f342afdf6fd26dc8/1?pq-origsite=gscholar&cbl=18750&diss=y.

Mejudhon, Ubolwan. "The Way of Meekness: Being Christian and Thai in the Thai Way." DMiss diss., Asbury Theological Seminary, 1998.

Nguyen, Ai Quoc. *Le procès de la colonisation francaise* [The process of French colonization]. Paris: Imprimerie et Librairie du Travail, Première Série, Mœurs Coloniales, 1926.

Nguyen, KimSon. "The Catholic Church in Vietnam: An Example of Contextualization." *Asia Journal of Theology* 29, no. 1 (2015): 74–87.

———. *Cultural Integration and the Gospel in Vietnamese Mission Theology: A Paradigm Shift*. Carlisle, UK: Langham Monographs, 2019.

Nguyen, Nam. "Writing as Response and as Translation: 'Jiandeng Xinhua' and the Evolution of the Chuanqi Genre in East Asia, Particularly in Vietnam." PhD diss., Harvard University, 2005. https://www.proquest.com/openview/b39ca0e43c6d6a21fa2e222b6cdbcc1a/1?pq-origsite=gscholar&cbl=18750&diss=y.

Nguyễn, Tài Thư. "'Tam Giáo Đồng Nguyên': Hiện Tượng Tư Tưởng Chung của Các Nước Đông Á" [Unified source of the Three Teachings: A common ideological phenomenon of East Asian countries]. *Tạp Chí Hán Nôm (Journal of Han-Nom Studies)* 3, no. 40 (1999): 11–17. New York: Ballantine, 2001.

Pannenberg, Wolfhart. *Systematic Theology*, vol. 1. Grand Rapids, MI: Eerdmans, 1991.

Phan, Peter C. "An Asian Christian? Or a Christian Asian? Or an Asian-Christian? A Roman Catholic Experiment on Christian Identity." In *Asian and Oceanic Christianities in Conversation: Exploring Theological Identities at Home and in Diaspora*, edited by Heup Yong Kim, Fumitaka Matsuoka, and Anri Morimoto. Studies in World Christianity and Interreligious Relations 47. The Church and Theology in Context Series, 57–74. Amsterdam: Editions Rodopi B. V., 2011.

———. *Christianity with an Asian Face: Asian American Theology in the Making*. Maryknoll, NY: Orbis, 2003.

———. *In Our Own Tongues: Perspectives from Asia on Mission and Inculturation.* Maryknoll, NY: Orbis, 2003.

Sanneh, Lamin O. Translating The Message: The Missionary Impact on Culture. American Society of Missiology Series 42. 2nd ed. Maryknoll, NY: Orbis Books, 2009.

Storkey, Elaine. "Evangelical Theology and Gender." In *The Cambridge Companion to Evangelical Theology*, edited by Timothy Larsen and Daniel J. Treier, 161–76. Cambridge: Cambridge University Press, 2007.

Sunquist, Scott W. *Understanding Christian Mission: Participation in Suffering and Glory.* Grand Rapids, MI: Baker Academic, 2013.

———. *The Unexpected Christian Century: The Reversal and Transformation of Global Christianity, 1900–2000.* Grand Rapids, MI: Baker Academic, 2015.

Thong, Chan Kei, and Charlene L. Fu. *Finding God in Ancient China: How the Ancient Chinese Worshiped the God of the Bible.* (Previously published as Faith of Our Fathers.) Shanghai: China Publishing Group Orient Publishing Center, 2006. (Originally published in simplified Chinese.) Grand Rapids, MI: Zondervan, 2009.

Walls, Andrew F. *The Cross-Cultural Process in Christian History: Studies in the Transmission and Appropriation of Faith.* Maryknoll, NY: Orbis, 2002.

Whitmore, John K. "Social Organization and Confucian Thought in Vietnam." *Journal of Southeast Asian Studies* 2, no. 15 (1984): 296–306.

Yao, Xinzhong. *An Introduction to Confucianism.* New York: Cambridge University Press, 2000.

Yeh, Allen. "Asian Perspectives on Twenty-First-Century Pluralism." In *The Gospel and Pluralism Today: Reassessing Lesslie Newbigin in the 21st Century*, edited by Scott W. Sunquist and Amos Yong, 215–32. Downers Grove, IL: IVP Academic, 2015.

Yong, Amos. "Whither Asian American Evangelical Theology?" *Evangelical Review of Theology* 32, no. 1 (2008): 22–37.

CHAPTER 16

AFTERWORD

BEYOND SOUTHEAST ASIA – SO THE WORLD MAY KNOW

R. Daniel Shaw

I am writing this as an American and thus an outsider to the Asian context. However, I spent my first eighteen years growing up as a missionary kid in India and later in the Philippines – a nation Narry Santos identifies as the only "Christian" nation in Southeast Asia. I also have an undergraduate degree with a double major in anthropology and "Asian studies." I have taught courses across the region, regularly mentor Asian students, and frequently visit my son and his family in Thailand. Thus as an "outside-insider," I hope to provide a unique perspective.

The Southeast Asia region, as noted by all the authors, is extremely complex, a mix of social, religious, economic, and political concerns that reflect an interaction of history, colonialism, and contemporary responses that boggle the mind. As I write this in 2021, we are all in a panic over the global pandemic that is COVID-19. No nation has been left untouched, yet the responses have been widely varied. The region is also very much in the news as Myanmar endures yet another coup after the re-election of 1991 Nobel Peace laureate Aung San Suu Kyi with much fear and upheaval among the population. In the United States, once again we are reeling from racial unrest after multiple incidents involving the shooting of African Americans by white police officers to the politicization of COVID-19 as the "China flu" lead to a dramatic increase in violence against Asian Americans.[1] This is our contemporary world, and Southeast Asia is very much a part of it.

In this afterword, I wish to appreciate the complexity of the region and reflect on what that means for the rest of the world, thereby helping non-Asians apply what they read here to enhance their own contexts. Doing so

---

1. Nicole Chavez, "2020: The Year America Confronted Racism," CNN (2020).

may demonstrate how the unchanging message of the Bible, God with us, can be applied to the ever changing conceptual environments that represent the sociospiritual complexity of our twenty-first century world.

In Part I, though emanating from a historical focus, each of the national overview authors demonstrate the foreign path by which the church in their nation became the way it is. Clearly, these histories demonstrate that Christianity throughout the region "was associated with Western culture and politics, and therefore suspect."[2] Despite the diversity, these authors present a symmetry that recognizes the need for a complex systems approach in the midst of socioreligious structures dominated by Islam, Buddhism, or Catholicism.

At its heart, Samuel K. Law's chapter is designed to help us recognize the necessity of revitalizing Christianity to its biblical, incarnational intent to be considered relevant in Southeast Asian contexts. The book is organized on a twenty-first century complex systems framework with the vignettes reflecting multidimensional networks. The chapters by John Cheong, Andrew Peh, and Robert Solomon emphasize the dynamics of pluralism in local contexts. Yet each context must be fit into a larger regional and global environment which accounts for what is relevant and contextual as well as universal and relational. Finally, Kiem-Kiok Kwa and KimSon Nguyen challenge us to go beyond the evolving realities that were created from what the colonial powers, foreign missionaries, and globalization brought.

Law's introduction to the complex systems approach is specifically designed to help us understand all the historical, contemporary, and contextual issues of Southeast Asia that reflect pluralism. Pluralism by definition exudes complexity, as Newbigin noted over thirty years ago.[3] There is need then to move beyond Western logic with its linear product of the Enlightenment approach to something that accounts for a conceptualization that assumes "multi": multi-cultural, multi-religious, multi-economic, multi-political, and multi-lingual. All of these factors account for the need to network interactive relationships that bring the many parts of what is Southeast Asia together. Such an "emergent" perspective goes beyond pluralism to recognize what was always there but that foreigners with their simple, linear, positivist, and reductionist thinking missed.

---

2. Karl Dahlfred, chapter 8, pg 119.
3. Lesslie Newbigin, *The Gospel in a Pluralist Society* (Grand Rapids, MI: Eerdmans, 1989).

Afterword

Ben Ramalingam notes that in order to move forward, we must explore complexity in the region,[4] while Homi Bhabha recognizes that to advance beyond the myopia of former mentors, Asians must now draw from the well of both contexts. In order to understand themselves, they interact with others; those who share their involvement in the region as well as those who made a strong historical impact on creating what is today – what Bhabha calls the "third space."[5] To do so, Law takes a page from Ramalingam to emphasize the value of "process rather than goal," "diverse solutions not right answers," and "knowledge transfer rather than knowledge creation."[6] Law looks to connect the issues essential to surviving personal, national, regional, and global concerns that impact us all – of which COVID-19 is an example. Because this collection realistically deals with complexities in one of the world's most diverse regions, the rest of the world can benefit. It is this benefit I wish to highlight.

Peh's broad strokes history of Christianity in Southeast Asia is a chronicle of colonialism, economic intrigue, and Christianity following closely on the heels of exploration and exploitation. Is it any wonder that Christianity in Southeast Asia has been considered irrelevant, foreign, and insidiously exploitative by local people who were well-served by the extant religious expressions before outsiders arrived in the sixteenth century? Sadly, "aspirations for God, gold, and glory" established a global pattern of dominance. These outside expressions were characterized by divisions between Christian manifestations of national, ecclesial, and denominational concerns that made them appear to be splintered rivals, competing for the souls of the few who were already disenfranchised. Hence Christianity was viewed as a religion of the minority or marginalized rather than those in the mainstream of society.

Solomon reminds us that Christians in the region need to develop their own theologies, systematized from an Asian perspective rather than the usual, but less relevant, Western systematics. As long as Asians depend on Western-derived approaches to organizing biblical information it will, in large measure, not make sense to local congregations – a position Kosuke Koyama arrived at in northern Thailand where people with a Buddhist framework forced him to view life from a perspective much more like his Japanese assumptions

---

4. Ben Ramalingam, *Aid on the Edge of Chaos: Rethinking International Cooperation in a Complex World* (London: Oxford University Press, 2014).
5. Homi Bhabha, "In the Cave of Making: Thoughts on Third Space," in *Communicating in the Third Space*, eds. Karin Ikas and Gerhard Wagner (London: Routledge, 2009), ix-xiv.
6. Ramalingam, *Aid on the Edge*, 26.

indicated rather than his Western-dominated theology dictated.[7] Such reflection encourages me to cheer for developing biblical theologies that match local religious experience and cultural expectations.[8] As Asian students minister where the real people of Asia live – whether in the urban contexts, the slums or the paddy fields – they must with Koyama "see the face of God in the faces of the people."[9] Those who teach in Asian seminaries and Bible Schools must reflect on their Asian perspectives, not merely the theology of their mentors.

I am reminded of Lesslie Newbigin, who retired to England only to realize that the issues he had grappled with in the pluralist environment of India had become the issues with which Christians in England were struggling. The lessons he learned as the bishop of South India could also be applied in my home, America.[10] Similarly, the issues the authors of this book grapple with are critical for those of us who are now experiencing rapid paradigm shifts in the West. We who are part of the body of Christ must get beyond globalization.[11] As Christians we must anticipate our presence in heaven as described in Revelation 7:9. Together we are the universal church in all its diversity yet all focused on glorifying the one true God.

I urge my Asian friends to avoid being clones of Western thinking and seek to help other Asians make sense of the biblical precepts for their context: holistic, naturalistic, spiritual, and relevant.[12] For example, my student in Myanmar is seeking to understand common Burmese beliefs associated with invisible spiritual beings called *nat*. If people can understand the role of the Holy Spirit, who energizes human beings much like the *nat* impacts human

---

7. Kosuke Koyama, *Waterbuffalo Theology*, 25th Anniversary Edition (Maryknoll, NY: Orbis, 1999).
8. R. Daniel Shaw, "Beyond Syncretism: A Dynamic Approach to Hybridity," *International Bulletin of Mission Research* 42, no. 1 (2018): 6–19.
9. Koyama, *Waterbuffalo Theology*, xv.
10. See Ryan K. Bolger, ed. *The Gospel after Christendom: New Voices, New Cultures, New Expressions* (Grand Rapids: Baker Academic, 2012).
11. The general assumption has been that globalization would provide people of the world with a commonality, thus making them more like each other by means of the internet, international commerce, geopolitics, and ease of travel. Salvador Babones, "Studying Globalization: Methodological Issues," in *The Blackwell Companion to Globalization*, ed. George Ritzer (Malden, MA: Blackwell, 2008), 146. Despite such benefits, however, the more people are exposed to such trends, the more they become aware of their own inadequacies and their identity. Therefore, my objective is not to ignore globalization but to recognize the pros and cons of its impact on how people perceive themselves and others.
12. R. Daniel Shaw, "Ritual as Worship: Toward Authentic Christian Worship in Asia," in *Christian Mission in Religious Pluralistic Society*, eds. Eiko Takamizawa, David S. Lim, and Daniel J. Kim (Seoul: Asian Society of Missiology, 2019), 65–93.

Afterword

existence, from a Burmese perspective, the Burmese may appreciate God in their context much more than they would from a penal-substitutionary presentation of Christ's sacrifice derived from a Western, Protestant theological understanding, which in the Burmese cognitive environment makes no sense at all. Because they understand *nat* spirituality, contextualizing God within the framework of the Burmese worldview will center their attention on what is meaningful to them.[13]

Kwa makes clear the importance of taking the whole person into account in the context of community. The community structures and concomitant relationships recognize self-worth and identity that is much closer to the intent of the biblical authors who reflected God's intent in their contexts. I believe Westerners can learn much from Asians who reflect perspectives about relationship with God and about giving honor to God as well as to each other, thereby broadening the one-dimensional guilt paradigm that so dominates Western thought.[14] Kwa further reflects on mission in the public square, thereby going beyond the individual to use language that reflects the sociolinguistic context and avoids Westernized Christianese that only brings confusion. Approaches such as business as missions, dialogue with people about their faith rather than dogmatism, utilizing emotive narrative styles, incorporating music, and using local art forms such as Indonesian *Wajang* shadow puppets, dance, and mime all go far beyond Western-style propositional proclamations or apologetics that are less than effective in Southeast Asian cultures.

As the Western church edges toward being marginalized by society, and as church attendance declines, we in the so-called "Global North" can follow the lead of authors in this volume who point toward ways Christians can survive, and thrive, as a minority. By bringing biblical solutions to societal issues such as endemic corruption, racism, and social deconstruction, to name a few, Southeast Asians point the way for us in the West to move closer to God's intentions for living in our contemporary, post Enlightenment, world. And what can the migrant phenomenon with its blend of mutual experience, rich heritage, and vibrant relationships bring to the way the larger Christian community reflects on God? From diversity comes unity through which each community can learn new things about God from others.

---

13. Nok Kam, "Toward Constructing a Hybridized Pneumatology for Transforming Christian Mission among the Burmese in Myanmar" (PhD Research Proposal, Fuller Graduate School of Intercultural Studies, 2020).

14. Christopher Flanders and Werner Mischke, eds. *Honor, Shame, and the Gospel: Reframing our Message and Ministry* (Littleton, CO: William Carey, 2020).

Southeast Asians and those who will be serving in Southeast Asia, or any other region in the world, must not copy Western Enlightenment approaches that are not designed for the diversity and complexity of their region. Rather, I implore Asians to develop complex, "glocal" approaches as demonstrated throughout this book. Doing so will enable Asians to make the Bible's message of relationship to God and to other human beings the center around which the diverse elements of Asian conceptual grids revolve. Allow deeply held beliefs and values to integrate with others thereby benefiting from socio-religious structures that interface with biblical principles on one hand and societal concerns on the other. Allow the Bible to be the framework that organizes each perspective while valuing others. Doing so will enable Asian approaches to be a beacon for the rest of the world as together we navigate our identity as human beings who will one day gather around God's throne and shout a collective "hallelujah" in our respective languages and styles of worship. To God be the glory.

REFERENCES

Babones, Salvador. "Studying Globalization: Methodogical Issues." In *The Blackwell Companion to Globalization*, edited by George Ritzer, 144–61. Malden, MA: Blackwell, 2008.

Bhabha, Homi. "In the Cave of Making: Thoughts on Third Space." In *Communicating in the Third Space*, edited by Karin Ikas and Gerhard Wagner, ix–xiv. London: Routledge, 2009.

Bolger, Ryan K., ed. *The Gospel after Christendom: New Voices, New Cultures, New Expressions*. Grand Rapids, MI: Baker Academic, 2012.

Chavez, Nicole. "2020: The Year America Confronted Racism." CNN (2020). https://edition.cnn.com/interactive/2020/12/us/america-racism-2020/.

Flanders, Christopher, and Werner Mischke, eds. *Honor, Shame, and the Gospel: Reframing our Message and Ministry*. Littleton, CO: William Carey, 2020.

Kam, Nok. "Toward Constructing a Hybridized Pneumatology for Transforming Christian Mission among the Burmese in Myanmar." PhD Research Proposal, Fuller Graduate School of Intercultural Studies, 2020.

Koyama, Kosuke. *Waterbuffalo Theology*. 25th Anniversary Edition. Maryknoll, NY: Orbis. 1999.

Newbigin, Lesslie. *The Gospel in a Pluralist Society*. Grand Rapids, MI: Eerdmans, 1989.

Ramalingam, Ben. *Aid on the Edge of Chaos: Rethinking International Cooperation in a Complex World*. London: Oxford University Press, 2014.

Afterword

Shaw, R. Daniel. "Beyond Syncretism: A Dynamic Approach to Hybridity." *International Bulletin of Mission Research* 42, no. 1 (2018): 6–19.

———. "Ritual as Worship: Toward Authentic Christian Worship in Asia." In *Christian Mission in Religious Pluralistic Society*, edited by Eiko Takamizawa, David S. Lim, and Daniel J. Kim, 65–93. Seoul: Asian Society of Missiology, 2019.

Asia Theological Association
54 Scout Madriñan St. Quezon City 1103, Philippines
Email: ataasia@gmail.com Telefax: (632) 410 0312

OUR MISSION

The Asia Theological Association (ATA) is a body of theological institutions, committed to evangelical faith and scholarship, networking together to serve the Church in equipping the people of God for the mission of the Lord Jesus Christ.

OUR COMMITMENT

The ATA is committed to serving its members in the development of evangelical, biblical theology by strengthening interaction, enhancing scholarship, promoting academic excellence, fostering spiritual and ministerial formation and mobilizing resources to fulfill God's global mission within diverse Asian cultures.

OUR TASK

Affirming our mission and commitment, ATA seeks to:

- **Strengthen** interaction through inter-institutional fellowship and programs, regional and continental activities, faculty and student exchange programs.
- **Enhance** scholarship through consultations, workshops, seminars, publications, and research fellowships.
- **Promote** academic excellence through accreditation standards, faculty and curriculum development.
- **Foster** spiritual and ministerial formation by providing mentor models, encouraging the development of ministerial skills and a Christian ethos.
- **Mobilize** resources through library development, information technology and infra-structural development.

To learn more about ATA, visit www.ataasia.com or facebook.com/AsiaTheologicalAssociation

Langham Literature, along with its publishing work, is a ministry of Langham Partnership.

Langham Partnership is a global fellowship working in pursuit of the vision God entrusted to its founder John Stott –

> *to facilitate the growth of the church in maturity and Christ-likeness through raising the standards of biblical preaching and teaching.*

Our vision is to see churches in the Majority World equipped for mission and growing to maturity in Christ through the ministry of pastors and leaders who believe, teach and live by the word of God.

Our mission is to strengthen the ministry of the word of God through:
- nurturing national movements for biblical preaching
- fostering the creation and distribution of evangelical literature
- enhancing evangelical theological education

especially in countries where churches are under-resourced.

Our ministry

Langham Preaching partners with national leaders to nurture indigenous biblical preaching movements for pastors and lay preachers all around the world. With the support of a team of trainers from many countries, a multi-level programme of seminars provides practical training, and is followed by a programme for training local facilitators. Local preachers' groups and national and regional networks ensure continuity and ongoing development, seeking to build vigorous movements committed to Bible exposition.

Langham Literature provides Majority World preachers, scholars and seminary libraries with evangelical books and electronic resources through publishing and distribution, grants and discounts. The programme also fosters the creation of indigenous evangelical books in many languages, through writer's grants, strengthening local evangelical publishing houses, and investment in major regional literature projects, such as one volume Bible commentaries like the *Africa Bible Commentary* and the *South Asia Bible Commentary*.

Langham Scholars provides financial support for evangelical doctoral students from the Majority World so that, when they return home, they may train pastors and other Christian leaders with sound, biblical and theological teaching. This programme equips those who equip others. Langham Scholars also works in partnership with Majority World seminaries in strengthening evangelical theological education. A growing number of Langham Scholars study in high quality doctoral programmes in the Majority World itself. As well as teaching the next generation of pastors, graduated Langham Scholars exercise significant influence through their writing and leadership.

To learn more about Langham Partnership and the work we do visit **langham.org**

www.ingramcontent.com/pod-product-compliance
Lightning Source LLC
Chambersburg PA
CBHW051628230426
43669CB00013B/2225